Bread and Authority in Russia, 1914–1921

Studies on the History of Society and Culture
Victoria E. Bonnell and Lynn Hunt, Editors

Bread
and Authority
in Russia,
1914–1921

LARS T. LIH

University of California Press

BERKELEY LOS ANGELES OXFORD

University of California Press
Berkeley and Los Angeles, California

University of California Press, Ltd.
Oxford, England
© 1990 by
The Regents of the University of California

Library of Congress Cataloging-in-Publication Data

Lih, Lars T.
  Bread and authority in Russia, 1914–1921 / Lars T. Lih.
     p.   cm. — (Studies on the history of society and culture)
  Includes bibliographical references.
  ISBN 0-520-06584-0 (alk. paper)
  1. Food supply—Soviet Union—History. 2. World War, 1914–1918—
Soviet Union. 3. Soviet Union—History—Revolution, 1917–1921.
I. Title. II. Series.
HD9015.S652L54   1990
947'.084' 1—dc20   89-20151
                                                             CIP

Printed in the United States of America
1   2   3   4   5   6   7   8   9

To Bjorn and Mary Lih

Thanks to my friends for their care in my breeding
Who taught me betimes to love working and reading.

Isaac Watts

The food-supply question, on which the whole conduct of a war of unexampled dimensions in one way or another depends, inevitably raises in Russia the political question.

Peter Struve, February 1917

He who thinks that socialism can be constructed during peaceful, untroubled times is deeply mistaken; it will everywhere be constructed in a time of breakdown, in a time of hunger, and that is how it has to be.

V. I. Lenin, July 1918

And then came the bourgeois war—
People became mean and ugly.
And screw by screw, brick by brick
They tore apart the brick factory.

Russian popular song

Contents

Illustrations

Acknowledgments

A Bolshevik food-supply official gave the following advice to his colleagues: you can learn a lot if you listen to the peasants as they argue about how to distribute the grain assessment. That describes my basic method: I have listened to, and learned from, the passionate arguments of Russian political activists trying to avert a food-supply crisis. Some of the finest economic minds of their generation contributed to this policy debate, and I find it a matter of great encouragement that their homeland is now clearing them of the villainous charges brought against them during the Stalin era. A. V. Chaianov and N. D. Kondratiev have already been rehabilitated, and it seems that rehabilitation will soon follow for V. G. Groman and N. Sukhanov. I would also like to express my gratitude to some lesser-known sources: N. Dolinsky, V. Martovskii, A. V. Peshekhonov, N. Orlov, P. K. Kaganovich, M. Vladimirov, the American journalist Ernest Poole, and the contributors to the journal *Food Supply and Revolution*. There is more recovery than originality in this book.

My research in the Soviet Union in 1980–1981 was supported by a grant from the International Research and Exchange Board. I was given immense assistance by the coworkers of the Central State Historical Archive in Leningrad and the Central Military-Historical Archive in Moscow. Some of the ideas presented in the last chapter were discussed at the Colloquium on the History of Ideas at Wellesley College. The accuracy and clarity of the final copy was helped by Richard Miller's careful editing. Sheila Levine of the University of California Press has been such a patient and encouraging friend of the book and its writer that it is now hard to think of the manuscript separately from her.

I owe much to my friends in Washington, D.C. The first drafts of this work were written while I was living with Tom, Jane, Caitlin, and Nicholas

Earley. While Caitlin Earley learned how to walk, I learned how to write a scholarly work: I can only hope my further success matches hers. George Withers has helped me in ways that go greatly beyond the usual duties of friendship, and I can give only pale and inadequate thanks here. Margaret and Chris Kobler, Julie Scofield, and their wonderful families have been a needed point of stability in what was long an unsettled life.

This book has benefited from a number of careful and sympathetic readers. My sister Nora Lih is close to my ideal reader: a critical but involved nonspecialist. Her professional copyediting skills and her enthusiasm for the subject have greatly improved the presentation of the book. Among specialist readers I received valuable suggestions from an anonymous referee of the University of California Press. My greatest debt is to Victoria Bonnell and William Rosenberg. Each of them spent much time and energy giving suggestions to a scholar whom they did not know personally for no other motive than to ensure that readers got the best book possible. I learned from them not only about the Russian time of troubles but also about the nature of a scholarly community.

This book is a product of my graduate training at Princeton University, where I was privileged to be at the same time as a remarkable group of graduate students and teachers. Among my teachers I am grateful in particular to Harry Eckstein, Stephen Cohen, and Richard Wortman, all of whom sought to impart a sense of the mutual dependence of the comparative and the historical outlooks. I owe the greatest debt of all to Robert C. Tucker, who has helped me in all the ways one scholar can help another, from loaning books and giving truly sage advice to offering insightful criticism and encouragement at difficult moments. My intellectual debt to him goes beyond Soviet studies, as anyone who has read *Politics as Leadership* will realize.

I have worked long enough on this project to have a basis for comparison, and so I can say with assurance: it is better with Julie Cumming than without her. She has been as merciless to the defects of any one sentence as she has been generous to the overall spirit of the book. She has made the usual hectic completion of a manuscript seem almost peaceful. It is heartening indeed to think that everything I write in the future will profit in the same way.

Note on the Translation of Key Russian Terms

Prodovol'stvie is sometimes translated as "food," sometimes "supply." I have chosen the more inclusive "food supply." *Prodovol'stvie* has rich etymological overtones, including satisfaction, freedom, will, command, and power.

Golod covers hunger, starvation, and famine. S. G. Wheatcroft comments that "the concept of famine as used by Englishmen living in a low mortality society in the 1980s is very different and much narrower than the concept of *golod* used by Russians living in a relatively high mortality society before the Second World War."

Razverstka is best left untranslated, although "quota assessment" is close. It is derived from words meaning to equalize, measure, or compare. One of its etymological cousins is the Russian unit of length, the verst. It is pronounced "raz-VYORS-ka."

Uchet i kontrol' is often translated as "accounting and control," but that translation is misleading. *Kontrol'* is best translated as "monitoring." *Uchet* can be translated as either "inventory" or "registration." I have chosen "registration," partly to catch some of the overtones of social conflict in expressions such as "draft registration" and "gun registration." In their translation of Bukharin and Preobrazhenskii's *The ABCs of Communism* Eden and Cedar Paul manage to render *uchet* in the following ways in the course of the translation of a single sentence: "accurate reports . . . list . . . tabulated statements . . . account . . . definite idea."

The contrasted pair *soznatel'nost'–stikhiinost'* is central to Russian political culture. *Soznatel'nost'* is sometimes translated as "class consciousness," but that translation is too narrow. "Consciousness" is better, but unidiomatic in "the conscious worker" and unintelligible in "the unconscious worker." "Deliberate" and "purposive" give some of the connotations, but the best translation would probably be "enlightened," with its overtones both of religious insight and rational awareness. I have not dared to break with tradition, however, and *soznatel'nost'* is here rendered as "consciousness," although *bessoznatel'nyi* is translated as "unenlightened."

Stikhiinyi is usually translated either as "spontaneous" or "elemental." The second is much preferable. A *stikhiinoe bedstvie* is a natural disaster—the Russian idiom gives the proper connotation. For this study, the related term *stikhiia* is more important. It usually means native element, but in the key phrase "petty-bourgeois *stikhiia*" I have translated it as "disorganizing spontaneity." In 1921 Lenin commented that "petty-bourgeois *stikhiia* is not called *stikhiia* in vain since it really is something completely formless, indeterminate, and *bessoznatel'nyi*."

Melkaia burzhuaznaia is taken from the French *petit bourgeois* and is most accurately translated as "small bourgeois." In this study, however, it appears only as a term of Marxist rhetoric, and the connotation of contempt contained in the term "petty bourgeois" is entirely appropriate.

The political terms *gosudarstvo*, *pravitel'stvo*, and *vlast'* form a system and their meaning can only be understood in relation to each other. *Gosudarstvo* (state) is the enduring political community, whatever form it may happen to take; *pravitel'stvo* (government) is the executive branch; *vlast'* is the energizing center of decision making and power for both state and government. No single translation of *vlast'* will do: I have rejected the unidiomatic term "power" (as in "the soviet power"); "sovereignty" has been my first choice and "authority" or "political authority" my second choice. The difference between the February and the October revolutions is that the first gave rise to a *pravitel'stvo* and the second to a *vlast'*.

The word "state" is an overwhelmingly positive one for all Russian political activists in this study, including Lenin. A classic definition is given by the historian V. O. Kliuchevsky: "A people becomes a state when the feeling of national unity finds expression in political ties, in the unity of the supreme *vlast'* and of the law. In the state a people becomes not only a political but an historical individuality, with a more or less clearly expressed national character and a consciousness of its own global significance." In more ordinary rhetoric, "the state" represents the common interest and the valid claims of the whole against the part.

A pood is approximately 36 pounds; a funt is approximately one pound; a desiatin is 2.7 acres.

Imperial Russia was divided into provinces (*gubernii*); there were about fifty in European Russia. Provinces were divided into counties (*uezdy*), each with a town as administrative center. The next subdivision was the district (*volost'*), which dealt directly with the peasant villages. *Vlast'* and *volost'* were originally the same word—an appropriate connection for a period when the key test for a central authority was to make its presence felt in each individual village.

Introduction:
A Time of Troubles

A man may here object, that the condition of subjects is very
miserable; as being obnoxious to the lusts, and other irregular
passions of him, or them that have so unlimited a power in
their hands . . . not considering that the estate of man can
never be without some incommodity or other; and that the
greatest, that in any form of government can possibly happen
to the people in general, is scarce sensible, in respect of the
miseries, and horrible calamities, that accompany a civil war.

Thomas Hobbes, 1651

Is it Bolshevism that wrecked Russia? Or is it wrecked Russia
that created Bolshevism?

Maurice Hindus, 1920

During the years 1914 to 1921 Russia experienced a national crisis that
destroyed the tsarist state and led to the establishment of the new Bolshevik order. If we wish to understand the society that emerged from this
crisis, we must examine its entire course. The focus of this study is
therefore not the ten days that shook the world but the seven years that
devastated Russia.

One of the central features of this whole period of war, revolution, and
civil war was a food-supply crisis that was both symptom and intensifier of
the overall dislocation and then breakdown of national economic and social
life.[1] Until the end of the period food-supply problems were not caused by
an absolute lack of grain in the country. "There *is* grain in the country"—
this was emphasized by all three governments of the period (tsarist,
Provisional, and Bolshevik). The problem was getting it from the peasant
producer to the city dweller and the soldier, and here a whole series of

---

1. This study concentrates almost exclusively on grain and not on other important foodstuffs such as sugar, potatoes, vegetables, and meat. The technical and
institutional problems of the other foodstuffs are quite distinct, and grain had
overwhelmingly greater economic and political significance. On its cultural significance, see R. E. F. Smith and David Christian, *Bread and Salt* (Cambridge, 1984),
part 3.

obstacles intervened, including the breakdown in transport, the vicissitudes of the civil war, and the reluctance of the peasant population to market or deliver its grain. My real object of study is therefore not so much the food-supply crisis itself but the disintegration of Russian society and the struggle to reconstitute it.

The name I have chosen for this object of study is *time of troubles*. This is a term taken from Russian history: it is the usual translation of *smutnoe vremia*, the name given to the interregnum between the death of Boris Godunov in 1605 and the accession in 1613 of Michael Romanov, the founder of the Romanov dynasty that ended in 1917. It can be used to mean any period between the breakdown of one government and the founding of a stable successor regime.

For the purposes of this study, a wider definition of time of troubles is convenient: a period of disruption of societywide coordinating institutions, accompanied by a breakdown of central political authority. The coordinating institutions may include the market or state economic regulation, the transport system, and even the common norms of behavior. The definition is worded to avoid any prejudgment of the cause-and-effect relation between social disruption and political breakdown. It can only be justified in the course of the study that follows, but some important themes can be stated beforehand. These include uncertainty, the dilemma I call Hobbes's choice, and rhetoric.

The Russian word *smutnyi* connotes not only turbulence and strife but also confusion and lack of clarity. This connotation is appropriate as well to my wider definition: disruption creates uncertainty, perhaps more so than complete collapse. When the coordinating institutions that served as a basis for mutual reliability no longer work, individuals begin to lose control of their environment.

Political breakdown in particular creates uncertainty about the location of sovereign authority. The danger inherent in this situation led Pavel Miliukov in March 1917 to make a surprising plea to another Michael Romanov, in whose favor Nicholas II had just resigned his throne. Miliukov was the leader of the Constitutional Democrats (Kadets), whose ultimate aim was a rationalized and secular modern constitutional state. Yet alone among the parliamentary activists with whom Michael consulted, Miliukov appealed to him to accept the office of tsar, despite the personal risks involved. V. V. Shul'gin later recalled his plea:

> If you refuse, Your Highness—the result will be ruin! Because Russia—Russia will lose its axis. This axis is the monarch— the sole axis of the country! The masses, the Russian masses—around what—around what will they gather? If you

refuse, there will be anarchy . . . chaos . . . a bloody mess. The monarch is the sole center—the only one that everybody knows—the only one common to all. [It is] the only conception of sovereignty [that exists] so far in Russia. If you refuse, it will be horrible—a complete lack of knowledge—a horrifying lack of knowledge because there will be no—no oath![2]

When Miliukov asked Michael to help provide legitimacy for the interim revolutionary authority, he did not refer to any supposed monarchist values of the population but simply to the fact that "the monarch is the sole center that everybody knows." Miliukov's concern about "the horrifying lack of knowledge" that results from uncertainty was not unrealistic, even if the means he found to combat it were inadequate. At a session of the Petrograd Soviet that was just beginning to organize itself at that time, a soldier delegate exclaimed, "I don't know whom to deal with, whom to listen to. Everything is unclear. Let's have some clarity."[3] The events of 1917 only served to spread the confusion to wider circles; a Menshevik activist in Saratov reported in the fall that peasants were beginning to complain that "for a long time [the government] has not established order [and] it has reached the point where one doesn't know who governs whom and to whom one must subordinate oneself."[4] During the civil war the commander of a food-supply worker detachment was the only one in the group who owned a leather jacket, but he gave it in turn to each of his men who spoke at peasant meetings "for the sake of authority."[5] Wearing a leather jacket was a significant political act because it signaled the presence of an agent of the new sovereign authority and thus helped make clear who governed whom.

The philosophy of Thomas Hobbes is useful here because it is based on the contrast between a situation where an accepted sovereign exists and one where there is none. In addition, Hobbes described the difficult time when it is still unclear whether a sovereign authority will be able to maintain itself, so that each individual must decide whether or not to support it. The logic is the same as that of a run on a bank: though it would be better for each individual if the central authority continued to exist, it may still be rational for each individual to take action that will help destroy the authority.

This dilemma arises whenever any coordinating institution is disrupted.

2. V. V. Shul'gin, *Dni* (Belgrade, 1925), 297–98. The scene is described in Tsuyoshi Hasegawa, *The February Revolution: Petrograd 1917* (Seattle, 1981), chap. 28.
3. Hasegawa, *February Revolution*, 396.
4. Donald J. Raleigh, *Revolution on the Volga* (Ithaca, 1986), 289.
5. Vsevolod Tsiurupa, *Kolokola pamiati* (Moscow, 1986), 144.

Looking at it from the individual's point of view, we may call it Hobbes's choice: whether to take the risk of, on the one hand, remaining loyal to the institution or, on the other, striking out on one's own without the institution. From society's point of view the question is the balance between the centrifugal and centralizing forces created by these individual choices. Does the balance of social forces tend toward self-help and further disruption or toward reconstitution of the disrupted institution?[6]

These individual choices are not made by noncommunicating monads: choices are justified and urged on others by means of rhetoric. Rhetoric is not simply persuasive speech used by individuals to attain their private ends: it is a tool of collective deliberation through which communal values are applied to specific situations. If we go back to the *Rhetoric,* we find that Aristotle's advice to the aspiring rhetorician contains a large amount of information about the actual values of Athenian political culture. The study of rhetoric is thus a way of studying two of the most important questions we can ask about any political system or political culture: what arguments are effective within the system, and how do they change over time?

Rhetoric plays an even more vital role in a time of troubles when standard responses no longer achieve expected results and conscious choices must be made continuously about previously routine matters. Since basic communal values are now being contested, advocacy is put under closer scrutiny. And since the first application of new communal values to specific problems is apt to be particularly ambiguous, advocacy and justification are correspondingly more vital. All of this helps to explain why revolutionaries talk so much.

One way to study rhetoric is to focus on key rhetorical terms. These key terms are a kind of focus toward which many lines of argument converge, and indeed the simplest method of evoking the political atmosphere of a particular time and place is just to list the current terms of political discourse. André Mazon, a French linguist in Russia at the time of the revolution, noticed that each successive phase of the revolution had its own set of stock phrases; he felt that examining the impact of the revolution on the Russian language was a revealing way to chart the course of events.[7] Much of the present study analyzes the shifting meaning of the key terms

6. My argument is somewhat similar to that of Albert O. Hirschman, *Exit, Voice and Loyalty* (Cambridge, Mass., 1970).

7. André Mazon, *Lexique de la guerre et de la révolution en Russie* (Paris, 1920), 50. Mazon's material indicates that more new words were formed from *prod-* (short for *prodovol'stvie,* food-supply) than from any other particle. Among works that take a rhetorical approach to issues of Russian history are John D. Klier, "Zhid:

used to advocate different solutions to the food-supply crisis, such as *grain monopoly, kulak, registration,* and *razverstka.*

Rhetoric also helps us examine the self-understanding of a political class. The term *political class* is taken from the political sociology of Gaetano Mosca and refers to the middle level of policymakers and full-time activists that stands between the top leadership and the mass of the citizenry. In this study it refers specifically to those who held or aspired to responsible positions in any government food-supply organization. The idea of the political class serves as a link between two approaches sometimes artificially opposed to each other, political history and social history. A political class is defined by its mode of recruitment from wider social groups, the authority relations through which it coordinates its activities, and its shared vision of its own role in society.[8]

Mosca gave the name *political formula* to this basic self-definition of the political class. The present study concentrates on the part of the political formula that provides the political class with a strategy for responding to problems facing society. A particular way of solving political problems can enjoy intense loyalty. It is a central proposition of this study that at least in the area of food-supply policy this loyalty endured over a period that saw radical changes in other aspects of the political formula, such as mode of recruitment or internal authority relations.

At the conclusion of the study I will consider the advantages and disadvantages of viewing the period from 1914 to 1921 as a time of troubles in contrast to other ways of looking at the events of those years. For the present, the idea of a time of troubles can be summed up in a number of questions that I will ask at each stage of events. What caused disruption in coordinating institutions? How much uncertainty was created? What choices led to self-help and thus further disruption, and what choices led to reconstitution? How do we account for these choices? With what arguments and appeals did people justify their own choices and urge choices on others?

In 1917 a provincial journalist working for the Nizhegorod food-supply

---

Biography of a Russian Epithet," *Slavonic and East European Review* 60 (January 1982): 1–15; A. M. Selishchev, *Iazyk revoliutsionnoi epokhi* (Moscow, 1928); Roman Redlich, *Stalinshchina kak dukhovnyi fenomen* (Frankfurt, 1971); Stephen Cohen, *Rethinking the Soviet Experience* (Oxford, 1985), 208. I have found Edward H. Levi, *An Introduction to Legal Reasoning* (Chicago, 1949), very useful for thinking about these issues.

8. Gaetano Mosca, *The Ruling Class* (New York, 1939), 70ff; Harry Eckstein and Ted Robert Gurr, *Patterns of Authority* (New York, 1975). For a succinct modern restatement of the position of Mosca as well as of Vilfredo Pareto and Robert Michels, see G. Lowell Field and John Higley, *Elitism* (London, 1980).

committee, V. Martovskii, liked to report on life in the queues that were at that time establishing themselves as a feature of Russian life. He reported the following typical occurrence. A housewife asks the price of a funt of bread, and when she hears the astronomical price, she says, "Are you crazy?" But when the shopkeeper hears what the housewife believes is a reasonable price, he responds, "Are *you* crazy?" Martovskii asked himself, Well, which of them is crazy? His answer: Neither, the *times* are crazy.[9]

9. *Prodovol'stvie* (Nizhegorod), 3 December 1917, 5 (hereafter cited as *Prod.*). After carefully noting down the authors of each of the articles in this journal, I learned from the last issue of 1917, as the journal was closing down, that Martovskii had written all the articles himself.

1 Beginning of Troubled Times

> No one supposed at that time that the war would drag on and
> turn itself into a frightful war of peoples. No one supposed at
> that time that those tasks which were given to us at the
> beginning would become so complicated and become more and
> more difficult at each step.
>
> A food-supply commissioner, August 1916

When war broke out in the summer of 1914, the Russian government did
not feel that providing the army with food was a pressing priority: Russia
was after all a major exporter of grain. Germany might have to worry
about obtaining enough food to sustain its war effort, but not Russia.
Indeed, the extra purchases required by the army might prove to be a boon
since they would help avert a depression in agricultural prices that might
be caused by the cutoff of Russian exports.

Before the war, grain for the army had been purchased directly by the
army purchasing agency (Intendantsvo). It was an easygoing process, and
any controversy surrounding it had more to do with the distribution of
economic plums than with efficient ways of supplying the army. A few
days after the beginning of the war the task of making purchases was
suddenly given to the Ministry of Agriculture, which had no previous
experience in army purchasing.[1] The motive for this decision had little to
do with strictly military considerations and much more to do with long-
contemplated reforms of the grain trade, where the position of the middleman was strongly resented. The Ministry of Agriculture was given a
mandate to purchase grain from the immediate producers—the landowner
and the peasant. To help achieve this goal, it would call on the zemstvos

---

1. Technically speaking, Agriculture was not a ministry until 1915. Before that,
it was a main administration (Glavnoe Upravlenie Zemledeliia). According to a
book published in 1915, "Though food has remained cheap other things have
become dear. . . . So the middle and upper classes will feel the pinch of the war; but
the poor, who do not ask for anything more than food, will be better off." Stephen
Graham, *Russia and the World: A Study of the War and a Statement of the World-
Problems That Now Confront Russia and Great Britain* (New York, 1915), 54–55.
Graham was only a little less sanguine about the rising cost of living in *Russia in
1916* (New York, 1917), 38–48.

(local self-government organs) as well as a more recent arrival on the scene, the cooperatives. These organizations were regarded as associations of the immediate producers and not as middlemen.[2]

The casualness of the government approach was not justified. Although first regarded as an opportunity, food supply soon came to be seen as a problem, then as a crisis, and finally as a catastrophe. Instead of falling because of a glut on the internal market, agricultural prices steadily climbed until efforts to control them became one of the central questions of domestic politics. Not only was the army poorly supplied, but the cities and the grain deficit provinces (located for the most part in the north of Russia) began to feel the pinch and to fear for the future. In the last months before the revolution food-supply policy became the center of a pitched bureaucratic and political battle that led to drastic shifts of policy but not to alleviation of the people's hardships and insecurity. When the tsarist government fell in the depths of the winter of 1916–1917, it was the Petrograd crowds calling for bread that delivered the final blow.

What went wrong? The explanation must begin with the disruption of normal life caused by the outbreak of war. This disruption first expressed itself in the physical relocation of millions of men taken from productive activity at home and sent to the front. In early 1915 there was an answering movement in the opposite direction when millions of refugees from the war zones were uprooted and sent to the interior provinces, bringing disorder and uncertainty. "The elements have risen. Where they will stop, how they will settle down, what events will accompany them—all this is an equation with many unknowns. Neither governmental, public, nor charitable organizations have the forces to bring the elements into their proper course."[3]

Alongside this physical relocation came a massive redirection of productive activity. The scale can be shown by the example of food supply: almost

2. One motive for purchasing from the immediate producer was dislike of Jewish middlemen; see *fond* 456, *opis'* 1, *delo* 19, *listy* 126–27 in the Central State Historical Archive in Leningrad. (Archival references are hereafter cited in the following fashion: 456-1-19/126–27. All references are to the Central State Historical Archive unless otherwise noted.) For a description of cooperatives as immediate producers by an official of the trade ministry, see 457-1-255/14–15.

For other reasons behind the choice of the Agriculture Ministry, see K. I. Zaitsev and N. V. Dolinsky, "Organization and Policy," in P. B. Struve, ed., *Food Supply in Russia During the World War* (New Haven, 1930), 4.

3. This is a summary by the recording secretary of a cabinet meeting in August 1915. Michael Cherniavsky, ed., *Prologue to Revolution* (Englewood Cliffs, N.J., 1967), 45–46; see also 38–40, 56ff. T. M. Kitanina gives the figure of three million refugees. Kitanina, *Voina, khleb, i revoliutsiia* (Leningrad, 1985), 48.

half of marketable grain went to the army in 1916.[4] The necessary reorganization of the national economy was made even more difficult by a sudden isolation from the world economy. Losing Germany as a trading partner was a severe blow, soon compounded by the closing of the Straits and the consequent difficulty of maintaining economic ties even with allies.

This redirection of economic activity meant that the previous network of "paths of communication" (*puti soobshcheniia,* the transport system) was no longer adequate. The strain on the transportation network resulted from the attempt to supply the front in the far west of the country and the swollen capital city of Petrograd in the far northwest. The new demands on the transportation network were almost the reverse of the usual market pattern of peacetime transportation when grain was shipped to southern ports for export. The rail system matched the river system by having a north-south emphasis; it was simply not set up for east-west traffic. Difficulties were compounded by the enormous length of the front line, and when large-scale troop movements took place, the transport system failed to cope.[5]

In the long run the war would first remove the economic stimulus for productive activity, because of a lack of goods for civilian use, and then even the possibility of productive activity, because of a lack of raw materials and equipment. But in the first two years of the war these dangers were hardly thought of. The challenge facing society seemed straightforward enough: emergency mobilization for a short war. Proceeding from this diagnosis, state authorities reacted in a way that, far from lessening the disruption caused by the outbreak of the war, served to amplify it.

SUPPLYING THE ARMY:
EMBARGOES AND REQUISITIONS

None of the belligerent powers of 1914 realized that they were in for a protracted war that would call on all of society's resources—material, administrative, political, and social. The war could not be fought with stocks on hand, whether of ammunition, clothing, transportation, or patriotic support; government and society had to be transformed in order to manufacture all of these items in ever-increasing quantity. The warring powers recognized only slowly that business as usual and ad hoc intervention were insufficient and even dangerous.

4. Kitanina, *Voina,* 70–71.
5. Kitanina, *Voina,* 12ff; S. S. Demosthenov, "Food Prices and the Market in Foodstuffs," in Struve, ed., *Food Supply,* 343.

On the surface, the minister of agriculture could look back at the end of
the first year of the war with a sense of a mission accomplished. That was
the claim of Aleksandr Krivoshein, the minister of agriculture who was
also at that time the most prominent politician in the tsarist cabinet. The
main objective had been accomplished: the army had been provided with
the necessary grain. He said in a speech of July 1915 that despite mistakes,
the country was ready to sustain "years of struggle without the slightest
scarcity." He went on to quote British prime minister David Lloyd George
to the effect that victory now went not to the best army but to the most
highly developed productive technology; he amended this statement to say
that victory went to the country that could feed itself indefinitely, no
matter how big its army.[6] Krivoshein was especially proud of the "shining
example" that had been given of cooperation between the zemstvos and
the central government. The success of provisionment demonstrated the
soundness of turning with confidence to local activists (*deiateli*) and elim-
inating the we-versus-they mentality that was so widespread in Russian
political life. As his deputy G. V. Glinka put it, "To [our] cause [should] be
enlisted all economic, all activist Russia, so that each is given access and
means to serve the homeland in this difficult moment."[7]

Krivoshein did not deny that cost-of-living problems had arisen in the
consuming centers, especially Moscow and Petrograd: this difficult situation could only be eased by "systematic work [*planomernaia rabota*]" of all
government departments working together. It was also true that one cause
of this situation was trade disruptions due to embargoes, but, concluded
Krivoshein, priorities must be kept straight: civilian disruptions, bad as
they were, were preferable to any disruption in provisionment of the
army.[8]

The disruption of civilian trade had not been caused by the amounts
taken by military and civilian purchasing commissioners but by the methods they used. The commissioners shared Krivoshein's sense of priorities,
so that the damage done to the civilian economy was undervalued, and
their inexperience also helped to magnify inevitable dislocations.

But in the summer of 1914 the job of civilian purchasing commissioner

6. 456-1-19/104–6.
7. *Materialy po voprosu ustanovleniia tverdykh tsen na prodovol'stvie i furazh*
(Petrograd, 1916), 79–80. This is a report on the conference of August 1916. Glinka
was the "High Commissioner for Grain and Fodder Purchases for the Army (whose
condensed telegraphic address, *Khlebarmiia*, . . . was commonly used to designate
the entire organization)." Zaitsev and Dolinsky, "Organization and Policy," 5.
8. 456-1-19/104–6; 457-1-7/74–78.

(*upolnomochennyi*) had not seemed a difficult one, and Krivoshein made his appointments mainly among provincial zemstvo chairmen—people he had worked with and knew personally. The new commissioners promptly built up an apparatus of more than two thousand agents.[9] Left to their own devices, the commissioners showed considerable zeal but lamentable ignorance—they would buy a load of grain at what they felt was a bargain price and then discover that it was cheap because it was located far from rail stations and therefore expensive to transport.[10] The original policy of buying directly from the producers could not be sustained, if only because the commissioners did not have storage space for such large purchases. As a result, half of government purchases went through middlemen.[11]

When the commissioners began to experience difficulties in obtaining supplies (especially oats) at what they felt was a reasonable price, they blamed the middlemen. They were aided in their search for ways of dealing with the middlemen by regulations issued by the central government on 17 February 1915. These regulations had been proposed by the army purchasing agency; their effect was to extend powers already held by military authorities at the front to commanders of the military districts in other parts of Russia. These powers included the right to set prices for government purchases and enforce these prices by means of requisitions and embargoes that prevented shipment out of the local area. Although the military commanders issued the necessary orders, decisions were taken jointly with the provincial governor and the local purchasing commissioner.[12]

Neither the frontline military authorities nor the civilian purchasing commissioners actually resorted to requisitions to any great extent; the idea was to use the threat of requisition at a penalty price as an inducement to voluntary sale. But local embargoes were widely applied and by the

9. For administrative units and units of measurement, see the Note on Translation. Kitanina, *Voina*, 187, gives as the figure 2299 commissioners; according to N. D. Kondratiev, the figure was 3300. Kondratiev, *Rynok khlebov i ego regulirovanie vo vremia voiny i revoliutsii* (Moscow, 1922), 94–96.

10. A. V. Chaianov, *Prodovol'stvennyi vopros*, (Moscow, 1917), 7. Rudolph Claus, *Die Kriegswirtschaft Russlands bis zur bolschewisten Revolution* (Benn, 1922), 143.

11. Kondratiev, *Rynok khlebov*, 96–98; Kitanina, *Voina*, 73–74.

12. 1276-11-969/1–3, 12–17; Zaitsev and Dolinsky, "Organization and Policy," 7; V. S. Diakin, *Russkaia burzhuaziia i tsarizm v gody pervoi mirovoi voiny, 1914–1917* (Leningrad, 1967), 212. As of April 1915, districts in the theater of war included Kiev, Odessa, and Caucasian *okruga* and Kiev, Podolsk, Volynsk, Chernigov, Kherson, Bessarabia, Tauride, Poltava, Ekaterinoslav, Tersk, and Kuban provinces. 456-3-46/5.

summer of 1915 embargoes had been set up in most of the frontline and producing provinces.[13] Embargoes were much more disruptive than requisitions would have been since instead of inconveniencing an individual middleman, an embargo cut long-established links between regions and deprived the deficit regions of their normal sources of supply without warning. It is therefore surprising to discover that the commissioners saw the embargoes as a way of avoiding what they thought was the more drastic step of requisition. They reasoned that since an embargo deprived the grain dealer of alternatives by preventing shipment of grain out of the area, it made the threat of requisition more effective and increased the chance of voluntary sale to the government. An embargo would also disrupt trade within the province less than the use of requisitions would. This blatantly localist perspective meant that an embargo was placed on twenty million poods so that three million poods could be bought for a few kopecks a pood less.[14]

The rhetoric used to justify requisitions and embargoes introduces one of the most important rhetorical terms of the time of troubles, *speculation*. Speculative middlemen were seen as the cause of the rise in prices, and this view meant that requisition had not only an economic but also a moral rationale, for can a speculator justly complain if his goods are requisitioned? To some extent, then, the charge of speculation was a case of giving a dog a bad name in order to beat it, or rather, to take its bone. The case is precisely that of the term *kulak* later on. If the authorities were hostile to the grain holder, it was not because he was necessarily a villain but because he held grain. I will examine later the economic impact of speculation, but the impact of speculation as a rhetorical category was fully as important.

The local purchasing commissioners translated their feeling about speculation into hostility toward "specialists in the grain trade" (the euphemistic label given to private grain dealers). Even when the commissioners acknowledged the services and equipment provided by specialist middlemen, they still felt it was worth the trouble and expense to replace or duplicate them at least for government purchases. Local activists were much more confident than the government about their ability to do the job alone—especially since they themselves did not feel the pinch created in the consumer centers by the disruption of civilian trade.

13. A thorough examination by S. N. Prokopovich of the extent and effect of the embargoes can be found in *Trudy komissii po izucheniiu sovremennoi dorogovizny* (Moscow, 1915), 3:125–59. See also Kondratiev, *Rynok khlebov*, 102–5; Kitanina, *Voina*, 66.

14. Chaianov, *Vopros*, 7. Zaitsev and Dolinsky, "Organization and Policy," 8, put the blame on "military simplicity and finality," but the civilians were just as guilty. 456-1-18, especially *listy* 11–13; 456-1-19; 456-1-90/48–49.

Central officials had a different perspective on the use of specialists. The center had become keenly alive to the scarcity of administrative resources and realized that rejecting experience and talent was a luxury Russia could ill afford. It could also observe the performance of the system as a whole and so was aware of how inadequate that performance was. And as it came closer to dealing with the peasants directly, it began to understand the need for intermediaries. (At this early stage of the war the services asked of the intermediaries were mainly technical: gathering grain from scattered peasant villages as well as cleaning and drying the lower-quality peasant grain.) Of course the specialists had to be carefully watched, and this supervision required an activist state policy: "It is necessary to arrange things so that [the middlemen] do not fleece the people and sell cheaply." This could be done if the government properly used its strategic resources, such as control over rail transport.[15]

Whenever a representative of the War Industries Committees (an association of manufacturers organized to help the war effort) or of the Ministry of Trade and Industry addressed a conference of the purchasing commissioners, he was met with crackling hostility. The tone of Krivoshein or Glinka was defensive when they tried to make the case for using the specialists. They had to emphasize they only wanted to employ "honorable" ones and that the zemstvos themselves were not doing an efficient job of collecting, storing, and shipping grain.[16] This debate over the use of the specialists reveals a characteristic split between the center and the locals that continued throughout the entire time of troubles.

To accuse the speculator was to excuse the immediate producer. The head of the army purchasing agency stated that penalty prices would be a "threat only for speculators; the general mass of the population will not suffer from this since procurement experience has shown that the immediate producer is not only not avoiding [grain] deals but is also actively searching them out."[17] To accept that the population itself was capable of hardheaded and economically rational behavior would have meant facing the moral and practical difficulties of applying coercive measures to everybody. As soon as the government actually began to work directly with a particular group of "immediate producers," it rapidly became disillusioned. This process began with the big landowners. Glinka expressed his exasperation with unscrupulous landowners who sold grain they did not have and then tried to obtain it from the neighboring peasants: "Then the whole operation falls apart and a few noble ladies sustain a financial loss.

15. 456-1-19/137.
16. 456-1-19/141.
17. 1276-11-969/1–3 (report to Council of Ministers, January 1915).

They kick up such a fuss in all spheres and departments that all Russia shakes."[18] But even at this time we can see the beginning of a fear that later came to dominate Russian political thinking: the fear of the self-sufficient peasant in a position to cut off economic contact with the towns. At this early stage the reason assigned for peasant self-sufficiency was the vodka prohibition that was announced at the beginning of the war, which eliminated a major item of expenditure.

Bureaucrats and activists were not the only ones searching for explanations. Two commercial agents sent out by the railroads to investigate conditions discovered a wide range of opinions among people concerned with the grain trade. One of these agents felt that southern cities were indeed experiencing difficulties because of the "unbridled speculation" of "grain and flour kings," and he was quite cynical about regulatory attempts made by municipal councils in towns like Rostov and Novocherkassk. But he also reported many other opinions. The main impression from his reported conversations is confusion as people attempted to make sense of an economy that was beginning to go haywire. Everyone convincingly blamed someone else—either inexperienced government purchasers, or transportation delays, or the landowner and peasants who were beginning to get greedy, or of course speculative middlemen. The small-fry grain collectors (*ssypshchiki*) who hung around the stations and wharves denied that hoarding was even within their economic powers, for they depended on rapid turnover. They (and other observers such as tax inspectors and agronomists) pointed to the landowners and the well-off peasants. But these in turn claimed they knew of high grain prices only by report; all they could see was climbing prices for consumer items. More objective reasons such as massive army purchases or the difficulty of getting oats from outlying regions to the railroad stations were also mentioned.

The other agent disguised himself as a prospective buyer to get a more straightforward story from the grain merchants. According to these merchants, competition made any large-scale hoarding impossible, and anyway it was impossible to cheat the landowners and peasants because every one of them knew the latest market price and would accept no less. They also declared that all it took was rumors about the possibility of requisition to reduce the likelihood of finding supplies at major collection points: the risk was becoming too great. The landowners and the well-off peasants ran a smaller risk: they undoubtedly had reserves that mysteriously appeared

18. 456-1-90/46. Krivoshein's replacement as minister of agriculture, A. N. Naumov, also complained about the many titled petitioners who did not want their "darling little cows" requisitioned. Naumov, *Iz utselevshikh vospominanii* (New York, 1954–55), 2:391.

whenever a local embargo was lifted. The author then stated the necessity of using requisition measures against the actual grain holder—evidently not considering the possibility that requisition would dry up this source as well.[19]

The expectation of a short war gave rise to an attitude that consciously accepted a dualism between the army and the civilian population: government policy concentrated only on the army, and the civilians were left to fend for themselves. The regulations of 17 February 1915 amplified the consequences of this dualism by giving extraordinary powers to purchasing commissioners. But the commissioners' disregard of any interests but the army's or perhaps their own provinces caused enough damage to ensure that pressures to reestablish unity quickly came into being.

OVERCOMING DUALISM: PRICE REGULATION

In March 1915 the grain dealers Kurazhev and Latyshev bought more than eight hundred thousand poods of grain in Ufa province; the grain was intended not for the army but for the industrial city of Ivanovo-Vosnesensk in Vladimir province. The governor of Ufa put pressure on them to sell the grain voluntarily to the army and save him the trouble of requisitioning it. In response, the grain dealers turned to the governors not only of Vladimir province but of Kostroma province, where the flour mills of the area were located. In an effort to pry loose the grain, these officials bombarded with telegrams the Ufa governor as well as the purchasing commissioner and the relevant military authorities. These appeals finally succeeded, but the grain was still far from its final destination—the Kostroma governor now used his embargo powers to keep the flour in his own province, and the authorities in Vladimir had to start sending telegrams again.[20]

This story shows that pressures that had expressed themselves through the market did not go away when embargoes were introduced but instead were transformed into political ones. Defenders of the embargoes argued that the complaints of the consumer centers should not be taken seriously, but this argument did not lessen the intensity of the complaints. The mere existence of these consumer pressures made the embargoes less effective in inducing voluntary sale since the grain dealers now felt that sooner or later the embargoes would have to be lifted.[21] Since anything was preferable to

19. 456-1-1005/1–19.

20. V. Ia. Laverychev, "Prodovol'stvennaia politika tsarizma i burzhuazii v gody pervoi mirovoi voiny (1914–1917 gg.)," *Vestnik Moskovskogo Universiteta*, 1956, no. 1:177.

21. 456-3-46/9–12.

the free-for-all just described, attempts were made in the spring of 1915 to overcome the army-civilian dualism by means of bureaucratic reorganization.

The first result of this effort was the Main Food-Supply Committee (Glavny Prodovol'stvenny Komitet) set up in May 1915 under the chairmanship of the minister of trade and industry, V. N. Shakhovskoi. Shakhovskoi himself did not want the job and was not completely sure why his ministry had been given this task instead of the Agriculture Ministry. The Main Food-Supply Committee did not exist long enough even to set up any organizational apparatus for grain purchases, but Shakhovskoi did send around a circular lifting all embargoes then in force since his ministry was hostile to disruptions in trade.[22]

By August 1915 the task of overcoming dualism in food supply was given back to the minister of agriculture in his role as the chairman of the newly created Special Conference (Osoboe Soveshchanie) on food-supply matters. Shakhovskoi had lifted the embargoes simply to let normal trade operate more freely, but the political and social forces behind the creation of the Special Conference wanted to replace dualism with a more active regulation of the national economy. One of the slogans of opposition forces had been the need for a centralized ministry of supply, and in this demand they were seconded by the military. The result of all the political infighting over who would control such a ministry was a compromise system of not one but four special conferences with responsibility for food supply, transport, fuel, and the defense effort in general.[23]

The Special Conference on Food Supply tried to establish a new level of coordination in several spheres. In the political sphere it moved to overcome the split within the political class between the government bureaucracy and the public opposition. The partnership/rivalry between these two is the great theme of tsarist politics during the war years; the new forms of cooperation that had been evolving pragmatically during the first year of the war only took concrete institutional form when military defeats temporarily put Tsar Nicholas on the defensive.

The members of the special conferences from the legislature and the public organizations were true representatives since they were selected by

---

22. V. N. Shakhovskoi, "*Sic Transit Gloria Mundi*" (Paris, 1952), 68–74, K. A. Krivoshein, *A. V. Krivoshein* (Paris, 1973), 221–23. Shakhovskoi was said to have been a creature of Rasputin's.

23. For background to the Special Conferences, see Ia. M. Bukshpan, *Voenno-khoziaistvennaia politika* (Moscow, 1929), 307–17; Diakin, *Russkaia burzhuaziia*, 87–89. The official name of the Special Conference on Food Supply was "Special Conference for consideration and unification of measures relating to food supply."

the institutions that sent them. The Special Conference on Food Supply had seven representatives from the Duma, seven representatives from the State Senate, and one representative each from the Union of Towns and Union of Zemstvos. Since there were no representatives from the War Industries Committee, representation of public organizations was much less than on the Special Conference on Defense. Even so, the Special Conference on Food Supply had sixteen representatives from outside the bureaucracy and only nine or ten ministerial representatives. [24]

These numbers in themselves do not give an accurate picture of the actual relative influence of the two sides. The Special Conference on Food Supply was legally only an advisory organ; full decision-making power rested with the minister of agriculture, the ex officio chairman. The Special Conference could be seen as a bulky miniparliament with the expected consequence that most of the real work was done by its secretariat. The representatives of the legislatures decreased their influence by absentee-ism, whether or not the Duma was in session. But none of these factors canceled out the significance of the Special Conference. The chairman did not want even the appearance of conflict with public representatives so that at least until mid-1916 the Special Conference was de facto a decision-making organ, not just an advisory one. The representatives of the public organizations—Peter Struve from the Union of Zemstvos and especially Vladimir Groman from the Union of Towns—had a disproportionate influence stemming both from their personal activity and from the weight of the social groups in whose name they spoke. The main legislative development of the year—the price-regulation decision of February 1916—was pushed through by a coalition of the chairman, the secretariat, and Struve and Groman. [25]

The Special Conference was also meant to achieve coordination in the administrative sphere by creating a central authority responsible for all food-supply matters. In the spring of 1915 Krivoshein responded to a complaint about fuel for flour mills by saying, "In this connection I'm almost as helpless as you"; the most he could promise was to petition the appropriate authority. [26] The effect of the Special Conference system was to

24. Secondary sources give varying numbers for ministerial representatives: Bukshpan, *Politika*, 316–17; Kitanina, *Voina*, 137; Zaitsev and Dolinsky, "Organization and Policy," 10. From a list of members in 457-1-33/13–14 I count nine.

25. Naumov, *Iz vospominanii*, 2:346; P. B. Struve, *Collected Works* (Ann Arbor, 1970), vol. 11, no. 515. For other assessments of the Special Conference, see Laverychev, "Politika," 150–51; Kitanina, *Voina*, 124–44; Bukshpan, *Politika*, 377–401.

26. 456-1-19/185.

give this petitioning a more stable institutional form. Results were seen mainly in the area of transport policy. The first aim of the Special Conference was to get a top priority for food shipments for both the military and the civilian population. The transport bottleneck had become so tight that those without top priority simply would not get their shipment on the rails. Many horror stories were told in this regard; a zemstvo noted in August 1916 that they had just received a shipment that had been sent in December. The Special Conference had to petition long and hard just to get an appropriate priority for food shipments. The next step was what was called a transport plan, which simply meant matching available freight car space to available food shipments. Even this amount of regulation was not achieved in the case of the more decentralized river transport system, which was never used to its capacity during the war years. Despite constant squabbles and mutual accusations, some progress was made in the immensely complicated business of meshing food procurement and transport capacity.[27]

But otherwise the Special Conference did not gain full control even in food supply. A list of all the agencies with a role in food-supply policy includes local branches of the army purchasing agency; local towns and rural administrations; the food-supply section of the Ministry of Internal Affairs (whose prewar function had been famine relief); the military, directly intervening on the local level; central transport authorities; and various organizations attending to the needs of refugees.[28] The role of the Special Conference as a coordinating institution at the center was also challenged by various rivals mostly set up on an ad hoc basis as the result of bureaucratic infighting.[29] Even within the Special Conference system the Special Conference on Defense had final say on food-supply matters and used this prerogative in September 1916 on the politically explosive question of the level of fixed prices for grain. The efforts of the Special Conference to coordinate food supply finally ended in failure in late 1916 when it began to lose its political standing and as a result lost most of its administrative usefulness as well.

The main aim of the Special Conference was to achieve coordination in the economic sphere by overcoming the army-society dualism. This mission was reflected in its local organization. The Special Conference (or, to be more precise, its chairman) had a commissioner in each province; the organization below this level was vague and depended a great deal on the initiative of the provincial commissioners. In the surplus provinces the

27. Zaitsev and Dolinsky, "Organization and Policy," 62–81.
28. Kondratiev, *Rynok khlebov*, 80.
29. Bukshpan, *Politika*, 383–85.

zemstvo chairmen who had been serving as purchasing commissioners directly under the minister of agriculture often became Special Conference commissioners as well. In other provinces the Special Conference commissioner was usually the governor, the official with traditional responsibilities for public order.

Theoretically the purchasing commissioner was subordinated to the Special Conference commissioner who had the broader mission of alleviating food-supply difficulties as they arose; in practice there was a division of labor between the two kinds of commissioners: the purchasing commissioners took responsibility for procurement, and the Special Conference commissioners for distribution. (It is understandable that there were complaints about "these various commissioners who are propagating these days in such numbers.") Unity at the top was guaranteed by the fact that the minister of agriculture and the chairman of the Special Conference were always the same person.[30]

Merely by virtue of including the situation in the deficit areas within its purview, the Special Conference was led to continue the repudiation of local embargoes that Shakhovskoi had begun. The destructive impact of sudden embargoes was so clear that the Special Conference even got the support of Tsar Nicholas in this effort, and although there were isolated violations, by and large this problem had been overcome by early 1916. But when it abolished the blatant dualism of embargoes and reestablished communication between surplus and deficit regions, the Special Conference took on the imposing challenge of regulating their mutual relations. Krivoshein had preferred the embargo system, which isolated the surplus regions from the competitive bids of the deficit regions, because he felt it economized on administrative resources: "I can compel someone to sell, but it is hardly possible to compel a buyer not to offer a price higher than the established one."[31] Not until Krivoshein was replaced as minister of agriculture in October 1915 by A. N. Naumov were embargoes definitely abandoned. Naumov also gave much attention to ending direct purchases by the military behind the front.[32]

Dualism still existed in the price structure. The basic dualism between

30. Zaitsev and Dolinsky, "Organization and Policy, 5, 13–15; Kitanina, *Voina*, 142–43; Bukshpan, *Politika*, 385. According to Bukshpan, there were sixty-seven Special Conference commissioners, of which eighteen were zemstvo chairmen and thirty-five were governors. The comment on their proliferation comes from *Ekonomicheskoe polozhenie Rossii nakanune velikoi oktiabr'skoi sotsialisticheskoi revoliutsii* (Leningrad, 1957–1967), pt. 3, doc. 77 (hereafter cited as *Ek. pol.*).

31. 457-1-256/9–11.

32. 456-1-19/124–26 (July 1915); Naumov, *Iz vospominanii*, 2:347; Krivoshein, *A. V. Krivoshein*, 283–85; P. B. Struve, Introduction to Struve, ed., *Food Supply*, xiv–xv.

regulated prices and market prices at first existed in two forms: regulated government versus unregulated civilian purchases, and regulated retail versus unregulated wholesale prices. The logic of events drove the Special Conference to overcome this dualism and replace it with one regulated price for all grain transactions. Yet, as we shall see, the Special Conference only undertook the task of overall price regulation with great foreboding.

Dualism is created when a powerful actor protects its own interests by self-help actions that disrupt the normal activities of everybody else. When the government and its local agents used their power to set fixed prices for army food-supply purchases, a dualism was created between the government price and the unregulated market price. The market price was soon considerably higher than the fixed government price, partly because government purchases took a significant percentage of total supply—or, as it was usually put at the time, because the producers and the millers made up for losses on government purchases by overcharging the civilians. This dualism irritated both the government and the civilians. The civilians were irritated because they felt an undue share of wartime strain was being shifted to them, and the government was irritated because the seller much preferred the unregulated market and so began to flee when he saw the government purchaser approach.

A dualism of a different kind was created when municipal authorities tried to protect local interests by establishing a regulated price (*taksa*) for bread and other foodstuffs to keep the cost of living down—a dualism between regulated retail prices and unregulated wholesale prices. The cities were much less powerful than the central government, and their self-help actions failed to achieve the intended purpose. If the regulated price was simply based on the existing wholesale price, with the aim of controlling the profits of local tradesmen, it had little impact on the cost of living. If the cities tried to set a regulated wholesale price, they merely succeeded in drying up supply as wholesalers diverted their shipments elsewhere. When economic competition was transmuted into political competition, disruption was only amplified, as in the case of the meat war between Moscow and Petrograd: "When the regulated price was higher in Moscow, livestock was brought only there. Petrograd suffered from lack of meat and in its turn raised its regulated price, so Moscow was left without meat, and all the livestock went to Petrograd. Thus Moscow could do nothing but raise its regulated price in turn. She once more raised her price, and again Petrograd sat without meat."[33]

During the second year of the war both of these price dualisms were

33. Chaianov, *Vopros*, 8–9; Kondratiev, *Rynok khlebov*, 135–39.

overcome. The process began late in 1915 when the Special Conference imposed central control on fixed prices for government purchases. Empirewide prices for the various grain products were decreed and backed up with requisition powers. Price setting started with oats and ended with wheat flour, that is, it went from the grain product whose production was the least market-oriented and therefore hardest to procure to the one whose production was the most market-oriented. The government originally set the fixed prices on the basis of market prices, but dualism returned when the fixed prices stayed constant and the market price continued to rise.[34]

The next major decision of the Special Conference was to tie the many regulated prices set by local civilian authorities to the empirewide fixed price used for government purchases. The Special Conference undertook to review the civilian prices so as to coordinate them with each other and with the fixed prices offered by the government to sellers in the surplus regions. These prices were enforced through de facto government control over the transport bottleneck. In February 1916 rules were issued that instructed Special Conference commissioners to grant access to priority shipping (which in practice meant the opportunity to ship anything at all) only to those dealers who would promise to sell at regulated prices.

There was now one national price dualism: a government price system that tied together prices for both the army and the urban population coexisted uneasily with the prices created by the unregulated market. Despite their control over the transport system, political authorities still found this dualism a hindrance. Municipal authorities could now make sure that grain was sold at a reasonable price—but only if they succeeded in obtaining actual supplies at that price. In frustration they turned more and more to the central purchasing authorities to get these supplies. The central authorities, faced with an ever-increasing procurement target, were also frustrated. To be sure, the fixed government prices were backed up with requisition powers, but these could only be used with "visible supplies," that is, supplies already concentrated at transportation points, flour mills, and other places of storage. These supplies were noticeably drying up already in the summer of 1915, and by the end of the year the use of requisition had made dealers so cautious that all grain supplies were rapidly becoming invisible.[35]

These difficulties led to the final overcoming of dualism by making state grain prices mandatory for all transactions, public and private. Just as the

34. Kondratiev, *Rynok khlebov,* 141–47; Kitanina, *Voina,* 158ff.
35. 456-1-19/65; Kitanina, *Voina,* 161–67.

transport bottleneck had forced an increase in the scope of government regulation in February 1916, the bottleneck of the flour mills forced this final step. The millers were afraid of paying the market price for their grain since they could easily be compelled to sell their highly visible supplies at the lower government price. But they were unable to obtain supplies if they restricted themselves to the government price. In June 1916 the Special Conference decided that fixed prices should be extended to all supplies obtained by the mills and that the government "must create conditions which will assure the millers a sufficient supply of the grain they need, at fixed prices." Since the millers were the main buyers of commercial grain, there was little difference between extending fixed prices to their transactions alone and extending them to all grain transactions. The government had now undertaken to do what Krivoshein warned was not possible: to keep the buyer from offering more.

There was a certain logic to the steadily increasing government intervention. But there was also an alternative method of overcoming dualism, and that was the removal of regulated prices altogether. The government rejected this path only after much wavering and conflict. The reason for this ambivalence was that it was both necessary and impossible to regulate prices, and since the bureaucrats were experienced and clearheaded enough to see both the necessity and the impossibility, they could not be expected to be cheerful about their decision. They were forced to do what opponents of regulation had warned against: to take on the job of an "adequate and equitable provision of the population with food, while having a complete lack of confidence in the possibility of executing . . . these responsibilities."[36]

The crucial choice had been made in February 1916 when the Special Conference decided to tie civilian regulated prices to the fixed prices for government purchases. In the debate within the Special Conference that preceded this decision, both sides agreed on two things: the transport bottleneck was the "center of gravity of the whole food-supply question" (Struve, who supported regulation), and setting price rates could be effective only as a "component . . . of a whole system of measures" (the Pokrovskii committee, made up of opponents of regulation).[37] But the conclusions drawn by the opposing parties differed radically.

The debate in the Special Conference grew out of a report in late 1915 by the secretariat of the Special Conference on the chaos created by ad hoc price regulation by local authorities. This report (written by K. I. Zaitsev) had made a convincing case for the necessity of going further than simply

36. 457-1-256/9–11.
37. 457-1-256/9–12; Zaitsev and Dolinsky, "Organization and Policy," 46–49.

regulating prices at the local level: "On the state authority that regulates prices lies the responsibility either of ensuring that a sufficient quantity of the affected product appears on the relevant market or of regulating demand, since as soon as the prices are regulated, prices lose the ability to regulate supply and demand." It was the authorities who now had the job of "drawing out goods hidden from observation and getting them to the consumer." Not that the difficulties of further regulation were ignored: Zaitsev spoke at length about the difficulties of setting prices properly in a situation where production costs fluctuated because of inflation and wartime shortages. It had been difficult enough to determine a fair price for the middlemen: how much more difficult "to go deep into the hidden side of economic life and determine production costs."[38]

The Pokrovskii committee was a nonofficial grouping of Special Conference members headed by N. N. Pokrovskii, a member of the State Council. Though it agreed that uncoordinated local regulation was destructive, it recoiled from the prospect of "state monopolization" and "statization." It noted that the government was having difficulties coping just with the regulation of sugar production and distribution it had already undertaken: how could it possibly hope to take on economic life as a whole? Since transport was the origin of the difficulties, the committee advised concentrating on making improvements there; as for price-setting measures, they should all be rescinded (except perhaps for the capitals).

It was this last suggestion that moved Struve to make his one major intervention in food-supply policy making. Struve saw in the removal of local regulated prices a "purely negative measure" that would only discredit the state authority: "If it is possible to see danger in the sketching of theoretical schemes of state intervention and [in] the announcement of such broad tasks by the state authority [this is probably a reference to proposals advanced by Vladimir Groman], still it would be not less but perhaps even more dangerous in the present crucial moment for the state authority, consciously and on principled grounds, to remove itself from intervention in economic life, based on lack of confidence in its own powers." The breakdown in transport had to be taken as an inevitable feature of wartime, along with the "severe militarization of all of national life" that made free trade impossible.[39]

Struve's argument pointed to the consideration that finally led the

38. *Sovremennoe polozhenie taksirovki predmetov prodovol'stviia v Rossii i mery k ee uporiadocheniiu* (Petrograd, 1915), 66, 73–76. See also Struve, *Collected Works*, vol. 11, no. 501. The further course of the debate is described in Zaitsev and Dolinsky, "Organization and Policy," 37–61.
39. 457-1-256/11–12.

majority to accept the necessity of price regulation. It was unwise to rely on any substantial improvement in the transport situation, especially since transport was outside the mandate of the Special Conference on Food Supply. The Special Conference had fought hard to get access to priority transport: how could it avoid using this power to influence economic life? It was also clear that it would be impossible to get the cities to remove their price rates; but if price rates there must be, reasoned the Special Conference, they should be at least effective ones that did not damage national economic life. The hand of the Special Conference was thus forced by decisions taken earlier at all levels of government.

In response to the argument that the government was taking on a task that would be "impossible for any government on earth to carry out," Struve made a distinction between free trade and private trade. Free trade was dead, but the private trade apparatus would still be able to act as specialists in "concentrating and distributing goods." (There was never a whisper in these debates about any rights of the capitalists; the bureaucrats who opposed price regulation saw the capitalists purely as an apparatus that it would be inexpedient to destroy.)

Despite these arguments, the original decision of the Special Conference was to reject regulation. Only after the chairman of the Special Conference, Agriculture Minister Naumov, made his preferences known did the Special Conference reverse itself (thus sparing him the necessity of overriding its decision). When Naumov had taken over the ministry from Krivoshein in October 1915, he was appalled at the "chaos of decisions, opinions, and intentions" and at Krivoshein's casual attitude toward coordination and control.[40] Naumov heavily stressed the necessity for unity of action and for a planned approach to policy. Furthermore, he had political reasons for wanting to be able to point to a coherent program: criticism of the Special Conference's lack of system in food-supply policy was beginning to be heard not only from the Duma but also from the Ministry of Internal Affairs. Naumov himself was scheduled to meet the Duma on 18 February 1916. The decision to use control over access to transport as a means of regulation was made 16 February; hence Naumov was able to refer to it in his well-received Duma speech.

THE BATTLE OVER PRICES

After the decision to overcome dualism in grain prices by establishing a fixed price for all transactions, political battle began over the level of those

---

40. Naumov, *Iz vospominanii*, 2:468.

prices. This struggle went on throughout the summer of 1916 and was a much more passionate affair than the debate that had preceded the more fundamental decision to impose fixed prices. Naumov started the process of price formation by asking local commissioners of the surplus regions to consult local agricultural producers and set prices based on local conditions. Not surprisingly, these prices were placed rather high, and the officials of the Special Conference secretariat worked over them and reduced them noticeably. Meanwhile, a challenge to these prices was also being mounted by the commissioners of the deficit regions of the Moscow area. The prices finally approved by the Special Conference were between the high level proposed by the producers and the low level proposed by the consumers. But at this point the consumer interest gained a powerful ally: the army. Owing to the army's challenge, a unique meeting of all four Special Conferences took place in September, and prices were lowered still further. The Council of Ministers then made one final adjustment upwards.[41]

In this conflict over the level of fixed prices we can see the outlines of an alignment of social forces that lasted throughout the time of troubles. Leading the fight for low prices was Vladimir Groman. Groman was a Menshevik economist and statistician whose previous experience had been in the local zemstvos. He was a fascinatingly typical member of his generation of the Russian intelligentsia, a generation whose enthusiasm had been excited by the opportunities for reform first of the war period and then of the revolutionary period but which was disillusioned by Lenin and destroyed by Stalin.

Even before the beginning of the Special Conference Groman had been a powerful voice pushing for further regulation. In spring 1915 he presided over a multivolume study of the rise of the cost of living in which he called for the "self-organization of the nation" as an answer to growing economic dislocation. When the Special Conference was formed in August and the public organizations were asked to send representatives, "The Union [of Towns] happened to choose Groman, or vice versa."[42] The archives of the Special Conference are littered with his passionate and polemical memoranda, characterized by insightful rebuttals of his opponents and a visionary faith in economic regulation based on statistical data. The course of food-supply policy during the time of troubles cannot be understood without recalling this visionary faith, which did not wait for the revolutions of 1917 to make its influence felt. Naum Jasny, who at that time had

41. *Ek. pol.*, pt. 3, doc. 76.
42. Naum Jasny, *Soviet Economists of the Twenties: Names to Be Remembered* (Cambridge, 1972). Groman's 1915 remarks are in *Trudy komissii*, 3:362–63.

just joined Groman's staff, later described Groman in action at one of the conferences of the summer of 1916:

> The commissioners consisted mostly of wealthy landlords,
> with "your excellencies" and even princes richly strewn among
> them. It was fascinating to observe how Groman, in a suit
> which had never been pressed since he bought it off the rack,
> made himself heard. In spite of his immense drive, however,
> the commissioners decided on prices which he believed too
> high. Groman's continued pressure brought the Army's inter-
> ference in favor of his proposals.[43]

It may seem astonishing that Groman, the revolutionary statistician with a visionary dream of a planned economy, should have a major impact on the tsarist economic policy. Indeed it *is* astonishing, and for an explanation we must look at Groman's allies in forcing a lower price. First we see the Union of Towns, which hired Groman and put him on the Special Conference. Then there are several of the central ministries, including the Ministry of War, whose protest brought about the joint session, as well as the ministries of Finance and State Audit. A partial ally was liberal land-lords and merchants who "considered it their political duty to separate themselves from the narrow group interest in higher prices" and therefore voted for low prices or abstained.[44] Another ally was the specialists, both in the public organizations and in the Special Conference secretariat, who had their own ambitious dreams of economic reform. For example, Ia. M. Bukshpan of the Special Conference secretariat wrote in August 1916:

> The war has moved the state into center stage in social life,
> and made it the dominant principle, in relation to which all
> other manifestations of public endeavor [*obshchestvennost'*] are
> auxiliaries. . . . Industrial mobilization, regulated prices and
> requisitions, syndicates and monopolies, all of this has created
> a new current in the national economy and points to unheard-
> of possibilities for economic creativity. [The new organizations
> at the center and in the localities are] all cells of our national-
> economic organized nature and are a yet unappreciated foun-
> dation for the systematic [*planomernyi*] construction of our fu-
> ture external and internal commercial policy.[45]

43. Naum Jasny, *To Live Long Enough: The Memoirs of Naum Jasny, Scientific Analyst*, ed. Betty A. Laird and Roy D. Laird (Lawrence, Kans., 1976), 21. Jasny is rightly indignant that Zaitsev and Dolinsky gloss over Groman's role almost completely. On Groman's importance, see Chaianov, *Vopros*, 9–12.

44. Kondratiev, *Rynok khlebov*, 154.

45. *Materialy*, iii–iv. On the background of these specialists, see Jasny, *To Live*, 18.

On one side of the battle over prices was a coalition based on the consumer interest of the deficit regions, the mobilization needs of the military, and the dreams of ambitious specialists. On the other side were the landowners, who had not previously had much impact on the course of wartime economic regulation but were galvanized into action by the threat of low fixed prices.[46] The landowners believed intensely that the city was robbing the countryside and that, in the words of a landowner from Kursk, "when the town loots the village, when it demands this sacrifice, then I count this as a crying injustice." Under these circumstances, it was claimed, the landowners had a common interest with the mass of the peasantry. The Kursk landowner stated that he was the one and only representative of the rural producers at the provincial price-setting conference; all other participants were either bureaucrats or factory owners, whose only aim was to set prices as low as possible.[47]

The landowners argued that the consumer representatives had no conception of agricultural costs. A writer from Viatka named I. Sigov granted that in some cases gentry-dominated local conferences had exaggerated production costs, but he gave the following counterexample from Viatka: local residents calculated the average cost of producing a pood of grain to be two rubles and twelve kopecks at the place of production (that is, without including transport costs). It was probably an underestimation since weather conditions were worse than expected. Meanwhile the fixed price was set at one ruble and twelve kopecks—with no extra premium for the cost of transport.[48]

The fight over prices was thinly veiled by the pretense that it was a debate over the method of price calculation.[49] Some of the features of the "Moscow method" associated with Groman's name will give an idea of his style. The Moscow method was intended to correct for wartime speculative influences by a complicated system of proportions between production costs before the war and production costs in 1916. Groman had great confidence that his method would allow the central government to establish fair and efficient prices for the localities. As a pamphlet by one of his disciples stated, it was a "scientific method, with scientific positions, scientific premises and arguments of scientific value."[50] It was precisely this

46. Bukshpan, *Politika*, 392.

47. *Materialy*, 93. An opposing view of the local conferences can be found in a publication of the Union of Towns written by M. D. Farber, *Tverdye tseny na khleb* (n.p., 1916).

48. I. Sigov, *Arakcheevskii sotsializm* (n.p., 1917), 3–7.

49. A full discussion of all proposed methods can be found in Kondratiev, *Rynok khlebov*, 149–51.

50. Farber, *Tverdye tseny*, 15.

"theoreticalness" to which his opponents objected. A speaker at one of the Special Conference debates scoffed at the statistics on which Groman's calculations were based: "What are statistics worth at present? An absolute farthing—just as they are never worth anything. Statistical data are gathered by village elders and scribes, and these do as they wish."[51]

Groman also contended that the countryside would not gain anything from higher prices for what it sold since they would be matched by higher prices for what it bought. He stated that "there can only be one basic criterion: the equilibrium of the national economy"; high prices for grain would threaten this equilibrium since they would push wages up and thus increase the cost of all industrial products. This speech is one of the first appearances of the concept of equilibrium for which Groman became notorious in the late 1920s. It reflects well on Groman's integrity that the emphasis on equilibrium, seen as soft on peasants in the late 1920s, should make its first appearance as a defense of the urban consumer against high grain prices.[52]

Besides challenging Groman's arguments about the level of prices, the landowners also insisted that it was unfair to impose fixed prices on agricultural products but not on manufactured goods bought by the countryside.[53] This argument was seen as a conservative one in 1916, although it was later taken up by peasant spokesmen and supported by the left-wing parties. Even in 1916 the justice of the complaint was not denied by the opposing coalition, both because it was politically dangerous to raise up the countryside against the towns through one-sided regulation of agricultural products and because fixed prices for industrial items broadened the scope of government economic regulation. A conference of local commissioners in August 1916 went on record as favoring price regulation of industrial items so that there would be an equitable distribution of wartime burdens between town and country; this demand was supported by a Duma resolution in December.[54] The commitment to provide industrial items at fixed prices was also taken up as official policy by the Provisional Government and the Bolsheviks.

This commitment to further regulation revealed a feeling shared by both sides that the overcoming of dualism by means of fixed prices was incomplete and therefore unstable. Vladimir Gurko (an opponent of fixed

51. *Materialy*, 95.

52. *Russkie Vedomosti*, 23 August 1916. Jasny traces Groman's explicit use of the concept back to 1923 and says it was implicit earlier. (The term is also used in Farber, *Tverdye tseny*.)

53. Kitanina, *Voina*, 168.

54. L. L., *Prodovol'stvennyi vopros* (n.p., 1916), 13, 16–17. See also *Ek. pol.*, pt. 3, docs. 72, 73, 78, 83.

prices) felt that the extension of fixed prices to all transactions would have the same effect as local regulation—a drying-up of supply, only now the supply of the entire empire would be affected. He believed that the government should allow complete free trade (with occasional use of requisition powers) or institute a state monopoly: "there is no third solution."[55] Support for a full-fledged state monopoly was in fact gaining in strength. The first suggestions had been made by purchasing commissioners facing difficulties in the procurement of oats. By August 1916, partly at the instigation of Special Conference specialists such as Bukshpan, there was a widespread discussion in the press of the possibility of a state monopoly of the grain trade. At the September meeting of all four Special Conferences the prominent Kadet spokesman Andrei Shingarev argued that "the most correct and radical solution of the problem would be to establish a state grain monopoly." Shingarev meant what he said: six months later he was instrumental in setting up the grain monopoly of the Provisional Government.[56]

Behind the struggle over the level of prices was a more ominous debate on the efficacy of economic incentives in general. The Special Conference representatives of the Union of Zemstvos and the Union of Towns parted ways on this issue. Struve took a lonely position since he strongly supported the extension of fixed prices to all transactions but strongly opposed setting the level of prices too low: "If we have to choose between a high, even excessive, level of fixed prices and the mobilization of an enormous requisitioning organization directed against the mass of agricultural producers who hold a surplus of grain, it stands to reason that what we should fear most is the fixing of too low, or even merely inadequate, prices."[57] Groman objected that since peasants had only a limited need for money, higher prices might even decrease the amount of grain offered. He mentioned that soldiers often wrote home to their families saying, "Watch out, don't sell your bread, who knows what may happen!" and commented that this motive was not affected by high prices.[58] This reasoning came perilously close to arguing the necessity of force.

Decreeing a single price for all transactions was an attempt to overcome the disruption caused by dualism. But the very process by which grain prices were fixed had the unfortunate effect of increasing political and social disruption. Naumov's original reason for allowing the prices to be set through a broad open process was so that they would be perceived as fair to

55. 369-1-56/41.
56. 369-1-56/57–58; 456-1-90/49–50; Bukshpan, *Politika*, 390–91.
57. Struve, Introduction, xvii–xviii; Struve, *Collected Works*, vol. 11, no. 504.
58. *Materialy*, 110–12.

all parties. The result was just the opposite, for the prices were now viewed as the result of a power struggle between groups. Even though the public consultation with local assemblies about price levels was a concession to the demands of the landowners, Naumov himself left office in the summer of 1916, partly because of unpopularity earned by association with the whole policy of fixed prices.[59]

The delay caused by the price-setting process had a paralyzing effect on the market. As producers waited for the price to be set, they stopped selling. Not only government purchases but also the market as a whole were at a standstill. Local buyers had asked that prices be announced by July, yet they were not set until the middle of September. By September the Special Conference was inundated with frantic telegrams from purchasing commissioners asking for a definite price so that they could start buying.[60] This tardiness in the start of government purchasing operations was extremely harmful since supplies had to arrive in the north before the end of river navigation in the middle of October.

The economic standstill was easily perceived as deliberate blackmail. Local grain dealers had been listening to the local price-setting conferences, and they had concluded that the fixed price was going to be immense. Acting on this assumption, they bought grain from the peasants at fairly high prices and were shocked when the final fixed price was considerably below their expectations. They could not believe gentry opinion could be so easily flouted, so they waited for a change and in the meantime held on to their grain.[61]

To disabuse grain holders of the hope of any change, a telegram was sent out to local officials in late September over the signatures of Boris Sturmer (chairman of the Council of Ministers), Aleksei Bobrinskii (the new minister of agriculture), and Aleksei Protopopov (minister of internal affairs), saying that success now depended on convincing people of the fixity (*tverdost'*) of the fixed prices. Protopopov's signature was important since he was known to be an advocate of free trade as an answer to food-supply difficulties. The commissioners were to inform the population that under no circumstances would the prices be raised and were to induce them to cooperate by "knowing how to use the uplift of its patriotic feeling"; but they were also to remind them that the requisition power stood at the ready. This volley in the war of nerves between government and grain holders was not successful since the political challenge in high government

59. Kitanina, *Voina*, 167, 173.
60. 457-1-278/42, 48, 49, 55, 58; *Ek. pol.*, pt. 3, doc. 64, p. 134.
61. Chaianov, *Vopros*, 21–22.

circles to the policies of the Special Conference was hardly secret. The governor of Ekaterinoslav reported that the appeal to patriotism-cum-force struck many people as revealing not determination but rather the lack of it.[62] Earlier the embargoes and requisitions that created economic dualism had brought forth political counterpressures; now the politics of overcoming dualism in turn had economic consequences, which unfortunately only intensified disruption.

Although the breakdown of political authority was still in the future, the first two years of the war reveal the logic of a time of troubles almost as much as do the more dramatic events to come. The time of troubles first showed itself in small things—a shipment that failed to arrive because of a local embargo, a regulated price that made bread affordable and unavailable—but the logic was similar to that of the larger crisis ahead that indeed grew out of these small disruptions.

The expectation of a short war had led authorities to be casual about the costs of disruption so that they consciously created a dualism by which civilian society was to bear the entire burden of dislocation and readjustment. This policy could not be sustained indefinitely, and the second year of the war was spent in trying to overcome the dualism created during the first year. But the process of overcoming dualism itself created further uncertainty.

People had difficulty accounting for these unexpected developments. Why were there shortages and high prices in a country where there should have been a glut? In efforts to explain this puzzling state of affairs everybody blamed everybody else. Society was now forced to make conscious choices about what had previously been done routinely, but the knowledge to support these newly conscious choices was not forthcoming. To use the poignant commercial metaphor, visible supplies were quickly exhausted, and the government was forced to feel its way around on the hidden side of economic life.

Uncertainty gave rise to conflict, and conflict gave rise to uncertainty. The battle over fixed prices led to bitter disunity between the coalition of forces that wanted a cheap and reliable supply of grain and the rural producers who felt they were being exploited. The political struggle did not end with the final establishment of fixed prices in September 1916 but merely entered a new phase—and until the smoke had cleared and the outcome of the battle was known, the fixity of the prices and of everything else about food-supply policy was in doubt.

62. 457-1-40/174, 1291-132-428/21.

2 The Two Solutions

> The food-supply question has swallowed up all other
> questions. . . . And we see that as economic anarchy has
> spread, all the deeper is the process of the penetration of the
> state principle into all aspects of the economic existence of the
> country.
>
> An employee of the Union of Towns, fall 1916

By the fall of 1916 food-supply policy had become a central focus of
political attention.[1] The feeling was spreading that a drastic change of the
government's overall course was imperative and that any such change
would have to begin with food-supply administration. Two strong challenges arose to the middle course that had been pursued by the Ministry of
Agriculture and the Special Conference on Food Supply. One came from
within the government and was headed by the Ministry of Internal Affairs;
the other came from outside and was headed by the public organizations,
particularly the Union of Towns. The three-way struggle between these
two challengers and the Special Conference came to a climax in October
and November 1916.

I will not be concerned so much with the complicated infighting that
accompanied this struggle as with the solutions proposed by the challengers and the arguments they used to justify their approach. The deep
fissure within the Russian educated elite over the proper direction of the
future political evolution of the tsarist government showed itself in the
microcosm of debates over food-supply policy. Were the traditional methods of the government hopelessly outmoded and incapable of being up-
dated to meet the challenge of modern war and international competition?
Or did the demands of the educated public to be given a decisive voice in the
councils of government reflect only the ignorant amateurism of the frustrated outsider?

The clash of solutions was not only a partisan debate over the best

---

1. According to L. L.'s account, papers reported 98 sessions on food-supply
matters in September alone, most of them not coming to any conclusion. L. L.,
Vopros, 1.

approach to food-supply problems but also two opposing attempts to establish a basis of unity for the political class. Most people realized that the war could not be fought successfully unless the various elements of the Russian political class—the bureaucrats, the opposition activists, the "third-element" specialists, the military, and the landowners—achieved a greater working unity than they had been able to achieve in the first two years of the war. Yet this unity was almost impossible to achieve given the entire lack of consensus on the bases of legitimacy for the political class. Without agreement on a political formula the effort to overcome economic dualism would be defeated by lack of consensus on proper political methods. Since the beginning of the war, disputes over economic policy had reflected this deeper political conflict.

One possible strategy for a central political authority is to send an agent to a locality and give that agent full responsibility for maintaining order and in consequence full authority over other members of the political class in the area. In Russian history this agent has been the governor, and so I have named this strategy the *gubernatorial solution*. This term would not have seemed strange to political activists of the period. In 1914 Struve called the gubernatorial authority (*vlast'*) the main unhealthy element in Russian political life; even after 1917 and the disappearance of the governors, people understood what was meant when Bolshevik commissars were called Red governors.[2]

During the first years of the war the main advocates of the gubernatorial solution were to be found in the Ministry of Internal Affairs, the ministry to which provincial governors reported. The gubernatorial solution was advanced mainly by three ministers of internal affairs (there were six altogether between August 1914 and February 1917): Nikolai Maklakov, Aleksei Khvostov, and Aleksei Protopopov. All three were bizarre characters with close connections to the empress and to Rasputin; they were intensely hated by the public opposition. They were parodies of the reforming minister, filled with projects and plans that went nowhere. But the definition of the situation implied by their programs is consistent enough to warrant the assumption that it originated in something more enduring than three unstable ministers. Behind the gubernatorial solution was a great deal of accumulated experience on how to run a Russian government.

The gubernatorial solution arose out of a definition of the war situation

---

2. Struve, *Collected Works*, vol. 11, no. 461. On the similarity between the governors and today's provincial party secretaries, see T. H. Rigby, "The Soviet Regional Leadership: The Brezhnev Generation," *Slavic Review* 37 (1978): 1–24. For an instructive look at the real world of the governors, see Richard G. Robbins, Jr., *The Tsar's Viceroys* (Ithaca, 1987).

that emphasized the finite amount of administrative resources at the disposal of the government and the absolute priority of the war effort. A certain amount of dualism was therefore acceptable to shield the army from the inevitable disruption of national life. This acceptance did not mean acquiescence in the blind policy of the military leadership, who seemed to believe that taking any civilian interest into account was illegitimate.[3] But it did imply that the problem of provisioning the population should be considered only when food-supply problems threatened disorder, and even then attention should be given primarily to workers in defense industries.

Preventing disorder may have seemed an unambitious goal to opposition activists, but to gubernatorial advocates it was a worthy challenge. Maklakov, Khvostov, and Protopopov each put prevention of food-supply disorders at the center of their political program. Maklakov wrote:

> I assume that a revolutionary movement based exclusively on the preaching of the theories of learned socialists cannot present a serious threat to the system existing in the Russian Imperial state and society. . . . Such a movement will definitely be crushed by appropriate measures of the government authority.
>
> But much more dangerous are revolutionary outbreaks of the masses caused by economic reasons, the most important of which is the high price of objects of prime necessity and in the first place—bread. . . .
>
> The uncivilized [*nekul'turnyi*] mass of poor people in the capital, independently of their political outlooks, explain these oppressive phenomena in the most undesirable fashion, willingly taking as truth various dark rumors, which boil down to the following: the government is completely on the side of the well-off classes and the capitalists and therefore willingly gives the latter the possibility of "making a bundle" by exploitation of the poor people, to whose lot fall, even without that, the heaviest burdens of the present war. Reasoning like this so agitates the simple people that more and more often one hears that it is necessary to start pogroms, to "settle accounts with the parasites [*miroedy*] and the moneybags," and so forth. A mood is being created in which is hidden the embryo of all kinds of complications for the task of preserving necessary order and public tranquillity.[4]

3. Daniel W. Graf, "Military Rule Behind the Russian Front, 1914–1917: The Political Ramifications," *Jahrbücher für Geschichte Osteuropas* 22 (1974): 390–411.
4. 1276-11-975/2–6.

To fight these problems effectively, the political class had to be united around the gubernatorial authority that was traditionally responsible for order. In early 1915 Maklakov argued that he should not be expected to preserve order by purely repressive means and that regulatory authority should be given to organs of the Ministry of Internal Affairs, the only ones "having at their disposal data on the needs and moods of the population, as well as having sufficient authority for carrying out any kind of exceptional measure."[5] In late 1916 Protopopov also complained of the danger that the Ministry of Internal Affairs would turn into a mere police station. Only if the governor had local sovereignty could he impose a unified policy and be held responsible by the center for order in the provinces. If he were not given primary responsibility for food supply, the only result would be endless squabbles between him and the other local officials.[6]

Another advantage of gubernatorial authority was that it was supposed to be strictly subordinated to the center. Gubernatorial advocates were appalled at the manner in which the minister of agriculture relied on voluntary cooperation, as reflected in Glinka's words:

> I must point out that this whole organization [of purchasing commissioners] has one extraordinary feature: it is not definitely subordinated to the department, but rests entirely upon the free will of its members to render service to the cause of provisioning our gallant troops. My position as High Commissioner, called upon to furnish instructions and directions to the local commissioners, has been most unusual and might have been exceedingly difficult, when we consider that it lacks real authority.[7]

Gubernatorial advocates felt that more reliable means for ensuring cooperation were required. Protopopov, for example, realized the need for zemstvo participation in food-supply matters, and he asserted that the transfer of food-supply authority to the Ministry of Internal Affairs would broaden this participation. But he insisted that zemstvo activity would be productive only if the governor had more authority as well as control over the granting of contracts and financial aid.

These means of influence could also be used to lure the local zemstvos away from the national Union of Zemstvos. Protopopov felt that this

5. 1276-11-975/46–50.

6. *Padenie tsarskogo rezhima* (Moscow, 1924–27), 4:65–68; 1276-12-1288/2–5.

7. Zaitsev and Dolinsky, "Organization and Policy," 5. This statement was made in August 1916.

organization was dominated by a revolutionary salaried staff and that in general the demand of opposition activists for a role in food-supply matters was meant to further political, and not practical, aims. This reasoning led him to attempt to bring unity to the political class entirely through the negative policy of banning independent organizational initiative—in particular the food-supply congresses scheduled by the public organizations in late 1916.[8]

Although gubernatorial advocates sought a secure basis of unity for the political class, they continued to accept economic dualism. This acceptance led to a solicitude for the apparatus of private trade so as to disrupt peacetime arrangements as little as possible. This policy did not stem from any admiration of the market or respect for bourgeois law and order. On the contrary, the governors had a penchant for high-handed methods of dealing with "speculators"—having them whipped in the bazaars, for example.[9] The reason for relying on the "commercial apparatus" was to free the government to concentrate its attention and forces on the vital tasks of supplying the army while making sure through monitoring and punishment that "speculative" price rises did not cause disorder. Although Protopopov, for example, had a more sincere admiration of the banks and the large commercial firms than the previous ministers of internal affairs, it is still inexact to describe his program as simply free trade. His plan was to get what the army needed (plus a certain reserve to be used for civilian purposes) by imposing fixed prices and then remove all restrictions on trade. Even at that point the government was to use its reserves to moderate prices.[10]

Gubernatorial advocates did not necessarily restrict themselves to using the existing trade apparatus, and at times a more activist policy was put into effect. Khvostov in particular felt that such a policy was necessary. Believing that "politics depends on the stomach," Khvostov took over the post of minister of internal affairs in September 1915 with a list of projects that (he said later) struck his fellow ministers as equivalent to socialism.[11] Khvostov's formula for achieving a mass base without enlisting organized social forces was to demonstrate the concern of the government by vigorous and visible activity. Police made raids on railroad stations revealing unloaded wagons, and gubernatorial agents were sent out as troubleshooters, all to the accompaniment of much publicity.

Khvostov tried to invigorate the traditional assertion of the tsarist

8. 1276-12-1288/20–28; Padenie, 4:65–68.
9. Norman Stone, The Eastern Front, 1914–1917 (London, 1975), 288.
10. Padenie, 4:71–78; TsGVIA, 13251-40-140/13–17.
11. Padenie, 6:84–86; Diakin, Russkaia burzhuaziia, 130.

governors that they protected the people against economic exploiters. Food-supply difficulties were blamed on speculators in the form of citizens of German nationality, the syndicates, the banks, and of course the Jews. To show that he meant business, Khvostov ordered massive raids of the Moscow grain exchange, and in January 1916 he sent out a circular to the governors in which he accused dark forces of sabotaging the war effort.[12]

All this activity could also be used as an offensive weapon against opposition activists. The city councils that made up the Union of Towns could be pictured as hotbeds of speculators.[13] Deliveries to the cities would be distributed through the police rather than the city dumas, and within the government Khvostov tried to take coordinating authority away from the Special Conference and its agents in the localities and give this authority back to the governors.[14]

Khvostov had difficulty connecting his activity on the food-supply front to a wider worldview that could serve as the basis for a political formula. All that was available to a tsarist minister trying to reanimate the gubernatorial solution came from the Black Hundreds, extremely nationalist and anti-Semitic groups spurned by more traditional conservatives as rabble— "an army of *dvorniki* (concierges), cabbies, servants, peddlers and rag and bobtail."[15] The outlook of these groups is expressed in a letter sent to the chairman of the Council of Ministers by an Irkutsk schoolteacher, Ia. G. Fedin:

> The most important and essential defect of our food-supply setup consists in the fact that it was mistakenly given to the city self-governments, the majority of which consist of merchants who are therefore naturally interested in selling the objects of their trade at the highest price possible. This is the first and most important reason for speculation, and it is necessary to remove it.
>
> Claims that we do not have objects of prime necessity are completely unfounded—we have everything, but this "everything" is hidden and not allowed on the market in order that prices not fall. Set up a governmental dictatorship, appoint

12. The tepid response of the public opposition to the anti-Semitic content of this circular is described in Michael Hamm, "Liberalism and the Jewish Question: The Progressive Bloc," *Russian Review* 31 (1972): 163–72. It should be said to the credit of Protopopov that removing restrictions on the Jewish population was part of his program.

13. Diakin, *Russkaia burzhuaziia*, 207–16.

14. 1284-47-269/9–11.

15. Allan Wildman, *The End of the Russian Imperial Army* (Princeton, 1980), 80.

government and not elected food-supply commissars, and you will be convinced that those stocks hidden by the speculators can feed the population for a very long time. Of course it will be necessary to give these commissars a very large authority, so that besides requisitioning they can severely punish speculators: here there should be no coddling. The commissars should be subordinated only to the state and to you [the chairman of the Council of Ministers] personally; the commissar should be given the right to find assistants from the population, paying no attention to their social position—just so that they are honorable and wish to work for the good of the people and the government.

The moral significance of the appointment of the commissars will make itself felt immediately: even before they have time to show their authority there will be food products on the market in sufficient quantity and at reasonable prices. These products will only have to be used intelligently and distributed among the population—this already will be a secondary task. Do not delay, Your Excellency, in the institution of a food-supply dictatorship.[16]

A deep distrust of society's ability to govern itself, a romantic image of the virtue and vigor of the agents of the supreme authority, and the ideal of governmental service as the highest calling of a loyal subject—all these are combined in Fedin's letter with a disdain for the complicated job of economic regulation ("a secondary task"). But along with these traditionalist images are more radical overtones. Fedin was anticapitalist; he feared election because it led to domination by local elites; he had scant regard for bureaucratic rules and regulations; and he wanted the powerful agents of the center to be appointed without attention to social position.

But tsarism and a mass base were destined not to come together.[17] Khvostov's attempts to unify Black Hundred groups and make them somewhat respectable did not get far, and Khvostov himself fell from favor as a result of some bizarre intrigues concerning Rasputin. Looking at this effort to give a new energy to the gubernatorial solution, one is tempted to reverse Marx's epigram and say that history occurs first as farce and later as

16. 457-1-219/69–70. Fedin surprisingly included participation by the public organizations as part of his program. His letter was received in December 1916. There is some evidence of support for the Bolsheviks from right-wing extremists; see M. Agurskii, *Ideologiia natsional-bol'shevizma* (Paris, 1980), 52.

17. Earlier attempts to combine the two included the "police socialism" associated with the name of Zubatov. See Jeremiah Schneidermann, *Sergei Zubatov and Revolutionary Marxism* (Ithaca, 1976).

tragedy. It is certainly difficult to take seriously Maklakov (who did barn-yard imitations to amuse the Tsar), Khvostov (who tried to poison Rasputin's cat), or Protopopov (who got advice from the dead Rasputin at seances).[18] But despite their eccentricities, they were groping toward a vigorous application of the gubernatorial solution that would be possible only when a new political class was constituted.

Opposed to the gubernatorial solution was the solution based on enlistment [*privlechenie*]. The self-confidence of the "vital forces" of Russian society expressed itself in the view that the government could solve its problems only to the extent that it earned the confidence of society and enlisted its representatives into full membership in the political class. This was not only a technical but also a moral imperative: the government *should* solve its problems only by way of earning the confidence of society. This general view of the proper relation between government and society led to a definition of the food-supply problem as something that could be solved by what society felt it had to offer: expertise, the ability to mobilize support, and a sense of the reforms required by modernity.

The specific programs proposed by enlistment advocates varied widely, depending not only on what was seen as necessary for earning the confidence of the vital forces of society but also on different views of the precise identity of these forces. But moderate bureaucrats such as Krivoshein, the liberal public opposition, and the socialists all agreed that the key to the problem was earning the confidence of society through enlistment. A crucial role in providing continuity in the evolution of the enlistment solution in the food-supply area was played by Groman. As the representative of the Union of Towns on the Special Conference on Food Supply, Groman was undoubtedly the main spokesman on food supply of the liberal public opposition. But he was also a dedicated socialist, and after the February revolution he argued that the food-supply crisis demanded a socialist transformation of the economy. Groman's advocacy thus provided a bridge between the liberal public opposition of the tsarist government and the radical enlistment solution that became dominant after the February revolution. Groman was finally left behind by the radical extreme reached in the spring of 1918 when he opposed the Bolshevik version of the enlistment solution.

The logic of the enlistment solution was based on confidence—confidence *in* society and the goal of earning the confidence *of* society. It arose

18. Bernard Pares, *The Fall of the Russian Monarchy* (New York, 1939). For an unexpected tribute by a Soviet historian to Maklakov, see Diakin, *Russkaia burzhuaziia*, 77.

out of a definition of the situation that emphasized not only the urgent priority of the war but also the all-encompassing demands made by military mobilization in all phases of social and economic life. The war was seen as a challenge and an opportunity. Far from wishing to limit the impact of the war, enlistment advocates stressed the need for complete militarization of national life and mobilization of social forces.[19]

If the population at large was to be enlisted into the war effort, it had to have confidence in the government. This precondition implied what was called a government of confidence (the insistent slogan of the public opposition) or perhaps even a government responsible to society instead of to the Tsar. As a pamphleteer of the public opposition put it, "The food-supply question has long ago become and in essence will remain a political question. . . . To change the system of administration is the most necessary condition of a rational economic policy in time of war."[20] The new system of administration would rely not so much on agents of the central authority as on newly created councils such as the Special Conferences that included representatives from various social groups.

The population had to accept many hardships and sacrifices during wartime, and these sacrifices had to be distributed fairly if the government was to retain the confidence of the population. This meant a broad government commitment to ensuring not only that food was available but also that it was available at a reasonable price or, even better, rationed on an egalitarian basis. Then, as Groman argued, "Once it becomes necessary to regulate consumption, we must inescapably enlist the consumers themselves, who alone can organize distribution [by rationing]. We must not forget that if the mass of the population is not enlisted into regulatory activity, they will not understand it, and inevitably a feeling of deep dissatisfaction will result."[21]

The enlistment advocates wanted to expand the food-supply apparatus both vertically and horizontally: it was to reach down to lower levels than previously, and it was to include a wider range of public forces. The extension of the apparatus was defended by the pamphleteer L. L. in December 1916. L. L. wrote that the food-supply apparatus should consist of collegial organs resting on a wide range of social forces and empowered to elect the local commissioner. This meant that the representative of the central organs would be responsible to local forces. Only through such local collegial organs could the government carry out central measures

---

19. Struve, *Collected Works*, vol. 11, no. 510 (December 1916).

20. L. L., *Vopros*, 16–17.

21. TsGVIA, 12593-68-78/12. This memorandum was written in October 1915, which is very early to be thinking about rationing and shows Groman's continuous pressure on food-supply officials to extend the scope of their regulation.

"tied together by a common plan whose implementation depends on harmonious and coordinated actions of regional organs." Election instead of appointment of the local commissioners, L. L. continued, would assure that these commissioners would not be "infected with lack of confidence in public forces." In this way the apparatus would itself gain the confidence of the public forces and therefore be strong enough to carry out "the most serious measures, up to and including compulsory seizure of grain."[22]

We see here the ideal of a voluntary hierarchy. Of course such a hierarchy needs leadership from above, but it presumably would be in the form of guidance, not direct orders. As a writer in the newspaper Den' put it: "Healthy decentralization is the foundation of proper development of such a complicated matter as the organization of the population's food supply, but along with this a living regulatory activity by the central organs is also necessary."[23] One reason for rejecting appointment from above was not so much principled democratism as suspicion about who would be appointed. We may surmise that if a change of government had lessened the suspicion between the locals and the center, the locals would have shown less resistance to central direction.

The opposition activists agreed with Khvostov on the organizing potential of the food-supply question, and there were various attempts in 1915 and 1916 to set up independent public organizations to provide the cities and the workers with food. The hope was that such organizations would eliminate the damaging competition between consumer centers—in one town, for example, there appeared twenty-two purchasing representatives of cities and zemstvos.[24] Politically these organizations would not only shame the government but also help enlist worker groups into opposition ranks and provide a national umbrella organization for groups excluded from full membership in the tsarist political class. A police report claimed that "under the guise of regulating food supply . . . there was an intent to create a supreme leadership center that in reality would have been a parallel government."[25]

Given the ambition of enlistment advocates, it is not surprising that they pushed for a full grain monopoly. Under a grain monopoly the government would control all the grain in the country above a fixed minimum left with the producer. The surplus grain, however, was not simply taken: it was to be exchanged in return for town products needed by

22. L. L., Vopros, 4.
23. This article was written in May 1916 and can be found in 1291-132-12.
24. Deviatyi s"ezd predstavitelei gorodov Petrogradskoi oblasti, April 1916, 268–74.
25. 1276-12-1294e/7–23 (a memorandum on the cooperatives). See also Laverychev, "Politika," 166–69.

the peasant. Although the grain producer had to sell his grain at a fixed price, the government would undertake to regulate the price of goods bought by the grain producer and to see that those goods were actually available.

The monopoly strategy of the enlistment solution can be contrasted to the tax strategy of the gubernatorial solution. Gubernatorial advocates viewed the grain needed by the army (and perhaps defense industries as well) as an obligation (*povinnost'*) that the citizen owed the state in its hour of need and for which no direct recompense should be expected. The tax strategy demanded a specified amount, be it large or small, and afterward gave the producer free disposal of what was left of his surplus.

The ambitious monopoly strategy required a huge amount of information about the nation's economic resources, but the enlistment advocates felt that this information was obtainable in the form of statistics. Groman was a statistician by training, and his admiring disciple Naum Jasny said of him that "if Groman had been given a free hand, nobody would have been doing anything but collecting and processing statistics."[26] Overweening confidence in the new tool of statistics was undoubtedly one motive force behind the enlistment solution. Statistics offered control over a chaotic situation and the possibility of reconciling what otherwise seemed to be three contradictory demands: coordination of government action, expansion of government tasks, and expansion and decentralization of the administrative apparatus.

Statistics also challenged the claim of the Ministry of Internal Affairs to be the best-informed department because of its control of the police and the local administration. In the eyes of the governors, statistics was hardly to be distinguished from socialism. They viewed the statisticians on the staff of local zemstvos as a subversive element and did what they could to obstruct the remarkable studies of the peasant economy carried out by zemstvo statisticians.[27]

The logic of the enlistment solution thus described a full circle: to have equitable distribution, we need monopolized control of grain exchange; to carry out the monopoly, we need the confidence of the population; to earn this confidence, we need to have equitable distribution. The only danger was that enlistment advocates would be caught in this logic and forget why they embarked on economic regulation in the first place: to supply the army and preserve national independence.

26. Jasny, *To Live*, 19. For the similar background and feelings of the Bolshevik commissar of food supply, A. D. Tsiurupa, see V. Tsiurupa, *Kolokola pamiati*, 42–44.

27. Hans Rogger, *Russia in the Age of Modernization and Revolution* (London, 1983), 61.

The gubernatorial solution was openly based on special features of the Russian political environment, whereas the enlistment solution was much more influenced by Western models of democratic control of government. But the enlistment advocates unconsciously adopted in their view of the world certain structural features of the Russian polity in a way that weakened the relevance of Western democratic thought. In Russia the chain of authority went from tsar to governor down to peasant council; since there were few horizontal links at lower levels, this pattern resulted in a dominance of vertical communication over horizontal communication. In the West horizontal links between people independent of each other formed the basis of industries, classes, professions, and parties—the interest formations that were the basic political units of the parliamentary system. Although this type of communication was developing rapidly in Russia, coordination in the political system still took place overwhelmingly at the top.

The enlistment solution aimed at enlistment into vertical hierarchies, which helped preserve a pyramidal structure that lacked horizontal links at lower levels. The deep strain of alienation from the state in Russia's social thought that Robert Tucker has called the image of dual Russia emphasized the contrast between popular Russia and official Russia.[28] Yet the reformers' vision of a triumphant popular Russia also had an underlying structural similarity to its statist counterpoint, and this similarity created the possibility that a revolutionary new Russia might reproduce more than it realized of the old Russia.

In summary, here is a list of contrasts between the gubernatorial solution and the enlistment solution:

Gubernatorial	Enlistment
order	confidence
solidarity of political class	enlistment
limitation of task	expansion of task
control from above	voluntary hierarchy
centrally appointed agent	locally elected council
advisory organs	collegial organs
tax strategy	monopoly strategy
limit impact of war	mobilization/militarization of national life
surveillance	statistics
strict priorities	reform ambitions
prevention of disorder	equity

28. Robert C. Tucker, *The Soviet Political Mind*, rev. ed. (New York, 1971). For a discussion of an allegedly Russian tendency to reverse positive and negative evalua-

The two solutions had roots that went far deeper than an immediate reaction to food-supply problems. The loyalty they inspired was not due just to a belief in their technical efficacy as a response to current problems; the two solutions sprang from deep convictions about the proper way for the state to go about its political business. They were solutions in search of a problem since prior loyalty to a particular solution usually determined how a problem was defined. The food-supply crisis was seized on by advocates of both solutions as an excellent illustration of why their strategy was the only basis of unity for the political class.

CHALLENGES TO THE ENLISTMENT SOLUTION

Up to September 1916 the evolution of food-supply policy had been in the direction of the enlistment solution. There had been a steady move toward overcoming dualism and toward the enlistment of public forces. By October 1916 this evolution finally provoked enough opposition from gubernatorial advocates to check its course. The policies of the Special Conference had not achieved the results that would have disarmed this opposition.

Dissatisfaction with the Special Conference was revealed by an attempt to introduce dualism in civilian food supply by militarizing the provisionment of defense workers. The idea first appeared in a meeting at Stavka, army general headquarters, in July 1916. Minister of War D. S. Shuvaev (who had previously been head of the army supply organization) was then told to work out a more detailed project. The basic idea of the project was to provide selected factories with food supplies directly from the reserves of the army supply organization; the factories would then distribute them to the workers through its own facilities. Various mechanisms were set up for quality control and inspections (with worker participation). At the beginning this measure could not be extensively applied if only because few factories had canteen facilities, and those facilities that did exist were mainly for show. But the project would take in approximately seven hundred thousand workers, mainly in the Moscow and Petrograd regions, and was expected to have "serious significance in the struggle against the lack of material security of the factory workers and their families and against the strike movement."[29]

---

tions while retaining the same structure, see Iu. M. Lotman and B. A. Uspenskii, "Binary Models in the Dynamics of Russian Culture," in Alexander D. Nakhimovsky and Alice Stone Nakhimovsky, eds., *The Semiotics of Russian Cultural History* (Ithaca, 1985). For an example of Bolshevik susceptibility to the gubernatorial solution, see the hero-worshiping description of a food-supply commissar in S. N. Nevskii, ed., *Prodovol'stvennaia rabota v kostromskoi gubernii* (Kostroma, 1923).

29. 32-1-396/1–11; further information can be found in 1276-12-1294zh.

This project was having relatively smooth sailing through bureaucratic channels until it came to the Special Conference on Food Supply in late September 1916. Here the reaction was sharply and unanimously negative. In Struve's words, "To separate out one group in the population would create still more confusion in food-supply matters." He believed that it would be inequitable, as well as administratively and politically difficult, to provide food only for defense workers since they were not segregated residentially from the rest of the working population. It also seemed unfair to give a privileged status to the Moscow and Petrograd workers as opposed to those in other regions who had equal "state significance." It was thought the plan would increase class antagonisms, for what would the soldiers say when they learned that the *soldatki*, the soldiers' wives, were being discriminated against? Groman summed up the feelings of the Special Conference: "According to rumor, the government will take further measures to secure the food supply of railroad workers, employees, and then bureaucrats and so on, and all this in a scattered way, on separate bases and with different norms. . . . The food-supply plan should be single and completely the same for all classes of the population."[30]

The opposition of the Special Conference killed the plan. This hostile reaction to a mild attempt to impose priorities on civilian food provisionment can be contrasted to Bolshevik policy, which resulted in a crazy quilt of different statuses in relation to food distribution, not only between social classes, but also between military and civilian families and between occupations, depending on their importance to the war effort.

The people who rejected the war minister's project did so in the name of a unified "plan" of food-supply provisionment that would deal with the whole problem of food supply in a coherent way and would coordinate procurement, transportation, and distribution. The defenders of the war minister's project could—and did—make a telling reply. Where is your plan? they asked; we cannot wait on this urgent matter while you work out your schemes. Thus the Special Conference was under pressure to come up with its coordinated plan, which it did by early October. An important part of this plan was an outline of a system of local councils for purposes of both purchasing and distribution. This system was included in a set of new rules proposed by the Special Conference on 10 October which were the apogee of the enlistment solution under the tsarist government.

30. 32-1-396/5–11. Other objections to the project included protests from factory owners against the extra burdens and the internal interference, and suspicions that the army purchasing agency was not up to the job. The army lost prestige if food-supply difficulties continued after militarization; for an example from October 1916, see TsGVIA, 499-3-1634/38–39. T. M. Kitanina distorts Groman's objections in Kitanina, *Voina*, 360.

During its first year of existence the Special Conference had given provincial food-supply commissioners few directives on how to set up their local organizations. The structure that had developed was largely dependent on local circumstances and on the initiative of the local activists.[31] In September 1916 the extension of fixed prices to all transactions and the wider responsibilities of the government food-supply organization, as well as bureaucratic challenges from the War Ministry and the Ministry of Internal Affairs, convinced the Special Conference of the need for more stringent rules for local organization. The new rules mandated a purchasing committee in the surplus provinces at the level of the district, the lowest rung of the tsarist administrative hierarchy and the only one to have direct contact with the peasant villages.

The proposed committees, at provincial as well as lower levels, were bulky, and rightly so, since "the complexity and many-sidedness of the questions to be analyzed and decided . . . demand a very complete representation of interests." Furthermore, the new district units were necessary for the sake of "making a closer approach to the producer and of penetrating to the depths of the localities."[32]

The new committee structure was also intended as a substitute for the private commercial apparatus. The government purchasing organization would certainly be preferable to

> the haphazard middleman [*sluchainyi skupshchik*], sufficiently famous for his negative methods of activity and recently fading away in view of the exceptional circumstances experienced by the country in connection with wartime events. . . . In the scheme of economic measures designed to raise rural productivity and eliminate the middleman activities that make the labor of the producer valueless, the placing of purchasing organizations under the leadership of the government central authority will have a very great significance.[33]

All of the citations just given are from tsarist bureaucrats—officials of the Special Conference secretariat—and not from the public organizations or from points further to the left. In the original proposals of the secretariat it was even suggested that under some circumstances the zemstvos would elect the provincial commissioner. The privilege of election was not an unmixed blessing, for it was meant as an inducement to a further enlist-

31. L. L., *Vopros;* G. K. Gins, *Organizatsiia prodovol'stvennogo dela na mestakh* (Petrograd, 1916); 457-1-255, p. 61; *Obzor deiatel'nosti osobogo soveshchaniia* (Petrograd, 1916), 220. *Obzor* can be found in 1291-132-47.
32. 1291-132-18/45–48; *Materialy,* xiii–xxxi.
33. *Materialy,* xiii–xxxi.

ment of the zemstvos in times of difficulty, especially when it seemed that the producer would not deliver his grain voluntarily. In that case the zemstvos would move from "voluntary service" to an "official obligation" to provide the necessary grain.[34] Election of the provincial commissioner from below was not included in the final rules as published. A conference of the Union of Zemstvos in late October called for local election, but by that time the local committee rules as a whole were doomed. This de facto alliance between the specialists of the Special Conference secretariat and the specialists in the central bureaus of the public organizations is an indication of the complexity of the political forces and coalitions that influenced the course of food-supply policy.

The proposed rules would have marked a real step forward in the evolution of the tsarist government and an important attempt to bring the central administration and the population into direct contact. Its significance was not lost on Protopopov, who listed with horror all the local organizations to be included: three landowners, elected by the district zemstvo; three peasant representatives; representatives of cooperatives within the district; a representative of the tax inspectorate; the district peasant elder; members of local peasant institutions; the justice of the peace; a member of the district zemstvo board; zemstvo doctors, veterinarians, agronomists, and insurance agents; representatives of the local church hierarchy; representatives of the commercial and industrial classes; representatives of local branches of the public organizations (Union of Towns, Union of Zemstvos, War Industries Committees); and members of the Special Conference who happened to be in the area. Protopopov concluded, "Is it even necessary to mention that with this kind of composition the food-supply committees will be representative institutions, not of the zemstvos, but of the so-called third element [or professional staff] and that, inasmuch as the committees will obviously not work for the common good so much as for their particular goals, they deserve to be abolished?"[35] The result of Protopopov's accusation was a compromise: the bid by his ministry to take over the food supply was rejected, but the attempt by the Special Conference to expand the apparatus was also rejected. The rules of 10 October were quietly retracted even though they had been officially published, and things were left much as they were.

N. Kondratiev expressed the public opposition's view of this retreat: the government found the rules for local organizations "politically dangerous and in particular even saw in the district organizations a tendency to

34. 457-1-261/67–93.
35. 1276-12-1288/20–28.

implant in contraband fashion [the old liberal project of] a district zemstvo. A better illustration of the interference of the politically reactionary tendencies of the government in the business of supply [than the retraction of the October rules] would be hard to find."[36] Another view is put forth by Zaitsev and Dolinsky: it was not only political considerations that led to the conclusion that the bulky local committees would have been unworkable. Aleksandr Rittikh, the last tsarist minister of agriculture, preferred working with peasant elders to working with the proposed district committees because he believed that the peasant officials would be more "prompt executors" of his new policy. Zaitsev and Dolinsky also pointed to the bad experience of the Provisional Government with such committees.[37]

THE RITTIKH RAZVERSTKA

When Rittikh, a career official in the Ministry of Agriculture who had played an important role a decade earlier in the formation of the Stolypin reform legislation, took office as agriculture minister in November 1916, he was immediately confronted with an emergency. A telegram from General Aleksei Brusilov, commander of the southwestern front, described at length the miserable and inadequate food of the soldier. Brusilov stressed that the army had no reserves and was living hand to mouth on incoming shipments. This situation not only created an intolerable dependence on the flawless functioning of the railroads but demoralized the troops as well. The general demanded that the civilian authorities quickly build up reserves; otherwise he would authorize his officers to start foraging for grain.[38]

Rittikh immediately depleted available supplies of grain and sent 85 million poods to the army. But the need to build up army reserves meant that the order from the army was increased from the actual yearly use of around 485 million poods of grain to 686 million. At the same time, because of the extension of fixed prices to all transactions, central government purchases earmarked for civilian use went up from 411 million poods of grain to 420 million, and for a while the amount was thought to be much

36. Kondratiev, *Rynok khlebov,* 87.

37. Zaitsev and Dolinsky, "Organization and Policy," 22. Dolinsky the participant was less detached than Dolinsky the historian; in 1917, he blamed the gubernatorial authority for the demise of the October rules. *Izvestiia po prodovol'stvennomu delu* 1 (32): 5–7 (hereafter cited as *Izv. po prod. delu*).

38. 457-1-78. The relevant portions of this telegram can be found in A. L. Sidorov, *Ekonomicheskoe polozhenie Rossii v gody pervoi mirovoi voiny* (Moscow, 1973), 492. The food-supply situation in the army at this period is discussed in Wildman, *Russian Imperial Army,* 108.

higher. The total order for government purchases was thus 1,106 million poods of grain—that is, roughly equivalent to the entire commercial turnover in prewar years.[39]

At the same time as he was faced with urgent new demands, Rittikh had to address a deteriorating situation on the supply side. Time had been lost in the summer and early fall, before the close of river transport in mid-October. Besides terrible weather, a major problem was the tardiness in setting fixed prices for grain and disappointment caused by the prices when they were finally announced. Many middlemen had already built up stocks by paying prices higher than those the government was now willing to match. The requisitioning of these stocks by panicky purchasing commissioners meant the complete end of commercial operations, for the merchants were in no position to replace them.[40]

The government purchasing apparatus was also degenerating into a competitive free-for-all and an "unbelievable customs war of all the provinces among themselves." Bureaucrats of the Agriculture Ministry openly encouraged the consumer regions to send their own agents to the producing regions, saying, "Perhaps they will listen to you more than they do to us."[41]

If material incentives were unavailing, Rittikh realized that the use of force against the mass of peasant producers was hardly feasible,[42] as an incident in Viatka province in early December 1916 confirms. There a provincial levy had already been applied to obtain oats. A land captain (the tsarist official directly responsible for the peasantry) had gone out with a force of ten policemen (*strazhniki*) to Aleksandrovskaia, a village of about sixty-five households, since thus far no one had delivered so much as a single pood of oats. The peasants blandly informed him that the provincial levy was meant to apply only to surpluses, of which they unfortunately had none. The land captain tried to check the storehouses of the peasants, but in each case the owner never seemed to be around; so he broke in and took the appropriate amount. This action infuriated the crowd of peasants. At the end of the day, fearing bloodshed and not having sufficient carts and men, the land captain retreated and asked for further instructions from the chairman of the zemstvo of the county, the administrative unit between the

39. 457-1-78/10–20; Nicholas Golovine, *The Russian Army in the World War* (New Haven, 1931), 49.

40. TsGVIA, 369-1-376/92–106 (speech by Rittikh).

41. *Ek. pol.*, pt. 3, doc. 94; Chaianov, *Vopros*, 23–24; Sidorov, *Ekonomicheskoe polozhenie*, 486–91.

42. *Gosudarstvennaia duma, IV sozyv, sessiia V* (Petrograd, 1917), 1261–83 (hereafter cited as Duma). Speech of 14 February 1917.

district and the province. On their side the peasants sent in a complaint to Petrograd.

The zemstvo chairman saw a dilemma: "Without a doubt, if compulsory measures are not applied to the peasants of Aleksandrovskaia, the whole purchase of oats in the county will be stopped; even more dangerous in its consequences, however, [would be] any serious clash . . . between officials of the administration and the peasants." He was especially afraid of being accused of arbitrariness (*proizvol*) and reminded his local officials that "wide circles of the public" were taking an active interest in food-supply administration. His concrete suggestions were to seal off the storehouses and intensify efforts to persuade influential peasants.

The governor's response was only slightly more vigorous. He ordered that a detachment be sent in to inspire respect (*vnushitel'nyi otriad*) but also stated that on no account should there be bloodshed.[43] Besides all the other obstacles to the use of force, such as unreliable troops, the case of Aleksandrovskaia shows that one restraining factor was the hostility of public opinion, not to mention the administration's own scruples. The government had the unenviable choice of either appearing bloodthirsty or appearing foolish.

Faced with a situation in which neither material incentives nor force could meet the demands of urgency, Rittikh improvised a response based on moral incentives. "The idea of the razverstka . . . consists in the transfer of grain deliveries from the area of commercial transactions to the area of duty toward the homeland, a duty obligatory for every Russian citizen in the conditions of the war we are living through."[44] Out of the total government order of 1,106 million poods of grain, Rittikh took out 772 million to be subjected to a *razverstka*. A razverstka is a method for alloting shares: a total amount is determined first, and this amount is divided up among those concerned.[45] Rittikh's total of 772 million poods was divided up between provinces, after which the provincial zemstvos were to hand out fulfillment quotas to the county zemstvos, which in turn would do the same to the peasant organizations on the district level, and so on down to the peasant household.

The total of 772 million poods was based on the army order of 686 million, with the rest intended for workers in defense industries. Rittikh felt that this open return to dualism was necessary because only the direct war effort could justify making grain deliveries a matter of civic obligation. But he also felt he could not publicly explain the desperate situation of

---

43. 456-1-118/81, 102–11. ("Levy" is a translation for *razverstka*.)
44. 369-1-376/3–14 (Special Conference on Defense, 15 Feb. 1917).
45. For further discussion of the term *razverstka*, see Note on Translation.

army reserves, and thus much of his urgency could not be communicated to the public. Since the army order was so much larger than the army's actual yearly consumption, Rittikh has been accused of "lying grandiosely" and of surreptitiously including civilian procurement in the razverstka.[46] But although there were a few exceptions based on special circumstances or personal influence, Rittikh's razverstka really was intended only for the direct war effort.[47]

The real aim of the razverstka was to speed up deliveries. It was announced in early December, and the total process of allotting quotas, right down to the individual peasant, was supposed to be completed by 6 January 1917. This tempo would have been fast for any government and was unheard-of for the tsarist government; the deadline had to be extended until 1 March. These deadlines were only meant for the allocation of quotas, and actual deliveries were obligatory within a six-month period. Deliveries made at any time after 2 December 1916 would count toward one's razverstka quota, and special receipts were to be given out for this purpose. Any deliveries made before the quotas were determined would obtain better prices in the form of transport costs and bonuses for large shipments. Local officials were also told that if deliveries were not forthcoming, Rittikh would be forced to take dire, if still unspecified, steps, or (even more ominously) the entire matter would be handed over to the military to deal with as they saw fit.

The Rittikh razverstka was not based on the use of force; it was rather an attempt to impose "something of an obligatory nature" on grain deliveries.[48] This sense of obligation would be created by the allotment of a definite quota for each producer labeled "your contribution to national defense" and even more by the urgency generated by the campaign itself. Rittikh said that he did not care if the razverstka failed as long as grain was delivered; if a purchasing commissioner did not like the razverstka method and felt he could obtain his quota by regular channels—fine, let him do so.[49] The price bonuses and the threat of force were meant as supplementary motives backing up this sense of urgent civic duty. Requisition powers remained available, but at least they would now be applied more equitably instead of haphazardly to any grain holder whose stocks happened to be in a convenient place. Rittikh had in fact come up with the razverstka in the first place mainly to prevent the use of force by the military.

---

46. George Yaney, *The Urge to Mobilize* (Urbana, 1982), 433; Zaitsev and Dolinsky, "Organization and Policy," 95.

47. Kitanina, *Voina*, 254–64.

48. E. Iashnov, in *Izv. po prod. delu* 1 (32): 9–11.

49. Duma speech of 14 February 1917. Out of thirty provinces nine chose this option.

Rittikh failed in his primary objective of creating an atmosphere of urgency and self-sacrifice; instead, the razverstka gave rise to a storm of protest and criticism.[50] Rittikh was accused of reviving dualism and abandoning the cities to their fate, especially the provincial cities with few defense workers. A hostile source reports him as saying he was not going to worry about "some Tula or Orenburg or other."[51] In theory the razverstka did not imply a fundamental break with the existing procurement system, which was still based on fixed prices and the distribution of orders to purchasing commissioners. In reality the exclusive focus of government attention on the direct war effort and the headlong disintegration of the government purchasing apparatus meant that the cities were left to their own devices. Even Petrograd and Moscow were getting no more than one-tenth of their orders filled.[52] Rittikh could only have defended himself by saying that he was not throwing the cities overboard but rather, out of the shipwreck of food supply he discovered on taking office, he was trying to ensure that the army at least did not go under.

It was also charged that in the interests of speed Rittikh failed to consult with the provincial commissioners but instead hastily assigned razverstka quotas based on dubious statistics. Previously the determination of provincial purchasing targets had been accomplished through bargaining by the purchasing commissioners among themselves, which (it was claimed) led to the targets representing a moral authority that they lacked when they were merely handed down by the center.[53] The figures for the 1916 harvest were unreliable, even though they had been provided by the zemstvos themselves, and it was also difficult to determine how much grain had already been procured previous to the razverstka. Differences among provinces in the level of marketed grain were also not taken sufficiently into account; some provinces got off easy and others were unfairly burdened. Whatever the justice of these claims, the result was that zemstvo activists distributed quotas to lower levels only under protest and often disavowed all responsibility for the outcome.[54]

Rittikh's manipulation of the fixed prices by adding transport costs also provoked outrage from the public opposition. One observer, I. Sigov, reported that he "personally heard a passionate speech by a genuine Russian socialist intellectual, who in enumerating the genuinely horrible

50. Kondratiev, *Rynok khlebov,* 106–10; Bukshpan, *Politika,* 397–401; Zaitsev and Dolinsky, "Organization and Policy," 88–97.

51. Sidorov, *Ekonomicheskoe polozhenie,* 490, citing a Union of Towns report.

52. TsGVIA, 369-1-376/92–106.

53. Zaitsev and Dolinsky, "Organization and Policy," 88–97.

54. *Ek. pol.,* pt. 3, docs. 85, 86, 87, 88.

crimes of the old government included the fact that the government 'did not scruple to make the fixed grain prices flexible.' "[55] According to the more substantive objections by specialists, Rittikh had repealed the law of rent, so that grain farthest from transportation points was now worth as much as more conveniently located grain. Since every grain shipment had a different price, it was impossible to establish consistent regulated prices for consumers.[56]

Rittikh felt that under the battle cry of moderate prices the consumer interest had gone too far in dampening the economic stimulus of the producer to deliver his grain. In particular, the growing difficulties of cartage and the necessity of tapping grain supplies now held far from railroad station points was not taken sufficiently into account.[57] Beyond the political difficulties involved in raising the fixed price, it would not work because the psychological moment when peasants normally marketed in the fall had been wasted; besides, the peasants had enough money and were not feeling the economic pinch. Furthermore, they would interpret any price concessions as weakness and would hold out for more. Therefore Rittikh's price supplements were presented as strictly temporary and as a once-in-a-food-supply-campaign opportunity. The supplements were originally meant to expire on 6 January 1917, when the razverstka allotment process was to be concluded, but an extension was then made until 1 March. This extension undoubtedly weakened their credibility as an inducement to quick delivery.

The most fundamental objection to the razverstka was that it tried to avert the necessity of enlisting social forces. While Rittikh called for unity, his fellow minister Protopopov was closing down food-supply congresses right and left. Aleksandr Chaianov remarked a few months later that "the government feared hunger, but it feared public organizations even more."[58] The razverstka failed because "the absence of a base for food-supply organizations in the population itself and the prerevolutionary zemstvo's isolation from the peasantry [meant that] as the razverstka got closer to the producers, in their view it became more and more a simple seizure of grain by an unpopular state authority."[59]

The government had been on the verge of obtaining a base in the population with the district purchasing committees set up by the rules of

55. Sigov, *Arakcheevskii sotsializm,* 9.
56. Dolinsky, in *Izv. po prod. delu* 1 (32): 5–9; Zaitsev and Dolinsky, "Organization and Policy," 92–93.
57. *Ek. pol.,* pt. 3, doc. 81; Sigov, *Arakcheevskii sotsializm,* 9.
58. Chaianov, *Vopros,* 22.
59. Iashnov, in *Izv. po prod. delu* 1 (32): 9–11.

10 October, but then it had thrown this necessary institution away. Shingarev took up this point in a debate with Rittikh at the Special Conference for Defense on 15 February 1917:

> For A. I. Shingarev it remains incomprehensible how the influence of the conscious public forces on the peasant population, which the minister of agriculture tells us is desirable, is to be accomplished. The minister of agriculture places the implementation of the razverstka in its final and therefore crucial level on organs as inappropriate to the fulfillment of general state tasks as district and village assemblies. *Access to these assemblies is closed to representatives of the intelligentsia* and thus the latter are factually deprived of the means of influencing the course of the razverstka.
>
> The formation of all-class (*vnesoslovnyi*) district committees with wide participation by public elements was rejected by the minister of agriculture. It is the deep conviction of A. I. Shingarev that in order to attain that unification of which the minister of agriculture himself admits the necessity, the population must first of all believe in the existing state authority.[60]

In response Rittikh argued that enlistment was not without its difficulties. All the discussion leading up to the determination of fixed price levels in September had done little more than split up the country into the mutually antagonistic camps of producer and consumer. The proposed district committees would have been dominated by zemstvo staff, which approached "the estimation of local needs with a somewhat peculiar patriotism—and they are right, of course—the patriotism of their parish, their little region."[61]

Instead of enlistment Rittikh advocated political class unity based on acceptance of the central leadership's definition of priorities: "It would have great significance if all elements of the population and of the active public [*obshchestvennost'*] inspired the peasantry with the thought that [grain delivery] is their civic duty, that it is demanded by the war[as well as by] the decisive moment we are now living through." More of an obstacle than impassable roads was the "poison of doubt" that certain influential currents of public opinion persisted in injecting into political life. Rittikh's colleague M. A. Beliaev, the minister of war, later commented that "Rittikh continually turned to the State Duma with a request that it support him from their side and say the word that would compel the landowners

60. TsGVIA, 369-1-376/106 (emphasis added).
61. Duma speech of 14 February 1917.

and peasants to sell the grain [and] fulfill the quota division that had been introduced. . . . Evidently, it was impossible to count on [this support], and it was even said that there might be resistance."[62]

It is in principle impossible to measure the success of the Rittikh razverstka in terms of grain deliveries since it would not have been completed until the summer of 1917. Discussion of this question has usually relied on the amount assigned in quota distribution, not amounts actually delivered. The extent of even this distribution is unclear and becomes more so as we approach the individual producer. But the political failure of the razverstka is manifest in the protests of local activists and their refusal to cooperate. It partially failed as well in its primary aim of building up a military reserve. A reserve of eighteen to thirty days had been created by the middle of January, but the extremely harsh winter had led to transport problems, and the reserve had been dissipated.[63]

The razverstka also failed to obtain grain without the use of force. On 23 February 1917, frightened by the outbreak of disorder in Petrograd and by the oncoming *rasputitsa* (season of impassable roads), Rittikh and Beliaev sent out a telegram to all commissioners, governors, and zemstvo officials stating that deliveries had to be made within three days. During that period price concessions were to remain in force. Afterward, in any region that had refused or significantly lowered the razverstka, "all available reserves above seed and personal food-supply needs" were to be requisitioned: "To the county zemstvo is given the task of effective cooperation in the fulfillment of requisitions."[64] That same day Rittikh admitted his failure in the Duma: "I'm only human, only mortal, and Russia needs now to push forward everywhere—in the active public and everywhere—[people] of titanic strength. Yes, I'm to blame that I don't have this strength—in that respect I admit my guilt with complete openness."[65]

To acknowledge the failure of the razverstka is not to justify its critics. Rittikh's program was based squarely on the gubernatorial solution. He openly accepted dualism between the direct war effort and the home front, made grain delivery a matter of obligation rather than relying on material interest, tried to impose central unity on the political class, and rejected enlistment strategies as counterproductive. It is true that he relied on statistics, but to the extent necessary only for a tax strategy, not for a monopoly strategy. The many difficulties of this approach were pointed out

---

62. *Padenie*, 2:237.
63. TsGVIA, 369-1-376/92–106; Shingarev, in *Izv. po prod. delu* 1 (32): 13, 60.
64. 457-1-40/222. I have not seen this telegram mentioned in any discussion of Rittikh or the February revolution.
65. Duma speech of 28 February 1917, 1596.

by the critics, but their own alternative was weak—weaker than they knew. Their outrage at Rittikh's price manipulation reveals a fetishism of the fixed price that overlooked the genuine difficulties of price formation, especially in a highly charged political atmosphere. The promise of material equivalents for grain deliveries implied by the commitment to put fixed prices on industrial items was impossible to keep. Rittikh's warnings about localism should have been heeded: it would turn out to be harder than enlistment advocates realized to build a bridge to the peasantry through newly established councils and committees. The banned food-supply congresses obscured the fact that enlistment was not a straightforward answer to political class unity, given deep divisions in outlook and aim. Sooner than they knew, enlistment advocates were about to learn some bitter lessons on these matters.

The Soviet historian A. L. Sidorov wrote that "with the democratic-bourgeois revolution [fast approaching], only a bureaucrat with no contact with life could dream of a unification of 'all the vital forces of the country' around the thoroughly rotting autocracy."[66] Rittikh's efforts do seem naive in the doom-laden atmosphere of the winter of 1916–1917. At the top, officials spun confused intrigues around the uncomprehending figure of Tsar Nicholas and tried vainly to force him to show some leadership.[67] The public witnessed explosions of frustration such as the grotesque murder of Rasputin and the barely veiled accusations of governmental treason made by speakers in the Duma. At the bottom of society the strike movement picked up energy, and despair over the hardships of wartime grew stronger as the winter grew colder. The forces of disruption had gone beyond economic dislocation and had rendered helpless even the best intentioned of those who sought unity of the political class. Rittikh was only mortal, and his razverstka ended up intensifying political and economic disruption; but his improvisation still stands out as the only real effort made by the government to save itself from swiftly advancing destruction.

66. Sidorov, *Ekonomicheskoe polozhenie*, 493.
67. Nicholas himself stated in September 1916, "I simply understand nothing about these questions of food supply and provisionment." Kitanina, *Voina*, 301.

3   The Crisis of 1917: Bread

This morning I went with Lotte and Beaumont to the Duma,
which is open to everyone. The Palace looks like an immense
guardroom. Soldiers are everywhere, all unbuttoned and
eating at dirty wooden tables or sprawling on the floor round a
samovar. Others, still carrying arms, are asleep on top of
piled-up sacks of flour, brought there as food supplies for the
town, and which cover everything with white dust.

Louis de Robien, March 1917

In the fall of 1917 large rail shipments of grain on the way to Petrograd
failed to arrive. This breakdown in the transport network was caused by a
failure of political authority: not only were the authorities unable to
prevent the pillaging of the shipments by peasants in the northeast provinces, but they sometimes even cooperated with the peasants to prevent
further damage to the rail system. Yet the breakdown of authority in turn
was caused by the food-supply crisis since the peasants in these deficit
provinces did not see any way to acquire grain legally.[1]

The food-supply crisis of 1917 was thus part of a chain whose other links
consisted of the failure of basic societywide coordinating institutions: the
transport network, the market, and political authority. The failure at each
link intensified the failure at all the others. If it is true to say that the
breakdown in transport was a central cause of the food-supply crisis, it is
just as true to say that the food-supply crisis was a central cause of the
breakdown in transport.

It is difficult to find an adequate form for the presentation of this chain
of social crises. The best would be some equivalent of a split-screen effect,
where we could view harried food-supply officials, indignant peasants, and
desperate consumers all at the same time as the different story lines moved
toward a common climax. To get the sense of a time of troubles, we would
also need to use animation to portray a world where the usual laws of
behavior do not seem to apply: nothing can be trusted, but at the same time
everything seems possible. The soul of this animated world would be for
the most part malevolent so that just getting by would often require heroic
efforts. Lacking these means, we must view sequentially the different

1. *Ek. pol.*, pt. 2, doc. 536, pp. 359–61; Stone, *Eastern Front*, 297–300.

groups of Russian society as they struggle to impose order on a world spinning out of control—and sometimes, even as they do so, help to push the chain reaction of social disintegration closer to an explosion.

THE WAGER ON THE MONOPOLY

In the few months between the revolution in February and the end of the summer, policy-makers had to revise more than once their perception of the strategic bottleneck that had to be overcome to avert the disaster of starvation. At the beginning of the year officials were worried about the size of the harvest and focused their attention on making sure that all possible land was sown. It soon became clear that this worry was overly optimistic: there was no chance that the food-supply apparatus would be able to obtain enough grain to reach that particular ceiling. Officials realized that they first had to concentrate on getting the peasant producers to deliver their grain. But owing to the breakdown in the economy and the political system, the Provisional Government was hard pressed to provide either material or coercive incentives for grain delivery, and it was forced to make heavy use of appeals to loyalty and other ideal incentives, which became progressively less effective as the year went on.

Even when the peasants did deliver their grain, it was no simple matter to transport it to the northern consumer centers. Previously the phrase *breakdown in transport* had referred primarily to the railroads, but disorganization continued to spread, and there were now more links in the chain of transportation to be disrupted. During the course of the previous year reserves at transportation points and flour mills had been used up, and almost all available grain was in the hands of the actual producers. But the short distance covered by cart to the rail point had always been vastly more expensive than the long distance traveled by rail. The new dependence on cartage meant greater vulnerability to the rainy season, greater need for new collection points, greater difficulties in price setting, and greater chances for bottlenecks to develop in the provision of such mundane items as sacks.[2]

The collapse of the rail system had led to greater interest in the efficient use of river navigation. Not much had been done about improving efficiency in 1916 because of the tardiness in the final decision on fixed prices, but food-supply officials were determined to do better in 1917. The problems were great. It was harder to impose regulation on river traffic than on

2. *Izv. po prod. delu*, 2 (33): 6–12 (Jasny); *Prodovol'stvennoe delo* (Moscow), 23 July 1917, 6–7 (hereafter cited as *Prod. delo*); G. P. Pavlovsky, *Agricultural Russia on the Eve of the Revolution* (1930; New York, 1968), 31; Golovine, *Russian Army*, 172–75.

the railroads because of the smaller units and the greater role played by private owners. Consequently when the navigation season opened, first priority was taken by shipments of all kinds that had been piling up over the winter rather than by newly delivered grain. The geographic distribution of the 1917 harvest made matters worse since the provinces on the Volga itself had a poor harvest. In the name of the efficient use of river transport the authorities called on the Volga provinces to deprive themselves temporarily in return for grain from the northern Caucusus, but this sacrifice required more confidence in the Provisional Government than was forthcoming. As with cartage, there were also more things that could go wrong, from labor trouble with the Tsaritsyn stevedores to river piracy. "Failure to exploit the 1917 fall navigation season will inevitably lead to starvation in the northern regions": food-supply officials unfortunately had a chance to test the accuracy of this prediction made in May.[3]

To overcome these obstacles, the government needed three things: an apparatus of officials to collect and transport the grain, information about the location of the grain, and incentives for peasant producers to make deliveries. Government hopes were outlined in legislation passed in March 1917 setting up the grain monopoly. It stated that all grain in the country, including the upcoming 1917 harvest, now belonged to the state; the actual producer was no more than a temporary holder of the grain. The producer was allowed to retain a stated amount of grain; everything above this norm would be delivered to the state at a price fixed by the state.

The apparatus needed to enforce the monopoly was to be created by a thoroughgoing democratization of the previous system of commissioners. Local organs were given greater autonomy from the center, and organs at all levels were expanded to include wide representation of public organizations. The result was not a system of agents sent out from the center but a system of locally elected food-supply committees (*prodkomy*). The apparatus was told to get the necessary information by putting all the grain in the country on register (*uchet*) to ensure that the surplus above the consumption norm was actually turned over to the state. As an incentive for cooperation, the state undertook to put equitable fixed prices on industrial items and guarantee their availability. The apparatus would expedite their distribution to grain producers as well as provide assistance in increasing grain production.[4]

3. *Izv. po prod. delu*, 1 (32): 108; Zaitsev and Dolinsky, "Organization and Policy," 76–78; *Prod. delo* (Moscow), 23 July 1917; Kitanina, *Voina*, 45.

4. Partial texts of the grain monopoly legislation can be found in *Ek. pol.*, pt. 2, doc. 513 (commentary, doc. 515) and Robert Paul Browder and Alexander F. Kerensky, *The Russian Provisional Government 1917: Documents* (Stanford, 1961), 2:618–21.

Since the government was never able to make its control effective, a full grain monopoly remained only an ideal. The actual policy is better described as a state monopoly of the grain trade since the state's control over transportation meant that it could make a serious attempt to outlaw private grain transactions. This was in fact close to what tsarist policy would have been if the rules of 10 October had gone into effect and social forces had been enlisted into local food-supply committees. Opposition activists had protested when Rittikh made the delivery of grain a state obligation, but only because the government refused to expand the state food-supply apparatus to include public forces. Now that the apparatus was more thoroughly democratized than was possible under the tsarist government, these objections fell away.

The grain monopoly was a gamble, and perhaps the greatest risk was the creation of an apparatus by means of enlisting the peasants into the district-level food-supply committees. "The law gave precisely to these organs a whole series of functions on whose proper fulfillment depends in essence the fate of the grain monopoly"—putting the available grain on register as well as handling the technical operations of receiving and shipping grain deliveries to the center.[5] In lectures given in April 1917 to the "workers in cultural and enlightenment activities" who were to help set up the new system, Aleksandr Chaianov, one of Russia's foremost experts on the peasant economy, used the following allegory to explain the role assigned to the new committees. Imagine a large field covered with scattered grains of wheat. If a man tried to pick them all up, he would get nothing but a few handfuls and a strained back. But if he had an army of ants, they could gather the grains into small piles, and then the man could gather up these small piles.

The sheer number of ants was staggering. Chaianov calculated that there would be seventy provincial food-supply committees and seven hundred county ones. Since there were about fifteen districts in each county, there would be eight to ten thousand committees. Assuming about ten people on each of the district committees, Chaianov arrived at an estimate of an apparatus of seventy thousand people—just at the lower levels. He told his audience that "reading through the provisions of the law, you will see the colossal antlike work that the committees must carry out.

5. Bukshpan, *Izv. po prod. delu*, 3 (34): 1–9. For discussions of the food-supply committees, see Graeme J. Gill, *Peasants and Government in the Russian Revolution* (London, 1979); G. A. Gerasimenko, *Nizovye krest'ianskie organizatsii v 1917–pervoi polovine 1918 godov: na materialakh Nizhnego Povolzh'ia* (Saratov, 1974); John Keep, *The Russian Revolution: A Study in Mass Mobilization* (New York, 1976), chap. 14.

And this work must squeeze out of the village all the surplus grain—the village must put the entire surplus on the altar of the fatherland."[6]

Food-supply officials were conscious of the risks they were taking. As N. S. Dolinsky put it, "In the organized will of the peasantry—an elemental state force [stikhiinno-gosudarstvennaia sila]—we hope to find a way out of our difficulties."[7] In the Russian political vocabulary of the time the combination of "elemental" and "state" has the air of a deliberate paradox. Elemental usually conjured up images of an undisciplined, uncontrollable, parochial, and anarchistic Russian people. According to Chaianov, the very hugeness of the task required this wager on the enlistment of the peasantry. The necessary food-supply apparatus could not be "built and put into motion from the center, by appointing bureaucrats and agents— the state alone could not build such an apparatus. . . . Only the people [narod]—taking into its hands its food supply [and] its own fate—is capable of doing it."[8] The old regime never understood that the man—the state—had to rely on the ants—the peasant committees—"to penetrate to the very depths of peasant life."

The need to rely on the peasant committees was so evident that Chaianov was compelled to overlook the possibility that the ants might not find it in their interest to collect grain for the convenience of the man. The wager on peasant enlistment failed, for the district remained a "nest of peasant suspicion and separatism."[9] The food-supply committees as well as the other new local committees suffered almost immediately from a "poor parody of universal suffrage," which resulted in the exclusion of the rural intelligentsia, even those with useful skills such as consumer cooperative administrators. Food-supply officials traded stories about village meetings demanding that the local agronomists be replaced with less educated ones.[10] The district committees could not have done their job even if they had been able and willing. "The population . . . vigilantly follows the activities of these organs elected by it, and at any attempt of these organs to work in accordance with the law or the directives of the central authority,

6. Chaianov, Vopros. Chaianov never joined any political party. See V. V. Kabanov, "Aleksandr Vasil'evich Chaianov," Voprosy istorii, 1988, no. 6:151. See also Susan Gross Solomon, The Soviet Agrarian Debate: A Controversy in Social Science, 1923–1929 (Boulder, Colo., 1977), 214; Agurskii, Ideologiia, 19–20.

7. Izv. po prod. delu, 1 (32): 5–9.

8. Chaianov, Vopros.

9. O. Chaadaeva, Pomeshchiki i ikh organizatsii v 1917 godu (Moscow, 1928), 57 (report of Duma members).

10. "Mart–mai 1917 g.," Krasnyi Arkhiv 15 (1926): 50; Prod. delo (Moscow), 15 October 1917, 10–11; Raleigh, Revolution on the Volga, 174ff; Gerasimenko, Nizovye organizatsii, chap. 1.

the population removes them and disperses them, often to the extent of beating and even murder."[11]

The committee structure above the district level also bore little relation to what Chaianov had proudly described as a "colossal working system, subtly elaborated and provided with everything necessary for its work." Instead, it was an amalgam of committees that had existed previously, those that spontaneously grew up in the month after the revolution, those that were set up only in response to telegrams sent out by the center, and even those that tried to conform to the grain monopoly legislation. These committees never cohered into a working system, colossal or otherwise. Each level thought the committees above them or the ministry itself unresponsive or addicted to routine; each level thought the committees below them irresponsible and sloppy.

A provincial food-supply conference in Kostroma in late May revealed some of the tensions. Representatives of the county committees attacked the provincial food-supply committee for the way it distributed rights to obtain grain (nariady). It soon became clear that the provincial food-supply committee had no real data on which to base its decisions, so that the distribution depended on how insistent the county committees could be and how convincing their hard-luck stories were. The conference passed a resolution condemning the selfishness that painted too bleak a picture of local needs to the detriment of their brother counties. But the executive board of the province committee also came under heavy attack for its "chancellery" attitude and general lack of leadership. In reply it insisted that it was being blamed for failures that were beyond its control and due to general political and economic causes.[12]

Just as important as the vertical tensions within the committee hierarchy were the tensions between surplus and deficit provinces. The surplus provinces were hostile toward the agents sent out by the deficit provinces since they made the work of the local food-supply committees more difficult by bidding up prices and disrupting the local organizational framework. The deficit regions replied that to rely solely on the energy and competence of the surplus-region food-supply committees meant risking starvation. The officials of the center tended to agree: they wanted to make the food-supply apparatus more efficient by harnessing the energy and insistence of the consumers.

An unofficial meeting of provincial food-supply committee chairmen took place during September in Moscow. The chairman from the deficit

11. Izv. po prod. delu, 3 (34): 1–9 (Bukshpan).
12. Prod. delo (Kostroma), 1 July 1917, 28–29.

province of Kaluga attended the meeting and reported back home that other provincial representatives had been stirred by the desperate plight of Kaluga and had promised to help. But a closer look reveals that in each case the promised help was conditional. Poltava would help *if* the ministry gave it an order for Kaluga; Ekaterinoslav would help *if* enough paper money were sent to pay the local grain producers; Ufa would help *if* the ministry gave Kaluga priority over other deficit provinces; Voronezh would help *if* Kaluga did something about the disruptive flood of individual Kaluga residents trying to get grain for themselves.[13]

The sense of dependence could quickly lead to irritation and hostility. An article in the official publication of the Tver food-supply committee asked the question "On whom does the food supply of Tver province depend?" It answered as follows: "The fate of Tver province is in the hands of the agriculturists of the black-earth, southern region of Russia." The writer went on to stress that the problem was not a shortage of grain but a "shortage of conscious civil duty in the well-fed population of the grain-growing provinces." He noted that before the war Tver received 10 million poods of grain from the southern provinces; it was now asking for only 7.5 million but to date had only received 1.5 million.[14]

The consumer-producer split was thus a split within the peasantry itself. In Riazan the southern counties had enough food whereas the northern counties were starving. The northern peasants were getting angry at their brothers in the south, who had taken over the estates but were now refusing to divide the spoils. The northern peasants felt they had two choices: starve, or go south to smother the peasants there.[15]

The food-supply apparatus was further weakened by its inability to enlist the technical skills of the grain-trade specialists, as millers and merchants were now called. The designers of the grain monopoly had hoped to enlist the trade apparatus, but this policy ran into the usual conflict between the localities and the center. A telegram sent to local food-supply committees on 27 July noted that both the population and the committees were reluctant to use private firms. The central authorities tried to overcome this reluctance by arguing that the firms would be put under strict monitoring, thus ensuring that state purposes would be observed. Furthermore, the firms worked for commission, not profit; they did not enter into contractual relations with anyone but merely fulfilled technical functions.

13. TsGVIA, 13214-13-72/66.
14. *Prod. delo* (Tver), 25 April 1917.
15. *Prod.* (Poltava), no. 2, 9 September 1917.

The reasoning of the center was clear. In the words of one food-supply official, the private apparatus had looted the population both before and after the revolution, but at least before the revolution it had also delivered the goods. The state should now force it to do so again since unfortunately the democracy lacked competent people.[16] But local officials adamantly refused to allow the participation of private merchants, declaring that the merchants had so discredited themselves with previous profiteering that it was impossible to use them.

The grain-trade specialists originally accepted the grain monopoly; their growing opposition came from the realization that they would not be allowed to participate under any conditions.[17] They soon felt that they were being used as a scapegoat, to the point of "systematic instigation of the other classes of the population against [the business class]." One grain dealer frankly stated that the business classes should not get involved since all they would earn would be the "hatred of the starving population." His colleagues rebuked him, saying that it was their patriotic duty to help even at the risk of incurring popular wrath.[18]

Thus the apparatus was torn apart by the centrifugal forces it was intended to overcome. The food-supply officials also lost the gamble on registration of grain supplies as a source of information. The partisans of the monopoly had come to see registration as a moral imperative: "Remember, citizen peasants, that the enemy of freedom is he who resists these measures, who throws a spoke in the wheel, who resists the registration of grain, who hides the harvest surplus from the food-supply committee, who refuses to sell grain at the fixed price, who is concerned only with himself and not with the salvation of his tortured and writhing homeland."[19] Yet registration was bound to fail, not only for technical reasons but also because conflict with the population was inevitable. In the words of I. Sigov:

> How much work must there be simply in conducting registration of each muzhik in each hamlet, in each village, in each settlement—how much will it cost—how much time will it

16. TsGVIA, 12593-36-69/48–49.

17. 23-7-404/22–24; 32-1-391/197–206; TsGVIA, 13251-7-6/5–8; *Izv. po prod. delu,* 1 (32): 15–18, 3 (34): 56–59; *Ek. pol.,* pt. 2, docs. 518, 521; Kitanina, *Voina,* 346; V. Ia. Laverychev, "Krupnaia burzhuaziia i prodovol'stvennyi vopros v 1917 godu," *Istoricheskie zapiski,* 99 (1977): 312–21; Browder and Kerensky, *Provisional Government,* 2:631–32. A minority of "grain trade specialists" did call for a return to free trade.

18. 32-1-391/193–96, War Industries Committee memorandum, 9 October 1917; TsGVIA, 13251-7-6/5–8.

19. *Prod.* (Poltava), no. 3–4, 1 October 1917, citing the publication of the Moscow regional food-supply organization.

take—what an army of clerks and census takers will be required, and where will that army come from? Finally, even in normal times how many misunderstandings, mistakes, and therefore protests, revisions, disputes, offense, and indignation will there be? And when will the [actual] procurement of grain take place?[20]

The material incentives that were an inherent part of the monopoly strategy were also not forthcoming. The continual promise of industrial items, combined with the utter lack of results, must be accounted a centrifugal force rather than a force for reconstitution since it irritated peasant producers and gave them an excuse for noncooperation.[21]

The gamble on the monopoly strategy had failed, and the results were not slow in showing themselves. In 1917 the country began to wait anxiously for the results of each month's grain procurement. March and particularly April were bad months because of transportation difficulties caused by spring floods and because the peasants were preoccupied with the spring sowing. May was a successful month for grain procurements, and for a brief moment it looked as if a corner had been turned. But May turned out to be the only month when deliveries exceeded consumption. In Moscow, where the situation was much better than in provincial towns, the population was consuming more than it received: an average of twenty-five train cars a day had arrived over the summer, yet forty-two train cars a day had been distributed in May and thirty-seven a day in August. Reserves were almost depleted, and the daily ration had to be lowered at the beginning of September from three-fourths of a funt of bread to one-fourth of a funt.[22] The scene was set for the explosion of the fall.

When surveying the wreckage of their strategy, many food-supply officials fell back to blaming the darkness of the people. The attitude of these officials is portrayed in an account by the American journalist Ernest Poole:

> In true Russian fashion, [the food-supply officials] had built up a system so elaborate and complete that when you saw it on paper you felt all Russia's troubles were solved. If red tape could feed people, then the Russians were to be gorged. The plan included a network of committees large and small, in

20. Sigov, *Arakcheevskii sotsializm*, 12.

21. On the insufficiency of industrial items, see Keep, *Russian Revolution*, 175–77; P. V. Volobuev, *Ekonomicheskaia politika vremennogo pravitel'stva* (Moscow, 1961).

22. *Prod. delo* (Moscow), 3 September 1917, 4–5; *Ek. pol.*, pt. 2, docs. 496, 497; Diane Koenker, *Moscow Workers and the 1917 Revolution* (Princeton, 1981), 129–30.

cities, towns and villages, in every section of the land. But
then, also in true Russian fashion, some of the planners began
to despair. One, with whom my interpreter talked in the Ministry of [Food Supply], was a tall thin man with a hollow chest
and rather long dishevelled hair. . . .

"The general position is this," he said, in a tone which implied it was hopeless. . . . "My department of this ministry
controls all the agricultural tools, domestic or imported. Another has charge of the wheat and rye, and another of the oats
and hay. The plan is later to control all the cotton goods as
well, and leather, fuel and sugar. The scheme is so enormous
that to direct the work from here would take a perfect army.
So we are leaving things to be done by committees out in the
provinces.

"I hope it will go better," he continued patiently, "when the
entire mechanism of our plan is understood. But to tell you
the truth, we are getting but little co-operation yet; for the
country is quite unprepared for a socialistic plan of this kind. I
myself am a socialist, but in the last few months I have found
this is not a socialist country. Our people are not made like
that. Each one is greedy for his own and thinks very little of
the State. We discovered this almost at the start; but in the ex-
altation prevailing in those wonderful days, no one cared to
point out the fact. We had clothed the people with ideals, and
now we found them naked. . . .

"The revolution has shown to us that the layer of civilization here is about one thousandth of an inch. Some of us are
even afraid that our beautiful revolution, like a soap-bubble,
will suddenly burst."[23]

We seem to have come full circle: in his disillusionment the socialist official
now echoed the despised Rittikh. When Rittikh had been asked for an
explanation of popular unrest about food supplies on the eve of the February revolution, he had replied, "Gentlemen, [if you ask] what is the reason
for this panic—it's difficult to explain exactly, it's something elemental."[24]

POPULAR SELF-PROTECTION

Frustrated officials, whatever their political persuasion, painted a picture
of popular irrationality and selfishness, but the picture begins to fade when
we consider the options actually available to the "dark people," as they

23. Ernest Poole, *"The Dark People": Russia's Crisis* (New York, 1918), 105–7.
Bureaucratic self-confidence was lacking even before the revolution. Naumov
complains in his memoirs that he got depressed after hearing reports from Glinka,
who was always nervous and full of doubts. Naumov, *Iz vospominanii*, 2:347–49.
   24. Duma session of 25 February 1917 (pp. 1741–48).

were called by the educated classes. The story of the choices made by ordinary people in 1917 begins with the situation that baffled Rittikh: sudden panic among consumers in the days just before the outbreak of the February revolution. Official statements by Rittikh and by S. S. Khabalov, the top military authority in Petrograd, stressed that reserves of flour existed in the city, that deliveries were arriving by rail, and that no change had been made in the amount of flour issued to Petrograd bakeries.[25]

Although these statements were accurate as far as they went, they left much unsaid. Khabalov did not mention that the flour given to the bakeries was a lowered norm that had gone into effect at the beginning of February, when city authorities had been told that there would be no rail shipments for a while—Petrograd and Moscow would have to subsist for the duration on their reserves. Shipments had started up again, but only recently.[26] Rittikh had been more forthcoming and had described the exceptional weather conditions that had interfered with rail traffic; he admitted that no one had expected the halt in deliveries to last as long as it did. But Rittikh could not be completely candid in his Duma statements, as material from closed government meetings reveals. The halt in grain deliveries was due not only to weather conditions but also to a fuel crisis so that even passenger traffic was interrupted. The situation was serious enough that reserves for the front were allowed to run down to a dangerous level.[27]

Even though the daily norm had just been set at a very low level, there was no rationing system in Petrograd. At the same time as the government informed the city about the interruption of flour shipments, it recommended introducing rationing. But conflicting attempts to implement this sensible suggestion led to squabbles between the city administration and the Petrograd food-supply commissioner appointed by Rittikh. (This official had the unfortunately German name of Weiss and like most other top city officials had only been on the job for a month or two.) This conflict resonated with the wider conflict between Protopopov and the city administration over control of food-supply matters and especially over the role of worker's representatives. Officials only made matters worse by a sudden refusal to give flour, which they hoped to conserve, to the workers' cooperative system. All these actions were reported in a confused way in the press.[28]

25. E. N. Burdzhalov, *Vtoraia russkaia revoliutsiia* (Moscow, 1967–1971), 1:134; Hasegawa, *February Revolution*, 244–45.

26. *Velikie dni rossiiskoi revoliutsii* (Petrograd, 1917), 25; Sidorov, *Ekonomicheskoe polozhenie*, 495–96; Browder and Kerensky, *Provisional Government*, 1:69.

27. TsGVIA, 369-1-376/106.

28. Shingarev speech in Duma session of 24 February 1917, 1704–15; Hasegawa, *February Revolution*, 159–63; A. Shliapnikov, *Semnadtsatyi god*, 2d. ed.

Meanwhile the population of Petrograd had to deal not only with a low daily norm and the insecurity attendant on the absence of rationing but also with a lack of supervision of the bread shops, which led to well-founded suspicions of abuse by the bakers.[29] Price movements increased the sense of insecurity; for much of the Petrograd working class, the winter of 1916 brought the first drop in the level of real wages.[30] The population thus observed an extremely long interruption of rail traffic, a fuel crisis that threw many places in Russia literally into the dark, and an administration filled with new and far-from-reassuring faces that could not even carry out the simplest measures of expedient distribution. It was not, as Rittikh suggested, an unexplained panic that led to a run on the bread shops and genuine deprivation for those who came too late, but an unfortunately rational strategy of self-preservation.

The February days began with a walkout by women workers, triggered by the breakdown in bread distribution, on the occasion of International Women's Day. This event reveals the three strands of the popular movement: workers and their established methods of struggle, consumers and their less organized methods of pressure, and activists with their traditions of militancy and their political focus. All observers watched anxiously to see how these strands would interact and which would become dominant. The activists urged the demonstrators not to vent their wrath on small tradespeople, who were themselves victims, but to keep their attention focused on the criminal government.[31] But both the attackers and the defenders of the government felt that the movement would collapse if only the government succeeded in scraping together some bread to give to the Petrograd population. This proposition was never tested, however, since all the government could come up with was promises of reorganization. There was a steady shift in the slogans of the popular movement from an immediate demand for bread to a call for an end to the political causes of economic chaos. The result was pointed out by General Khabalov: "When they say, 'Give us bread,' you give them bread and it's done with. But when 'Down with the autocracy' is written on their banners, how is bread going to calm them?"[32]

(Moscow, 1924–27), 1:254–59; I. P. Leiberov, *Na shturm samoderzhaviia* (Moscow, 1979), 66–71; 456-1-1358/133–34.

29. *Padenie*, 1:184–92.

30. Rex Wade, *Red Guards and Workers Militias in the Russian Revolution* (Stanford, 1984), 21–22; Hasegawa, *February Revolution*, 201; Koenker, *Moscow Workers*, 95–96.

31. Burdzhalov, *Vtoraia revoliutsiia*, 1:119; Leiberov, *Na shturm*, 121; Leiberov, "Nachalo fevral'skoi revoliutsii," in *Iz istorii velikoi oktiabr'skoi sotsialisticheskoi revoliutsii i sotsialisticheskogo stroitel'stva v SSSR* (Leningrad, 1967), 8.

32. Burdzhalov, *Vtoraia revoliutsiia*, 1:168. See also George Katkov, *Russia*

In February insecurity about the food supply had found expression in a political program, and the result was the end of the autocracy. But after the prompt promulgation of the grain monopoly by the Provisional Government the struggle for bread reverted to a more personal level, and the issues of peace and land dominated the political struggle. Only at the end of the summer did the bread issue again become incorporated in a widely accepted political program.

Yet individual choices still had vast consequences. The response made by each person and each social unit to the challenge of Hobbes's choice created a balance of forces that contributed either to centrifugal self-protection or to reconstitution of the authority of society. Many activists felt that the outcome of the choice was dependent on a person's consciousness, whether defined in terms of class or citizenship: the greater the consciousness, the more unhesitating the choice for reconstitution. But the choice was even more dependent on the concrete possibilities open to each person and the available forms of cooperation with others in similar plight.

One familiar form of cooperation was the peasant *mir*, or commune, the institutional framework for concerted action at the village level. In 1917, after a decade of subversion by the Stolypin legislation, the commune experienced a resurgence.[33] This made sense: the commune had originally been developed partly for the self-protection of the village in a hostile or, at best, indifferent environment, both natural and social. The collapse of political authority in 1917 thus not only allowed but almost compelled the resurgence of the commune. Lancelot Owen wrote that in 1917 "the Mir was living and active though the State was in suspension"; perhaps *because* should be substituted for *though*.[34] Other elements in the countryside were less able to thrive in a time of troubles: landowner estates and farms of peasant separators lost economic viability because of the failure of the societywide market and lost political viability because of the failure of societywide law and order.

The commune (or, more broadly, the village meeting) proved to be an effective instrument in transforming the countryside in its own image. The methods used in the struggle against the landlords were adapted from methods traditionally used within the commune to keep recalcitrants in line. These methods started with social pressure, moved to withdrawal of

1917: The February Revolution (New York, 1967), 248–51; V. I. Startsev, *Vnutrenniaia politika vremennogo pravitel'stva* (Leningrad, 1980), pt. 1.

33. V. V. Kabanov, "Oktiabr'skaia revoliutsiia i krest'ianskaia obshchina," *Istoricheskie zapiski* 111 (1984): 100–150; Dorothy Atkinson, *The End of the Russian Land Commune* (Stanford, 1983).

34. Cited in John Maynard, *Russia in Flux* (New York, 1948), 181. There are some sensible remarks on this issue in Yaney, *Urge to Mobilize*, 464ff.

protection, then harassment and sniping, and if necessary went on to out-and-out terrorism. In 1917 they were used not only against landowners but also against peasants reluctant to join in the commune-mandated struggle.[35] Peasants who had left the commune got the same treatment. The struggle within the peasantry is sometimes called the second social war, but it was not a class struggle directed against the rich peasant; it was a struggle of the commune directed against the separator. There is little reason to equate the separator with the rich peasant and still less to label the separator a kulak. Once reabsorbed within the commune, the erstwhile separator was often able to exert influence in communal deliberations. The aim of the commune was less to expropriate a class enemy than (in the words of one peasant) "to correct the sins and the psychology of the commune members who left to become separators under the Stolypin law."[36]

The resurgence of the commune as an organ of self-protection weakened forces working toward reconstitution since it operated on the principle of suspicion of nonpeasants or, more precisely, of anyone who could not easily be submitted to communal discipline. Bolshevik propaganda was at its most successful not when it used the framework of class but when it appealed to this suspicion of outsiders. A set of instructions for Bolshevik agitators reads:

> It should be resolved by the village gathering that elected [representatives] of the poorest peasantry should keep a close eye on everything in the village: on the priest, so that he doesn't use hell to frighten those who don't want a tsar; on the teacher, so that he doesn't corrupt children [into believing] that it was better under the tsar and the landowners; on the clerk, so that he doesn't drink the people's blood with the kulak; on the doctor, so that he treats peasants and not just the rich.[37]

This principle of suspicion placed food-supply officials in a bind since the peasant's suspicion was awakened not only by the burdens imposed by the new government but also by its promises and urgent appeals. Nizhegorod

---

35. A description of peasant moral pressure can be found in John Rickman, "Russian Camera Obscura," in Geoffrey Gorer and John Rickman, *The People of Great Russia* (New York, 1962). See also I. V. Igritskii, *1917 god v derevne* (Moscow, 1967), 49; *Ek. pol.*, pt. 3, doc. 278.

36. *Ek. pol.*, pt. 3, p. 288; see also docs. 199, 330; V. I. Lenin, *Polnoe sobranie sochinenii*, 5th. ed. (Moscow, 1959–1965), 23:260–77 (1913) (hereafter cited as *PSS*); Atkinson, *Russian Land Commune*, 84–98.

37. *Ek. pol.*, pt. 3, doc. 272, p. 428.

journalist V. Martovskii analyzed the logic of the peasant outlook. For the peasant, the state was never the representative of the whole but something external and mainly hostile—a worker-master relation. The state had only one function that the peasants understood and approved of—protection from enemies, both internal (criminals) and external: "The state is an armed force that like it or not has to be paid for." Everything else, Martovskii argued, was thought up by the gentlemen (*gospoda*) to trick the peasantry into supporting them. The peasantry made no distinction among the nonpeasant classes: they were all *gospoda* who lived at the expense of the muzhik and only played at work. Obviously the state treasury had much more money than it needed if it could pay a young girl to sit in an office and plunk at a typewriter or to stand in a classroom and teach little girls. Therefore it was perfectly acceptable, he concluded, to cheat the treasury or take advantage of its handouts even if they were meant only for the needy. After the February revolution the village was inundated with appeals saying that the government now represented the sovereignty of the people—but all the peasants saw was the same old *gospoda*. There was, however, an important change: evidently the gentlemen no longer had force at their disposal, so they had to rely on trickery to get the muzhik to feed them. Appeals to support the grain monopoly because of national need fell into this category, and the more passionate these arguments became, the more convinced were the peasants of their interpretation.[38]

The village commune was not solely a force of local self-protection and did not automatically reject all the demands made on it for grain and other necessities. But in line with the view of the state as essentially a protector, the peasant producers made a sharp distinction between grain deliveries for the army and deliveries for the town. The peasants understood the necessity of supplying the army by giving up his grain without compensation, but they saw no such necessity to supply the town. What the town wanted, it had to pay for.

This attitude exasperated food-supply officials, who obviously felt the peasants were too backward to grasp that supplying the cities was a civic duty on a par with supplying the army. When peasants in Tver, for example, said they would sell hay at fixed prices only to the army, they were rebuked sharply by a food-supply official: "It is necessary to explain . . . that the fixed price is dictated by state necessity, that the peas-

---

38. *Prod.* (Nizhegorod), 17 December 1917. For tsarist difficulties with peasant egalitarianism, see Richard G. Robbins, Jr., *Famine in Russia, 1891–1892: The Imperial Government Responds to a Crisis* (New York, 1975), 150. For Bolshevik difficulties, see V. V. Kabanov, *Krest'ianskoe khoziaistvo v usloviakh "voennogo kommunizma"* (Moscow, 1988), 179–80.

ants will give the hay not to the army nor to the towns, nor to the factories, but to the state. It is not our business to whom the state then gives the hay: it will give it to whoever needs it. If explanation and persuasion do not work, the state is able to take what it needs by force."[39]

One reason for the peasants' lack of indulgence for the towns was exasperation with the workers, who demanded an eight-hour day, got enormous wage increases while the peasant had to sell his grain at a low fixed price, and went to political rallies instead of making the items needed by the village. In Kostroma in May 1917 the provincial food-supply committee debated whether to equalize the grain consumption norm in town and village. (Kostroma was a deficit province, so the peasants also received a ration from the committees.) The representatives of the workers argued that the availability of eggs, carrots, and other foodstuffs in the country meant that the peasant diet did not depend exclusively on bread; equal rations just meant that the peasants would sell back some of the grain they received to the town. Food-supply officials felt that the whole idea of distributing available grain in equal portions to everybody was wasteful since there was barely enough for the needy. The peasants rejected these arguments and asserted that they worked harder than the workers and had suffered more in the war; they also warned the committee that the slightest inequality would lead to peasant indignation that could cause all deliveries to stop.[40]

A similar debate broke out in Tver province over sugar rations after the city of Tver unilaterally increased the urban sugar rations. The debate covered the same charges and countercharges as in Kostroma: who had the harder life—the peasant, who had to work around the clock at harvest time, or the worker, who had to work day after day cooped up with "those damned machines"? The peasants were infuriated by what they regarded as urban privilege and stated, "The workers are the children of the peasants— but children who introduce for themselves the eight-hour working day [and thereby show] they are not thinking of helping their fathers. For this reason, among others, they do not deserve an increased handout of sugar." As an example of the kind of tactless argument that must have increased peasant hostility, I will cite the assertion of a town representative that before the war 85 percent of the sugar was consumed in the towns. Presumably this percentage reflected a natural law that it would be presumptuous for the peasant to transgress.[41]

39. *Prod. delo* (Tver), 30 July 1917.
40. *Prod. delo* (Kostroma), no. 1 (July 1917) (meetings of 18 May and 14 June). The final decision was to put everyone in the country automatically in the category receiving the highest ration, namely, hard physical labor.
41. *Prod. delo* (Tver), 30 July 1917 (meeting of 16–18 July).

If the peasant producers had organizational forms ready to hand with which to protect themselves, urban workers had to spend much time and energy creating new forms and coming to some consensus about their mutual relations. Factory committees, trade unions, local and central soviets, political parties—all these institutions had to create or recreate themselves in 1917 while at the same time struggling not only with the government and the employers but also among themselves. Recent investigations have shown that in this institutional shakedown a crucial role was played by Hobbes's choice, that is, the tension between centrifugal self-protection and centralizing reconstitution.[42] Workers had a direct stake in reconstitution of the economic unity of society in their status both as individual consumers of food and as collective consumers of the raw materials needed to keep the factories going. In both capacities they faced the choice of securing their own supplies to the detriment of general coordinating institutions or of supporting efforts to strengthen general coordinating institutions—often, unfortunately, to the detriment of securing their own supplies.

The outcome of this choice directly affected the balance of influence between the new institutions. The factory committees showed more vitality than the trade unions in 1917 because they put problems such as food supply at the center of their attention. Trade unions had an impact on workers' access to food only indirectly through wage contracts, yet these contracts seemed increasingly meaningless as the market collapsed and inflation wiped out nominal gains.[43]

In a longer perspective the factory committees of 1917 can be seen as one of a series of institutions created to protect food supply at the factory or other local levels. In 1916 workers' cooperatives had taken on the job of securing supplies and monitoring food shops, and in late 1918 trade unions took charge of sending worker detachments to obtain grain for both the state and the individual factory.[44] Whether these factory-level organizations worked on their own or in conjunction with a centralized food-supply apparatus depended on the institutional and political environment. In 1917 the factory committees were often a disruptive force since the unreliability of official food-supply channels forced them to strike out on their own.

42. S. A. Smith, *Red Petrograd: Revolution in the Factories, 1917–1918* (Cambridge, 1983), 145, 238–39; Raleigh, *Revolution on the Volga*, 158; Koenker, *Moscow Workers*, 180; R. G. Suny, *The Baku Commune, 1917–1918* (Princeton, 1972), 102–4; Alexander Rabinowitch, *The Bolsheviks Come to Power: The Revolution of 1917 in Petrograd* (New York, 1976), 158.

43. Koenker, *Moscow Workers*, 159–60; S. Smith, *Red Petrograd*, 86–88, 124; Raleigh, *Revolution on the Volga*, 120.

44. Browder and Kerensky, *Provisional Government*, 2:752; *Ek. pol.*, pt. 2, doc. 516; Leiberov, *Na shturm*, 66–71.

Food-supply officials felt they needed to discipline the factory committees and other localist institutions such as district soviets, but they also wanted to harness the energy of these enterprising consumer organizations to strengthen the food-supply apparatus in the surplus provinces.[45]

Other urban residents also turned to a familiar organizational form: the consumer cooperative. The time of troubles had its usual contradictory effects on the cooperative movement. On the one hand, the number of consumer cooperatives doubled and then tripled in the three years since the outbreak of the war. Urban residents saw the cooperatives as a weapon against high prices and a hedge against the government's failure to secure the food supply. On the other hand, this prodigious growth distanced the new cooperatives from the prewar ideals of the movement. The new members were called flour and sugar cooperators—their goal was food, not creative forms of social self-organization.

Two new types of consumer cooperatives also revealed the contrasting pull of centrifugal and centralizing forces. One was the closed (zamknutye) forms that served a single profession or even institution: journalists, artists, doctors, students, civil servants. The other new type moved in the opposite direction by including all classes and economic conditions, contrary to cooperative tradition. The worker cooperatives, which stood between these two types since they were open to all members of one class, also took on much greater prominence during the war years.[46]

Many urban residents had no familiar organizational forms to fall back on. Aleksei Peshekhonov concluded from his experiences in neighborhood government early in the year that other urban residents, deprived of this natural focal point, were truly "human dust" whom it was impossible to organize even with the best will in the world. The expression human dust was not one of contempt but rather a challenge to those who sought to reconstitute a new authority: how can people with no stable connections to one another be brought into a new centralized framework?[47]

45. Ek. pol., pt. 2, doc. 481; Keep, Russian Revolution, 81; Koenker, Moscow Workers, 183–86; Prod. delo (Moscow), 30 March, 7 May, 11 June 1917.

46. This account is based mainly on M. L. Kheisin, Istoriia kooperatsii v Rossii (Leningrad, 1926), 217ff. See also V. V. Kabanov, Oktiabr'skaia revoliutsiia i kooperatsiia (Moscow, 1973), 109–20, and Henri Chambre, Henri Wronski, and Georges Lasserre, Les coopératives de consommation en URSS ([Paris], 1969).

47. A. V. Peshekhonov, "Pervye nedeli," Na chuzhoi storone 1 (1923): 272. Roy Medvedev seems to interpret N. Orlov's use of the term in a description of sackmen as an expression of class hostility. Medvedev, The October Revolution (New York, 1979), 142. Sun Yat-sen used a similar expression, "a sheet of loose sand," according to Theodore Von Laue, The World Revolution of Westernization: The Twentieth Century in Global Perspective (Oxford, 1987), 84.

Often the only institution uniting these other urban dwellers was the dismal one of the queue. A food-supply official wrote that "one cannot calmly devote oneself to work, observing every day these endless queues; one cannot look without pain in one's heart at people who stand humbly and patiently throughout the night so that in the morning they can receive a slice of bread."[48] Martovskii has left us an account of how the queues served as a forum for popular deliberation on the source of Russia's troubles. He described how a craftsman swore up and down against the food-supply board, the "comrades," and the soldiers or how an old woman and a young worker debated the impact of the February revolution. The old woman repeated again and again, "Ivan Ivanych would always say, In a month they will cry: give us the old tsar and bread." "Hey," retorted the young worker, "did the tsar feed you or what, you old fool?" "There were no queues with the tsar." "Why don't you go give him a big kiss then?" At which the atmosphere lightened up a little, but not for long. According to Martovskii, the food-supply committees did occasionally find defenders, but victory in these deliberations usually went to the most persistent shouter.[49]

Some efforts were made to organize food distribution in a less destructive manner. In Moscow, building committees (*domovye komitety*) were created in the fall and given responsibility for bread distribution; these committees were the forerunners of the compulsory consumer societies of the civil-war years.[50] A more defensive measure undertaken by local soviets was to head off unorganized pogroms by carrying out organized searches of food stores and private homes.[51]

Despite these efforts, the queues remained politically a centrifugal force, fueling any and all resentment toward the authorities. As Martovskii observed, "Anyone who has had to stand for hours in a queue or run around town in a fruitless search for bread can tell you to what a state of free-floating annoyance and spite it can lead and what a fertile ground it is for pogrom agitation." Many observers concurred with John Reed that "dark forces" used the queues for counterrevolutionary agitation: "Mysterious individuals circulated around the shivering women who waited in queue long cold hours for bread and milk, whispering that the Jews had

48. *Prod. delo* (Moscow), 10 September 1917, 5; *Ek. pol.*, pt. 2, doc. 499.

49. *Prod.* (Nizhegorod), no. 12, 2 September 1917; no. 15, 23 September 1917.

50. *Prod. delo* (Moscow), 10 September 1917, and following issues. Food-supply officials preferred these committees to regular cooperatives. Kheisin, *Istoriia*, 261–62.

51. *Prod. delo* (Moscow), 27 August 1917, 5; Raleigh, *Revolution on the Volga*, 249.

cornered the food supply—and that while the people starved, the Soviet members lived luxuriously."[52] Lenin also tried his hand at mobilizing this resentment: " 'Everybody' suffers from the queues, but . . . the rich people send their servants to stand in line and even hire special servants for it! There's democracy for you!"[53] But he did not find it any easier when he was in power to get rid of the queues or the bitterness they engendered. An eyewitness described the queues in Petrograd a year later:

> Queues, mostly of working women, were waiting outside
> small stores with notices printed on canvas over the lintel
> "First Communal Booth," "Second Communal Booth," and so
> on. . . . There was rarely enough to go round, so people came
> and stood early, shivering in the biting wind. . . . One caught
> snatches of conversation from these queues. "Why don't the
> 'comrades' have to stand in queues?" a woman would exclaim
> indignantly. "Where are all the Jews? Does Trotsky stand in a
> queue?" and so on.[54]

The worst damage that an urban crowd could inflict was a local pogrom. The damage done by peasant consumers, forced to secure their food outside institutional channels, was nationwide. This new centrifugal force gave rise to a new word in the Russian language: *meshochnichestvo*, or "sackmanism." The sackmen (*meshochniki*) were men and women who went to the peasant villages of the surplus regions to obtain grain, which they carried back home on their person in a sack (*meshok*). Other terms for the same phenomenon were "pilgrims" (*palomniki*), "walking delegates" (*khodoki*), and "slicemen" (*kusochniki*). These names denote the long distances traveled and the small amounts of grain obtained.

The phenomenon of the sackmen is usually associated with the civil war, but it had already attained mass proportions by late 1917. This fact has been overlooked by most historians, partly because there is a tendency to equate peasant with grain producer and to see peasant mass action in 1917 mainly in terms of the expropriation of gentry land. But sackmanism was the revolt of the peasant consumer.

The sackmen were the bootleggers of the prohibition of private grain trade. Just as in the case of the prohibition of vodka, prohibition of the trade in grain led to the replacement of specialized and efficient experts with a democratized and hugely inefficient influx of amateurs. It is difficult to

---

52. John Reed, *Ten Days That Shook the World* (New York, 1960), 8, 9, 49; see also Raleigh, *Revolution on the Volga*, 263–66.

53. Lenin, *PSS*, 34:181.

54. Paul Dukes, *Red Dusk and the Morrow* (New York, 1922), 45–46.

categorize neatly the flood of buyers inundating the surplus provinces since the types blended into one another. At one end of the spectrum were agents of various organizations in the deficit provinces, sent south to act as expediters (*tolkachi*). These agents might accept the discipline of the local food-supply authorities, or (more usually) they might feel obliged to hustle on their own, thus earning the hostility of the local authorities. This type merged into the sackmen—although really obtaining grain for themselves, they had usually extorted certification as agents from district food-supply committees—then blended into the speculators, who were buying grain with the intention of reselling it. Often the only difference between a sackman and a food-supply agent was a scribbled signature on a crumpled piece of paper. Given this situation, it was impossible to tell where the black market began and where it ended.

In September a representative of the Ministry of Food Supply, N. Sheremetev, wrote a description of the situation in Kaluga province in the hope of getting central officials to reexamine their basic premises. Sheremetev marked three stages in the rise of sackmanism. In the beginning the food-supply committees sent out instructors to urge people to cooperate with the monopoly. At first these instructors were believed, but when the committees failed to make good on their assurances, the instructors became so unpopular that they had to assume the "name, far from popular in the village, of statistician."

In the next stage the food-supply committees were told not to hand out the purchasing certificates that gave a semilegal cover to individual purchases. These directives had little effect. The district committees caved in to the sackmen quickly; the county committees held out a little longer, but after an incident in late August they changed their attitude. A crowd seized the members of a county food-supply board and paraded them down the street, their hands tied behind their backs, with the intention of tossing them in the river. After this incident the county committees offered no resistance. The sackman movement began to grow to enormous size and involve tens of thousands of peasants.

In the third stage a food-supply militia was formed. It had some effect but usually only against the weakest of the sackmen—widows or soldiers' wives. At journey's end, after incredible exertions, these people saw their bread confiscated by the militia. Hence their reproach to food-supply officials: "Now tell us, Mr. Chairman, what are we to do: go out looting, or murder our own children?" And how could the chairman answer? commented Sheremetev bitterly. Could he say, "Do neither the one nor the other, but bravely and tranquilly die a death by starvation, for the good of the country?" No, that would require an excessive belief in the monopoly.

To demonstrate how hated the *monopol'ka* was, Sheremetev related that once a telegram from the center was misinterpreted as announcing its repeal: "The news was greeted with such joy by the population that you would have thought it was the emancipation from serfdom." There was an immediate mass attack on the trains, and it took three weeks to get things back to normal, or what passed for normal. Sheremetev sided with the sackmen, who refused to starve quietly. Why should they be sacrificed to the "stubborn doctrinairism" behind the monopoly? What purpose was served by turning people, to their own surprise, into criminals and smugglers?[55]

The same story repeated itself in most other deficit provinces. Martovskii described one Nizhegorod district, where things were quiet until a prominent citizen said in public, "All is helpless—every man for himself." This declaration created a panic, and no one was left in the area except the rural intelligentsia. The district committees put up no resistance to the peasants' illegal demand for certificates; if anyone criticized their actions, the committees could easily turn the hostile attention of the crowd toward the critic. The committees even gave a certificate to the kulak (Martovskii's word) who sauntered in and announced, "I've got enough rye, but I need wheat for pirozhki." Martovskii did not blame the committee members, who were average semiliterate peasants capable perhaps of going to town to get food to distribute but not of carrying out the complicated organizational work required by the monopoly. In any event, not only organized food-supply work but all civilized values as well were being trampled by the crowd, whose attitude was, "Who cares about honor if there is nothing to eat? [*Chto za chest', koli nechego est'?*]."[56]

The wave of sackmen had a devastating impact on the surplus provinces. The sackmen bid up the prices and made it impossible for the local food-supply committee to obtain grain. A ministry official noted that Cheliabinsk had given fifty thousand poods a day in October 1917 but only three or four thousand a day in November, the reason being "whole crowds of peasants and people in soldiers' greatcoats" who undermined the fixed prices.[57] Indeed, many places began to fear they would not be able to provide for their own needs. In Eletsk county in Siberia, inundated with peasants from Kaluga and Smolensk, the use of force against the sackmen

55. TsGVIA, 13214-13-72/162–66. Sheremetev uses the term *palomniki* rather than *meshochniki* to describe the sackmen. For the situation in Kaluga, see *Ek. pol.*, pt. 2, doc. 479; pt. 3, doc. 94, 277.

56. *Prod.* (Nizhegorod), 12 November 1917, 30 November 1917.

57. 32-1-394/22–23. Speech of 19 November 1917.

had been endorsed by all the local organs of the democracy. In this case, however, the soldiers of the garrison still refused to confiscate the grain.[58]

The sackmen, who had used violence to extort certificates from their local committees, did not hesitate to use violence in the surplus provinces. A representative from Tver, returning from a trip to Voronezh, described an incident in which a band of sackmen got thirty-five thousand poods of grain in one village, hijacked a train, and were stopped only after a pitched battle with garrison soldiers up the line, in which three sackmen were killed.[59] Moreover, the hordes of sackmen presented a health hazard. The chairman of the Ekaterinoslav committee spoke of huge crowds, with women and children, living around railroad stations under the open sky "in horrifyingly unsanitary conditions that threaten every sort of epidemic."[60] No wonder a hostile attitude grew up in the surplus provinces, not only against the sackmen but also against the deficit provinces that could not restrain their population.

In response to the violence of the sackmen the food-supply committees increasingly demanded a get-tough policy. A conference at the Ministry of Food Supply on 18 October on the problem of sackmanism suggested the following measures: (1) to put blockade detachments on railroad lines; (2) to reduce formalities on searches (*osmotr*) of train passengers; (3) to restrain the lower committees from handing out certificates; (4) to crack down on open trade in the large cities; (5) to give wide publicity to the requisitioning of products from sackmen; (6) to increase penalties for speculation; and (7) to improve procurement in the surplus regions.[61]

Many local committees urged similar measures. One telegram that came into the center is of special interest because it came from Aleksandr Tsiurupa, then a food-supply official in Ufa but later the Bolshevik commissar of food supply. Tsiurupa said the following measures must be vigorously applied, by force if necessary: categorical refusal to allow sackmen to leave the deficit provinces, armed search of trains to eject sackmen, and legal penalties for any official who gave out certificates.[62] These proposals, which are redolent of the civil war, hardly stand out from other proposals by food-supply officials in the fall of 1917.

58. 1276-14-483/172. Ministry memorandum, 11 October 1917.

59. *Prod. delo* (Tver), 1 January 1918.

60. 32-1-394/34–35.

61. 1276-14-483/191–92.

62. 32-1-394/34–39. In view of this telegram it is ironic that a Soviet novelization of Tsiurupa's career starts off in November 1917 with Tsuriupa protesting against a railroad guard's refusal to let a Petrograd woman take a sack of grain back to the capital. V. Krasil'shchikov, *Intendant revoliutsii* (Moscow, 1967).

The sackmen phenomenon reached a height of destructiveness when it was intensified by the disintegration of the army. The February revolution had led to an abandonment of the previous dualism that gave exclusive priority to the army since the new food-supply system was meant to take care of the needs of the country as a whole, with the army seen as only one component.[63] At first it seemed that the prestige of the army would help strengthen the new food-supply apparatus since soldier delegates were among the most successful in persuading peasant producers to comply with the demands of the grain monopoly.[64] But the new system could not give the army what it needed, and individual military units began to strike out on their own. The desperate food-supply situation was one reason commander in chief Lavr Kornilov began to turn his attention to civilian questions and demand militarization of defense industries.[65] By October it was clear to military authorities that food-supply difficulties mandated a de facto demobilization even in the unlikely event that the Ministry of Food Supply managed to deliver what it promised. Unfortunately the spontaneous demobilization often took the form of sackmanism, as all over the country appeared "masses of soldiers, furnished with certificates from their military units, . . . who demand the release of food-supply products and fodder without regard to any official distribution orders."[66] Deserters often became full-time sackmen, earning their living by defying the monopoly. Soldier sackmen were the most destructive kind of all, wrecking the rail system and spreading violence and chaos. Dualism before the revolution had been a centrifugal force, but its abandonment, unsupported by central institutions capable of supplying the economy as a whole, led not to reconstitution but to a frightening disintegration of the army, the final guarantee of a unified political authority.

Sackmanism showed the dilemma of Hobbes's choice at its sharpest. Food-supply officials saw the sackmen's attempt to solve the food-supply question by themselves as the main obstacle to the proper functioning of the apparatus. Officials in the deficit areas felt that this was the equivalent of saying, "First stop being hungry, and after that we'll give you some bread."[67] Only desperate need could drive people to take time off at the

63. Kondratiev, *Rynok khlebov*, 169–72; Zaitsev and Dolinsky, "Organization and Policy," 27–29.

64. *Prod. delo* (Moscow), 28 May–4 June, 14–15.

65. Browder and Kerensky, *Provisional Government*, 2:653–58, 1024; M. Frenkin, *Russkaia armiia i revoliutsiia* (Munich, 1978), 468–89; *Ek. pol.*, pt. 2, doc. 459–69.

66. Kitanina, *Voina*, 332–33, citing army supply officials, 13 October 1917; see also Golovine, *Russian Army*, 175–76; Frenkin, *Russkaia armiia*, 484–88; *Ek. pol.*, pt. 2, p. 358.

67. TsGVIA, 13214-13-72/162–66.

height of the harvest season, run the gamut of food-supply committees like beggars, steal away in the dead of night, bully their way onto a train, and at the end have their grain confiscated by the food-supply militia of the surplus provinces. It was often only the strong and comparatively well-off who could risk this adventure, whereas the poor peasant or the widow had perforce to rely on the meager official rations.[68] This differential impact of economic breakdown caused perhaps more bitterness within the village in 1917 and 1918 than long-standing class hostilities.

In 1917 all the groups we have observed—peasant producers, workers and other urban consumers, peasant and soldier sackmen—made choices that on balance strengthened centrifugal forces. The result was unsatisfactory to all, and great potential support existed for new institutions that could reconstitute the shattered unity of the economy and the political system. Yet reconstitution required not only popular cooperation but also a working consensus among leadership groups on a strategy for creating the new institutions.

68. TsGVIA, 13214-13-72/216–20.

4   The Crisis of 1917: Authority

The first state matter in which Russia will face a test on its economic maturity and organizing ability will be our food-supply question.

Aleksandr Chaianov, April 1917

As 1917 wore on, more and more people shared a feeling expressed by Martovskii in Nizhegorod: the Provisional Government was not a new order but a formless transition period—the continuation of the "disintegration of the state organism" that had already begun before February.[1] The political disintegration can be expressed in numbers: the Provisional Government lasted 237 days, of which 65—more than one-fourth—were spent in search of a cabinet. The total amount of time spent without a government was longer than any one of the four cabinets during the months between February and October.

The grain-monopoly legislation of March 1917 was as much a response to the crisis of political authority as it was a response to the food-supply crisis. The legislation itself may not be a good guide to actual food-supply policy, but the arguments used to attack and defend the monopoly do reveal the outlook of the enlistment advocates as they strove to reconstitute the unity of the political class and the economy in the face of powerful centrifugal forces.

The monopoly legislation was the result of a liberal-socialist consensus that had been achieved under the old government. This consensus is symbolized by the merger in the first days of the February revolution of the food-supply commissions created by the ad hoc committee set up by the Duma Committee and the newly formed Petrograd Soviet. This merger—a harbinger of eventual coalition—was eased by the experience of the two chairmen, Shingarev and Groman, in working together on the tsarist Special Conference.[2]

1. *Prod.* (Nizhegorod), 15 October 1917.
2. Peshekhonov, "Pervye nedeli," 261; Hasegawa, *February Revolution*, 334–35; Burdzhalov, *Vtoraia revoliutsiia*, 1:219; Shliapnikov, *Semnadtsatyi god*, 3:26–29.

The consensus that gave rise to the monopoly is already evident in a document that predates the revolution. In December 1916 Groman had prepared a report for a conference scheduled by the Union of Towns. Although the tsarist government then prohibited any conference on the food-supply question, the main theses of Groman's report were accepted by the executive board of the union. The Union of Towns was a liberal organization, and Groman soon became the chief spokesman of the Petrograd Soviet on food-supply matters. His report of late 1916 thus shows the starting point from which the two sides later diverged.[3]

Groman began by reducing all economic difficulties to one fundamental flaw, the lack of "conscious adaptation of all of national economic life and the state economy to the demands of the war." Since the food-supply question was only one manifestation of this general crisis, "both the system of measures aimed at easing the crisis and the organizational apparatus must be parts of a general system of measures and an integrated organizational apparatus." This reform required overcoming the disunity caused by the existence of four separate special conferences. A single Ministry of Provisionment (*snabzhenie*) would eliminate dualism by supplying both army and population as well as regulating all aspects of the economy.

The job of this regulatory structure was to "coordinate the activities" of all the vital forces of the country by means of enlistment: "the regime of free trade must be abandoned and replaced by a system of state-public organizations, constructed on principles of the predominance of representatives from public institutions and from cooperative, industrial, trade, and worker organizations. These organizations would enlist to the task of provisionment public institutions, cooperatives, and trade organizations— either on the basis of commission payments or as a publicly responsible task." This enlistment would have two guiding principles: the subordination of private interest to the demands of the national whole, and the reliance on the spontaneous initiative (*samodeiatel'nost'*) of all sections of the population. In Groman's thinking these two principles were not contradictory but mutually reinforcing.

In the realm of food-supply policy the right of the government to requisition grain not voluntarily delivered by the producer was to be applied in a systematic and all-embracing manner. Although grain delivery would be compulsory, every effort would be made to provide material incentives for voluntary delivery, and industry was to be mobilized to

3. Vserossiiskii Soiuz Gorodov, *Organizatsiia narodnogo khoziaistva* (Moscow, 1916), 5–10.

provide industrial items for the agricultural population. The food-supply apparatus in the localities would still be based on commissioners working with advisory organs; but the advisory organs would include wide representation of public organizations, and the commissioners had to work through them, not through their own agents. The presence of appointed commissioners in Groman's 1916 program is the only major difference between it and the actual grain-monopoly legislation, but the thrust of Groman's proposals is clearly toward full democratization.

Groman's report to the Union of Towns reveals that the grain monopoly was not simply a response to the food-supply crisis but also an attempt to reconstitute the economy and the political system. All-embracing state economic regulation would overcome the dualism of army versus civilian population and restore unity to an economy shattered by insistent state demands. In the case of the political system Groman felt that the war had greatly exacerbated the disunity that had existed previously but that the food-supply crisis presented an opportunity to create a new unity by means of enlistment of social forces.

It is sometimes said that the monopoly was adopted by the liberal majority of the Provisional Government only under pressure from the Petrograd Soviet. Nikolai Sukhanov asserted this in his memoirs and at the Menshevik trial in 1930: "Groman was the author of war communism. When did he proclaim it? He proclaimed it soon after the February revolution. . . . He took the Kadet Shingarev by the throat and squeezed out of him the basic element of war communism, namely, the grain monopoly."[4] In reality Shingarev had long been an advocate of the enlistment solution. In September 1916 he had called for a grain monopoly, and in February 1917 he had called for a more direct partnership with the peasants. In May 1917 he commented on the unanimity of the monopoly decision and predicted that state monopolies would become increasingly common as a means of fighting the disintegrating influence of "individual self-protection." A temporary improvement in grain deliveries allowed him to argue that the "country understands the voice of its leaders and civic feeling is growing"—all that was needed was for the government to meet the peasants halfway with an "organized answer."[5] Even after disillusionment set in, Shingarev fought the good fight for state regulation of industry and agriculture in an increasingly hostile Kadet environment.[6]

4. Jasny, *Soviet Economists*, 100; N. Sukhanov, *Zapiski o revoliutsii* (Berlin, 1922–1923), 2:271–75; Z. Lozinskii, *Ekonomicheskaia politika vremennogo pravitel'stva*, (Leningrad, 1929), 128, 131–32. Liberals also blamed Groman; see Alexis N. Antsiferov et al., *Russian Agriculture During the War* (New Haven, 1930), 284–86.

5. *Izv. po prod. delu*, 1 (32): 64–66.

6. Antsiferov et al., *Russian Agriculture*, 284–86; William Rosenberg, *Liberals*

Despite this consensus, the grain monopoly soon became a symbol of opposition to the Provisional Government on the part of both socialists and liberals. For Groman, the halfhearted implementation of the monopoly was proof of the "icy indifference and practical sabotage" not only of the Provisional Government but the Petrograd Soviet as well.[7] Groman's definition of the situation remained the same as it had been in 1916, although he dropped terms such as *interdependence* and *equilibrium* and indulged in some low-level rabble-rousing by arguing that regulation was needed to eliminate superprofits and improve working conditions.[8]

What was new in Groman's outlook in 1917 was a great enthusiasm that led him to downplay practical problems. He now felt that his schemes for all-embracing economic regulation had a chance of practical realization, and for this very reason he became a more bitter critic of the Provisional Government than he had been of the tsarist government. When Naum Jasny expressed skepticism over Groman's bold plans, Groman would complain, "No revolution happened to Jasny." And in response to Jasny's query "Who will work out the plan? I do not see the competent people," Groman blithely answered, "You and others." In 1925 Nikolai Kondratiev looked back and quoted Groman as saying, "I shall not distribute a single pair of shoes until the national economy as a whole has been regulated." Many of Groman's actions reveal a man ill-adapted to the daily improvisations of a revolutionary government. Later in the year, as head of the Petrograd Food-Supply Board, Groman refused to obtain grain by paying more than the fixed price on the grounds that doing so would further disrupt the economy and the grain monopoly, thus severely handicapping the Petrograd board in the competition for grain.[9]

From his base as a Menshevik member of the Petrograd Soviet, Groman had created around himself a "compact and harmonious group of soviet

---

in the Russian Revolution (Princeton, 1974), 203; Yaney, Urge to Mobilize, 457; Ek. pol., pt. 2, doc. 515; Kitanina, Voina, 130; Sukhanov, Zapiski, 3:428–29; Browder and Kerensky, Provisional Government, 3:1270. On Shingarev's disillusionment, see V. N. Nabokov, "Vremennoe pravitel'stvo," Arkhiv russkoi revoliutsii 1 (1922): 50–52; S. I. Shidlovskii, Vospominaniia (Berlin, 1923), 2:114–15; Ernest Poole, The Village: Russian Impressions (New York, 1918), 58–63.

7. Sukhanov, Zapiski, 2:69–77.

8. Compare the presentation to a soviet audience in Vserossiiskoe soveshchanie sovetov rabochikh i soldatskikh deputatov. Stenograficheskii otchet, ed. M. N. Tsapenko (Moscow, 1927), 202–4, 257–60, with Groman's article in Izv. po prod. delu 1 (32): 2–5.

9. Jasny, To Live, 301; Jasny, Soviet Economists, 99; Izv. po prod. delu, 3 (34): 60–63. Soviet historians have interpreted Groman's leadership of the Petrograd board in different ways: compare Kitanina, Voina, 368, to Volubuev, Ekonomicheskaia politika, 418–19. Groman's own account is in Protsess kontrrevoliutsionnoi organizatsii men'shevikov (Moscow, 1931), 377–78.

economists." Ernest Poole had a conversation with one of these Groman followers at the headquarters of the Moscow Food-Supply Committee:

> I found him in a building whose long dark halls were filled with soldiers and civilians, men and boys and student girls. Some carried trays with glasses of tea, and all were talking rapidly and with the greatest good humor. The man whom we had come to see was a thin, ungainly chap, red haired, freckled and washed out, a thoroughly uninspiring sort, until he got into his subject. But then I forgot his unpleasant voice, and saw only his eager friendly smile.
>
> "All this work of ours," he said, "is under one great national plan, which reaches through committees to every village in the land." And he displayed a Russian map all speckled with committees—and committees by the thousands, specks of every color and size. It really was a beautiful plan. . . .
>
> "We need only to have patience," he said. "Here in Moscow you go out on the streets and find that prices are still way up; you see long lines of people in front of the stores; and when they get in they find little there. But when our whole plan has gone into effect and our government controls our life, these troubles will all be remedied. At such a job you cannot expect speed, for we have to implant in men's old minds new ideas, and that takes time. Then, too, the mails and railroads are so slow it makes it hard for us. In short, *you must get the whole system going before you can make a real success of any one of its separate parts.* Things here may seem bad enough, but without the work that we have done you would find things infinitely worse. We have at least made a start."[10]

The power of Groman's definition of the situation appears in the food-supply congress of late May, although Groman himself was already seen even within socialist circles as part of the opposition from the left. This congress, held in Moscow, had heavy representation from soviets around the country.[11] The congress saw the grain monopoly as a step toward socialism: "The time has come to move from anarchic production and distribution, from trusts and syndicates, from free trade, to the work of a productive organism according to state tasks, under the monitoring of the state and even its immediate direction." As the editor of the Moscow food-supply journal remarked, "genuine state socialism" was being created not

10. Poole, "*Dark People*," 108–11 (emphasis added).
11. *Prod. delo* (Moscow), 28 May–4 June 1917, 40. Of 740 voting delegates, 311 were sent by soviets, 129 by food-supply committees, 135 by cooperatives.

because of revolutionary abstractions but because of the practicalities of a pressing crisis.

Accordingly the concerns of the congress went far beyond food-supply policy in the strict sense. There was a transportation section, a section devoted to agricultural production, an industrial section that called for rationing on all consumer items as a step toward replacing trade with direct exchange, and a social section that took up such matters as the regulation of profits and wages. Later in the year socialist critics identified the failure of the Provisional Government and its supporters in the Petrograd Soviet to carry out this ambitious program as the cause of food-supply difficulties: the monopoly would only succeed if industrial items were made available to the peasantry, and this could only be done through all-embracing state regulation.[12]

It was these ambitious claims rather than actual food-supply policy that provoked the most opposition. One fierce critic, I. Sigov, condemned the attempt "to put on register and under the bureaucratic monitoring of the state the everyday economic life of each and all." Sigov went on to argue that "history does not know a law that has been less thought-out. . . . Almost two months have already passed, and perhaps no small number of months will pass, before the activists of the monopoly finally admit, with shame and despair, to their impotence in scrambling out of the chaos and omnipresent all-Russian confusion that is just now becoming implanted."[13]

Despite the heated rhetoric, even Sigov did not advocate a return to an unregulated grain trade. Criticism of the grain trade monopoly from the right in fact almost never meant a defense of free trade. Ideological attitudes toward property did not play the same centrally divisive role in food-supply matters that they did elsewhere. Notions of property determined access to basic resources in agriculture and the nature of authority relations in industry. By contrast, no one much cared about the property rights of the middleman. The state's demands on the grain producer were seen either as a tax or as an enforced exchange transaction, both traditionally accepted limitations on property especially in time of war. The dispute over food-supply policy was much more about the expediency and fairness of the state's methods than its right to mobilize grain.

Many liberal activists did feel that socialism was a doctrine destructive of civic discipline since it encouraged class selfishness, exorbitant demands

12. *Prod. delo* (Moscow), 20 August 1917, 3–4 (Shefler); *Ek. pol.*, pt. 3, p. 414 (peasant *nakaz*); Sukhanov, *Zapiski*, 2:271–75, 4:48, 106–28.
13. Sigov, *Arakcheevskii sotsializm*, 12.

by workers, and utopian expectations of state planning. Some, like V. A. Stepanov, the Kadet minister of trade and industry, felt that an official rejection of socialism would therefore strengthen "state consciousness." But even while insisting on the principle of private property, Stepanov argued that existing circumstances "would turn the free play of private interests (permissable under normal conditions) into economic chaos."[14] Stepanov's condemnation of socialism did not imply a defense of laissez-faire or a rejection of extensive state regulation; it was more an expression of frustration than a positive program.

AN UNRECONSTITUTED POLITICAL CLASS

The original liberal-socialist consensus on the grain monopoly seemed to have split wide apart since one side was calling for movement toward socialism and the other for a rejection of socialism. Yet it is difficult to pinpoint what this dispute actually meant for practical food-supply policy. On two key controversies in food-supply policy—the use of the private trade apparatus under state monitoring and the refusal to raise the grain prices announced in March—the liberal-socialist consensus held through the summer, at least in the statements of spokesmen in the center.[15]

The original policy consensus might have provided the basis for unity of the food-supply question, but the two sides chose to emphasize the most divisive themes. In April 1917 Chaianov argued that political questions were easier to solve than economic ones since "in the area of political construction . . . almost everything is within our power and the power of human laws." By the end of May he felt differently: "We need not only a single plan but also a single will to carry out that plan."[16] Chaianov had come to realize that the unity of the political class was a more basic challenge than consensus on the details of any particular policy.

A debate in the State Duma on the eve of the February revolution revealed some of the roots of political class disunity. When the Petrograd crowds demanded bread, the instinctive response of both liberals and socialists was to call for enlistment of the vital forces of society—specifically for the transfer of control over Petrograd food supply to the elected city authorities. This action would not only ensure better monitoring of

14. Browder and Kerensky, *Provisional Government*, 2:672–77 (8 June 1917). Background can be found in Bukshpan, *Politika*, 460–66; Rosenberg, *Liberals*, 140–42.

15. See Chkheidze in Browder and Kerensky, *Provisional Government*, 3:1483, and Shingarev in *Ek. pol.*, pt. 2, doc. 517.

16. Chaianov, *Vopros; Prod. delo* (Moscow), 28 May–4 June 1917, 10–12. Chaianov praised Groman in April but was rather critical of him in May.

distribution but also give those authorities the right to ask the population to go hungry in a disciplined manner (*soznatel'no golodat'*).[17]

The unanimous support for this policy measure concealed profound differences in political outlook. An optimistic liberal such as the left Kadet Nikolai Nekrasov felt that the local elite could handle the job; he stressed the "creative and organizing role of the very idea of self-administration" as well as the confidence given by the local population to the city administration. Nekrasov's fellow Kadet Shingarev was more pessimistic about the liberal elite's ability to function under conditions of chaos and warned that given the general breakdown, the transfer to the city might merely be a way of shifting the blame for inevitable food-supply difficulties.[18]

An optimistic socialist politician such as Aleksandr Kerensky could express confidence that self-organization by the people would overcome the elemental force (*stikhiia*) created by hunger: "Organize yourselves; without waiting for permission, create public and worker organizations; demand that the question of your very existence, the organization of your nourishment, be given over to you." Nikolai Chkheidze, soon to be chairman of the Petrograd Soviet, injected a pessimistic note: "Gentlemen, we are not great admirers of the city self-administration that functions at the present time, but even this city self-administration will be forced to act in accord with the interests of the masses when they exert pressure, through their own organized cells." The strategy of distrust that soon gave rise to divided sovereignty (*dvoevlastie*) was thus in evidence even before the Petrograd Soviet was considered a possibility.[19]

Even after the February revolution efforts continued to be made to give at least a working unity to the political class. "One of the most tragic documents of that epoch," wrote Bukshpan, "is the minutes of the Economic Council and the Economic Committee [which had been given the responsibility for general economic regulation. The minutes show] members of the government, economists, experienced bureaucrats from the old regime, and representatives of the [mutually hostile] revolutionary forces trying to find some kind of common ground for living together and making effective policy."[20] But these efforts seemed feeble in the face of powerful centrifugal forces.

The underlying consensus on the enlistment solution may paradoxically have strengthened centrifugal forces within the political class. When

17. Duma session of 23 February 1917, 1649–53 (Kerensky speech).
18. Duma session of 25 February 1917, 1748–52; Shliapnikov, *Semnadtsatyi god*, 1:254–59.
19. Duma session of 24 February 1917, 1728, 1719–24.
20. Bukshpan, *Politika*, 461.

the enlistment solution failed to work, neither side really examined the assumptions behind it; instead they complained about the lack of "conscious" cooperation with state policy, and this lack in turn was blamed on the moral and intellectual failures of their opponents. The liberals blamed class selfishness, intelligentsia demagoguery, and socialist utopias; the socialists blamed capitalist sabotage, bureaucratic timidity, and free-trade utopias. It was easier to cast blame than to acknowledge that the enlistment solution was unlikely to overcome the centrifugal forces of rational self-protection.

Distrust within the political class was compounded by disagreement on the key question of how to contain the pressures of the population. Socialists felt that reform was a necessary precondition for political reconstitution; liberals felt that a reconstituted political authority must precede reform. On this crucial question the socialists remained loyal to the enlistment solution, whereas the liberals showed a preference for the gubernatorial solution.[21]

By the time of the food-supply conference in late May the effect on food-supply policy of this disagreement was out in the open. Despite his belief in state regulation, Shingarev argued that it was unwise to rely on popular gratitude: "Regardless of how deep was the confidence expressed by the masses, regardless of the endless number of welcoming telegrams they sent to the Provisional Government, these are nothing but words." He was pessimistic about political class unity: "In the localities there are either no [qualified] people, or they busy themselves with quarrels and arrest each other, bringing confusion and disintegration into the common cause." Russia would be lucky to emerge from the crisis "without fratricidal war, without anarchy, without social breakdown, bankruptcy, and blood."[22]

Shingarev's analysis was supported by Sergei Prokopovich, who told the food-supply congress that Groman's program of extensive state regulation was too ambitious, given the shakiness of the state's authority. (Although Prokopovich was technically a socialist, he was regarded as being to the right of the consensus of the congress.) Prokopovich's views were supported by V. I. Anisimov, who rejected fashionable terms of both left and right such as anarchy and revolutionary democracy but still felt that disorganization and multiple sovereignty (mnogovlastie) were the key problems. These arguments were unavailing: the congress overwhelm-

21. Rosenberg, Liberals, 11–20.
22. Prod. delo (Moscow), 28 May–4 June 1917, 1–5; Browder and Kerensky, Provisional Government, 2:632–33.

ingly supported Groman's view that the only way for the state to obtain authority was through successful economic regulation.[23]

This dispute over the priority of effective state regulation versus firm political authority may have been tragically beside the point. Economic breakdown prevented satisfaction of popular demands, and political breakdown prevented reconstitution of authority. The chain reaction of disintegration seemed unstoppable.

UNSOWN LAND: A CASE STUDY

Thus far I have examined separately the intertwining strands of the crisis of 1917. In reality the difficulties of food supply, the self-protection actions of the population, and the failure to create effective unity for the political class all interacted with one another to intensify the crisis. This interaction can be seen at work in the case of policy toward unsown land.

At the beginning of the year food-supply officials felt that the crucial question was whether all available land would be utilized. As Chaianov declared in April 1917, "One may say with confidence that the most basic question in Russian life now consists in this: will the Russian democracy and its local organs cope or not with the spring sowing? . . . Our success now is being decided not so much on the front, not so much in our political life, as in the fields being sown."[24] One result of this concern was a desire to avoid disruptive trouble in the countryside, and under the circumstances this meant protecting the landowners. But even stronger was a desire to ensure the unsown land was utilized by *somebody*, which meant empowering peasant committees to take over private property. This double concern found expression in the legislation of 11 April 1917 entitled "On the Protection of Crops," which explicitly tied its promise of protection of landowner property to an insistence on the full use of available land. Unsown land was subject to compulsory transfer to local committees.[25]

Commentary on this legislation has traditionally stressed its solicitude

23. *Prod. delo* (Moscow), 28 May–4 June 1917. Prokopovich and Anisimov represented cooperative organizations. See also Prokopovich's speech to the congress of cooperatives in September 1917, S. N. Prokopovich, *Narodnoe khoziaistvo v dni revoliutsii: tri rechi* (Moscow, 1918), 24–35.

24. Chaianov, *Vopros*, 16–17. See Groman's remarks at the all-Russian conference of soviets in April 1917 (Stenographic report, 259–60); Struve's remarks in Samuel Hoare, *The Fourth Seal* (London, 1930), 193; *Ek. pol.*, pt. 3, doc. 77.

25. *Ek. pol.*, pt. 3, doc. 118; Browder and Kerensky, *Provisional Government*, 2:621–25. Some Soviet historians have recognized the break with property rights inherent in the crop-protection legislation; see Kitanina, *Voina*, 306; Startsev, *Vnutrenniaia politika*, 229–30.

for the landowner, but the mandate to take over unsown land made sense to the peasants, who used it to justify their actions. In turn the central ministries did not feel they could retreat from the imperative of full utilization even after they became worried about land seizures. In July the three socialist ministers Viktor Chernov (agriculture), Iraklii Tseretelli (interior), and Aleksei Peshekhonov (food supply), sent out circulars warning against illegal land seizures—but all three felt compelled to reiterate that "nonutilization by landowners of free lands and fields is impermissible."[26] At the end of the month Peshekhonov issued a further decree on the "compulsory maximum utilization" of agricultural equipment as well as land. Landowner organizations protested against this decree as a violation of property rights.[27] So it was, but although the mobilizing bureaucrats might on occasion protect a landowner's property, they were not particularly interested in his property rights.

In the case of unsown lands, actions taken to fend off the bread crisis intensified the authority crisis. A further paradox reveals itself on examination of the rhetoric surrounding unsown lands: the government bureaucrats and the peasants seemed to be talking in one language, and the socialists and the landowners in another.

A distinction can be made between a rhetoric based on property and one based on utilization of resources. A property perspective looks primarily at human subjects and inquiries about the proper relationship between them: should it be based on some principle of distributional equality or rather on contract and the rule of law? A utilization perspective looks primarily at the available economic resources and asks how they can be used to the fullest extent.

Both the peasants and the bureaucrats felt more at home with the rhetoric of utilization. The peasant commune had always been more interested in maximum utilization of available resources than in any rights of the individual because the central imperative of survival in a harsh environment so determined.[28] Full communal membership was granted only to those who fulfilled the duty to utilize one's own capacity for physical labor. The representatives of the Russian state had also always been inter-

26. *Ek. pol.*, pt. 3, docs. 137, 138, 139 (the cited remark is by Tseretelli). For a retreat from this position by the Main Land Committee in September 1917, see *Ek. pol.*, pt. 3, p. 503 (footnote to doc. 269).

27. Browder and Kerensky, *Provisional Government*, 2:638–39; Chaadaeva, *Pomeshchiki*, 128–29. This decree was actually aimed at the peasants; see *Ek. pol.*, pt. 3, p. 314; Golovine, *Russian Army*, 175.

28. Edward Keenan, "Muscovite Political Folkways," *Russian Review* 45 (1986): 115–81. See also Yaney, *Urge to Mobilize*, 161ff., esp. 178–84.

ested primarily in the mobilization of resources, and this outlook was strengthened by the pressures of total war.

By contrast, both landowners and socialist intellectuals spoke in the more alien rhetoric of property. There were some surprising points of resemblance between Bolshevik and landowner views on agricultural development since both saw the natural next step in the countryside as a division between a productive bourgeoisie controlling large productive units and a propertyless agricultural laboring class. The Bolshevik slogan of land nationalization was intended not to prevent this development but instead to accelerate it.[29] The only difference—not a minor one, to be sure—was that the Bolsheviks assigned the role of the bourgeois not to the landowners but to the peasants after the revolutionary expropriation of the landowners.

The Socialist Revolutionaries (SRs) seemed closer to the utilization perspective since in their rhetoric the language of property seemed to self-destruct: land became the property of no one (*nich'ia zemlia*). But nevertheless the SRs still thought in terms of egalitarian distribution and the creation of fraternal relations rather than full utilization of resources, leaving them with curiously little to say about the realities of 1917.[30] The peasant activists willingly accepted the SR shibboleths as the preamble to their statements but then went on to speak in the more natural accents of communal localism and full utilization.

The rhetorical clash over unsown lands shows some of the constraints and opportunities created by the crisis of 1917. Peasant rhetoric kept the question of unsown lands in the forefront, both at the local level, when peasants justified their claims against particular landowners, and at the national level, in programmatic statements such as the "Peasant Instructions" that became the basis of the original Bolshevik land legislation. In these statements the radical demand for transfer of all land to the land committees was based squarely on the imperative of full utilization of all lands.[31] In the peasant customary law that governed internal communal relations, he who sowed the land of another had as much, or more, claim to the eventual product as the owner of land, contrary to the principles of

29. Lenin, *PSS*, 16:413 (1917), 34:35; P. N. Pershin, *Agrarnaia revoliutsiia v Rossii* (Moscow, 1966), 1:339. For acceptance by a landowner of the nationalization slogan, see Chaadaeva, *Pomeshchiki*, 61.

30. Oliver Radkey, *The Agrarian Foes of Bolshevism* (New York, 1958). Radkey notes that the main SR theorist, V. Chernov, was not fully committed to the commune and did not completely reject the Stolypin reforms (26ff., 84).

31. *Ek. pol.*, pt. 3, docs. 185, 195, 210, 220, 232, 237, 254, 257, 269. See also 412 (peasant *nakaz*); I. V. Stalin, *Sochineniia* (Moscow, 1946–1953), 3:34–36; Lenin, *PSS*, 32:44.

common jurisprudence.[32] In 1917 the peasants applied this standard to the landowner as well—at the invitation of the government.

Government bureaucrats could not sound too convincing defending property rights in a rhetoric so heavily weighted toward the utilization perspective. The political bind was even worse for Kadet officials such as Shingarev and Stepanov, who adhered in essence to the utilization perspective: in industry, as in agriculture, the liberals' natural constituency adopted the property perspective, whereas the utilization perspective was adopted by constituencies that the liberals had little hope of reaching.

The landowners' vulnerable position was exposed by their rhetoric: the defensive insistence on private property could not help sounding rather feeble. The Western bourgeois rhetoric of property sounded strange on the lips of Russian noblemen; the term *pomeshchik* (landowner) itself bespoke the time when estates had been autocratic grants in return for political loyalty and services.[33] Landowner organizations wanted the Provisional Government to declare the right of private property "holy and inviolable" just when all belligerent governments were making unparalleled inroads into private property.[34]

The standard of full utilization imposed by the food-supply crisis hurt the landowners. The breakdown of the market reduced their incentive to produce and left them without needed resources such as migrant labor or artificial fertilizer. They themselves had never owned the machinery to make full use of their own land resources but had relied on leasing peasant machinery.[35] During the war landowners became dependent on state-provided sources of labor such as prisoners of war; this dependency certainly did not fit in with an ideology of private property, and it aroused peasant resentment because of unfair distribution of the available prisoners. As a result, the percentage decline in their sown acreage during the war years was twice that in the peasants'. Landowners thus exercised their property rights in the negative form of preventing use of their land until satisfactory terms were offered. The peasants regarded refusal to cultivate as the equivalent of a workers' strike in wartime; they strongly rejected the legitimacy of both the one and the other.[36]

32. Maurice Hindus, *The Russian Peasant and the Revolution* (New York, 1920), 166–67; *Ek. pol.*, pt. 3, doc. 235.

33. Lenin noted the evasiveness of the term *landowner (chastnovladelets)* in *PSS*, 34:430; see also Chaadaeva, *Pomeshchiki*, 98.

34. Chaadaeva, *Pomeshchiki*, 99; *Ek. pol.*, pt. 3, docs. 125, 144, 196, 248.

35. Kitanina, *Voina*, 22; Chaadaeva, *Pomeshchiki*, 54–55; *Ek. pol.*, pt. 3, doc. 190.

36. In 1980 I heard a talk in the Soviet Union that justified the absence of strikes by using the analogy of a peasant harvest.

Bolshevik loyalty to the property perspective also proved a stumbling block to their plans. Lenin insisted on seeing the peasant world in terms of class and property rather than in terms of the commune or full utilization. He argued that the objective content of the peasant revolution, despite the peasants' own view of the matter, was land nationalization, a bourgeois measure that admittedly would bring no benefit to the vast majority of peasants since it implied distribution of land to those who controlled other means of agricultural production such as livestock or machines. The only way poor peasants could derive any benefit from such a policy would be to preserve each landlord estate intact and work there under the direction of agronomists. In this way they would have the option of being wageworkers for the state rather than for other peasants. Intrapeasant conflict was a matter for the future, and it would be based on class: Lenin makes no mention of the conflict between the commune and the separators.[37]

Although the peasants willingly listened to Bolshevik encouragement of immediate action, they continued to rely on institutions and worldviews far removed from Bolshevik prescriptions. In the second half of 1917 Lenin dropped most of his scheme of intrapeasant dynamics and simply used the term *poorest peasantry* without further analysis; this "timely shift of accent" allowed Lenin to use the peasant revolution as a support for the Bolshevik insurrection.[38] His newly simplified scheme was sufficient as long as he required no more from the peasants than what they wanted to do anyway.

Underneath the rhetoric lies a crucial dilemma for the government: it had to rely on peasant cooperation in food-supply matters while at the same time denying long-standing peasant desires on the land question. It

37. Lenin, *PSS*, 31:115, 271, 416–28; 32:163–89, 376–80; 34:108–16; Esther Kingston-Mann, *Lenin and the Problem of Marxist Peasant Revolution* (Oxford, 1983), 150. Although Kingston-Mann shows the limitations of Lenin's sociological analysis of the peasantry, she believes him "unequalled in his political insight" (175). I cannot agree: (1) Kingston-Mann does not bring out the political nonsense of Lenin's idea that the "center of gravity" in the countryside should be the rural proletarians (whom Lenin did *not* see as peasants); (2) she exaggerates Lenin's belief in the socialist potential of the peasantry, sometimes relying on inaccurate quotation (143 n. 40); (3) she misrepresents Lenin's argument with other Bolsheviks, who needed no urging to support peasant demands for land (144); (4) she seems to absolve Lenin from the errors of Bolshevik peasant policies after 1917 despite the fact that they were deeply influenced by Lenin's 1917 political analysis (193–94). One of the few places Lenin's vision of independent organization of rural proletarians acquired some reality was Latvia; see Pershin, *Agrarnaia revoliutsiia*, 1:333–34; Stanley W. Page, "Lenin's April Theses and the Latvian Peasant-Soldiery," in R. C. Elwood, ed., *Reconsiderations on the Russian Revolution* (Columbus, Ohio, 1976).

38. P. V. Volubuev, in *Kommunist*, 1987, no. 5:66.

had to empower and repress at the same time. The government would not have escaped its dilemma even it if had taken the plunge and carried out a radical land reform. Gratitude is a notoriously weak force in politics: when the Bolsheviks gave the land to the peasants, they were still faced with the task of creating an effective political authority to mobilize needed peasant resources.[39] To reconstitute the economy and political authority, the Provisional Government needed incentives, either material or coercive, but none was available: the government could not provide the peasants with exchange items nor punish their land seizures.[40] It had to rely on exhortation, and even its mobilizational rhetoric proved double-edged and easily turned against it.

But the rhetoric of utilization also confirmed the existence of values held in common by the peasants and the government. Observers both in 1917 and later have often felt that the language of utilization was hypocritical on both sides: the Provisional Government used it to protect the landowners, and the peasants used it to expropriate the landowners.[41] No doubt the peasants themselves often prevented landowner utilization and then used landowner inactivity as an excuse for expropriation. But hypocritical manipulation of a rhetoric need not detract from its importance. Although the peasants and the bureaucrats argued with each other, they did so in a language they both understood, and together they accomplished something—the drop in sown acreage was almost halted in the most important food crops.[42] This positive achievement should be remembered in a year otherwise marked by economic disintegration and political conflict.

The paradoxes created by the crises of 1917 came together in Aleksei Peshekhonov, the socialist minister of food supply who defended the liberal viewpoint and later supported the Bolsheviks. A central reason for the creation of the Ministry of Food Supply in May 1917 was to put a socialist in charge of food supply. The ministry was the old Special Conference on

39. The dilemma is presented in general terms by Mancur Olson, *The Logic of Collective Action* (Cambridge, Mass., 1965); for the specific case of war, see Arthur Stein, *The Nation at War* (Baltimore, 1978), and for the even more specific case of civil war in Russia, see Gerasimenko, *Nizovye organizatsii*, chap. 5. A similar argument is made by N. Orlov in *Izvestiia Narodnogo Komissariata po Prodovol'stvennomu Delu*, August 1918, 4 (hereafter cited as *Izv. NKP*).

40. Kondratiev, *Rynok khlebov*, 112–20; Zaitsev and Dolinsky, "Organization and Policy," 106–8.

41. Sukhanov, *Zapiski*, 2:69–77; *Ek. pol.*, pt. 3, docs. 261, 186 (p. 314); Pershin, *Agrarnaia*, 1:363; Chaadaeva, *Pomeshchiki*, 66–67; Keep, *Russian Revolution*, 166.

42. Browder and Kerensky, *Provisional Government*, 2:634, 644–45; Kitanina, *Voina*, 21. Sown acreage went up slightly for food crops and down slightly for fodder crops. According to Antsiferov et al., *Russian Agriculture*, 278–79, sown acreage went down mainly in export crops such as wheat or barley.

Food Supply and its secretariat, henceforth to be independent of the Ministry of Agriculture. The new arrangement was due in part to the size of the food-supply apparatus but also to coalition politics. Liberal politicians would not have tolerated Agriculture Minister Chernov's control of food supply as well as agriculture, and socialist politicians insisted that the new post be given to a socialist.[43]

Peshekhonov was the leader of the Popular Socialists (*narodnye sotsialisty*), an offshoot of the SRs usually regarded as the most moderate of the socialist groups.[44] Peshekhonov at first saw his task as carrying out the original Groman-Shingarev consensus on the grain monopoly, but as time went on, he tilted more and more toward the liberal view that popular indiscipline, rather than elite sabotage, was the main obstacle to success. But although Peshekhonov agreed on the priority of reestablishing an effective state authority, he was still disillusioned with the Provisional Government: it did not show the "systematic persistence that does not stop before repression, [nor] the stern decisiveness [needed] for taking on this 'dirty business.'" To his disgust, the government seemed to content itself with admonitions and excuses for delay. Such was his frustration that he resigned from the cabinet in August 1917. In later years, even though Lenin's government exiled him in 1922, Peshekhonov felt compelled to defend the Bolsheviks—he felt that despite the cruelty and absurdity of their methods, they at least succeeded in restoring the state authority (*gosudarstvennost'*) that Russia had lacked since February 1917.[45]

A RECONSTITUTED POLITICAL CLASS?

All political parties (except of course the anarchists) agreed on the need to reconstitute a firm political authority (*tverdaia vlast'*). The Bolsheviks were no exception. Their distinctiveness lay in their political formula, which outlined a strategy for reconstitution that made sense to the population while providing a basis for unity of the political class. A central element in this political formula was sabotage.

43. Zaitsev and Dolinsky, "Organization and Policy," 24–25. The organizational continuity is overlooked by Keep, *Russian Revolution*, 498 n. 12.

44. Radkey, *Agrarian Foes*, 65; Raleigh, *Revolution on the Volga*, 111.

45. A. V. Peshekhonov, *Pochemu ia ne emigriroval* (Berlin, 1922), 51–60. Material on Peshekhonov's outlook can be found in Rex Wade, *The Russian Search for Peace* (Stanford, 1969), 24; Rosenberg, *Liberals*, 229; Browder and Kerensky, *Provisional Government*, 2:633–36, 3:1640–41; Kitanina, *Voina*, 328; Roger Pethybridge, *The Spread of the Russian Revolution* (London, 1972), 98–99; Sukhanov, *Zapiski*, 4:236–37, 5:70–75; Prod. delo (Moscow), 28 May–4 June 1917, 10; 11 June 1917, 7–8; 25 June 1917, 7; 20 August 1917; Agurskii, *Ideologiia*, 21.

When coordinating institutions that are usually taken for granted no longer perform properly, theories based on conspiracies, stabs in the back, and other forms of conscious wrongdoing are apt to flourish. Sabotage theories were no monopoly of the Bolsheviks. Since the beginning of the war conservative circles had worried about German control of the economy (nemetskoe zasil'e). Jews were another popular target not only of the Black Hundreds but also of tsarist generals who thought it politic to uproot the Jewish population of the front regions and intensify chaos in the rear zones by sending a wave of refugees eastward.[46] The liberal opposition had also been willing to believe halfheartedly, and utilize wholeheartedly, suspicions of German sympathizers in high court circles; these suspicions were inflamed by speeches such as Miliukov's in late 1916 asking whether government policy was stupidity or treason.

Food-supply difficulties strengthened the attractiveness of sabotage theories. Even before the revolution Peter Struve observed that the food-supply problem made the political stubbornness of the tsar seem like a "consciously designed policy directed towards creating insuperable internal difficulties."[47] After the revolution both liberals and socialists tended to explain the failure of the grain monopoly by speaking of the agitation of "dark forces," although socialists were more apt to use the word sabotage. If the nonelite classes made heavy use of sabotage theories, they did not do it without the instructive example of their educated leaders.

Sabotage was the popular explanation for food-supply difficulties, and the party that gave this explanation its most vigorous and coherent expression was the Bolsheviks: only the Bolsheviks made sabotage a central theme in their political outlook and the crushing of sabotage a key plank in their political platform. The Bolsheviks' general outlook in 1917 was a radical version of the enlistment solution, stressing both popular participation and extensive regulation by the state.[48] Lenin was aggressively unoriginal in his vision of state economic regulation, declaring that the Bolsheviks wanted no more than what even the tsarist or German governments had seen was necessary, or at most the economic program adopted by the moderate majority of the soviets in spring 1917.[49]

Economic analysis was secondary in the Bolshevik response to the food-

46. Cherniavsky, ed., Prologue to Revolution.

47. Hoare, Fourth Seal, 194–95.

48. Alfred B. Evans, "Rereading Lenin's State and Revolution," Slavic Review 46 (1987): 1–19; S. Smith, Red Petrograd, 153–56.

49. Lenin, PSS, 32:247–49, 195–97, 292–94, 443–44; 34:155–61. This continuity between Groman and the Bolsheviks was pointed out by Sukhanov in Protsess, 386–87.

supply crisis and required no more than vague phrases lifted from elsewhere. At the May food-supply congress the Bolshevik contingent did not offer any alternative economic program. Its spokesman Vladimir Miliutin associated himself with the resolution proposed by Groman, and Bolshevik representatives abstained in the final vote on the congress resolution only because they felt that the measures called for could only be realized by a proletarian state authority.[50]

It was political analysis that was primary in the Bolshevik answer to the question, "Why are there no goods in the village or bread in the towns?"[51] Lenin's stress on consensus in regard to the content of state regulation was meant to suggest the following question: if the way out of the economic crisis was straightforward and obvious to all concerned, why was the situation getting worse, not better? His answer was sabotage by people whose interests were threatened since any effective regulation meant limitation of profits and an end to commercial secrecy. Therefore it was not experts in the required economic measures who were needed to solve the crisis but experts in political will and decisiveness.

This analysis was elaborated in a pamphlet by Emelian Iaroslavskii. After admitting that the war was part of the answer, Iaroslavskii went on to assert:

> The reason lies in the intentional derangement of all of economic life by the messieurs capitalists, factory owners, plant owners, landowners, bankers, and their hangers-on; the reason for the high cost of living, lack of goods, and lack of bread lies in the intentional hiding of bread and goods in warehouses and storage points, in the intentional closing of mines and factories [and in the intentional breakdown of transport]. All this is done intentionally so that the bony hand of hunger and poverty will grab the working class by the throat [as Riabushinskii said at the Moscow congress—see below].[52]

In explaining this intentional sabotage, the Bolsheviks projected their own intense political focus onto their opponents: Iaroslavskii argued that the main reason that landowners demanded high prices, for example, was not just to receive twice or three times as much money, eager as they were to enrich themselves—no, their main calculation was to create disunity between workers and peasants.

50. *Prod. delo* (Moscow), 28 May–4 June 1917 (Nogin).

51. E. Iaroslavskii, *Otchego net tovarov v derevne, khleba v gorodakh* (Moscow, 1917). The work was written in the fall of 1917.

52. Iaroslavskii, *Otchego*, 17–19.

Sabotage was the cause of the shortages, and therefore vigorous political action was the solution: "If we carry out a thorough search and registration of all warehouses, goods storehouses, basements, cellars, and grain-dealer depots, then it will be seen that [hidden] reserves are much greater than the amount put into circulation. But this search and registration must be carried out everywhere. Sooner or later the food-supply committees and the soviets will have to do it; better to do it now than later."[53]

The sabotage theory also made the task of reconstituting society along noncapitalist lines entirely unproblematic: "We must tear the matter of exchange out of the hands of the parasites and speculators and turn over the whole matter of distribution to democratic consumer and producer societies and cooperatives. The peasants and workers themselves must [create the framework of] exchange between town and village. Then there will be cheap bread; then there will be cheap goods."[54]

Iaroslavskii's rhetoric gives an indication of why many observers in 1917 dismissed the Bolsheviks as irresponsible demagogues. Yet events seemed to confirm the Bolshevik analysis. One strong piece of evidence was a speech given by the prominent Moscow industrialist Pavel Riabushinskii. Riabushinskii had long been a leader of the liberal wing of the bourgeoisie in its opposition to tsarism; he was a founder of the War Industries Committees, one of the public organizations interested half in cooperation, half in opposition. The speech included a phrase that became one of the most notorious of the revolutionary era, "the bony hand of hunger"; it appeared in the context of a violent attack on the soviets:

> Our commercial and industrial class will do its job to the end
> without expecting anything for itself. But at the same time it

53. Iaroslavskii, *Otchego*, 13–14. For examples of such searches, see *Prod. delo* (Moscow), 24 September 1917, 6–8; Koenker, *Moscow Workers*, 129–30; *Ek. pol.*, pt. 3, doc. 110.

54. Iaroslavskii, *Otchego*, 17–19. Continued food shipments to the Allies also strengthened the sabotage outlook; see *Ek. pol.*, pt. 2, doc. 475; Kitanina, *Voina*, 350–54. For other examples of the sabotage outlook, see Alexander Rabinowitch, *Prelude to Revolution* (Bloomington, Ind., 1968), 118; *Ek. pol.*, pt. 2, doc. 535 (M. Vladimirov); Stalin, *Sochineniia*, 3:210–12, 251–52. The workers' suspicion of sabotage is a major theme in David Mandel's two-volume study of the Petrograd workers; see especially *The Petrograd Workers and the Fall of the Old Regime* (New York, 1983), 137–48, and *The Petrograd Workers and the Soviet Seizure of Power* (New York, 1984), 211–12. The sabotage outlook has dominated much of Soviet historiography. See Lozinskii, *Ekonomicheskaia politika*, chap. 4, esp. 143–44; Volubuev, *Ekonomicheskaia politika*, esp. 410–11, 429–30. Kitanina and Laverychev are less constrained by the sabotage outlook; see also A. I. Suslov, "Sovremennaia anglo-amerikanskaia burzhuaznaia istoriografiia o prodovol'stvennoi politike v pervye gody sovetskoi vlasti," *Istoriia SSSR*, 1978, 3:188–95. Marc Ferro is one of the few Western historians to give credence to accusations of sabotage. Ferro, *La révolution de 1917* (Paris, 1967–1976), 2:242–43.

feels that at present it is unable to convince anybody or influence people in leading positions.

Therefore our task is very difficult. We must wait—we know that the natural course of life will go on its way and unfortunately it will severely punish those who destroy economic laws. But it is bad when we have to sacrifice state interests to convince a small group of people. This is unforgivable. It is just like the sacrifices we have had to bear at the front. It was necessary that several armies be destroyed and that our valiant officers suffer before the soviets of workers' deputies changed their convictions in time. Therefore, gentlemen, we are forced against our will to wait; a catastrophe, an economic and financial defeat, will be inevitable for Russia, if we are not already in the midst of a catastrophe, and only when it becomes evident to everybody, only then will people feel they have gone down the wrong path. Toward that time we have to ready ourselves in a practical manner so that our organizations will be up to the situation.

We feel that what I have said is inevitable. But unfortunately it is necessary for the bony hand of hunger and the people's poverty to grab by the throat the false friends of the people, the members of various committees and soviets, before they come to their senses. The Russian land groans in their comradely embrace. The people at present do not understand this, but they soon will, and they will say: "Away, deceivers of the people." (Stormy applause) . . .

All that is pure and clean is cursed, all cultured people are thrown out, mutual hate and fury reign, there is no feeling of national responsibility even for the state's existence, honor, and unity. When will arise, not yesterday's slave, but the free Russian citizen? Let him come soon. Russia awaits him. All around we hear the satanic laughter of those who scorn to pronounce the word *homeland*. In this difficult time, when a new time of troubles is approaching, all vital cultural forces of the country must become one harmonious family. Let the firm merchant's nature show itself. People of trade, the Russian land must be saved![55]

55. *Ek. pol.*, pt. 1, doc. 80. For Riabushinskii's political activity before the February revolution, see Lewis H. Siegelbaum, *The Politics of Industrial Mobilization in Russia* (New York, 1983). In 1921 Riabushinskii did approach the American Relief Agency to suggest that control of food distribution might allow the agency to become the actual governing body of Russia. Benjamin M. Weissman, *Herbert Hoover and Famine Relief to Soviet Russia* (Stanford, 1974), 49–50. Riabushinskii's ghost continued to vex the Soviet government. The defendants in the "industrial party" show trial of 1930 were accused of plotting with Riabushinskii in 1928, although he had been dead for some years.

Despite the violence of the rhetoric, Riabushinskii's speech is not good evidence of sabotage. According to Riabushinskii, the business classes saw that the country is going toward disaster, but their warning voice was unheeded—the people would have to learn through bitter experience that they had listened to false leaders. Obviously, there is no call here for any action to make food supply worse; indeed, the import of the speech is that the business classes must keep trying to help, despite the hostile attitude shown toward them. Nevertheless, Riabushinskii's intent to starve the revolution seemed clear enough to the Russian people. As a Soviet study of Bolshevik propaganda remarks, Riabushinskii's "bony hand of hunger" was "often cited in propagandistic literature and therefore well known to the masses; it demonstrated better than any other argument that the struggle with hunger was a class struggle."[56]

The rhetoric of sabotage offered great advantages to the Bolsheviks, for it tied them to the common discourse of the other Russian political parties while emphasizing their distinctiveness. The Bolsheviks could argue that extensive economic regulation was clearly realistic and not overambitious—otherwise it would not have been endorsed by the vast majority of moderate socialists and many of the liberals. Groman and his friends themselves documented the refusal of the governing elite to take the steps that would resolve the crisis. The political implication was clear: the crisis could be overcome without undue difficulty by a party with the courage and commitment to make refusal impossible.[57]

The sabotage outlook could easily be couched in the Marxist rhetoric of class, and this allowed the Bolsheviks to give expression to deep popular feelings of suspicion and outrage.[58] In turn a sabotage theory was needed to support the position that class struggle was an adequate response to pressing practical problems. In the fall of 1917 Lenin asserted: "Which class holds sovereign authority [*vlast'*]—that decides everything."[59] These words make sense only if economic and administrative solutions are already available but are not being adopted solely for reasons of class interest.

56. A. P. Kupaigorodskaia, *Oruzhiem slova: listovki petrogradskikh bol'shevikov 1918–1920 gg.* (Leningrad, 1981), 49. The Bolsheviks themselves were responsible for one documented case of sabotage. A. D. Tsiurupa, at this time a food-supply official in Siberia, kept back food shipments to Petrograd in October until after the Bolshevik takeover. M. I. Davydov, *Aleksandr Dmitrievich Tsiurupa* (Moscow, 1961), 38–39; V. Tsiurupa, *Kolokola pamiati*, 78.

57. Lenin, *PSS*, 34:158; Sukhanov, *Zapiski*, 6:93–94. For the same argument in Bolshevik debates over the armed uprising, see Rabinowitch, *Bolsheviks*, 197–99.

58. Ferro, *La révolution*, 2:422–27; S. Smith, *Red Petrograd*, 167; Koenker, *Moscow Workers*, 132, 251–52; Raleigh, *Revolution on the Volga*, 272; *Ek. pol.*, pt. 3, docs. 219, 271.

59. Lenin, *PSS*, 34:200.

Any version of the enlistment solution—perhaps like most democratic theories—contained a large component of distrust and suspicion.[60] In the radical Bolshevik version the proposed scope of enlistment was much broader than the educated "vital forces" championed by the prerevolutionary opposition: "The miraculous means [of increasing the strength of the state apparatus] is the enlistment of the toilers, the enlistment of the poor to the everyday work of state administration."[61] This step was necessary not only for the usual reasons (ending irresponsible government, obtaining social trust and cooperation) but also because the new state authority could act like proletarians (*po-proletarski*) and show the saboteurs that it meant business.

Lenin's insistence on the necessity of an act of decisive violence has been shown to be an important theme in his campaign in the fall of 1917 for an armed uprising.[62] The same insistence is found in the economic sphere. In a discussion of bread rationing, Lenin brought out the underlying motive: to point up the contrast between "reactionary bureaucratic methods of struggle with [economic] catastrophe—methods that try to limit transformations to a minimum—and revolutionary-democratic methods. To deserve the name, revolutionary-democratic methods must make their primary task a violent break with the old and outmoded and [by so doing] the quickest possible movement forward."[63] Violence was the most visible form of decisiveness, and visible decisiveness could solve the crisis almost by itself by inspiring loyalty and confidence while ensuring the enforced cooperation of erstwhile saboteurs. This reasoning supported Lenin's contention that the soviets could form a solid foundation for a reconstituted political authority. The soviets gained prestige from this proposed role: the power of the term *sovetskaia vlast'* (political authority based on the soviets) stemmed just as much, or more, from *vlast'* as from *sovetskaia.*[64]

For Peshekhonov, the paradox was that the Bolsheviks, a politically destructive force in the short run, was the only available force capable of reconstituting political authority. The sabotage outlook contributed to this paradox. Accusations of sabotage helped tear apart Russian society, and the

60. Jane J. Mansbridge, *Beyond Adversary Democracy* (New York, 1980).

61. Lenin, *PSS*, 34:313.

62. Sergei Mstislavskii, *Five Days Which Transformed Russia* (1922; Bloomington, Ill., 1988), 113; Ferro, *La révolution*, 2:366–68; Robert Vincent Daniels, *Red October: The Bolshevik Revolution of 1917* (New York, 1967), 53, 75–77, 157–58.

63. Lenin, *PSS*, 34:179. Lenin refers to an armed uprising as the "most decisive, most active policy" (34:395). A similar argument is made by Mao Zedong in "Report on an Investigation of the Peasant Movement in Hunan" (1927).

64. Lenin, *PSS*, 34:200–207, 340; Koenker, *Moscow Workers*, 253, 267; Ferro, *La révolution*, vol. 2, chap. 7; Raleigh, *Revolution on the Volga*, 202, 254; *Ek. pol.*, pt. 3, doc. 107; Chaadaeva, *Pomeshchiki*, 122–23.

belief that sabotage was the cause of economic difficulties led to some disastrous policy choices. But the sabotage outlook, since it viewed opposition or even simple lack of cooperation as a crime, gave the Bolsheviks the moral fervor and the popular support necessary to fulfill and overfulfill the task of imposing order and reconstituting political authority. Sabotage linked together the fight against enemies of Bolshevik political reconstitution (called counterrevolutionaries) and the fight against enemies of Bolshevik economic reconstitution (called speculators). To a greater extent than is realized, the popular meaning of the revolution is accurately summed up in the full title of the first Soviet secret police, the Cheka: the Extraordinary Commission for the Struggle Against Counterrevolution, Sabotage, and Speculation.

5 The Elemental Whirlpool

The state authority . . . must direct all its strength to avert
the final phase of the rapidly approaching famine. Otherwise
no authority will be able to exist in the country, and the
country itself will toss like a chip of wood in the elemental
whirlpool.

N. Dolinsky, fall 1917

In fall 1917 the chain reaction of social disintegration led to a series of
explosions—in the countryside, on the front lines, and in the capital cities.
In the area of food supply the event that lit the fuse was the doubling of
fixed prices at the end of August. Generally overlooked amid the high
political drama of those days, the decision to double the prices paid to grain
producers was not only a signal of the imminent collapse of food supply; it
destroyed the morale of the existing political class while confirming the
political formula of the Bolshevik contenders.

THE FIXED PRICES COME UNSTUCK

The level of fixed prices had already created difficulties for the Provisional Government. In March it raised the fixed prices decreed by the
tsarist government in September 1916 by 60 percent. This decision led to a
falling-out with Groman. Though admitting that the earlier prices were
now out of line with prices for industrial items, Groman wanted to lower
the industrial prices, not raise grain prices. Since this could not be done
immediately, Groman proposed to give grain producers temporary certificates. When the Provisional Government rejected this proposal as impractical, he decided that Shingarev was just another tsarist official like Bobrinskii and Rittikh.[1]

The decision of the Provisional Government was not a complete victory
for peasant producers. In 1916 Rittikh had surreptitiously raised prices by
paying them at the producer's storehouse rather than at the railroad station
or wharf, so that transport costs were borne by the government instead of

1. Sukhanov, *Zapiski*, 2:271–75; Jasny, *Soviet Economists*, 29–32.

the producer. This move had infuriated opposition activists, and when the Provisional Government raised prices, it went back to the old system. Accordingly the further away a producer was from transportation points, the less benefit he received from the new prices. Sigov quotes the commissioner of Viatka as saying that, on average, prices were lowered ten kopecks a pood in his province.[2] Thus one of the first acts of the new revolutionary government was to lower the prices paid to many producers.

The Provisional Government assured the peasants that it was useless to hold out for better prices since the March prices would not be raised under any circumstances. Despite the growing urgency of the food-supply situation, Peshekhonov ruled out the possibility of a change in prices. He therefore sent a telegram on 20 August telling the local committees not to shrink from the use of force. Speed was essential: if grain were not shipped north by the middle of September, many northern provinces would have no way of getting food, and all consumer regions would be threatened, given the wretched state of the railroads and the coming end of navigation on the river system. Grain was to be taken first of all from large firms and from producers who were closest to transportation points since the next two or three weeks would decide everything. The telegram went on to say that "extreme measures are dictated by a state necessity that is the equivalent of military service."[3]

Meanwhile other forces within the Provisional Government sought another way out of the crisis. On 23 August a meeting of the Special Council of Defense observed that the food-supply crisis was now threatening the entire economy and the war effort. Lack of flour and grain in the Donets and Baku regions was causing a mass exodus of workers from the mines and oil fields, which in turn meant no fuel, no railroads, and no defense production. The council also felt that the "existing organization of the general food-supply system does not correspond to present circumstances": despite the availability of adequate grain supplies as well as transport capacity, producers had no motivation to part with their grain. And since this motivation had been destroyed by the lack of correspondence between the fixed grain prices and the price of everything else, the solution seemed obvious.[4]

This pressure from the right wing of the government coalition came at the very time that Kerensky (the closest person the Provisional Government had to a head of state) was accusing his own commander in chief, Kornilov, of a counterrevolutionary plot. The urgency of the situation, the small likelihood that Peshekhonov's use of force would be successful, and

2. Sigov, *Arakcheevskii sotsializm*, 9–12.
3. *Izv. po prod. delu* 3 (34), ofitsial'nyi otdel (O.O.), p. 38.
4. TsGVIA, 369-13-62/7; *Ek. pol.*, pt. 2, doc. 491.

Table 1. Fulfillment of Government Targets

	Grain for Population (%)	Grain for Army (%)
May	80	100
June	60	70
July	46	50
August		
1st half	15	28
2d half	40–43	23 (NW and SW front)
		44 (Rumanian front)

Source: 1276-14-483/106–14.

the precariousness of his own political position all pushed Kerensky to what Bukshpan called the "complete capitulation of the Provisional Government before the peasantry of the producing provinces."[5]

The price-doubling decree was issued 27 August when Kornilov's troops were still approaching Petrograd. The official excuse was that doubling the fixed price restored a town-country equilibrium that had been destroyed "by the uncontrollable (*stikhiinyi*) course of events." In an attempt to save face a warning was also issued: "The government will show firmness both in resisting any unfounded pressure to increase the income of the non-agricultural population and in using force against grain producers [to ensure] timely and exact fulfillment of their responsibilities in the delivery of grain needed to prevent starvation by the Army and the population."[6]

It is difficult to assess the impact of the new prices. The center pointed to increased deliveries, but skeptics claimed that the increase was due to the harvest. The skeptics are borne out by figures showing the increase starting before the announcement of the new prices (see Table 1).[7]

By heightening the atmosphere of uncertainty, the sudden doubling of prices provided an incentive not for delivering grain but for holding on to it. The new prices even upset many of the grain producers and dealers, who had called for higher prices but had not expected a clumsy across-the-board doubling.[8] When the peasants themselves were ready to sell the grain, the food-supply apparatus often ran out of paper money (or "money tokens"

5. Bukshpan, *Politika,* 516; see also *Ek. pol.,* pt. 2, p. 356.
6. *Prod.* (Poltava), no. 2, 9 September 1917. The price doubling was made retroactive to 1 August. The decree also made more generous allowances for transport costs. *Ek. pol.,* pt. 2, doc. 522; Browder and Kerensky, *Provisional Government,* 2:641–43.
7. See also Lozinskii, *Ekonomicheskaia politika,* 139.
8. *Izv. po prod. delu* 3 (34): 56–59.

[*denznaki*], in the professional jargon). Other bottlenecks developed—in carts, bags, storage space, and rail space.[9]

Whether because of the new prices, the harvest, or the growing effectiveness of local committees, grain deliveries did in fact increase. But this change brought little consolation to the starving cities because river navigation had come to an end and rail transport was in terrible shape. Little more than one half of the September grain procurement had left the area of procurement by the middle of October.[10]

In Petrograd, officials felt that difficulties within the city—unloading the congested railroad warehouses, setting up a tolerable distribution system—were at least as severe as the problem of getting grain delivered to the city in the first place. At a meeting of the Petrograd City Duma in October speakers declared the situation "very close to catastrophe": there was a real possibility that the city would soon be without flour. It was an open secret that the northern front had no reserves, and that soldiers in the Petrograd garrison were upset by a lowering of their ration. The situation in the army constituted a direct threat to civilian order since soldiers had physically threatened city officials to ensure that military needs were met first of all.[11] The garrison proved a key supporter of the Bolshevik takeover.

If the sudden doubling of prices did not avert the collapse of food supply, it actively hastened the collapse of political authority. It was a heavy blow to the morale of the food-supply officials. Having vociferously assured everybody that there was absolutely no chance of any price rise, they were "stunned" by the announcement and deeply humiliated. The first issue of the Poltava food-supply publication contained a strong assurance to the peasant producers that the fixed price was stable. In the very next issue the chairman had to eat his words: "In the life of the state there are moments when the most firm of governmental intentions must be modified by the force of events. To our great and general sorrow, such a moment has come."[12]

The life of a food-supply worker was not enviable: it was hard work for which the reward was hatred, baseless accusations, and physical danger. Food-supply workers felt more and more threatened by pogrom violence

9. *Prod.* (Tobolsk), no. 2, 12 October 1917; *Prod. delo* (Moscow city), no. 21, 17 September 1917.

10. *Ek. pol.*, pt. 2, pp. 356–58; Frenkin, *Russkaia armiia*, 479–80; *Prod. delo* (Moscow), 22 October 1917.

11. *Prod. delo* (Moscow), 15 October 1917, 13; *Ek. pol.*, pt. 2, doc. 535. This situation may have contributed to the decision to move the garrison that touched off the chain of events leading to the Bolshevik takeover.

12. *Prod.* (Poltava), no. 1, 26 August 1917; no. 2, 9 September 1917.

from below and more and more abandoned by the center. Peshekhonov had resigned in protest and the new minister, Sergei Prokopovich, was perforce preoccupied with forming a cabinet. Paralysis at the top was matched from below by a wave of resignations of local officials or by actions such as that of the Tobolsk committee, which refused "moral responsibility for implementation of the grain monopoly" under the new prices.[13] In October one food-supply official asserted that none of the proposals for reform of the monopoly would work: "With complete clarity I affirm this, and I feel that the one way out of the food-supply problem from the side of the population will be for them to come to me, beat up the whole board—and then hang me."[14]

The demoralization of one political class was matched by the growth of support for another. The dramatic political events of the capital city could not match the societywide impact of the doubling of prices, which communicated its antigovernment message, day in and day out, better than any press campaign. In an article written in late October one writer stated that "the price doubling for grain continues to disturb all Russia" and that the question had only grown sharper. He asserted on the basis of a questionnaire sent out by the newspaper *Narodnaia vlast'* that in all social classes the reaction was unanimous condemnation. A common formulation was that the doubling of grain prices had undermined the foundations of everyday life.[15]

The doubling of prices seemed to confirm the Bolshevik diagnosis of sabotage. It was more than the closeness of dates that indicated a connection between Riabushinskii's outburst about the "bony hand of hunger," Kornilov's attempted coup, and the price-doubling decree. Both Riabushinskii and Kornilov were horrified at the disintegration of the country and put the blame squarely on the soviets. Riabushinskii supported higher grain prices, and he had been among those who gave Kornilov a ringing public endorsement in early August. When the Menshevik minister Matvei Skobelev moved against the factory committees, the picture seemed complete. A worker resolution stated, "We are forced to conclude that in the present context [of the Kornilov mutiny] the ministry for the 'protection of labor' has been converted into the ministry for the protection of capitalist interests and acts hand in hand with Riabushinskii to reduce the country to famine, so that the 'bony hand' may strangle the revolution."[16]

When a predominantly socialist government suddenly doubled the price

13. *Prod.* (Tobolsk), no. 2, 12 October 1917 (resolution of 27 September 1917).
14. TsGVIA, 12593-36-69/45–47, 54–56, 52–54, 59–62.
15. *Prod. delo* (Tver), 22 October 1917.
16. S. Smith, *Red Petrograd*, 180–81; *Ek. pol.*, pt. 2, doc. 486; Rabinowitch, *Bolsheviks*, 105–6.

of a basic staple, it seemed to indicate either criminal weakness or actual connivance with counterrevolutionary sabotage. For years to come, the necessity of a firm state authority based on the soviets was most easily proved by pointing to Riabushinskii and Kornilov.

RETHINKING THE MONOPOLY

The collapse of the monopoly forced food-supply officials to rethink their basic assumptions. Their painful disillusionment can be seen in the pages of the Ministry of Food Supply's short-lived official publication, *Izvestiia po prodovol'stvennomu delu*.

Spring 1917. In the first issue editor Ia. M. Bukshpan contemplated the new grain monopoly with confidence. The monopoly would be only the "first step on the path of the statization (*ogosudarstvlenie*) of the immense field of provisionment" since "the food-supply question must be tightly tied to a single plan of the whole national economy." The new apparatus would be coordinated in the following manner: "To fill up this scheme with living day-to-day work, to elect practical people enjoying wide confidence, to subordinate local interests to general state ones, and to enlist in the service of these interests all creative forces—all this depends not so much on the center as on organized democratic work in the localities." The economic key to obtaining grain was to provide the peasants with the goods they needed; this task undoubtedly presented "uncommon difficulties under present conditions," but precisely these difficulties confirmed the need for a state takeover. [17]

Summer 1917. Bukshpan's editorial in the second issue was entitled "On Vacillations in Food-Supply Policy." The tone had become defensive: Bukshpan complained that in food supply, as in no other economic area, people blamed the whole situation on the state authority and its policies without taking objective difficulties into consideration. He tried to show that without the monopoly the situation would be even worse: prices would skyrocket, and there would be even less grain. Even as it was, "the village is cutting itself off from the city as if to bottle itself up in a subsistence economy." The village would not hand over grain without manufactured goods, but these could not be manufactured unless the workers got grain immediately. "The indubitable weakness of the local committees must [also] be admitted, [for they are] motley in their makeup, not rarely arbitrary in local food-supply policy, and often simply do not exist as agents of the central state authority"; in particular "the district

17. *Izv. po prod. delu* 1 (32): 1–2.

committees have failed, so that producers and holders of grain remain as before, almost without monitoring or compulsion." Bukshpan ended by warning his readers that under present circumstances even the best food-supply policy would not lead to satiation.[18]

Fall 1917. Ministry official N. Dolinsky summed up the situation in the third and final issue of the journal:

> We are used to the tragic background of our life; tragedy has become our everyday reality. Nevertheless, even on this general background a small group of phenomena stand out from the framework of daily life, and our consciousness, although dulled to the perception of catastrophe, experiences sometimes the approach of something frightful, fateful, unconquerable.
>
> To this group of phenomena belongs first of all the food supply of the population. One only has to read the provincial and metropolitan press for a short period to feel that ordinary labels, such as *crisis, catastrophe,* and so on, by themselves sufficiently specific and decisive, pale before the frightful hue of reality. Famine, genuine famine, has seized a series of towns and provinces—famine vividly expressed by an absolute insufficiency of objects of nutrition already leading to death from exhaustion and malnutrition. . . .
>
> From the frightful experience of every day, it is clear that the satisfaction of the population's food requirement is determined by an aggregate of chance circumstances and causes outside the control of authority, [so] that there is no support for even the most elementary assurance of receiving the minimum amount of products necessary to sustain oneself. Losing the assurance of being able to eat tomorrow, the hungry crowd searches for guilty parties. A primitive and excited psychology is convinced that food products are available [but that] greedy merchants, speculators, and dealers have hidden them. Searches are made, almost always without result.[19]

These words, taken not from opposition elements but from the pages of an official journal, express the inner abdication of the Provisional Government. It speaks well for the resilience of many food-supply officials that they did not simply give up but continued to search for a way to overcome what Dolinsky called the elemental whirlpool of social and political breakdown. Within the ministry and generally among those professionally concerned with food supply there were intense discussions in the fall of

18. *Izv. po prod. delu* 2 (33): 1–2.
19. *Izv. po prod. delu* 3 (34): 9–12.

1917 aimed at reversing the slide to disaster. The final collapse of the Provisional Government meant that these discussions did not result in practical measures, and for this reason they have largely escaped the eye of the historian. But they hold great interest for this study because they mark a definite move away from the enlistment solution and toward the gubernatorial solution.

The greatest source of frustration was the failure of the local committees to enforce the monopoly. Throughout 1917 various central agents—emissaries, instructors, inspectors, delegates, commissioners—had been sent out to strengthen central influence over local activity. Central control was further tightened with a decree of 24 August that gave the center the right to rescind any directive issued by lower authorities or even to remove a specific task from the sphere of a committee's responsibilities. Shortly before the Bolshevik coup the ministry sent out a circular to local committees outlining two possible deviations (to use a word applied later to these situations): lacking energy in fulfilling directives from higher officials, on the one hand, and exceeding their authority with local embargoes, fixed prices, and the like, on the other. The circular reminded the committees that although they were not technically on state service, they were still officials (*dolzhnostnye litsa*) and as such they were responsible for the correct execution of food-supply policy. It followed that the two deviations just mentioned would be punished as dereliction of duty. Thus the Ministry of Food Supply was driven to adopt the argument made by the Minister of Internal Affairs a year earlier: it was dangerous to have policy carried out by local activists who were not directly responsible to the center.[20]

Reformers at the center were also contemplating a more radical rehaul of the committee structure: "We must realize that the wager on the autonomous activity of wide strata of democratic circles and on their state feeling has been lost. . . . The closer the food-supply organs are to the population, the less they are concerned with general state considerations." To do their job, the procurement organs would need to apply "great pressure [*nazhim*] on the population, [but] there have been no psychological stimuli [to produce] this pressure." Therefore the center would have to create its own procurement apparatus.[21] Distribution could be left in the hands of local authorities since it required less independence to give than to take.

---

20. *Izv. po prod. delu* 3 (34), O.O. 26–27; 1276-14-483/200–201 (23 October 1917); Kondratiev, *Rynok khlebov,* 91–92; Bukshpan, *Politika,* 510–11.

21. 1276-14-483/67, 148–51 (speech of Anisimov to the Congress of Inspectors and Instructors, 24 September 1917). The effort of the Provisional Government to overcome the previous weakness of its food-supply apparatus was noted by N. Orlov, *Prodovol'stvennoe delo v Rossii* (Moscow, 1919), 20–21.

This move away from the enlistment solution was challenged by many liberal reformers at a conference of the Union of Towns held in October. Centralized procurement threatened a long-standing reform that was just being completed—the transference of authority over food supply to the new democratically elected zemstvo organ of local self-government. In the original monopoly legislation the food-supply committees had been seen as no more than provisional organs that would remain independent only until the new zemstvo structure was set up. The zemstvo ended up playing the same role on the local level as the Constituent Assembly did on the national level—an excuse for delaying both social reform and the imposition of order. Food-supply officials let themselves assume that the stability and authority so lacking in local food-supply committees would be created by the new, all-class democratic structures. In reality the new zemstvo inspired almost no loyalty from the population. By the fall the central authorities had a new view of the helpfulness of local influence and began to drag their feet on the actual transfer of food-supply matters to the new zemstvo.[22]

The Union of Towns conference resented this lack of confidence by the center in the new self-government organs and felt that the gains of the revolution were being lost. If the local zemstvo could not get all the available grain, the bureaucrat from the center could get even less. One speaker acidly remarked that it was not usually the first-raters who were sent out by the center to the provinces.[23] The final resolution of the conference stated that the new local organs should continue to have responsibility for both procurement and distribution and expressed confidence in their ability to do the job. The conference was forced to admit, however, that too often in the past "the most democratic organs could not raise themselves higher than their parish"; hence the central authority still had to be ready to guarantee that procurement tasks were really carried out.[24]

The move to tighten discipline over the committees had its counterpart in efforts to provide material incentives in a more controlled and expedient way. The original plan of ensuring the availability of industrial items at low fixed prices was abandoned as food-supply officials realized that they could not expect to increase the limited supply to any great extent. But the Provisional Government moved only slowly toward a coherent policy of

22. *Prod. delo* (Moscow), 30 August 1917; Gerasimenko, *Nizovye organizatsii*, 176–99; William Rosenberg, "The Zemstvo in 1917 and Its Fate Under Bolshevik Rule," in T. Emmons and W. S. Vucinich, eds., *The Zemstvo in Russia* (Cambridge, 1982), 383–421.

23. TsGVIA, 12593-36-69/38–41, 51–52.

24. *Izv. po prod. delu* 3 (34): 59–60.

commodity exchange (*tovaroobmen*). In a speech in October ministry official A. A. Titov noted that direct exchange would not work because of the extremely short supply. The real motivation for cooperation would continue to be "state awareness" and the organized application of force.[25] But industrial items would remain useful as a psychological stimulus for selling grain at a reasonable price and as a measure of justice to attain equality of sacrifice between village and town.

Thus these efforts are still in the realm of the enlistment solution: the distribution of scarce industrial items was a gesture that would help the government receive the confidence of the population. But the actual principles of distribution policy show that the Provisional Government was feeling its way beyond the enlistment solution. Cloth goods were to be assigned to provinces on the basis of population, but the first shipments were to go to those provinces that had delivered grain. Within the province the cloth goods would not be given to any district that had not registered grain supplies or delivered any grain. Individual distribution would be on the basis of need. Under these principles provision of cloth goods would be used as a direct incentive to deliver the grain. The policy was still quite relaxed: distribution was still according to population and need, and a laggard province was only penalized by a delay in receiving the cloth.

Another aim of distribution policy was to avoid speculation, that is, the resale of government-issued goods at a great markup. The only way to avoid this problem was to make the original distribution so close to actual consumer desires that there would be no cause for further redistribution. Titov did not shrink before this task: a table was to be prepared showing the requirements for the next half year for every man, woman, and child, and goods would be distributed according to certificates based on this table. "To those who one way or the other are able to manage without the purchase of cloth, no cloth will be given." This pronouncement was a fantastic overestimation of administrative capacities: Titov admitted that the district committees simply passed the goods around.[26]

A more sober view of the need to economize scarce administrative resources was expressed by Nikolai Kondratiev, a high ministry official who later became one of the stellar Soviet economists of the 1920s. The Ministry of Food Supply controlled only 60 percent of the output of cloth goods. Kondratiev agreed with the general feeling that splitting the cloth supply between the government and the private commercial apparatus was unsatisfactory. There were two ways to unify distribution: transfer it com-

25. TsGVIA, 12593-36-69/37–38.
26. TsGVIA, 12593-36-69/31–38.

pletely to private trade, which would be supervised by the state much more closely than heretofore, or give it over into the hands of the state. Kondratiev contended that the ministry had an open mind on the question, but he himself was clearly in favor of transferring distribution to private trade. He stressed the disadvantages of giving the job to an "all-embracing" governmental body and argued that the combination of capitalist trade and strict state monitoring was appropriate for Russia's bourgeois revolution. The basic monitoring method would be mutual responsibility (*krugovaia poruka*), a method of organizing trade in the national interest that Kondratiev felt would still be useful after the war.[27]

Both of the solutions had a vision of the proper role of commodity exchange. Advocates of the enlistment solution saw it as part of the monopoly strategy and perhaps even as a step toward socialist distribution. For gubernatorial advocates the idea of a commodity-exchange policy was not to provide a full exchange equivalent of grain delivery; it was rather to withhold extremely scarce industrial items as a penalty for nonpayment of a tax obligation. The commodity-exchange policy of the Provisional Government was still at an embryonic stage and had strong elements of both solutions. But on the whole it represented a move away from the idea of exchange toward the idea of a tax.

Since food-supply officials were no longer sanguine about either state consciousness or material incentives, the role of coercive incentives began to take on greater importance. The possibility of using force against the grain producers had never been completely denied in 1917, although there had been hope in the beginning that the new solidarity and civic maturity of the Russian population would make it unnecessary. Especially after the price doubling, food-supply officials felt that (as one remarked in November) "all means [of moral influence] have been exhausted": having gone the extra mile to respond to the producers' interests, they now claimed the right to use force.[28] All in all, however, the attempts of the Provisional Government to use force were not impressive. Most were like the incident in Samara that took place in September, when peasants collected themselves together by means of the alarm bell and announced to the authorities, "You'll get our bread only over our dead bodies." So the local food-supply officials and a military detachment left without getting any bread.[29]

The inability of the Provisional Government to use force effectively was due not only to inner inhibition but to lack of a reliable armed unit suitable

27. 1276-14-483/12 (speech of 12 October 1917).
28. *Prod.* (Tobolsk) no. 4, 1 December 1917 (meeting of 17 November 1917).
29. TsGVIA, 13251-2-40/25–33. For attempts of the Provisional Government to use force, see Volubuev, *Ekonomicheskaia politika*, 452–55.

for domestic purposes.[30] Food-supply officials were already beginning to feel the necessity of a central militia on the grounds that it would be "expedient to transfer [procurement] to a special organ of the militia tied not so much to the population as to the central apparatus of the central state authority since it is necessary [in this area] to carry out one general line and to carry it out especially insistently."[31]

The most urgent of proposals in this direction was made by military supply officials. In September the chief supply officer, General Bogatko, argued that the ministry should send out inspectors with the power to force local committees to follow central directives. But he felt these inspectors needed to be backed up in each province by a governor-general, who should be someone who enjoyed the full confidence of the popular organizations so that he could not be accused of any counterrevolutionary intentions. He also should be given full authority, including the right to impose the death penalty for failure to carry out directives essential to the existence of the republic: "If such a governor-general is not present in the localities, we cannot even speak of the possibility that the proposed inspector—authorized to compel a provincial food-supply board to immediately implement this or that measure—will be able to compel anybody to do anything at all."[32] In this argument we see an old-line military official who wants to obtain the confidence of the "democratic organizations," but only because that confidence seemed to be indispensable for establishing a vigorous central authority. His appreciation of the need to revitalize the gubernatorial solution harks back to Khvostov and also provides an intimation of the future.

The lack of an available armed force was not the only obstacle. In an article written in December, Martovskii analyzed in Nizhegorod the difficulties of using force against the peasants. He noted that for the Bolshevik-dominated soviets (and to some extent for the earlier soviets of the SRs and Mensheviks) the problem seemed simple: take from the kulaks, the well-off minority, and give to the worse-off majority: "If that's the way it's going to be, there's no point in being shy about it." But if the application of force was easy enough in a village that consisted mainly of net consumers, it would get harder and harder until it was next to impossible in a village consisting mainly of net producers. Unfortunately it was precisely the latter type of village that had general state significance since grain requisitioned in consumer villages would mostly stay in the area. The application

30. Wade, *Red Guards*, 69; Startsev, *Vnutrenniaia politika*, 167–93.

31. TsGVIA, 12593-36-69/1–25 (Iurovskii, Union of Towns Conference, 15 October 1917).

32. TsGVIA, 499-3-1726/2 (18 September 1917).

of force was in the best of cases a tricky business. A mere show of force was inadequate: soldiers were reluctant to obey orders, and peasants were experts in concealing grain. It was also dangerous to apply these policies through undisciplined local organs. Martovskii's analysis was later borne out by events.[33]

Despite the explosion of discontent that surrounded them, many food-supply officials continued to search for a way out. A painful rethinking of the basic assumptions of the enlistment solution led to the realization that the monopoly strategy could not work with available resources of exchange items, administrative capacity, and "state consciousness." But time had run out for the Provisional Government, and the effort to work out a policy that took account of these scarcities had to wait until the new rulers of the country went through their own painful learning process.

THE PROBLEM OF AUTHORITY

Food-supply officials realized that efforts to reform food-supply policy in isolation always led back to the same problem: "We have to be able to order the grain-holder to hand the grain over, and to back up that order if it is not fulfilled. This is the general problem of a political authority [*vlast'*]."[34] How far the Provisional Government was from solving the problem of authority is evident from the testimony of Prokopovich, who had been appointed the new minister of food supply. Prokopovich's guarded optimism about grain deliveries was undermined by his unrelieved pessimism on the political side. In his description of centrifugal forces Prokopovich made a distinction between civil war (the regional and class separatism of the peasant producer) and anarchy (individual lawlessness), even though both represented a similar logic of rational self-protection. In speaking of separatism in the Kuban area, Prokopovich asked, "What do they want? They want to remain intact in that sea of anarchy that is flooding the country; they want to save themselves, like an island."[35]

What was needed was a central political authority capable of showing peasant separatists, by force if necessary, that "yes, [the peasants] are brothers of the workers [and] of the town dweller." But the Provisional Government was helpless to provide this forcible demonstration of brotherhood. In the center the political class was hopelessly divided, making

33. *Prod.* (Nizhegorod), 10 December 1917. Peshekhonov was already complaining in June 1917 that local committees were acting only in deficit areas.
34. TsGVIA, 12593-36-69/1–25 (Iurovskii, Union of Towns Conference, 15 October 1917).
35. *Ek. pol.*, pt. 2, p. 365.

formation of a cabinet almost impossible. Prokopovich complained that instead of dealing with pressing matters, the government was forced to respond "now to pressures from the right, now to pressures from the left. It is impossible to work this way."[36] In the localities the Provisional Government could not even protect its own agents. During a trip around Russia Prokopovich met a stationmaster who had barely escaped being lynched just two hours before. He had been saved only by members of the local committee surrounding him and forming a human shield, for the local militia had been run off by the lynch mob. The stationmaster had incurred the wrath of the mob by telling peasant and soldier sackmen that they could not take any grain out of the area by train; the sackmen had told their story to soldiers being transported on the train, and these soldiers, bored with sitting in train cars, ran out and started a riot.

Prokopovich told his audience in the capital of the shame he felt when a faithful executor of his orders had to take such risks and he, the minister, was unable to provide any protection. His only response to the stationmaster was to suggest a compromise: allow people to carry five poods as personal baggage. At this the stationmaster brightened up and said, yes, maybe that would help. Prokopovich concluded, "We have to stop being wheedlers in chief or subwheedlers because as long as we are wheedlers, we will burn with shame just as I burned with shame before the stationmaster."[37]

Prokopovich knew that the Provisional Government had little chance of becoming the boss (*khoziain*) that he felt was necessary. He even declared that he would support the Bolsheviks if he thought that they could really create a strong political authority without risking civil war by alienating the peasant producer. But Prokopovich's alternative of a firm political authority based on coalition seemed just as unrealistic; when he spoke of the necessity of coercion, a voice from the floor asked sensibly enough, "What will the comrades say?"[38] The choice seemed to be between a nonexistent state authority and one obtained at a terrible price.

In late October 1917 the Bolsheviks made their bid to tame the elemen-

---

36. Prokopovich, *Narodnoe khoziaistvo*, 68, 29.

37. Prokopovich, *Narodnoe khoziaistvo*, 62–69. This speech to the Council of the Republic, given on 16 October 1917, is reprinted in *Ek. pol.*, pt. 2, doc. 536. *Glavnougovoriaiushchii*, the sarcastic name given by army officers to Kerensky, is more neutrally translated as "persuader in chief," but "wheedler" captures the spirit better. Prokopovich's later discussion of Bolshevik food-supply policy fails to bring out this desperate situation to which he himself gives such eloquent testimony. See Prokopovich, *Narodnoe khoziaistvo SSSR*, (New York, 1952), 1:145–60; Prokopovich, *The Economic Condition of Soviet Russia* (London, 1924), 101.

38. *Ek. pol.*, pt. 2, p. 365.

tal whirlpool. Food-supply officials were immediately faced with a dilemma. Disgusted as they were with the Provisional Government, they felt the Bolshevik coup could only make things worse. Yet the food-supply situation limited their freedom of action, and they could not imitate the many civil servants who greeted the new authority with strikes.[39] Support for the Bolsheviks and struggle against them seemed to strengthen centrifugal forces.

As much as the food-supply officials insisted on the need for a generally recognized state authority, they felt it was dangerously unrealistic to try to build one on the basis of the soviets. As Anisimov said in November, "We cannot speak of a dictatorship of a class [in the sense of an] organized part of society. The dictatorship of a class is turning into the dictatorship of each proletarian separately or of several handfuls or of chance assemblies." Anisimov went on to say that a strong authority with organized coercion was a necessity, but although Russia now had plenty of coercion, little of it was organized.[40]

The new authority also lacked any sensible or practical program in food supply. Officials lamented the "obvious ignorance of the Bolsheviks, their obvious illiteracy" in food-supply matters. There were solid grounds for this impression, for the Bolsheviks presented no coherent food-supply program until the spring. Before then, Bolshevik policy was mainly determined by the political imperative of providing for "the proletarian centers" to the detriment of everyone else. But this attitude of the food-supply officials also reflected a general feeling among the trained experts and bureaucrats (the so-called bourgeois specialists) that they were indispensable and that any viable revolutionary authority must recognize this. Indeed, many Bolsheviks secretly agreed, and Lenin had found that one of the greatest difficulties he faced in persuading the party to overthrow the Provisional Government was Bolshevik timidity on this score.

The food-supply officials therefore had to decide the tactical question of how best to ward off the menace of Bolshevik disorganization. One possibility was for the food-supply workers to see themselves purely as a technical apparatus and to bow to the Bolsheviks' brute force as an unavoidable part of getting the job done. Groman put this point of view at a conference of food-supply officials in November:

> If the factual situation of a country in a state of civil war
> pushes me up against the representative of some commissar,

39. For Bolshevik accusations of sabotage, see John Keep, ed., *The Debate on Soviet Power* (Oxford, 1979), 110–12, 235, 249; A. S. Iziumov, ed., *Khleb i revoliutsiia* (Moscow, 1972), 53–57.
40. 32-1-394/12–14.

calling himself the commissar of a military revolutionary committee and demanding to talk with me so that he will not interfere with the job of food supply, then I will not disdain to
talk with him. If some commissar comes to me, and I am not
in a position to eject him by physical force, and if I am unable
to carry on the business of food supply without his presence, I
will say to him, "Sit. I will do what the business at hand demands, and if you want to endorse it, endorse away."[41]

Those at the conference who opposed this position argued that there was no
alternative to a walkout. A speaker told the conference that this was
no longer the autocracy, when responsible workers could be treated like
pawns; that working conditions were intolerable—ministry officials were
forced to work in the stairways—and that the conference had no right to
ask them to be indifferent while their civil liberties were trampled under
soldiers' boots.[42]

The final decision of the conference was to select a middle course. On
the one hand, to go on strike not only would be almost criminal in itself but
would play into the hands of the Bolsheviks by allowing them to blame the
growing chaos on sabotage.[43] On the other hand, the food-supply workers
could not bring themselves simply to recognize the Bolsheviks, especially if
the Bolsheviks were to interfere with the elections to the Constituent
Assembly. Since the Constituent Assembly and a "generally recognized
authority" were technical necessities for food supply, anyone who continued to work after the Constituent Assembly had been aborted would be
drawing his pay but doing nothing to avert famine.[44] Therefore to continue work but maintain independence from the Bolsheviks, a proposal of
Groman's was adopted: create an All-Russian Food-Supply Council of Ten
that would direct the food-supply policy of the country and maintain
political neutrality. The idea was to preserve "the authority of the state
food-supply apparatus" so that food-supply workers could continue to
work without flagging until such time as the Constituent Assembly made
its will known.[45]

41. 32-1-394/3–4.
42. 32-1-394/9–11.
43. 32-1-394/6–7, 18–19. The second speaker (Shub) added that the real danger was not the Bolshevik Council of People's Commissars, who had no interest in
destroying the food-supply apparatus, but ignorant local commissars.
44. 32-1-394/13.
45. The text of the resolution is in *Prod.* (Tobolsk), no. 5, 31 December 1917.
The resolution passed by officials in the localities shows greater enthusiasm about
continuing to work until the Constituent Assembly than does the resolution passed
by the central branch of the Employees Union. 32-1-394/20.

This strategy of neutrality was doomed to failure, for the Bolsheviks had no intention of letting something as vital as food supply out of their hands, and the food-supply officials did not have the political resources to resist encroachment, especially since they rejected the strike weapon. The result of complicated maneuvering between November and late January was the dominance at the center of the Bolshevik People's Commissariat of Food Supply.[46]

The food-supply officials were completely helpless by themselves in the face of the elemental whirlpool of social breakdown. Their attempts to reform food-supply policy amid the collapse of the Provisional Government and remain above it all in the power struggle that followed came to nothing. The "general problem of a political authority" had to be solved first.

BREAD AND AUTHORITY IN THE LOCALITIES

Neither the Bolsheviks nor the food-supply apparatus were in a position to exercise national leadership in the fall of 1917, and the localities were left to fend for themselves. The challenge they faced can by gauged from a survey by the Ministry of Food Supply for the period of 2 September through 20 September:

> The process of running down all foodstuff reserves goes forward, and as a result hunger is advancing on the cities (Penza, Simbirsk, Mogilev, Smolensk, Astrakhan, Novgorod, Nizhegorod, Orel, Vladimirov, Turkestan).
>
> The system of compulsory alienation of grain as a temporary intervention continues to be the most practical way of realizing the grain monopoly (Viatka, Chernigov, Saratov, Samara).
>
> Speculation, finding for itself ever-new possibilities, disorganizes the market (Moscow, Kharkov, Turgaiskaia, Kuban).
>
> Liquor distilling is growing and is a serious reason for the destruction of all plans for supplying the population with grain (Mogilev, Voronezh, Tula, Taurides, Viatka, Riazan, Tambov, Kherson).
>
> Mass destruction and violence determine the course of local

46. Z. Serebrianskii, "Sabotazh i sozdanie novogo gosudarstvennogo apparata," *Proletarskaia revoliutsiia,* no. 10 (57), 1926: 5–17; Iu. K. Strizhkov, "V. I. Lenin— organizator i rukovoditel' bor'by za sozdanie sovetskogo prodovol'stvennogo apparata," in *Bor'ba za pobedu i ukreplenie sovetskoi vlasti* (Moscow, 1966), 236–85; Keep, *Russian Revolution,* 422–26; T. H. Rigby, *Lenin's Government* (Cambridge, 1979), 44–50.

life and pose questions that cannot be decided by the forces of
local food-supply organs (Kiev, Kazan, Baku, Kostroma, Orel,
Moscow, Vladimirov, Simbirsk, Voronezh, Turkestan, Astrakhan, Viatka, Smolensk, Saratov, Ekaterinoslav, Amur, Samara).

Every sort of public group applies efforts to restore the regular course of life: food-supply committees, worker and peasant soviets, town and zemstvo self-government, army soviets,
medical societies.

Measures [indicative of] breakdown are practiced: rations
are lowered, emissaries are sent out, appeals, exchange of
bread for other products, formation of flying detachments with
the participation of the military command.

A clear expression of a negative attitude toward the new
measure of doubling the prices (Don region, Saratov,
Ekaterinoslav, Tula, Kherson, Tambov, Samara, Astrakhan,
Taurides, Poltava, Yenisei, Omsk, Kursk).[47]

Events in the northern deficit province of Tver illustrate the struggle that took place after the Bolshevik coup between the forces of self-
protection—the sackmen swarming across the land and the local organizations grabbing what they could—and the forces working for a strong
central authority. In its first session after the coup (5–7 November) the
food-supply committee in Tver had to find its bearings in circumstances of
complete breakdown. The food-supply apparatus at lower levels was completely demoralized; deliveries from the southern surplus provinces had
stopped; the situation at the center was so uncertain that the committee
decided it was not time to send the delegation that they had earlier selected.
The comments by representatives of the county committees were uni-
formly grim:

Krasnokholm county: It is no longer possible for the board to
function properly. "Yesterday a whole village appeared at the
board, and under pressure from the crowd we were forced to
change the distribution [*razverstka*] of grain. In the county
and in the city there are in all around 150,000 people going
hungry. There is no bread, and how we will exist tomorrow—
we do not know."

Zubtsov county: the board is closed. Members of the board
are afraid to show themselves on the street. "We await the destruction [*razgrom*] of the board."

47. TsGVIA, 13251-2-40/32–33. A similar survey can be found in *Ek. pol.*, pt.
2, doc. 506, pp. 315–22.

Rzhev county: A little boy shot a little girl because she took an extra piece of bread.[48]

Already refugees from the turmoil in the capitals, Petrograd and Moscow, were exacerbating difficulties in the provincial towns. The committee discussion was also marked by the usual hostility between workers and peasants.

The first reaction of the committee was to declare itself above politics. This was not the anti-Bolshevik neutrality of the center but one that stemmed from the desire to keep working even though the outcome of the political struggle was uncertain. The committee next decided that Tver province had to work out its own relations with the surplus provinces. This had to be done on the basis of commodity exchange since money could no longer be obtained from the center owing to the Finance Ministry strike. One factory offered to contribute goods to the committee so that they could be exchanged for grain; all that the factory requested in return was to have its own representative in the purchasing organization. This offer was gratefully accepted. It was decided to organize a delegate bureau that would operate collection points in the south; one half of what was collected would go to the specific organizations contributing to the bureau, and the other half would go to the provincial food-supply committee.

By December a number of modifications in this plan had been made. The delegates had discovered that the southern provinces were not ready for commodity exchange; the peasants there still wanted money. The only source of money was now the population of Tver province itself, and accordingly an appeal was published explaining the situation and urging the population (especially the peasants) not to take their money out of the banks. However, peasant suspicion in Tver was easily aroused and hard to overcome, and (it was asserted) if food supply were transferred to the county zemstvo as planned, the peasants would take back their money, saying, "We trusted you, but on the zemstvo board are Bolsheviks, and them we don't trust."[49]

The desire for a central authority that could deal with the southern provinces was strengthened by the threat of Ukrainian separatism, which seemed to leave Tver in a "bitter position of helplessness and isolation." Kudriashev (the chairman of the provincial food-supply committee) felt that the northern provinces must band together to form a unified state authority: "We must go to this future authority and say to it: we are unable to receive grain by peaceful methods—help us take it by force."

48. *Prod. delo* (Tver), no. 13–14, 15 December 1917.
49. *Prod. delo* (Tver), no. 15, 1 January 1918 (appeal of 18 December 1917).

Later in the debate someone objected that it would hardly be possible to take food from the south by force, and Kudriashev rather weakly replied that he meant the force of organization. The hope of creating an effective central authority by a voluntary coalition of provinces did not seem promising.

The committee also realized that preparations had to be made for surviving on the provinces' own resources. To mobilize internal resources, a second registration (*pereuchet*) was proposed. An appeal to the peasants contained a threat that it would be better for them to share now, before hunger "darkened the minds" of grain consumers.

During the December meeting of the provincial food-supply committee (7–8 December) an arrangement was worked out with the provincial soviet. Chairman Kudriashev had declared that they must decide who was the master in the business of food supply. There were three choices: the soviets, the sackmen, and the food-supply apparatus, seen as a nonpolitical organization. Kudriashev admitted that politics was hard to avoid—like a fly waved out the door that returns through the window—but still suggested that a regional organization of deficit-province food-supply committees could perhaps deal with the Ukraine as an equal.

The result of negotiations between the soviet and the food-supply committee was far from the clear-cut choice asked for by Kudriashev. Tver did decide to join the proposed regional organization of deficit-province food-supply committees. Attempts were also made to organize the sackmen: as a representative of a county peasant soviet said, "Sackmanism is a good thing, if only it is done well." The food-supply organization also agreed to work in close contact with the provincial soviet. This cooperation was possible because both the soviet and the food-supply committee shared the same "faith": the grain monopoly, fixed prices, and struggle with the sackmen. (There were different nuances in the formulations of this common faith: the food-supply spokesman emphasized the struggle with sackmanism, and the soviet spokesman referred to the merciless struggle with speculation.) The food-supply apparatus wanted the soviet to share responsibility for food supply and not just to criticize. The food-supply workers were also worried about the situation of multiple authority (*mnogovlastie*) at the local level: a representative of Rzhev county reported that there were at least seven bosses in Rzhev besides the food-supply organization and that carrying out food-supply policy was comparable to tacking between seven sharp rocks.

What the soviet from its side wanted from the agreement was for the committee to declare that soviet sovereignty meant the sovereignty of the people's authority and that only the soviets could deal with the economic breakdown. The provincial food-supply committee did pass a resolution to this effect but could not refrain from adding the phrase (over the objection of the soviet representative) "up to the creation by the Constituent Assembly of a generally recognized state authority." Although the food-supply committee—whose dominant orientation seems to have been moderate socialist—had to deal with local power realities, it still was not reconciled to the idea of a Bolshevik-led state authority based on the soviets.[50]

The January meeting of the committee (9–11 January) took place days after the dissolution of the Constituent Assembly, and the committee, eager not to get involved in larger political questions, agreed by a large majority not even to discuss the political situation. But before debate was cut off, two opposed points of view found expression. Both sides agreed that the worst evil as far as food supply was concerned was the civil war and anarchy that resulted from the struggle for sovereignty. But one side drew the conclusion that "we must firmly and specifically demand the end of civil war" by getting the Bolshevik Council of People's Commissars to come to an agreement with the other socialist parties. The other side argued that the only way to avoid civil war was to line up behind the present government: "Two tendencies cannot live together; the political quarrel can only be decided the same way it began. Salvation . . . rests only in a strong state authority that has mastery over the entire territory of the country." Since the only realistic candidate for this authority was the soviets, the Bolshevik presenting this argument told his audience to forget about the Constituent Assembly and declare "sovereignty to the soviets." This is an unusually frank exposition of a Hobbesian calculation that must have influenced the thinking and actions of a great many people at that time.[51]

The meeting went on to discuss new ways of getting the information necessary for an effective registration of grain. A proposal was made to use the poorer half of the village to get information and possibly even use force against the richer half of the village. Local representatives discussed their experience with so-called registration-requisition commissions and cited the following advantages: a voluntary registration was absurd, and searches by soldiers gave only "pitiful results," so the only effective source of information was hungry fellow villagers. These registration-requisition commissions were a forerunner of the Committees of the Poor introduced by the Bolsheviks, but the justification was on strictly practical grounds and not yet in terms of class war.

50. *Prod. delo* (Tver), no. 15, 1 January 1918.
51. *Prod. delo* (Tver), no. 16–17, 1 February 1918.

After February the committee publication no longer contained the minutes of monthly meetings. A note in a later issue reports that actual absorption of the food-supply organization into the soviets took place at the county level in February and at the provincial level in early March. We are also told that all the old employees stayed and there were new workers from the soviets, so work continued without a halt.[52] It is likely that this last assertion was more pious hope than fact.

Local activists made brave efforts, and many of their improvisations foreshadowed future policy. But they were in no position to cope with accelerating breakdown or produce a coherent nationwide response. A national response had to come from a national authority. If the Bolsheviks wanted to make good their claim to such authority, they could no longer delay in presenting a full-scale response to the food-supply crisis.

THE FOOD-SUPPLY DICTATORSHIP

The response unveiled by the Bolsheviks in the spring of 1918 was called the food-supply dictatorship. The legislative underpinnings of the food-supply dictatorship were set forth in a series of dramatic decrees passed in late May and early June, and this timing has led many people to see it as a response to the loss of the Ukraine and the outbreak of civil war. In reality the outlines of the food-supply dictatorship were evident from the beginning of the year. Its aim was to reconstitute authority in the face of the spiraling growth in intensity of centrifugal forces that had continued since the fall of 1917.

Bolsheviks gave these centrifugal forces the general label *separatism*. The most flagrant case was the rural soviets. The center had worked for the incorporation of local food-supply committees into the soviet system as food-supply sections of the local soviets, but this policy strengthened rather than reduced separatism. The local soviets were determined to protect their own locality: they refused to export grain outside their region, interfered with grain transports, and raised fixed prices or rejected the grain monopoly altogether. The efforts of local authorities often degenerated into armed struggle over a carload of grain.

If the local soviets did try to represent state authority, they encountered the same violent hostility faced by food-supply committees in 1917. In the words of an observer reporting to the central Bolshevik authorities about the situation in Tver, "An intensified bitterness against the soviets can be observed. At the district level, soviet executive committees are reelected

---

52. *Prod. delo* (Tver), no. 20, 15 March 1918, 1–3. The true situation in Tver is discussed below.

just about every week. The best workers are thrown out or leave themselves. In their place are former peasant elders, merchants, well-off peasants. . . . Even party workers are removed, and they are often threatened by the rioting of the hungry and incited masses."[53]

The plague of separatism was carried not only by rural soviets but by urban consumers. Local factories would use their products to conduct direct exchange with the peasants, either by distributing items to individual employees so that they could conduct barter on their own or by sending factory delegations to the grain surplus regions. This group sackmanism deprived the Food-Supply Commissariat of the goods needed to carry out a centralized policy of commodity exchange, and the flood of factory representatives bartering on their own led to further disorganization of local grain procurement. The revolutionary takeover of the factories by the worker committees only accelerated what the center saw as insubordination. For the Bolsheviks, it demonstrated a general "falling apart of authority. . . . Many organs of authority, not sufficiently imbued with a consciousness of state unity and the necessity of acting according to a general state plan have come forward now with a narrow, local, and amateurish point of view."[54]

Separatism was not confined to the population. The Food Supply Commissariat applied the same label to central government institutions, especially the industrial committees loosely grouped under the Supreme Economic Council. These committees, each in charge of a separate industry, existed in uneasy interdependence with the food-supply authorities. The industrial committees needed agricultural raw materials and food for their workers, and the food-supply officials needed industrial products to exchange for grain.

The relations between the Supreme Economic Council and the Food Supply Commissariat never got beyond suspicion and mutual recrimination, and food-supply officials tended to blame much of their difficulties in dealing with the village on the "departmentalism" of the industrial committees.[55] To a large extent it was the Food Supply Commissariat that set

53. T. V. Osipova, "Razvitie sotsialisticheskoi revoliutsii v derevne v pervyi god diktatury proletariata," in *Oktiabr'i sovetskoe krest'ianstvo* (Moscow, 1977), 58–59. Detailed figures on the dimensions of the economic breakdown in the spring of 1918 can be found in Silvana Malle, *The Economic Organization of War Communism 1918–1921*, (Cambridge, 1985), chap. 7, and Keep, *Russian Revolution*, chap. 31.

54. Central Executive Committee, 4th *sozyv,* 1 April 1918, 75–84 (report by Briukhanov).

55. Iziumov, ed., *Khleb,* 58–61; *Tri goda borby s golodom: kratkii otchet o deiatel'nosti NKP za 1919–1920 gg.* (Moscow, 1920), 58–59.

the tasks for the industrial committees. Its mission was to keep town and village from falling apart; its dominance over the industrial committees reflected the priorities of the time of troubles.[56]

If the crisis of political authority intensified the food-supply crisis, the reverse was also true. In the cities there was a strong anti-Bolshevik backlash; in the villages there were not only constant reelections but also armed resistance. One Soviet historian has counted more than thirty cases of armed resistance to food-supply policy in March and April alone, concentrated in the central surplus provinces.[57]

The Bolshevik response was the food-supply dictatorship. Although the word *dictatorship* has many overtones, its central meaning in this case was not depriving the population of its rights so much as unifying and disciplining all state agencies dealing with food supply. Ever since 1916 there had been persistent calls to imitate the food-supply dictatorship set up by the Germans in May of that year. In the Bolsheviks' case the target was not only the food-supply apparatus but also separatism of all kinds. This double target was announced in January 1918 by the All-Russian Food Supply Congress, which resolved that the only way to enforce the grain monopoly was through uncompromising centralization and war with separatism.

The central goal of this dictatorship was to build up a food-supply apparatus that was under the control of a secure political authority in the center. The greatest difficulty was at the lowest rung of the apparatus: creation of a permanent and reliable base (*opora*) in the peasant population itself. This base was needed to give the apparatus a continuing presence in the village so that food-supply officials did not simply descend out of the blue at irregular intervals. In addition the apparatus wanted a source of valuable information that would act both as the alert eyes of grain registration and as a source of real force independent of village grain-holders. To sum up these tasks in a single formula, the apparatus wanted a base in the village that would be more loyal to the apparatus than to the village.

A candidate for this base immediately suggested itself: the "village poor," that is, everybody except the people to whom pressure would be applied. This use of poor peasants was enveloped in a cloud of rhetoric about "class war in the villages," but (as Tsiurupa said explicitly in July) the food-supply officials themselves were not so much interested in the

56. Lev Kritsman, *Geroicheskii period velikoi russkoi revoliutsii* (Moscow, [1924]), 208.
57. T. V. Osipova, *Klassovaia bor'ba v derevne v period podgotovki i provedeniia oktiabr'skoi revoliutsii* (Moscow, 1974), 315, 317, 321. Osipova reports a total of 120 antisoviet risings in the first half of the year.

political side of committees of the village poor as in the "purely technical" need for them.[58]

Material incentives would be needed to enlist a reliable base for the apparatus. The Bolsheviks saw the importance of combining force and material incentive. One Bolshevik publicist, R. Arskii, declared:

> We will only be able to conduct the struggle against the with-holding of agricultural products by the kulaks if we succeed in giving the village something useful, something necessary. And when we do this, then we will be able to present revolutionary demands to the village. Only in that case will it be possible to apply coercion and force in relation to the village. . . . If we do not give [anything], it is unthinkable for us to collect grain from the village. The rich [peasants] will find some tricky way of hiding grain.[59]

This task required centralized control over commodity exchange: the village must not be able to obtain exchange items through other channels. But "in order for commodity-exchange to have organized forms instead of an elemental and separatist character—which at present can be observed among individual factories and enterprises—what is needed is a regulating principle such as state intervention."[60] In short, the Bolsheviks returned to the slogan of organizing the sackmen: "There is only one way of stopping this elemental process: organizing it on a state scale and changing it from a means of disorganizing food supply into a mighty tool for [ensuring] its success."[61]

Urban consumers could also be used to create a force independent of the village and, just as important, independent of the local food-supply apparatus. From the point of view of the food-supply officials, enlistment of the urban workers was not attractive because the workers were by nature the progressive revolutionary class. Rather, the idea was (as one food-supply official put it) to let two parochial interests—consumer and producer—cancel themselves out to the benefit of the general state interest.[62]

58. 9 July 1918, Fifth Congress of Soviets, 135–45. The phrase *alert eyes* comes from this speech.

59. *Trudy pervogo vserossiiskogo s"ezda sovetov narodnogo khoziaistva* (Moscow, 1918), 31 May 1918, 417–18.

60. Central Executive Committee, 4th *sozyv*, 1 April 1918, 75–84 (report by Manuil'skii).

61. A report of the People's Commissariat of Food Supply to the Council of People's Commissars prior to the goods exchange decree, in Orlov, *Prodovol'stven-naia rabota sovetskoi vlasti: k godovshchine oktiabr'skoi revoliutsii* (Moscow, 1918); 179–82.

62. Central Executive Committee, 4th *sozyv*, 27 May 1918, 326–28 (Sviderskii).

Thus the Bolshevik food-supply commissar, Aleksandr Tsiurupa, was correct to argue that it was unfair for the opposition to maintain that the Bolsheviks relied solely on force: the food-supply dictatorship constituted a system none of whose parts could succeed in isolation. It included centralized control of the apparatus, material incentives, and the enlistment of urban consumers and poor peasants. Aleksandr Shlikhter, a senior Bolshevik food-supply official, announced in January that the foundation of food-supply work would be "organized revolutionary violence."[63] Another way of putting it is that violence would be used in the service of organization.

The outlines of this strategy for reconstitution are already evident in the resolution of the food-supply congress in January. War on separatism meant no independent purchases outside the food-supply apparatus and no separate goods exchange between individual regions. To strengthen centralization, representatives from the soviets of the grain-deficit provinces were allowed to join the food-supply committees of the grain-surplus provinces. The resolution also foreshadowed the enlistment of the village poor: "The Congress finds it necessary to assign to local soviets of workers', soldiers', and peasants' deputies the task of taking the most decisive measures against large-scale sowers who hide grain or refuse to deliver it."

A proclamation issued to the peasants by the food-supply congress showed how a straightforward directive to take grain from those who had it became clothed in an elaborate class-war interpretation. The proclamation announced, "Struggle, brothers, with your village bourgeois just as we are struggling with them in the towns." What the official resolution called large-scale sowers now became "malicious kulaks" who hid grain. Opposition to the monopoly was declared a provocation by the bourgeoisie, which tried to blame the current food-supply crisis on the soviet political authority even though in actuality the crisis was caused by its own sabotage. Nor does Riabushinskii's "bony hand of hunger" fail to make an appearance. Even so, the class-war interpretation was not yet all-embracing. In the resolution the distilling of home vodka was not yet blamed on a kulak plot but on "ignorant citizens who have not risen to a correct understanding of the interests of the working people."[64]

It was one thing to outline the strategy in resolutions and another to actually put the system in place. The first challenge to Tsiurupa and his

63. Third Congress of Soviets, 71–72.
64. Material on the food-supply congress comes from Orlov, *Rabota*, 36–37; *Prod. delo* (Tver), no. 18–19, 1 March 1918, 1–2, 13–20; Third Congress of Soviets, 71–72. Improvisation and unjustified optimism mark Shlikhter's presentation of food-supply policy in December in Keep, ed., *Debate on Soviet Power*, 252–55.

colleagues was to take over the old Ministry of Food Supply of the Provisional Government and install a unified Bolshevik leadership without sharing any authority with the previous food-supply officials. The drive to establish the personal authority of the people's commissar over the entire food-supply apparatus could hardly begin until his authority was recognized at least by the central ministry itself.

The next brick in the food-supply edifice was Lev Trotsky's appointment at the end of January as head of an extraordinary commission for expediting grain transport on the railroads. Despite the specific focus of this assignment, Trotsky was called a food-supply dictator because of the unlimited powers given to him. Since his involvement in food-supply matters was short-lived, it has been mostly forgotten that the term *food-supply dictatorship* was first used by the Bolsheviks at this point and not in May.

The immediate impetus to Trotsky's appointment was a drop in deliveries to Petrograd due to train seizures by local soviets and other less official armed bands. Trotsky's projected program contained the usual mixture of force and material blandishments: he wanted to crack down on unauthorized transport of grain on the railroads as well as mobilize all available industrial items for commodity exchange with the peasant. To protect the trains, "flying detachments" consisting of soldiers, sailors, and unemployed workers were formed. Trotsky's crackdown also included a get-tough policy toward the sackmen. The army detachments who had been given the job of enforcing the antisackman policy had evidently been "indecisive," and special detachments were required. As a Kadet critic said, thus began "the first war of the [s]oviet power—the war with the railway passengers."[65]

The Bolshevik food-supply system eventually relied on several different kinds of armed force. But the type most irritating to the population at large—the blockade detachments (*zagraditel'nye otriady*) that harassed people carrying grain and other foodstuffs by rail—was created first, long before the May decrees. For the Bolsheviks (as well as for many other food-supply professionals), the war on the sackmen was a necessary implication of any real commitment to the grain monopoly.

The next important measure was a decree of 26 March on commodity exchange. A person looking at a list of Bolshevik food-supply measures might deduce that in late March the Bolsheviks were still relying on

65. A. Tyrkova-Williams, *Why Soviet Russia Is Starving* (London, March 1919), 5–8; information from an article in *Nash vek*, cited in *Prod. delo* (Tver), no. 18–19, 1 March 1918; also *Prod. delo* (Kharkov), no. 5–6:8–10. Newspaper reports on the war against the sackmen can be found in James Bunyan and H. H. Fisher, eds., *The Bolshevik Revolution* (Stanford, 1934), 656–68.

peaceful measures of material incentive such as commodity exchange but that six weeks later, in May, they drastically changed course and resorted to class-war measures such as worker detachments and Committees of the Poor. That conclusion would be mistaken. The March decree was fully consistent with the strategy of the food-supply dictatorship. It was aimed mainly at the undisciplined (*samochinnyi*) and separatist attempts at commodity exchange made by local authorities and factories. Those who indulged in unpermitted exchange of goods for grain were threatened with arrest.[66] In a talk to the Kostroma province food-supply committee the Bolshevik food-supply official D. P. Maliutin traced the poor performance of the state food-supply system to a lax attitude toward the semiorganized sackmanism of individuals and groups: "They say that the voice of the people is the voice of God. We hearkened to the voice of the people, and for a period of time we allowed the population to make independent purchases, but what came of it all? The most pathetic results possible." Where monthly quotas had previously been fulfilled by 40–50 percent, fulfillment had plummeted in December and January to 10–15 percent, in places to 5 percent. Maliutin added, "This isn't a fairy tale, this isn't an invention or an empty phrase, but the plain truth." Thus for Maliutin the commodity-exchange decree was a continuation of Trotsky's fight against the sackmen.[67]

The decree also showed the continuing interest in the use of poor peasants to force the grain-holding peasants to cooperate. The decree itself mentions the "enlistment of the village poor" only in passing, but the instructions sent out to the provincial committees insisted that industrial items should not be given to individuals on the basis of how much grain they delivered—rather, they should be given to groups of poor peasants to distribute as they saw fit. The idea was to give poor peasants both an incentive to put pressure on their well-off fellow villagers (since the village as a whole would get the goods only after deliveries were made) and a means of doing so (through control of distribution). The local food-supply committees were also urged to "create a cell from the poorest elements that can be relied on in [the committee's] work among the village masses."[68] Thus material incentive was to be used not for encouraging individual exchange with the actual producer but for splitting the village.

Despite the chaos around them, the food-supply officials seemed to have

66. *Dekrety sovetskoi vlasti* (Moscow, 1957–), 2:23–24. This decree is usually dated 2 April 1918, when it was published in *Izvestiia*.

67. *Prodovol'stvie i snabzhenie* (Kostroma), no. 2, 1 May 1918, 24–26 (talk given 3 April 1918) (hereafter cited as *Prod. i snab.*).

68. *Prod. i snab.* (Kostroma), no. 2, 1 May 1918, 24–26 (Maliutin speech of 3 April 1918), 2–3 (telegram from Manuil'skii, 7 April 1918). *Prod. delo* (Tver), no. 22, 15 April 1918, 12–13.

been fairly optimistic in early April 1918—just as the Provisional Government had been for a fleeting moment in the spring of 1917. Centralization and commodity exchange were well begun, and the peace treaty and the opening of river navigation seemed to promise an easing of earlier pressures. As Maliutin declared in his talk in Kostroma, "I have to say that never has the soviet authority felt so strong and secure as at the present moment. The cause of the toiling masses is in reliable and strong hands." In line with the logic of the enlistment solution a strong political authority would be the consequence of the "full confidence" enjoyed by soviet organizations, allowing them to take the tough decisions that would be necessary.[69] This sense of security—if in fact it was ever more than a brave front—was gone by May. Instead of a hopeful feeling that the worst was over, food-supply officials were possessed by an anxious concentration on being able to hold out until August and "the first soviet harvest." Although their basic strategy did not change, they now laid most emphasis on getting immediate results.

The reason usually given for this loss of security is the civil war, but a closer look shows this view to be incorrect. An outline of all the measures of May and June was given by Tsiurupa on 9 May in the legislature of the new state, the Central Executive Committee. In particular he mentioned that worker detachments would be used for getting immediate results by providing "physical incentives" for the kulaks to deliver grain. Although the hurriedly prepared decrees were presented and passed later, the full food-supply dictatorship system cannot therefore be dated later than 9 May. According to William Chamberlin, the soviet regime, although still unpopular and shaky, seemed free of actual military threat in early May; the Czech uprising in Siberia on 26 May changed the outlook "with dramatic suddenness."[70] There is no reference to civil-war pressures in the decrees and debates in May (leaving aside the flamboyant rhetoric about "civil war in the villages"). Perhaps the best demonstration that it was not the threat of civil war that led to the food-supply dictatorship comes from a document written by Lenin on 26 May, the day of the Czech uprising, in which he proposes that the army itself be turned into a grain-collecting apparatus: "Change the War Commissariat into a War–Food-Supply Commissariat—that is, concentrate nine-tenths of the work of the War Commissariat on remaking the army for the war for grain and on conducting this war for three months."[71] Thus Lenin assigns a nine-to-one ratio to the urgency of food supply and the urgency of all other military pressures.

69. Maliutin speech of 3 April 1918; Central Executive Committee, 1 April 1918, 79–84 (report by Manuil'skii).
70. W. H. Chamberlin, *The Russian Revolution* (New York, 1935), 2:1–2.
71. Lenin, *PSS*, 36:374.

Another reason given for the changed atmosphere was the unavailability of grain from cut-off regions such as the Ukraine. There is no doubt that it was a blow, but it need not have crippled Bolshevik grain procurement. The Bolsheviks themselves did not lay heavy emphasis on it, partly because the German occupation of the Ukraine could plausibly be seen as the result of the Bolshevik capitulation at Brest-Litovsk: the Bolsheviks felt vulnerable here, and so they tried to show that other regions could make up the deficiency caused by the loss of the Ukraine. According to the figures of the People's Commissariat, even without the areas lost as a result of the peace treaty, there remained 330 million poods of grain available to cover a total of 321 million poods needed by the deficit provinces (not counting a substantial amount left over from previous harvests).[72]

This relatively optimistic outlook was based on the expectation of obtaining large amounts of grain from Siberia and the northern Caucasus. Even after those regions were cut off by the outbreak of civil war in late May, the Bolshevik leaders tried to put up a brave front. As late as 9 July, in his speech to the Fifth Congress of Soviets, Tsiurupa stressed that there remained enough grain in regions controlled by the Bolsheviks. Combined with the grain that could be expected shortly from the Caucasus, it would be enough to last the short period to the new harvest, "even at a well-fed standard [*po sytoi norme*]."[73]

The main cause of the Bolsheviks' desperation was their failure to get grain from the population still under their control. The grain-surplus provinces of Russia proper—the central agricultural region and the Volga provinces—had traditionally been the ones to supply the northern grain-deficit region because the outlying regions had produced mainly for export. Furthermore, as the Bolsheviks themselves pointed out, the very poor performance of the food-supply apparatus over the past year or so meant that there was considerable grain from previous harvests still in the countryside. Yet the Bolsheviks failed to get even a small percentage of the available grain. Their failure here makes it more than doubtful that they could have obtained much grain from the outlying regions even if these regions had remained under nominal Bolshevik control.

The basic reasons for the Bolsheviks' miserable performance on their home ground were clear to all concerned. The Bolsheviks had not succeeded either in creating a reliable apparatus or in combatting separatism. Because of this failure, measures such as the massive shipment of goods to

72. I. I. Mints, *God 1918* (Moscow, 1982), 362–63.

73. Fifth Congress of Soviets, 9 July 1918, 135–45. See also Lenin, *PSS*, 36:424, 452.

the villages in April 1918 may have even strengthened centrifugal forces. Local committees were unable to unload the goods, much less distribute them, and the goods often ended up in the hands of speculators masquerading as food-supply officials.[74]

The use of force was no more successful in overcoming separatism. In early June a village in Orel province surrounded itself with trenches and barbed wire, and a requisition detachment sent against it narrowly avoided being massacred.[75] Villages all over Russia were similarly trying to cut themselves off. The basis of the Bolsheviks' provisional optimism in April was gone: the soviet system had been unable to sustain a strong central authority.

The Bolshevik food-supply officials concluded there would have to be an emphasis on measures leading to quick results. Their thinking was based on the assumption that a small minority of kulaks had substantial reserves from previous harvests. Although the Bolsheviks maintained a studied ambiguity on the point, it seems that at this time the word *kulak* still connoted someone who was in the peasant estate but was not really part of village society. He was either a small landowner or a grain merchant, someone who might plausibly have not just a small excess over the consumption norm but an enormous reserve measured in thousands of poods. Both Tsiurupa and Shlikhter referred to their experience in western Siberia, where they had managed to uncover such reserves.[76] It is possible that the Bolsheviks were sincere in hoping that large reserves held by a small and unpopular minority would be enough to get them through the crisis and that they did not fully realize what they were getting into when they applied a strategy based on Siberian experience to the central provinces and unleashed "class war in the villages."

Both urban workers and poor peasants would be enlisted to overcome the expected resistance of these large grain holders. Most of the poor-peasant organizations that had sprung up by that time were in fact armed detachments, although not used systematically against grain holders.[77] A primary task of the new Committees of the Poor was to serve as a local base for the worker detachments, which would also be used for the central task of creating a disciplined apparatus. The detachments would not only re-

74. Orlov, *Delo*, 22–23; M. Frumkin, *Tovaroobmen, kooperatsiia i torgovlia* (Moscow, 1921), 5; Medvedev, *October Revolution* (New York, 1979), 136–43.

75. Osipova, *Klassovaia bor'ba*, 314–15.

76. Central Executive Committee, 4th *sozyv*, 9 May 1918, 241–52, 258–59. Reserves had built up in Siberia during the war because of transport difficulties. Kitanina, *Voina*, 286.

77. Osipova, *Klassovaia bor'ba*, 312–13.

move lax local officials but also provide reliable personnel for the technical tasks of the apparatus.[78]

All the seemingly new measures of the decrees of 13 May, 27 May, and 11 June—the pressure on kulaks, the worker detachments, the Committees of the Poor—were implied in the original strategy outlined in January. The immediate crisis meant that force was needed to obtain quick results, but food-supply officials had known all along that it would be required to impose discipline on their own unruly apparatus. Centralization could also be defended because of the need for speed and unity of action: the keynote of all three decrees was ending the independence of local organs and subordinating them to a hierarchy controlled by the People's Commissar.[79] The crisis was thus used to justify measures that food-supply officials had wanted all along.

In the fall of 1917, when both food supply and political authority had collapsed, the Bolsheviks had hoped, or at least had promised, that democratic soviets would provide a basis for a vigorous central authority that could overcome the food-supply crisis by crushing the sabotage that was its main cause. But events quickly revealed that the soviets and other local organizations would not make real sacrifices to support the new authority unless the direct local benefit was obvious.[80] The Bolsheviks continued to account for this indiscipline by sabotage and lack of class awareness, but in reality it was caused by the dilemma of Hobbes's choice and the dictates of rational self-protection.

The central food-supply authorities saw the wave of separatism as a distortion of the real nature of soviet sovereignty, which did not mean "all power to the localities" but instead meant the disciplined implementation of the line established by the central soviet authorities—the Congress of Soviets and the Central Executive Committee elected by the congress. The paradoxes of this position were scornfully pointed out by the Mensheviks. The new soviet constitution gave the local soviets power over local affairs—certainly keeping the local population from starving should be considered as a local affair. And when the Bolsheviks labeled the majority of peasant soviets as kulak soviets that had to be purged, they were denying legitimacy to the Congress of Soviets, the very body from which the Bolsheviks claimed to derive their authority.

Although Bolshevik food-supply officials were disappointed by the lack of disciplined soviet support, they did not let that stop them: they would

78. See especially Tsiurupa's remarks at the Central Executive Committee, 4th *sozyv,* 11 June 1918, 399–402.

79. Central Executive Committee, 4th *sozyv,* 9 May 1918 (Tsiurupa).

80. Gerasimenko, *Nizovye organizatsii,* chap. 5.

build with the soviets if possible, but against them if necessary. They felt that what Maliutin said about independent purchase could be applied to the whole idea of soviet sovereignty: "They say that the voice of the people is the voice of God. We hearkened to the voice of the people, . . . but what came of it all? The most pathetic results possible."

6   The Food-Supply
Dictatorship:
A Rhetorical Analysis

A man forgot about nature in those days. Words thundered
over the country, insistent summonses to struggle, impatient,
exultant, accusing, threatening enemies. Millions clustered
around these words as if they were magnetic poles. They were
challenges to destroy and at the same time challenges to
create. Those were days of sudden decisions and of constant
agitation.

Konstantin Paustovsky, recalling spring 1918

In the period between May and July 1918 food-supply policy became one
of the central political questions of the day and the subject of impassioned
partisan clashes in the legislature of the soviet system, the Central Executive Committee. The debates occurred at the end of the brief period when
the new soviet-based political authority was still a genuinely multiparty
system. The food-supply decrees were not only a response to the food-
supply crisis but also an assertion of the viability of the Bolshevik vision.
This assertion was not left unchallenged: the Bolsheviks had to defend the
food-supply dictatorship in the new forums of the soviet system against
those who remained loyal to other visions of the Russian revolution.

An understanding of the debates requires a close examination of the
meaning of the key rhetorical terms employed by the contending parties.
The attention given in this study to rhetoric should not imply that the
contending parties were responding only to their own imaginary con-
structs. The severity of the crisis in food supply and the crisis of authority
was no illusion; but a coherent collective response to circumstances is
possible only after they have been given meaning by political leaders.[1]
Rhetorical advocacy is needed to fit the response to any particular problem
into the larger framework of a general political outlook. This task is
especially important for a new political class whose claim to authority is
based on a novel and untried political formula.

1. Robert C. Tucker, *Politics as Leadership* (Columbia, Mo., 1981), 49.

DIVISIONS AMONG THE PEASANTRY

Each of the parties had a different terminology to describe the peasantry, and each terminology implied not only a different way of dividing the peasants but different theories about relations among them. The debates of 1918 were conducted by socialist intellectuals with a long tradition of dispute on this question; they were alive to the nuances of terminology, and so should be the observer who wishes to understand them.

	SR	Bolshevik	Menshevik
Top	kulak	well-off (*zazhitochnyi*)	rural bourgeoisie
Middle	laboring peasantry (*trudovoe krest'ianstvo*)	middle peasant	———
Bottom	poor peasant	rural proletariat (*batrak*)	rural proletariat

For the SRs, the center of attention was the laboring peasantry: groups above and below were residual and indeed not genuinely peasant. The laboring peasant was one who lived by applying his own labor to his own land; the kulak was one who did not live by his own labor but exploited others, either by hiring them or by using his strategic access to the cash economy (shopkeepers, usurers, and other middlemen). Similarly, the poor peasant was someone who was unable to live on his own land by his own labor. The poor-peasant group had no unity beyond this negative description since there were a wide range of reasons for someone's failure to succeed as a genuine peasant: he might make his living as a craftsman; he might be lazy or alcoholic; he might be suffering from a temporary poor harvest, or she might be a widow struggling on her own. Once land was equally distributed, members of this group would either become real peasants, leave the village altogether, or suffer the consequences of their refusal to work.[2]

This division of the peasantry was probably closest to the division made by the peasants themselves. The kulak, who (in the peasant's view) got rich not by honest labor but by manipulating the cash economy and duping his neighbors, was indeed the peasant's enemy. Since the kulak embodied the individualizing influence of the market (which affected both agricultural

2. The clearest exposition of the Left SR view is V. Trutovskii, *Kulaki, bednota i trudovoe krest'ianstvo* (Moscow, 1918). The origins of the SR outlook are described in Maureen Perrie, *The Agrarian Policy of the Russian Socialist-Revolutionary Party* (Cambridge, 1976).

products and land), the SRs felt that he was subverting peasant solidarity. The SR definition of the kulak also reflected the abstractions of the socialist intellectual when it put the usurer on the same footing as any peasant who hired labor. It is my impression that a peasant who hired a number of workers but worked in the field himself was not regarded automatically as an enemy by other peasants. The peasant made his division not by the SRs' abstract concept of exploitation but by whether a person truly *earned* his living, which he could only really do by physical labor. It is also my impression that the SR division was already dated by 1918. The kulak of old—usurer, shopkeeper, grain dealer, or land speculator—was a transitional figure at a time when the village was making the painful move to integration within the market economy. As that integration proceeded and the peasantry as a whole became more attuned to the market with its dangers and opportunities, the kulak was less able to exploit a monopoly position or peasant ignorance, and he gradually developed into a normal and useful part of the village scene.[3] But compared to the social democratic analysis, the SR view may be a better place to start a sociology of the Russian village.

The social democrats—Bolsheviks and Mensheviks—gave their main attention not to the central group of peasants but to the groups below and above. It was these groups, they believed, that had reality and the central group that was residual. This view resulted from their absolute confidence that the peasantry was undergoing a process of class differentiation (*rassloenie*) that would eventually end the existence of the peasantry as such and leave only a rural bourgeoisie and a rural proletariat. The "middle peasant" was simply someone who was not yet a member of these two groups.[4] The difference between the Menshevik and Bolshevik views consisted in a tactical question: to what extent could this process of differentiation be useful to the revolution? The Mensheviks tended to look on the middle peasant as a future member of the rural bourgeoisie and therefore wished to make no concessions to him for fear of strengthening the enemy;

3. See the descriptions of the Russian village by Ernest Poole in *"Dark People"* and *The Village: Russian Impressions* (New York, 1918). For SR ambivalence about the kulak, see Perrie, *Agrarian Policy*, 74–85. See also Teodor Shanin, *Russia as a "Developing Society"* (London, 1985), 156–58; Manfred Hagen, *Die Entfaltung politischer Öffentlichkeit in Russland 1906–1914* (Wiesbaden, 1982), 51–52.

4. See Chantal de Crisenoy, *Lénine face aux moujiks* (Paris, 1978), and Kingston-Mann, *Lenin and Peasant Revolution*. De Crisenoy might be said to adopt a Left SR standpoint. She brings out one central point better than Kingston-Mann: Lenin felt the "rural poor" had socialist revolutionary potential only insofar as they were proletarians, not peasants. For a discussion of the debate over *rassloenie*, see Teodor Shanin, *The Awkward Class: Political Sociology of the Peasantry in a Developing Society* (Oxford, 1972).

they considered the rural proletariat too isolated in rural society to be of much use as an ally of the working class.

The Bolsheviks (that is, in this case, Lenin) postulated a double soul within the middle peasant: one yearning toward the delights of being a petty bourgeois and the other accepting the honorable and progressive status of proletarian. This double soul allowed the party to use the revolutionary energy of the peasants' fierce desire for land to destroy the tsarist regime without fear of strengthening an implacable enemy, for soon the middle peasant would see that mere possession of land could not give him the secure petty-bourgeois status he longed for. In the second stage of the revolution independent organization of the rural proletariat would provide a pole that would attract and strengthen the proletarian side of the middle peasant's soul.

Nonetheless, the Bolsheviks were intensely suspicious of the middle peasant. The Left SR V. Trutovskii made fun of the Bolsheviks by remarking accurately that "it is ridiculous to look around every minute at the laboring peasantry, [asking] as the Bolsheviks do, Won't they suddenly deceive us? Won't they suddenly follow the kulaks?" But while the Bolsheviks always worried about this, the Mensheviks had no doubts at all: they knew ahead of time that the middle peasant would follow the kulak.[5]

All of these clashing schemes are based on the assumption that class can be used to predict political behavior, even though each party had a different theory about the nature of those classes. But class interpretations—especially ones worked out a decade or so earlier—are not helpful in understanding behavior in a time of troubles. Party intellectuals saw the self-protective reactions of localism as emanations of a class nature rather than understandable responses to a breakdown in social order. But the division between grain consumers and grain producers was more important in 1918 than the class divisions postulated by the intellectuals. There was no particular connection between those who happened to have access to grain in the spring of 1918 and any long-term class dynamics however interpreted. The debate over food-supply policy was therefore conducted in language that was not appropriate to the subject at hand.

The Bolshevik scheme may have been the least descriptively accurate of the three, but it was also the most useful as a basis for political action. The doctrine of the double soul (like many other Leninist concepts) allowed political flexibility while preserving the appearance of doctrinal consistency. The Bolshevik view was that the middle peasant wavered throughout the civil war as one side or another of his soul gained the upper hand

5. Trutovskii, *Kulaki*, 13. For the Menshevik view, see Martov's remarks in the Central Executive Committee, 20 May 1918, 300–301.

until he was finally persuaded that Bolshevik firmness could be relied on. A more realistic view shows the peasant as remarkably persistent in protecting his own basic goals—which were not necessarily the ones attributed to him by socialist intellectuals—with whatever means were available. It would also show the Bolsheviks in an undignified flurry of retreats, compromises, and maneuverings culminating in the decriminalization of the grain trade in 1921. Still, the doctrine of the double soul allowed the Bolsheviks to maneuver.

In 1917 and 1918 the Bolshevik view of the peasantry went through substantial changes under the impact of the food-supply crisis and the partisan debates of the spring of 1918. Bolshevik rhetoric moved away from a bipolar model that emphasized the conflict between bourgeoisie and proletarian to a tripartite model that underlined the crucial importance of a large swing group within the peasantry. At the same time the claim that a revolutionary majority existed among the peasantry was quietly retracted as it became clear that the food-supply crisis could not be solved simply by expropriating a small minority. The Bolsheviks also took over a number of terms associated with the SRs and afterward discarded some (*laboring peasantry*) and retained others (*kulak*). A detailed examination of these changes will show how rhetoric can serve as a barometer of the pressures exerted on political activists.

Before 1917 *kulak* was used by Lenin in its classic strict sense of village middleman between the peasants and the larger cash economy. It was then a small subset of *well-off peasants*, one that was not of great interest for revolutionary strategy. Lenin saw the kulak as the exploiter of even the protobourgeois well-off peasant and assumed therefore that he would be disposed of in the first phase of the revolution, when the peasantry was still acting as a united group. (The association of the term *kulak* with the SRs probably made it even less attractive to Lenin.)[6]

The Bolsheviks adopted *kulak* in 1918 partly because the word had become more popular in 1917 in connection with the food-supply crisis. The kulak in his role as shopkeeper and small grain dealer was one of the "dark forces" who opposed the grain monopoly. As a grain speculator who brought up and hoarded grain, he was seen as both a cause of the shortage and a potential solution to it. Of course, this use of *kulak* by frightened and famished city dwellers was emotional and vague. The political coalition between Left SRs and Bolsheviks also influenced Bolshevik terminology. While this coalition was in effect (October 1917 to March 1918), the Bolsheviks adopted SR terminology in deference to their partners, who

6. Lenin, *PSS*, 1:18, 227, 259; 2:426–27, 535–36; 7:158, 189.

were assumed to be the specialists in the peasant wing of the revolution. After the Left SRs quit the government, and as relations between the two parties degenerated into open conflict, the Bolsheviks used SR terminology to bait the Left SRs and to steal their thunder.

Kulak was the correlative term of *laboring peasantry.* The latter term implied the SR view of the revolutionary potential of the great majority of the peasantry, a view the Bolsheviks were pleased to make their own for a time. But the Bolsheviks differed with the Left SRs on the meaning of this revolutionary potential. For the Left SRs, it meant one could rely with confidence on the spontaneous action of local forces; for the Bolsheviks, it meant that the majority of the peasantry would accept the discipline of the central workers' and peasants' authority. The Bolsheviks' assertion that they believed in the revolutionary discipline of the vast majority also fit in with their assertion that they could alleviate the food-supply crisis by expropriating the large reserves of a tiny minority.

Since the Bolsheviks still wished to talk in terms of a clear class struggle in which a large majority was pitted against a small minority, it would have spoiled this picture to dwell on the existence of a large swing group among the peasantry. The evolution of Bolshevik rhetoric can therefore be traced by the attention given to the middle peasant. In Lenin's writings of 1917 the middle peasant is conspicuous by his absence, and all the attention is concentrated on the two poles of attraction at either end of the class spectrum. On the bourgeois side, Lenin's original term *well-off peasant* is replaced simply by *rich peasant* after April; the term *kulak* is used in 1917 rarely and almost always in connection with the price-doubling decree. (As late as April 1918 food-supply official D. P. Maliutin defined the *kulachestvo* as the private trade apparatus.)[7] On the proletarian side, the original term *batrak* (rural laborer) was felt to be insulting—this should have been a clue that something was wrong with the political dynamics of the model—and was dropped after April 1917 in favor of *sel'skokhoziaistvennyi rabochii* (agricultural worker).

The rest of the peasantry was seen as tending toward these two poles. For those closer to the proletarian side, a new term was coined: *bedneishee krest'ianstvo,* or "poorest peasantry." This term was criticized both by Left SRs and Mensheviks for vagueness, and it is hard to escape the conclusion

---

7. *Prod. i snab.* (Kostroma), no. 2 (May 1918): 24–26. *Kulak* did not usually mean "well-off peasant" in 1917. Pershin notes that the proceedings of the Main Land Committee in 1917 reveal no mention of the kulak. Pershin, *Agrarnaia revoliutsiia,* 1:311. Uses of the word *kulak* in 1917 can be found in *Ek. pol.,* pt. 3, doc. 94, 228, 260, 262, 272, 274; Sukhanov, *Zapiski,* 3:196; Lenin, *PSS,* 34:184, 235.

that it was precisely this vagueness that commended it to the Bolsheviks. The poorest peasantry was defined mainly by its assumed willingness to accept proletarian political leadership. It included peasants who owned some land but not enough to avoid the necessity of hiring themselves out. In Lenin's eyes this characteristic made them not incomplete peasants but incomplete proletarians or "semiproletarians."

In 1917 Lenin implied that the peasant-as-such, the peasant owner (*khoziain*), would follow the lead of the well-off peasants. One of the few explicit references to the middle peasant I have found in Lenin's 1917 writings refers to him as a little capitalist on the side of the well-off peasant. But in general the Bolsheviks downplayed the question of possible peasant allies of the well-off peasant, and the picture drawn in 1917 is of a sharp unambiguous clash between the majority of poor peasants and a minority of rich peasants.[8]

Lenin's emphasis on class conflict within the peasantry is accompanied by scorn toward the populist "laboring principle" that postulated the solidarity of the peasantry as a whole. It is thus a surprise to see *laboring peasantry* used as a synonym for the poorest peasantry soon after the October coup. But this terminological concession to his Left SR coalition partners did not mean that Lenin abandoned his two-part conflict model: the laboring peasantry simply stood in for the poorest peasantry for a while. The high point of Bolshevik acceptance of this vocabulary was in late May: in response to Left SR criticism, the Central Executive Committee employed *laboring peasantry* in a resolution (although Sverdlov still felt that *poorest peasantry* was "more exact"), and the Left SR term was also used in one of the food-supply dictatorship decrees. But under the pressure of events in the spring and summer of 1918 the differences between the two conceptions of the peasantry became more pronounced, and the referent of *laboring peasantry* in Bolshevik rhetoric slowly gravitated from the poorest peasantry to the middle peasantry and finally to the rich peasantry, at which point the Left SRs were accused of defending the kulaks.[9]

A term that became central to Lenin's rhetoric starting around April 1918 expressed the Bolshevik conception of the peasantry: *melkoburzhuaznaia stikhiia*, or "petty-bourgeois disorganizing spontaneity." To some extent this is simply a Marxist euphemism for backward peasantry. A Menshevik writer scornfully observed that Lenin avoided the very word *peasant* in his discussion of *stikhiia*.[10] This avoidance was probably of set

8. Lenin, *PSS*, 31:21–22, 52, 64, 92, 113–15, 136, 163–68, 188, 241, 272, 419; 32:44, 166, 184–86; 34:184, 235, 330, 400–401.

9. Lenin, *PSS*, 35:64; 36:504; Ia. Sverdlov, *Izbrannye proizvedeniia* (Moscow, 1976), 181–84.

10. *Vpered*, no. 71, 25 April 1918 (Martynov). Martov called it the "new Leninist word." *Vpered*, no. 72, 26 April 1918.

design, for in the drafting of the decree of 13 May the word *peasant* is dropped from any accusatory formulation: "peasant predator" is changed to "village kulaks" and the phrase "not one pood will remain in the hands of the peasant" is softened to "in the hands of its holder." But the concept of disorganizing spontaneity meant that the kulaks were more to be feared than the Left SR outlook allowed, since they were not simply an unpopular minority facing a spontaneously revolutionary majority but also the most vivid expression of a disease to which the whole peasantry was susceptible.

The ranks of the revolutionary majority were being thinned at the same time by a new definition that eliminated anyone with a grain surplus. This definition helps answer the question, Who was the intended constituency of the Committees of the Poor? Were the middle peasants included from the outset? In various decrees and resolutions both *poorest peasantry* and *laboring peasantry* were used to indicate the constituency of the new committees. The Left SRs told the Bolsheviks that notwithstanding these formulations, the committees were obviously based on "your *batraki*" and represented Lenin's old strategy of organizing the agricultural wage laborer.[11]

Some Soviet historians maintain that on the contrary the Committees of the Poor were meant to include the middle peasant. They point to Lenin's correction of the decree setting up the committees: in place of the original definition of a poor peasant he substituted a more inclusive definition that left out only "notorious kulaks." This argument overlooks the fact that Lenin's definition also excluded anyone with a grain surplus.[12]

The Bolsheviks were indeed eager to cloud over the differences between the image of a revolutionary class struggle of the majority against the minority and the reality of enforcing the grain monopoly against much larger groups. Tsiurupa faced up to the terminological difficulty when he responded to a statement by a Left SR speaker that many peasants with surpluses could not be called kulaks: "What happens to these surpluses? Clearly they must be handed over to a state storehouse. Anyone who has surpluses and does not hand them over to a storehouse is subject to confiscation—to him will be applied the same measures that are applied to the kulaks. How can you fail to understand that anyone who has surpluses and hides them and is evasive is of course subject to pressure, no matter who he is."[13] This statement reveals that the kulak was not yet simply equated with the uncooperative possessor of a grain surplus—at least not

11. Kamkov, Fifth Congress of Soviets, 74–77.
12. Osipova, "Razvitie," 61; Mints, *God 1918*, 387–88. Lenin's definition includes newcomers (*prishel'tsy*), who were important for centralizing purposes and in many cases actually ran the Committees of the Poor.
13. Central Executive Committee debates on the Committees of the Poor, 11 June 1918, 407–9.

in a debate that was relatively sophisticated. But it also shows a terminological gap for this uncooperative peasant, who lay somewhere between the categories of poorest peasantry and kulak.

Thus the original conception of the Committees of the Poor depended on a bipolar conflict model of the peasantry since the middle swing group had not yet achieved rhetorical prominence. The constituency of the Committees of the Poor was supposed to be as inclusive as possible, but only on the assumption that the majority of peasants was revolutionary in the Bolshevik sense—hence they would fight the disorganizing spontaneity of the petty-bourgeois kulaks and accept the organizational discipline of the center. In particular this assumption meant that they would hand over grain surpluses to the authorities. But it turned out that there was no such revolutionary majority. The Bolshevik leadership registered this fact by moving from a two-part conflict model to a three-part neutralization model. July 1918 marked the return to Bolshevik rhetoric of the middle peasant, who became the center of strategic attention.

The first appearance of the middle peasant was in response to the accusation of the Left SRs that the food-supply dictatorship was aimed (in practice if not in theory) against the broad mass of the peasantry. Maria Spiridonova, leader of the Left SRs, asserted in early July that the Committees of the Poor had alienated a peasant majority that otherwise consisted of natural supporters of a revolutionary regime: "[This legislation] strikes hard [*bol'no b'et*] not at the kulak but . . . at the broad masses, the strata of the laboring peasantry."[14] The Bolsheviks were defensive on this point, and in their resolution on food supply they echoed Spiridonova by using the same expressive word, *bol'no*, but refused to admit that a naturally revolutionary laboring peasantry had been alienated. Instead they used a hybrid transitional term when they granted that certain unworthy worker detachments had indeed "hit hard [*bol'no udariaet*] at the middle laboring peasantry," as well as at the kulaks, and that these abuses must be corrected.

In his speech following Spiridonova's, Lenin used the three-part model to retain the idea that the enemy was a small minority even while admitting that the majority was not automatically revolutionary:

> A thousand times wrong is he who says (as do sometimes careless or thoughtless Left SRs) that this is a struggle with the peasantry. No, this is a struggle with an insignificant minority of village kulaks—this is a struggle to save socialism and distribute bread in Russia. . . .
> It is untrue that this is a struggle with the peasants. Any-

14. Fifth Congress of Soviets, 5 July 1918, 58–59.

one who says this is the greatest of criminals, and the greatest
of misfortunes will happen to the person who lets himself [or
herself] be hysterically carried away to the point of saying
such things. No, we are not only not struggling with the poor
peasants, we are also not struggling with the middle peasants.
In all Russia middle peasants have [only] insignificant grain
reserves.[15]

The speech goes on to paint an unconvincing portrait of the middle peasant
as "our most loyal ally" who has the "sound instinct of a laboring person"
and who will not only sell his grain at the official price but even admit the
justice of having to pay higher prices than the poor peasant for industrial
items.

Lenin's ambivalent view of the middle peasant is also shown by a
statement at the end of July: "There is no longer a single village where a
class struggle is not taking place between the poor population of the village,
along with part of the middle peasantry that does not have any grain
surpluses, that ate them up long ago, that does not participate in speculation—a class struggle between this overwhelming majority of the toilers
and an insignificant handful of kulaks."[16] We are naturally led to ask, What
happened to the other part of the middle peasantry? And does the middle
peasant reject speculation only because he has nothing at present to speculate with?

In July 1918 a new wave of peasant revolts occurred at the same time as
the prospect of a long, hard-fought civil war opened up. What Lenin later
called the July crisis forced him to move the middle peasant to center stage.
The so-called kulak revolts led him to admit that owing to peasant darkness
"in many cases everybody [in the village] is united against us." The civil
war meant that even more pressure would have to be put on the war-weary
peasantry, yielding a new definition of the problem: "The kulaks know that
the struggle is over the middle peasantry, for whoever obtains the support
of this large section of the Russian peasantry wins." The key to success was
thus no longer the enlistment of a revolutionary majority. Following from
this new definition of the problem, the decision was made on 2 August to
make "neutralization" of the peasantry the basis of food-supply policy, and
shortly thereafter Lenin made the first public reference not just to avoidance of conflict but also to concessions to the middle peasant.[17]

Under the impact of the rhetorical evolution of 1917 and 1918 key

15. Lenin, PSS, 36:507–11.
16. Lenin, PSS, 37:11 (19 July 1918).
17. Lenin, PSS, 36:504; 37:14; 36:532; 37:37.

Bolshevik terms for the peasantry took on new meaning. The term *middle peasant* of August 1918 was not the same as in Lenin's previous scenarios in which the middle peasantry would soon be attracted to one pole or the other on the class spectrum. Moreover, the food-supply crisis and the civil war forced the Bolsheviks to deal not with the peasant as protoproletarian but with the peasant as peasant. The attitude toward the peasantry often seen as originating after the civil war and in reaction to it should be seen as originating during the civil war and because of it.

When the decree on the Committees of the Poor appeared, *poor peasants* could still be taken to mean the vast majority of the peasantry. Only later, when it became clear that the peasant majority would never be eager supporters of Bolshevik food-supply policy, did the term shrink to include only those whom the Bolsheviks continued to regard as their natural allies and as semiproletarians, namely, landless and destitute peasants. Once this happened, *class conflict in the village* meant everybody against the poor, not everybody against the rich. As this balance of forces did not help food-supply policy, the Committees of the Poor were abolished. These policy changes show that at no time did the Bolsheviks seriously try to realize Lenin's pre-October vision of a socialist transformation of the village based on independent organization of the rural proletarians and semiproletarians.

Kulak had now become the permanent name for the Bolsheviks' reprobate class. (The Calvinists divided up mankind much as the Bolsheviks divided up the peasantry: the reprobates, who are surely damned; the elect, who are surely saved; and the redeemed, who are caught in between.) The connotations of the term *kulak* by now contained many not entirely compatible elements: the SR image of a parasitic and exploitative minority roundly hated by the peasantry as a whole; the Bolshevik image of an economically progressive capitalist class that offered an attractive alternative political leadership to the village; the image created by the food-supply crisis of a ghoul who laughed at the groans of the starving and wanted to choke the revolution with the bony hand of hunger.

STATE CAPITALISM AND CLASS WAR

In Lenin's rhetoric the grain monopoly and the food-supply dictatorship were directly tied to the question of state capitalism. State capitalism in 1918 had little to do with what it came to mean after the New Economic Policy, or NEP, was introduced—namely, tolerance of market forms and other mixed-economy institutions.[18] Instead, the term before 1921 im-

18. Laszlo Szamuely, *First Models of the Socialist Economic System: Principles and Theories* (Budapest, 1974), 58–59; L. D. Shirokorad, "Diskussii o goskapi-

plied organization of the national economy as a whole by the state. State capitalism was treated as a necessary historical stage in the prerevolutionary writings of both Lenin and Nikolai Bukharin. According to them, the internal laws of capitalist development were creating a movement away from the decentralized market toward state organization of the economy. This movement, accelerated by the demands of the war, was basically a progressive one, even though for the present the capitalists dominated the state and used its economic organization for their own ends. Lenin wrote in 1916:

> When a large-scale enterprise becomes gigantic and systematically [*planomerno*] organizes the delivery of primary raw material on the basis of an exact registration of mass data, providing two-thirds and three-fourths of demand for tens of millions of the population, [and] when distribution of these products to tens and hundreds of millions of consumers takes place according to a single plan (as does the American kerosene trust in both America and Germany)—then it becomes evident that what we have in front of us is socialized production, and not just "interlocking directorates."[19]

Even earlier Bukharin had discussed "state capitalism, or the inclusion of absolutely everything within the sphere of state regulation." He cited as an example the German food-supply dictatorship, under which "the anarchic commodity market is largely replaced by organized distribution of the product, the ultimate authority again being state power." Despite his eloquent denunciation of the militarized bourgeois state, he felt that the "material framework" of the state's organization of the economy could be used by the revolutionary proletariat.[20]

In 1917 this theory was easily fitted into the sabotage outlook: the otherwise inevitable progress toward all-embracing regulation of the economy was being thwarted by the frightened bourgeoisie. Lenin could use state capitalism as an argument for an armed uprising:

talizme v perekhodnoi ekonomike," in *Iz istorii politicheskoi ekonomii sotsializma v SSSR 20–30e gody* (Leningrad, 1981).

19. Lenin, *PSS*, 27:425 (*Imperialism*).

20. N. I. Bukharin, *Selected Writings on the State and the Transition to Socialism*, ed. Richard Day (Armonk, N.Y., 1982), 16–17, 22–23, 32–33. See also Bukharin, *Ekonomika perekhodnogo perioda* (Moscow, 1920), 69–72; Bukharin and E. Preobrazhenskii, *Azbuka kommunizma* (Petrograd, 1920), 88–91. Lev Kritsman called the Supreme Economic Council the "proletarian inheritor of finance capital" (*Geroicheskii period*, 198). For a discussion of Bukharin's attitude toward the state, see Stephen F. Cohen, *Bukharin and the Bolshevik Revolution* (New York, 1971), 31–32.

> Well, what if, instead of a Junker-capitalist state, instead of a
> landowner-capitalist state, we tried to establish a
> revolutionary-democratic one that would destroy all privilege
> in a revolutionary way, fearlessly implementing the most com-
> plete democracy? You will see that state-monopoly capitalism
> under a genuinely revolutionary-democratic state will inevita-
> bly and unavoidably signify more than one step toward social-
> ism! . . .
>
> For socialism is nothing more than the very next step for-
> ward from state-monopoly capitalism. In other words: social-
> ism is nothing other than state-monopoly capitalism that is
> made to serve the whole people and to that extent ceases to be
> a capitalist monopoly.[21]

In the spring of 1918, after the Brest-Litovsk treaty was signed, Lenin
reverted to this theme, although he no longer used the term *state capitalism*. He argued that the new state authority now faced the "organizational
task" of imposing "the most strict and universal registration and monitoring" and of creating "an extremely complicated and subtle network of new
organizational relations, embracing the systematic [*planomernoe*] production and distribution of products necessary for the existence of tens of
millions of people."[22] Lenin had not abandoned the sabotage outlook, but
the identity of the main saboteur had changed: "We must not forget that it
is precisely here that the bourgeoisie—in particular the numerous petty
and peasant bourgeoisie—will present us with the most serious struggle by
undermining the monitoring we are establishing—for example, the grain
monopoly." The postrevolutionary emergence of the peasant bourgeoisie
as the main enemy of further progress toward socialism was consistent
with Lenin's long-held views on the subject.[23]

Lenin thus seemed inclined to drop the term *state capitalism*, but it was
reintroduced into Bolshevik rhetoric by the Left Communist opposition
that had originally formed during the Bolshevik debate over the Brest-
Litovsk treaty. The Left Communists did not object to centralized economic
organization in itself; their protests were primarily directed against the
participation of capitalists in administration. They could not understand
how the saboteurs of 1917 could be trusted with economic authority in
1918. They also objected to the "bureaucratic" nature of Lenin's centralizing policies, by which they seem to have meant hindrances to the participa-

21. Lenin, *PSS*, 34:190–93. This whole passage is crucial. For other references
to state capitalism in 1917, see 32:293–94; 34:160, 173, 310, 373–74.

22. Lenin, *PSS*, 36:138, 171.

23. Lenin, *PSS*, 36:182, 122, 131–32, 141.

tion of workers and the independence of local soviets. We can therefore assume that they were opposed to the food-supply dictatorship, even though they seem not to have proposed a food-supply policy of their own. The Left Communists remained loyal to the Bolsheviks' 1917 version of the enlistment solution—an unproblematic combination of state regulation and widespread participation, together with a great emphasis on capitalist sabotage.[24]

In response Lenin pugnaciously took up the term *state capitalism* and extolled its virtues, partly out of polemical verve. In his dispute with the Left Communists he quoted his own 1917 statements praising state capitalism, but he distorted his own earlier views by leaving this sentence out of his self-citation: "Socialism is nothing other than state-monopoly capitalism that is made to serve the whole people and to that extent ceases to be a capitalist monopoly." This statement concedes one of the Left Communists' central points, namely, a government monopoly used for the benefit of the people ceases by that very fact to be capitalist. But in his debate with the Left Communists Lenin wanted to drive home the similarities between state capitalism and socialism rather than the decisive political differences.[25]

Lenin could also use state capitalism to illustrate his new theme of the dangers of the peasant bourgeoisie. State capitalism was good because it was "something centralized, something allowing for calculation and monitoring, something socialized, and that is exactly what we lack, [for] we are threatened by the atmosphere [*stikhiia*] of petty-bourgeois sloppiness."[26] The real enemy was not the "cultured capitalist," whose propensity for sabotage could easily be checked by the proletarian state authority and whose aid was necessary for economic regulation; it was the "uncultured capitalist," whose resistance to measures like the grain monopoly needed to be crushed "with methods of merciless violence."[27]

The term *state capitalism* soon became a liability for Lenin. It was serviceable enough in polemics within the Bolshevik party among sophisticated and like-minded socialist intellectuals but less effective in disputes between parties. Some of them, such as the Left SRs, began to act lefter-than-thou and say that the state-capitalist doctrine meant that the Bolshe-

---

24. Lenin, *PSS*, 3d. ed. (Moscow, 1935), 22:569–71. On the Left Communist challenge, see R. V. Daniels, *The Conscience of the Revolution: Communist Opposition in Soviet Russia* (Cambridge, Mass., 1960), chap. 3.

25. Lenin, *PSS*, 36:302–3; Bukharin, *Ekonomika*, 106–8; *Leninskii sbornik* 11 (1937): 369.

26. Lenin, *PSS*, 36:255–56 (29 March 1918).

27. Lenin, *PSS*, 36:305, 293–99.

viks were losing their revolutionary prowess. Others, such as the Mensheviks, began asking embarrassing questions about the justification of a soviet-based political authority and a socialist revolution if Russia was only at a state-capitalist stage. Worse, they began to contend that a capitalist stage implied such bourgeois democratic concepts as sharing power and imposing fewer restrictions on political opposition. Lenin dropped state capitalism and now began to argue that the "agonizing famine has moved us by force to a purely communist task."[28] But on closer inspection we find that this purely communist task is defined as the "correct distribution of bread and fuel, their intensified extraction, the strictest registering and monitoring of them *on the part of the workers* and on a general state scale."[29] The content of the terms *organizational task, state capitalism,* and *purely communist task* are thus all equivalent, given the different rhetorical contexts.

It is customary to describe Lenin's outlook in the spring of 1918 as moderate and as the forerunner to NEP.[30] Moderate is an odd description of a rhetoric whose key term seems to have been *merciless:* "We will be merciless to our enemies and just as merciless to all wavering and harmful elements from our own midst who dare to bring disorganization to our difficult creative work of constructing a new life for the working people."[31] Neither would Lenin's "organizational task" have seemed moderate to the "uncultured capitalists" whose lives he intended to transform—and since Lenin saw lack of cooperation as sabotage, he was prepared to use violence. When in early May he summed up the basic idea of the food-supply dictatorship as "merciless and terroristic struggle and war with the peasant bourgeoisie and [any] other that retains grain surpluses," he once again showed the intrinsic connection in his thinking between class war and the task of imposing registration and monitoring.[32]

THE PARTISAN CHALLENGE

The Bolsheviks' rhetorical presentation of the food-supply crisis cannot be separated from the partisan challenge from the other socialist parties in the spring of 1918.[33] After the signing of the Brest-Litovsk peace treaty,

28. Lenin, *PSS*, 36:405.
29. Lenin, *PSS*, 36:362.
30. In Western writings this tradition goes back at least to Maurice Dobb, *Russian Economic Development Since the Revolution* (New York, 1928).
31. Lenin, *PSS*, 36:235–36. See also 35:311–13 (January 1918).
32. Lenin, *PSS*, 36:316 (first published in 1931).
33. For a study of the partisan conflict in this period, see Vladimir Brovkin, *The Mensheviks After October: Socialist Opposition and the Rise of the Bolshevik Dictatorship* (Ithaca, 1987), esp. chap. 3.

that challenge concentrated its fire on the food-supply crisis. In March and April the Bolsheviks had been inclined to be self-critical and stress the problems arising from indiscipline on the part of their own constituency. But this stopped when Mensheviks in the Central Executive Committee debates began to use these Bolshevik statements as proof of the Bolsheviks' complete helplessness before the food-supply crisis. The Bolsheviks also became more defensive as the food-supply crisis began to chip away at their central base of support, the urban soviets. The interaction between partisan considerations and food-supply matters was intensified by the fact that two of the obstacles to centralized unification of the food-supply apparatus— the regional food-supply committees and the village soviets—were political strongholds of the Mensheviks and Left SRs respectively. Thus the Bolsheviks needed a rhetorical definition of the food-supply crisis that shifted blame away from themselves and as much as possible onto the shoulders of the other parties; accounted for the wavering and defections in the Bolshevik constituency; and promised a short-term solution to the crisis that would provide outlets for hungry workers other than sackmanism, speculation, and political protest.

These needs were met by the class-war definition of the food-supply crisis, which ran as follows. The Bolsheviks were not to blame for the food-supply crisis. Rather, it was caused by the bourgeois war and was being further intensified by kulak hostility to the revolution. The only reasons anyone would be reluctant to hand over his grain was speculative greed and a desire to choke the revolution with the bony hand of hunger. The socialist parties who weakened soviet authority by criticizing the grain monopoly were objectively part of the counterrevolutionary front that also included foreign and Russian capitalists and the petty-bourgeois kulaks. Some workers indeed had lost their revolutionary good sense because of the famine and because of the infection from the old system's rotting corpse. But the truly conscious workers would continue to rally round the Bolsheviks and in particular join the worker detachments that would serve the revolution by confiscating the grain of the kulaks. Such action was not an attack on the village but participation in a class war within the village. The creation of the Committees of the Poor as the lowest rung of the centralized apparatus of the People's Commissariat of Food Supply represented not bureaucratism and old-regime police methods but the armed people.

These themes appear again and again in speeches by Lenin, Trotsky, Grigorii Zinoviev, Iakov Sverdlov, and others in the spring of 1918. (Not all the Bolshevik leaders agreed with the analysis of Lenin and Tsiurupa; Aleksei Rykov and Lev Kamenev in particular advocated a softer line.) A few citations will give the flavor of them. In late May Lenin offered an incisive one-sentence analysis of the food-supply crisis: "The famine does not come from the fact that there is no grain in Russia, but from the fact that the bourgeois and all rich people are making a last decisive battle against the rule of the toilers, the workers' state, the soviet political authority."[34] Zinoviev, always the most straightforward and crude of the Bolshevik orators, elaborated further on the problems of bourgeois sabotage: "There is no doubt that this is a definite plan, worked out in the quiet of bourgeois offices a long time ago." And this, he continued, should not be news to anyone, for recall what Riabushinskii had said: "Gentlemen workers and sailors, you think to wear us out with bayonets and your majority, but remember, we have a way of controlling you: the bony hand of hunger, and it will smother your revolution." Zinoviev's speech is littered with references to "Riabushinskii's agents" and "Riabushinskii's program"— for example, in speaking of the necessity of "holy violence on those kulaks who fulfilled Riabushinskii's program." More important were the references to Riabushinskii's *parties*—that is to say, the SRs and Mensheviks, who opposed such holy violence.[35]

Bolshevik rhetoric on the food-supply crisis took place in a growing atmosphere of invective and threats against the other socialist parties. The tone can be sensed in Lenin's reaction to Right SR and Menshevik criticism of Bolshevik implementation of the grain monopoly: the only distinction between them and the openly capitalist Kadets is that the Kadets were straightforward Black Hundreds.[36] According to Lenin, the conclusion was obvious: only fools could dream of any kind of united front of all soviet parties.

But the Bolsheviks did not content themselves with rejecting the possibility of sharing power. They moved on to open threats against the other parties—threats that were soon carried out. In a speech in early June Trotsky warned that unless the parties stopped making trouble on the food-supply issue, a terror would be unleashed against them. Up until then terror had been avoided, but "now the soviet political authority will act more decisively and radically. . . . Don't poison the worker masses with lies and slander, for this whole game might end in a way that is to the highest degree tragic." In another speech, after the inevitable reference to

34. Lenin, *PSS*, 36:357 (*O golode*, 22 May 1918). The words *last decisive battle* are in Russian a clear allusion to the apocalyptic vision of the Internationale.

35. G. Zinoviev, *Khleb, mir i partiia* (Petrograd, 1918), 22–30 (speech of 29 May in Petrograd). According to Trotsky, the kulaks were the "advance detachment of the counterrevolution . . . the support and hope of the counterrevolution." Lev Trotsky, *Kak vooruzhalis' revoliutsiia* (Moscow, 1923–25), 1:81–83, (speech of 9 June 1918) (hereafter cited as *KVR*).

36. Lenin, *PSS*, 36:402 (speech of 4 June 1918). I regard this statement as a masterpiece of invective even for Lenin.

Riabushinskii, Trotsky asked if there was any line that divided counter-revolutionaries, monarchists, exploiters, and kulaks from the Right SRs and Mensheviks. "No, there is no such line: they are united in one black camp of counterrevolutionaries against the exhausted worker and peasant masses." He then went on to wonder at the patience of the Moscow workers, who allowed, in what was supposed to be a workers' soviet, five to ten Right SR representatives.[37]

In this way the food-supply crisis, caused by a Riabushinskian conspiracy that included the other socialist parties, justified the repression of all political opposition. Class-war rhetoric also transferred any faults of the workers to the other classes. Thus Lenin explained away the cases where worker detachments got drunk and looted the peasants by stating that "when the old society perishes, you can't nail up its corpse in a coffin and bury it. It disintegrates in our midst; this corpse rots and infects us."[38] If the workers showed their dissatisfaction with Bolshevik performance on food supply by going out on strikes, Zinoviev could argue that "it could not be otherwise: in our petty-bourgeois country there would be groups that decide that the revolution means 'give, give, give' and to whom the revolution means two pounds of bread, complete provisionment, and so on." Zinoviev combined his condemnation of petty-bourgeois influence with a certain flattery of the conscious worker who was free from these influences and should be able to rise above desperate women workers and the average member of the mass (*srednyi massovik*) and see the deeper causes of the food-supply crisis.[39]

The Bolshevik rhetoricians saw the food-supply dictatorship as an excellent example of the organizational task that the revolutionary movement had to solve, whether that task was called state capitalism or a specifically communist task. As Lenin said:

> Our revolution has now come straight up against the task of implementing socialism in a concrete practical way—and in this lies its inestimable service. It is precisely now, and particularly in relation to the most important question—the question of bread—that the necessity [of these things becomes] clearer than clear: an iron revolutionary political authority; the dictatorship of the proletariat; the organization of the collection, transport, and distribution of products on a

37. Trotsky, *KVR*, 1:68–72 (speech of 4 June 1918), 90–91 (speech of 9 June 1918). The Bolsheviks' attitude toward the Left SRs was more lenient: they were generally seen as sincere but stupid.

38. Lenin, *PSS*, 36:409 (speech of 4 June 1918).

39. Zinoviev, *Khleb, mir i partiia*, 12–13, 18–20 (speech of 18 May 1918).

mass, national scale with a registration of the consumption
needs of tens and hundreds of millions of people and with a
calculation of the condition and results of production for this
year and for many years ahead.[40]

The class-war definition of the food-supply crisis not only gave the
"conscious workers" and other supporters of the soviet authority a visible
enemy in the form of kulak saboteurs; it also gave the central authority a
rod of discipline to apply to these same supporters since indiscipline in time
of war is unforgivable. Thus Lenin, in the same paragraph as that of the
passage just quoted, used the necessity of a grain monopoly to refute those
who did not see the necessity of a state power in the transition from
capitalism to communism—a state power that would be mercilessly severe
not only to the bourgeoisie but also (perhaps more important) to all the
"disorganizers of authority."

All these themes were combined in an appeal issued by the Council of
People's Commissars on 29 May. After noting how the bourgeoisie was
trying to use the famine to enslave the workers even further, the appeal
went on to explain that the grain monopoly was needed to resolve the
crisis. And if the monopoly was necessary, a further conclusion was ines-
capable: "Only the state in the person of the central authority can cope
with this most difficult task." And the state could only do its job if independent purchases were not allowed, for this would merely represent one
group of starving people tearing food away from another. "Sensible centralization" required discipline: "The grain monopoly will give positive
results only when all directions coming from the center are unques-
tioningly fulfilled in the localities [and] when local organs of the authority
carry out, not an independent food-supply policy, but the policy of the
central authority in the interests of the whole starving population."

By way of compensation for this renunciation of independent purchases, the appeal opened the possibility of actively joining in a crusade
against the kulak:

> The kulaks do not want to give grain to the starving, and will
> not give any, no matter what concessions are made by the
> state.
>   Grain must be taken from the kulaks by force.
>   There must be a crusade against the village bour-
> geoisie. . . .
>   Merciless war against the kulaks!
>   In this slogan—salvation from starvation in the immediate

40. Lenin, *PSS*, 36:358–59 (*O golode*, 22 May 1918).

future; in this slogan—salvation and deepening of the conquests of the revolution![41]

The worker detachments were also seen as a means of building a new state organization. Lenin called on the "advanced worker" in the food-supply detachments to be a "leader of the poor, chief (*vozhd'*) of the village laboring masses, builder of the state of labor."[42] Trotsky exhorted the workers to emulate Western superiority in organization. Although all belligerents had been devastated by the war and were low on grain supplies, the Western countries had avoided famine by weighing available supplies to the last ounce and distributing them according to the directives of the state authority. As for Russia, "there *is* grain in the country, but to our shame, the working class and the village poor have not yet learned the art of administering state life."[43]

This perspective was a wider reflection of the food-supply officials' goal of using the worker detachments as a means of disciplining the food-supply apparatus. In a similar way the food-supply officials' professional view of the Committees of the Poor as a continuing base for the food-supply apparatus was generalized by the Bolshevik leaders, who saw the committees, potentially at least, as "secure cadres of conscious communists."[44]

The Committees of the Poor were an attempt to bypass or discipline the peasant village soviets, and class-war rhetoric performed its greatest service for the Bolsheviks in justifying this embarrassing attack on "soviet sovereignty." In practice the Bolsheviks were conceding the validity of the criticism of the whole idea of a soviet-based political order, namely, that local soviets were an entirely inadequate base for a centralizing "firm authority." By labeling the peasant soviets as kulak soviets, they could picture a retreat as a forward movement. A centralizing bureaucrat like Tsiurupa was happy to use revolutionary phrases about civil war to accomplish his own pressing purposes. In response to Left SR criticism of the attack on the local soviets, Tsiurupa said he would be happy to rely on the soviets, but "if the soviets call congresses that remove the grain monopoly and the fixed prices—if they refuse to carry out the state plan in the name of purely local interests—if they gather up grain in their own hands and continue to hold this grain in their hands—then it is clear that we must fight with such soviets, [and] we will struggle with such congresses right

41. *Dekrety,* 2:348–54.
42. Lenin, *PSS,* 36:363 (22 May 1918).
43. Trotsky, *KVR,* 1:76–77 (speech of 9 June 1918).
44. Sverdlov, *Izbrannye proizvedeniia,* 181–84 (Central Executive Committee speech of 20 May 1918). This speech was given prior to the legislation on the Committees of the Poor, but its theme was the need for splitting the village.

up to imprisonment and the sending of troops, to the final and extreme forms of civil war."[45]

Class-war rhetoric also covered up a profound suspicion of the political tendencies of the poor peasants and a fear that the kulaks could provide an alternative leadership for the peasants. Food Supply Commissariat official Aleksei Sviderskii justified the "material incentives" given to peasant informers in these terms:

> The village poor, not understanding their own interests or the existing situation, and in general very often not realizing what is really happening, very often act at the behest of the kulaks. They help and defend the kulaks so that no grain is taken, since [otherwise] they themselves will have no bread. The kulaks seek to use this; they start selling grain at a low price in an attempt to give the poor peasant an interest in having grain surpluses remain with the kulaks.[46]

So it seems that the only thing worse than a kulak selling at high prices is a kulak selling at low prices. The same analysis is given in more general terms in Sverdlov's speech: the reason, says Sverdlov, that we must hasten to split the village and integrate the peasants into our own organization is that otherwise the kulaks will get there first and unite the village against us. Perhaps because Sverdlov, an urban party organizer, was further removed from village realities than the food-supply officials, the incongruity in his speech between two images of the poor peasants is so pronounced as to be comic in effect. On the one hand, they were disciplined fighters for the revolution and worthy brothers in arms of the urban workers; on the other hand, they had to be kept by force of arms from turning into a drunken mob.[47]

Bolshevik class-war rhetoric was ultimately based on the essentially political nature of the Leninist terms for the peasantry: the peasants were divided according to their attitude toward the revolution and toward those who spoke in its name. It is inexact to say that these terms were politicized: they had never been anything but political. Their sociological content simply offered clues on where to look for friends or enemies. The kulaks could almost be defined as the natural organizers of village solidarity against the outside world, and as the above citations show, the Bolsheviks not only accepted this view but made it the basis of their policy toward the village.

45. Central Executive Committee, 4th *sozyv*, 9 May 1918, 259–61.
46. Central Executive Committee, 4th *sozyv*, 11 June 1918, 406–7.
47. Sverdlov, *Izbrannye proizvedeniia*, 181–84.

If there is one term that sums up the interconnection between the themes I have been discussing, it is *registration.* Starting as a technical term, registration came to symbolize many of the hopes of the Bolshevik movement, and it was a constant refrain in Bolshevik rhetoric in 1918. It was first of all an integral part of the grain monopoly: enforcing the obligation to sell to the state all surpluses required accurate knowledge of each person's supplies. Moreover, the loss of the Ukraine and the deepening food-supply crisis made "clearer than clear" the need for "the strictest possible registration." But registration also linked the grain crisis to the general state-capitalist task of a centralized organization of the economy since the content of state capitalism could be briefly summarized as "registration and monitoring." This formulation also showed why state-capitalist organization was the threshold of socialism: a proper registration of available supplies was needed for truly socialist distribution. Not only grain was to be put on register; industrial items were also to be mobilized in this way and made available for commodity exchange, and this required more centralization of control over these items. In addition, registration pointed toward the class struggle since the kulaks and other disorganizers were hostile to registration and likely to sabotage it. The main purpose of splitting the village was to gain "alert eyes" for registration: the class war was primarily a war for information.

CRITIQUE OF THE FOOD-SUPPLY DICTATORSHIP

The rhetoric used by the Bolsheviks to present and justify the food-supply dictatorship reflected their whole view of the revolution. The same can be said of the critique of the Bolshevik program put forth by the Left SRs and the Mensheviks, who constituted the loyal soviet opposition at this point and were still able to present their case in the Central Executive Committee. These two opposition parties were themselves deeply opposed in outlook, and it is probably true that each of them had more in common with the Bolsheviks than they had with each other. But their critique of the food-supply dictatorship had one point in common: they both lashed out at the Bolsheviks' primitivism and propensity to solve complex problems by means of crude force and heavy-handed centralization. The two parties had very different ideas about where the important complexities lay, and each defended the claims of their own specialists to be able to handle these complexities. The Left SR specialists were members of the SR-dominated village soviets, whom the Left SRs regarded as experts in peasant class relations, whereas the Menshevik specialists were economists and food-supply experts like Groman.

The essence of the Left SR position was the defense of the independence of the village soviets, the latest incarnation of the village solidarity that the populist tradition had always celebrated. The Left SRs felt that the kulaks were an isolated and hated minority and hardly likely to dominate free soviets. The majority of the peasants—the "laboring peasantry"—genuinely supported worker-peasant sovereignty, and it was a mistake to stifle their initiative by imitating tsarist bureaucratism or, even worse, to antagonize them by sending out requisition squads. The proper course was rather to carry out energetically the laws on land equalization and to rely on the "state sense" of the local democratically elected authorities. Let policy be determined at the center, the Left SRs argued, but let it be carried out in a decentralized manner.

What particularly pained the Left SRs was the Bolsheviks' irresponsible use of the SRs' two-part division of the peasantry. The SRs used the model to emphasize the *unity* of the majority of the peasantry; the Bolsheviks temporarily adopted it to stress the sharpness of the *split* within the peasantry (without the fuzziness created by the assumption of a large swing group in the middle) and thus to stress the necessity and expediency of resorting to splitting tactics and the use of force. But the Bolsheviks were hardly likely to apply force constructively, said the Left SRs, as long as they relied on such a vague and inaccurate understanding of the kulak as they displayed in the Central Executive Committee debates. Obviously not everyone with a marketable surplus was a kulak: only those totally ignorant of the village would so believe. Who was or was not a kulak was a question to be decided by knowledgeable experts, namely, the local soviets, who would decide "on the basis of a whole range of complicated and delicate considerations" of which only locals could be aware. But the Bolsheviks proposed to send detachments composed of the dregs of the working class, people whose hunger had overcome their sense of honor to such an extent that they were ready to attack the laboring population of the villages.[48] Of course force should be applied against the real kulaks, acknowledged the Left SRs, but to do that in a crude and ignorant way would surely lead to a general throat cutting and discredit the revolutionary authority.

The Left SRs asserted that if the Bolsheviks were absolutely determined to split the village along class lines, they should do it in a respectable way and divide the classes by means of production (land and equipment), not by means of consumption (grain surpluses). As a result of Bolshevik bungling and paranoia about kulak influence on the peasantry, the exact opposite of

48. Central Executive Committee, 4th *sozyv*, 9 May 1918, 254–56 (Karelin).

what they intended would be achieved: the otherwise isolated kulaks would get a new lease on life as the village formed a united front against what would be perceived as a marauding band from the cities. As the Left SR B. V. Kamkov summed it up: "Out of all the ways to fight with the famine, [the Bolshevik food-supply dictatorship] is the least likely to achieve its aim. . . . You do not know the village and you do not know how to fight the kulaks and as a result you are supporting them."[49]

Beyond these tactical arguments, the Left SRs had a deeper objection to what they regarded as Bolshevik dogmatism. They felt that the Bolshevik class-war rhetoric betrayed a willingness to shove alien urban schemes down the throats of the villagers. The Left SR V. A. Karelin interpreted the Bolshevik slogan *class war in the villages* to mean "up against the wall, I'm applying the principle of class struggle to you."[50] And Spiridonova parodied Bolshevik determination to clothe their emergency measures in revolutionary rhetoric: "Comrade Bolshevik-peasants, take these thick books of the Marxists and you will understand why punitive expeditions are being sent out." At bottom was the vindication of the peasants' right to full political and cultural equality with the urban workers: "We declare that the peasantry also has an independent way of life and a right to a historical future."[51]

The Mensheviks did not share the Left SR enthusiasm for the local soviets and wondered why the Left SRs could not see the necessity of preserving the "ties that united the different parts of Russia into one integral organism."[52] Although accepting the Bolshevik goal of centralization and organization, the Mensheviks felt that the Bolsheviks were entirely incapable of achieving it because of their political methods. The heart of the Menshevik critique was the assertion that Bolshevik exclusiveness and demagoguery on the political level made effective economic organization impossible. The Bolsheviks rejected a broad socialist coalition, harassed the opposition press, restricted the electorate, and in general resorted to "civil-war methods." At the same time they proclaimed "all sovereignty to the soviets," a policy that had the predictable result of destroying the ability of the center to carry out effective policy. And in their desperate attempt to save the situation, the Bolsheviks continued to refuse to share power; hence recentralization led to heavy-handed and ineffective bureaucratism.

49. Fifth Congress of Soviets, 5 July 1918, 74–77.
50. Central Executive Committee, 4th *sozyv,* 9 May 1918, 262.
51. Fifth Congress of Soviets, 5 July 1918, 58–59. "Independent way of life" is a desperate paraphrase of *zhizneustoichivo.*
52. Central Executive Committee, 9 May 1918, 256–58 (Dan).

Certainly localism was a problem, but the Bolshevik diagnosis of that problem as stemming from kulak influence was simply mythology. Any democratically elected local government would show the same localist tendencies, said Iulii Martov, and there was only one weapon against them: "independent and free deliberation, and most important, the independent manifestation of public opinion." Unwilling to countenance this openness, the Bolsheviks overreacted to localism: "Without enlistment of the broad masses [that is, without universal suffrage], you will be tossed like a squirrel in a treadmill between ultra-anarchist ideas and a bureaucratism that sounds like a sour joke in the ear of the workers to whom you promised to give 'all sovereignty to the soviets.' "[53]

One political advantage of the Mensheviks was that their specialists in food supply and other economic areas were clearly a more prestigious group than the Bolsheviks could produce—indeed in 1917 the Bolsheviks had simply taken over the program of Groman and his followers. The Mensheviks tried to press their advantage by stressing the technical incompetence of the Bolsheviks: what good was centralization if the Bolsheviks did not have the bureaucratic wherewithal to make use of the opportunity? "Why your bureaucrats [*chinovniki*] should be more skillful and intelligent than the old ones, we do not know: practice has shown that they are much more venal, more dishonorable, and more corrupt than the old bureaucrats." (The speaker here, Rafael Abramovich, was called to order at this point by Sverdlov.)[54]

The Bolshevik response was to extol the virtues of the "modest workers [*rabotniki*]" who were "pushed forward [*vydvinutye*] by the masses." Lenin admitted that "the workers begin to learn slowly and of course with mistakes—but it is one thing to spout phrases and another to see how gradually, month after month, the worker [*rabochii*] grows into his role, starts to lose his timidity, and feels himself the ruler."[55] A remark made by N. Orlov about the first food-supply congress in January expresses the underlying clash of attitudes:

> One of the authoritative food-supply officials [Groman?] attached to the group that walked out of the Congress announced in a session of the socialist group of employees of the old Ministry of Food Supply that members of the Congress

53. Central Executive Committee, 4th *sozyv*, 27 May 1918, 328–30 (Martov).
54. Central Executive Committee, 4th *sozyv*, 27 May 1918, 330–32. Abramovich's attack was even more embarrassing because he quoted an intra–Bolshevik party circular confirming his analysis.
55. Shlikhter, Third Congress of Soviets, 15 January 1918, 71–72. Lenin, *PSS*, 36:515, 5 July 1918.

"were people who sincerely despised all knowledge and hated all bearers of knowledge." In that heated time, it was difficult to expect an objective appraisal from people, especially from those who had chosen the enviable part of "sincerely not understanding" any creative outburst and who were deeply contemptuous of people striving to realize their desires in reality.[56]

The Mensheviks felt that energetic ignorance was no substitute for competent experts responsive to informed public opinion. The Bolsheviks were returning to an illusion of tsarism when they relied on giving wide power to commissars—a sort of food-supply governor-general—and sending them out as troubleshooters, acting in defiance of economic laws and the need for careful coordination.[57] Given their reliance on these methods, the Bolsheviks were incapable of actually carrying out the grain monopoly. Although the Mensheviks were even more closely associated than the Bolsheviks with the monopoly and the need for extensive economic organization, they reluctantly concluded that a paper monopoly was worse than none at all: why prohibit the people from providing for themselves if the government is incapable of providing them with the food they need? The Mensheviks therefore advocated certain concessions in regard to prices and the right of independent purchase; the Bolsheviks seized on these and called the concessions a capitulation to the capitalists and the kulaks.

Just as Bolshevik political methods made economic recovery impossible, Bolshevik economic methods made further political degradation inevitable. In particular, the accelerating inflation provided an economic analogue to the disintegration of central authority. Semyon A. Falkner, one of Groman's group, argued that the inflation created an irresistible economic pressure to break the increasingly unrealistic prices fixed by the state and that this pressure realized itself in the sackmen:

> True, the fixed price usually entails a *personal* responsibility for breaking it, established by penal sanction in the law. But the realization of these threats requires a powerful state organization that penetrates into all cells of the social organism. [It must be] powerful not only from the physical volume of forces and means at its disposal but from the psychological training and unbribability of its agents.
>
> But it is in the epoch of revolution and the reconstruction of the state mechanism that these forces are weakened and the

56. Orlov, *Rabota*, 38.
57. Central Executive Committee, 9 May 1918, 256–58 (Dan).

> threats merely hang in the air, only haphazardly striking down
> this or that chance victim.[58]

This description of a coercive apparatus that is both all-embracing and ineffective does seem to apply to the Cheka, which never succeeded in damming the pressures leading to a speculative black market.

A brief mention should be given to critiques advanced by the Right SRs and the Kadets. Only one Right SR put in an appearance during the Central Executive Committee debates on the food-supply dictatorship. This speaker, Disler, boldly accused the Bolsheviks of creating the famine—through the inflation that they had intensified in a desperate attempt to stay in power, through the Brest-Litovsk peace, which deprived Russia of grain areas, through the civil war provoked by Bolshevik methods (the Czech troops in Siberia had just revolted), and finally through the proposed food-supply dictatorship: "These armed detachments will be able to alleviate your thirst for blood, but not the hunger of the population." At this point, as can well be imagined, Disler was deprived of the floor.[59]

I take the Kadet critique from a pamphlet written in England in early 1919 by the émigré Ariadna Tyrkova-Williams. She viewed the Provisional Government's original grain monopoly as a painful wartime necessity, one that later turned out to be a mistake since it was clearly beyond the capacity of the government machinery. The Bolsheviks retained it even after the peace treaty for ideological reasons, although they rejected most other Provisional Government reforms. Tyrkova-Williams also attacked the harassment of the sackmen train passengers by the lawless blockade detachments. (None of the socialist parties raised this point in the spring Central Executive Committee debates, although it had been going on since January.) Similarly, Tyrkova-Williams did not condemn the Committees of the Poor because they distorted the class struggle: rejecting the idea of class struggle altogether, she maintained that the Committees of the Poor were making orderly life impossible by introducing violence into village affairs and giving an opportunity to the village rabble to settle accounts: "Vio-

58. *Trudy pervogo s"ezda*, 31 May 1918, 395–404. To combat inflation and the incoherent system of fixed prices, the Gromanites brought up their old program of an economic regulatory council (to be called the Price Center) on which the various economic interests would be represented so that an "equilibrium" would be established.

59. Central Executive Committee, 4 June 1918, 386–87. This was a joint meeting with the Moscow Soviet and worker groups. The next speaker was Trotsky, who erupted with rage at the implied charge that he was responsible for the Czech uprising; in a speech later that week he called for the removal of the Right SRs from the Moscow Soviet. According to Osipova, the SRs were instigators of peasant revolts. Osipova, *Klassovaia bor'ba*, 317ff.

lence was everywhere rampant, there was no one to complain to, and in any case complaint was useless. When utter lawlessness reigns, people do not complain but fight over their differences." In sum, "The commissaries themselves are powerless amid the anarchy they have created."[60]

How should we evaluate the critique advanced by the parties of the soviet opposition, the Left SRs and the Mensheviks? It cannot be doubted that many of their criticisms of the Bolshevik food-supply dictatorship were well aimed and that the Bolsheviks were forced, in practice if not in words, to recognize the accuracy of their predictions. The "class struggle in the village" did turn into a "throat cutting"; the worker detachments did disintegrate into drunken bands; bureaucratic red tape did damage commodity exchange with the village. But the positive alternatives put forth by the opposition parties were also weak, especially those of the Left SRs, who wanted to rely on independent local soviets and saw a complete solution only in a revolutionary war against Germany to regain the grain-rich regions. The Menshevik contention that only extensive economic regulation in the style of Groman could solve the problem may have been correct, but it was an irrelevant counsel of perfection under the circumstances. The Mensheviks had begun to understand this flaw and were advocating a retreat from attempts to enforce the grain monopoly in its full rigor. The real question is whether Menshevik demands for a government of socialist unity and for unfettered political freedom were compatible with the imperative of imposing order.

Impractical as the positive suggestions of the Left SRs and the Mensheviks may have been, they were at least couched in language that corresponded to the actual content of the proposed programs. The same cannot be said of the Bolsheviks: the rhetorical dissonance between the class-war rhetoric and the actual program of disciplined centralization was vast and difficult to bridge. Having staked their political reputation on "all sovereignty to the soviets," the Bolsheviks could not say out loud that as predicted, it had all been a terrible mistake and sovereignty would now have to be taken away from the soviets. Their rhetorical cover-up was something more than the usual political hypocrisy and euphemism, and it had important consequences. One has already been mentioned: the opposition parties had to be excluded from the soviets so that they would not "sow panic," that is, so they could not point out that the Bolsheviks' new rhetorical clothing was threadbare. The Bolsheviks were caught in a bind:

60. Tyrkova-Williams, *Why Soviet Russia Is Starving*, 11–13, 5–8. The Mensheviks also saw the village soviets as one armed group lording it over the rest. Tyrkova-Williams is somewhat coy about Kadet responsibility for the introduction of the grain monopoly in the first place.

their effort to overcome the crisis of authority depended on public loyalty to a political formula that they themselves no longer fully believed in.

The debates over the food-supply dictatorship in the spring of 1918 have special historical resonance because they mark the point where three visions of the Russian revolution finally parted ways. The intensity with which the Russian intelligentsia believed in the idea of revolution had come in large part from the clash and interplay of these partially conflicting visions of the tasks of the revolution. The spring of 1918 was the end of the road for two of these visions. The revolutionary vision defended by the Left SRs contended that the Russian peasant had something of positive value to contribute to the Russian future. The vision of the February revolution defended by the Mensheviks asserted that the Western model of constitutionalist civilization—not just the technological and organizational dynamism admired by the Bolsheviks—contained many things that Russia must adopt if it were to reach greatness. These visions could not survive the pitiless environment of the time of troubles. The food-supply crisis of 1918 revealed the impoverishment not only of the Russian people but also of the Russian revolution.

1. Bolshevik propaganda poster, 1920: "The workers and the peasants are finishing off the Polish gentry and the barons, but the workers on the home front also have not forgotten about help to the peasant economy. Long live the union of the workers and peasants!" At the bottom: "Week of the Peasant." (From N. I. Baburina, ed., *The Soviet Political Poster, 1917–1980, from the USSR Lenin Library Collection* [Harmondsworth: Penguin, 1985], plate 18.)

Без пилы, топора и гвоздей
ИЗБЫ НЕ ПОСТРОИШЬ,
а их делает рабочий, кото-
рого нужно накормить.

2.   Bolshevik propaganda poster, 1920: "Without a saw, axe, or nails you cannot build a home. These tools are made by the worker, and he has to be fed." (From N. I. Baburina, ed., *The Soviet Political Poster, 1917–1980, from the USSR Lenin Library Collection* [Harmondsworth: Penguin, 1985], plate 21.)

3. "Milk was very hard to get, and the women and children waited sometimes overnight for a small supply." (From Orrin Sage Wightman, *The Diary of an American Physician in the Russian Revolution, 1917* [Brooklyn: Brooklyn Daily Eagle, 1928].)

4. "Tobacco, like bread and other necessities, was secured by ticket. This offered a profitable field of speculation for the soldiers." (From Orrin Sage Wightman, *The Diary of an American Physician in the Russian Revolution, 1917* [Brooklyn: Brooklyn Daily Eagle, 1928].)

5. "At Nijni-Novgorod they had established small markets where you could buy almost anything the other man did not want." (From Orrin Sage Wightman, *The Diary of an American Physician in the Russian Revolution, 1917* [Brooklyn: Brooklyn Daily Eagle, 1928].)

6. "At every station the peasants would meet the passing trains with food and milk, often cooked fowl and chicken wrapped in steaming hot towels." (From Orrin Sage Wightman, *The Diary of an American Physician in the Russian Revolution, 1917* [Brooklyn: Brooklyn Daily Eagle, 1928].)

7   Retreat to the Razverstka

I am surprised by the absence of news. Inform me
immediately how much grain has been collected, how many
carloads have been sent, how many speculators and kulaks
have been arrested.

Lenin, to officials in Tula, June 1918

At the end of May 1918 the Council of People's Commissars issued a long
appeal to the population on the subject of food-supply policy. It ended with
these ringing words, which set forth the foundations of the food-supply
dictatorship: "Not one step away from the grain monopoly! Not the
slightest increase in fixed prices for grain! No independent procurement!
All that is steadfast, disciplined, and conscious in a single organized food-
supply order! Unhesitating fulfillment of all directives of the central authority! No separate actions! War on the kulaks!"[1]

But by September these brave slogans could not have been repeated.
The fixed price had been tripled. The grain monopoly had been officially
relaxed to the extent that workers in Moscow were temporarily allowed to
go to the countryside to buy one and a half poods of grain per person—a
measure that disgusted food-supply officials referred to as legalized sackmanism. On a more permanent basis, the worker detachments were allowed to give half of the food they obtained directly to the organization
that sent them: this was in reality heavily taxed independent procurement
rather than state-monopoly purchases. And although the kulaks were still
treated as deadly enemies of the people, the emphasis of peasant policy had
been switched to "neutralization" of the peasant producer, that is, the
middle peasant who was not so much as mentioned in the May appeal.
Attempts had been made to restrain the blockade detachments and the
requisition detachments, and the Committees of the Poor were on the
verge of being disbanded. The only plank that remained of the food-supply
dictatorship was the insistence on a centralized apparatus.

A new system of food supply was built up starting from that one

1. *Dekrety*, 2:353–54.

remaining plank. This system—which I shall call the razverstka system—was the one actually used by the Bolsheviks during the civil war. It was constructed in the period between August 1918, when a spate of new decrees were issued to undo the damage already caused by the food-supply dictatorship, and January 1919, when a national food-supply congress declared that the razverstka would be the basis of future food-supply work.

The turning point can be conveniently dated 2 August 1918, when Lenin wrote a series of "food-supply theses" that guided the drafting of the August decrees on food-supply policy. The Bolsheviks could not afford to call general attention to what they were doing because of the potential political embarrassment caused by the retreat from the food-supply dictatorship, announced with so much fireworks in the spring, and Lenin prefaced his August theses with the remark that "part of these measures should be in decrees, part in enactments without publication."

Most of the features of the new system are at least foreshadowed in Lenin's August theses. His basic goal is in sharp contrast to the crusade of the spring—"to neutralize the greatest possible number of peasants during the civil war." Lenin went on to advocate higher fixed prices for grain; a greater use of cooperatives and a greater reliance on commodity exchange; a tax in kind (*naturnalog*); temporary permission for workers to get a personal supply of one and a half poods; greater discipline in blockade and food-supply detachments; and concessions to railroad workers in view of their economic importance. His reluctance is revealed in the many ways these concessions were hedged: a concession was to be only temporary, or only for certain groups, or under careful monitoring, or taken back in some other way.[2]

The new political orientation was thus declared at the top levels of government, but the practical methods used to build up the razverstka system came out of local experience in food-supply work. Shlikhter's efforts in Viatka province in the summer of 1918, written up two years later by N. Orlov, reveal the problems that faced the early pioneers of the razverstka method.[3] Orlov begins by describing the collapse of the food-supply mechanism during the chaotic summer of 1918. Local food-supply organs were hardly working, and the city population strongly resented any interference with local trade, saying of the Bolsheviks that "they themselves give nothing, while interfering with private deliveries." In the city

---

2. Lenin, *PSS*, 37:31–33. In Baku the failure of the Bolsheviks to carry out an effective retreat from the food-supply dictatorship was one reason for their political isolation and defeat. Suny, *Baku Commune*, 297ff.

3. N. Orlov, *Sistema prodovol'stvennoi zagotovki* (Tambov, 1920). Further details can be found in Iu. K. Strizhkov, "Iz istorii vvedeniia prodovol'stvennoi razverstki," *Istoricheskie zapiski* 71 (1961).

there were strikes, and in the village there were riots. One main reason for the riots was the worker detachments, which were sent out barely prepared and which abused the authority given to them. These abuses created fertile ground for anti-Bolshevik agitation against "those Jews and Germans sitting in Moscow," agitation that found willing listeners among those who "easily confused the soviet authority with some drunken vagabond, accidentally occupying the post of commander of a requisition detachment." Prices had skyrocketed; in the first half of 1918 the price of rye went up 178 percent and oats 161 percent. But the peasants quickly learned that money was depreciating in value and grain appreciating; it was best to hold on to the latter.

Viatka province was an especially clear example of disintegration. The main brake on procurement was the food-supply organs themselves, which completely ignored directives from above and set their own prices. Two provincial soviet congresses called for the removal of fixed prices altogether. Sackmanism took on vast proportions and even found official protection: when Viatka tried to set up border patrols, the soviet of neighboring Kazan province protested and even sent troops to make sure the sackmen were not hindered. (Kazan was already notorious for declaring free trade within its borders.)

In late June Shlikhter arrived on the scene with special powers as an agent of the center. Few forces were available for him, and he quickly decided that the worker detachments were not an appropriate procurement apparatus. The detachments could serve as a "real force" (coercive backup) but not as procurement agents themselves. The most experienced available force was the seventeen agents of the Moscow Region Food-Supply Committee, an organization dominated by anti-Bolshevik socialist food-supply professionals from the Provisional Government period. They advocated a centralized apparatus but saw themselves playing a leadership role that Shlikhter (who called them ideologues of sackmanism) was reluctant to grant them. There was also an inefficient delegation of the food-supply organization of the railroad workers, Prodput'. Finally, there were ten to fifteen "instructors" sent out to the detachments by the Food-Supply Commissariat. Orlov pays them a rather cool compliment by saying they were interested in an honorable career, and Shlikhter in a footnote took even that back, saying that with only one exception they were "worthless trash." Shlikhter's conclusion: "Without the assistance of the peasantry it would be impossible to accomplish anything, and the practice of simple raids on the village and of armed requisition was a bad one."

Perhaps overdramatically, Orlov traces the idea of the razverstka to a meeting of representatives of all these forces held in Sarapul'skii county on 22 July 1918. (Shlikhter himself was not present.) Local officials gave various excuses for the hopeless food-supply situation. Work on registration had started late. A commodity-exchange policy was required, except that there were no commodities to exchange, and besides, as one of Shlikhter's men said, "We as socialists cannot practice individual commodity exchange."

Then stepped forth a "food-supply Columbus"—S. A. Sukhikh, chairman of the county peasant soviet. Sukhikh started off with a declaration characteristic of the early soviet period but soon to go out of style: he would recognize the decrees of the central soviet authority only insofar as they coincided with the interests of the peasantry. He went on to criticize the detachments who took grain without distinguishing between rich and poor and thereby discredited soviet sovereignty. He noted that the local soviets had been successful in obtaining grain at the uncontrolled market prices until this practice was forbidden by higher officials.

Sukhikh then made the following suggestion. The revolutionary government should retreat from its principles a bit for the sake of the revolutionary cause. It should assign a grand total to each district soviet and tell them that if this amount is not turned in by a certain date, everyone on the executive committee will suffer. Both money and goods would be given in exchange for the grain, and the district soviet would control their distribution. A small force would be sent around to inspire respect (*dlia ostrastki*). The logic of the new method was to deliver an ultimatum but also to show a willingness to meet the peasant halfway: force would only be used if no corresponding willingness was shown on the other side. Sukhikh's suggestion was accepted on an experimental basis.

Orlov goes on to describe the negotiation between the food-supply officials and the peasant representatives about the total amount of the razverstka and the distribution of this amount to lower levels. Shlikhter agreed to leave a considerable percentage of the razverstka for local needs. Shlikhter's basic principles were "a razverstka based on approximate data and the razverstka's reliance on the assistance of local revolutionary forces." These local forces did not include the Committees of the Poor. A Shlikhter memorandum noted that in one county "there are few poor peasants and almost no village Committees of the Poor." Orlov felt that this description could be generalized to all the southern grain-surplus counties of Viatka so that the food-supply authorities had to do without an "internal tax screw [*nalogovyi press*]."

Results were good, and promised to be better, but the whole process was cut short by a peasant uprising. Orlov is frank about the reasons for this uprising. Viatka province had never had many landlords, thus removing one motive for loyalty to the soviet authority. Then the food-supply dictatorship sent in the requisition detachments. Orlov's language in criticizing the detachments is strong but shows as well the ambivalent attitude of even a sympathetic townsman toward the peasantry: the detachments "did not even explain what was going on or ask the advice of his majesty, the peasant with grain [*khlebnyi muzhichok*]." The detachments also caused scandal by drunkenness and disrespectful behavior. The peasants were especially infuriated at being forced to make deliveries at the height of the harvest season.

The harassment of the sackmen also angered the peasants. Unlike most Bolshevik accounts, Orlov did not explain this reaction merely as a lament for losing a chance to speculate—the peasants saw many of the sackmen as hungry individuals trying to survive. It was not only greed that caused protests but "the just indignation of an honest man." The peasants could not understand how the food-supply authorities could profess to be taking the grain for the hungry when they were persecuting these obviously hungry people. Thus (in the words of a local observer) "as soon as it became known that a detachment had appeared in one county, in another county the organization of resistance began."

Peasant dissatisfaction meant that a minor case of insubordination in a military unit turned into an uprising that swept across the province and made contact with a major SR uprising in Ufa. The search was on for Shlikhter and his friends, who had to leave the province in a hurry. Orlov concluded that it was too bad Shlikhter and his razverstka methods could not have come earlier, for the government might have avoided both drunken commissars and wild, aimless uprisings.[4]

In Shlikhter's Viatka experiment we see already the central features of the razverstka system and its contrasts with the food-supply dictatorship. Instead of a strategy based on class struggle and overcoming sabotage, the razverstka system aimed at neutralization of the peasantry and possibly even a partnership with it. Instead of registration of each producer's grain supplies, it started with an approximation of the total amount needed by the state, which was divided up and assigned to lower levels until it reached the individual peasant. Instead of relying on enlistment of popular forces, it resorted to methods of collective responsibility and put its main effort into building up a professional, centralized apparatus.

RELATIONS WITH THE PEASANTRY

Because of the chaos of revolution and then the pressures of civil war, the Bolsheviks had to take much from the peasants and give little in return.

4. Sukhikh was himself killed in the fall. L. A. Zubareva, *Khleb Prikam'ia* (Izhevsk, 1967).

For this reason they were anxious not to irritate the peasants any more than was absolutely necessary. In the rhetoric of class relations this caution was signified by the return of the middle peasant, a figure conspicuous by his absence during the phase of the food-supply dictatorship. The theory of the wavering middle peasant allowed the Bolsheviks to come to grips with the real peasant who was not particularly interested in a socialist revolution but was willing enough to fulfill his obligations to the state if they seemed at all reasonable or (perhaps more important) if the state promised not to harass him after they were fulfilled.

The middle peasant also allowed the Bolsheviks to switch to a longer-term orientation toward the peasant as producer. The food-supply dictatorship had been based on the assumption that a small minority of semipeasants had for commercial purposes collected huge reserves of grain from previous harvests. As the horizons of the Bolsheviks expanded beyond survival until the next harvest, they realized that it would take "whole decades" to get beyond single-owner farming, and therefore they had to increase productivity on single-owner farms now, in order to "mitigate the food-supply crisis . . . that cursed question."[5]

This new line on the middle peasant was ratified in general political terms by the Eighth Party Congress in 1919, but concrete measures to conciliate grain producers had been taken since August 1918, when the fixed price for grain was tripled. Because the Bolsheviks had strongly criticized the Mensheviks in May for suggesting an increase in the fixed price, this move was potentially embarrassing. But in general no one noticed, and the price tripling did not become a political issue. This lack of response shows the acceleration of the economic breakdown. In 1916 a major political battle had been fought among the elite over price raises of 10 to 20 percent. In 1917 the price doubling caused a political convulsion and provided a powerful argument for the overthrow of the Provisional Government. In 1918 the price was tripled; not only was there no protest, but when Zinoviev referred to the issue in a speech before Petrograd workers—hard-pressed consumers—he apologized for the delay in raising the price.[6]

The Bolsheviks also relied more heavily on the cooperatives and went out of their way to advertise this reliance as a concession to the middle peasant. It was an attempt to get extra political mileage out of a policy that would have been adopted anyway for technical reasons. The state food-supply apparatus simply could not take on the entire task of the collection

5. Eighth Party Congress, 227–42 (Kuraev).
6. G. Zinoviev, *O khlebe nasushchnom* (Petrograd, 1918).

and, especially, distribution of a whole range of foodstuffs and industrial consumer items. Relations between local food-supply committees and the cooperatives duplicated the relations under earlier governments between local officials and private dealers—much suspicion and hostility, despite the urgings of central authorities. Even before the Bolshevik revolution the breakdown of the market had made the cooperatives economically depen-dent on the state; their absorption into the Bolshevik food-supply appara-tus completed the process.[7]

Within the limits of their power the Bolsheviks tried to cut through their own red tape and mobilize available industrial items to exchange for grain. In a December speech Lenin demanded that the amount of goods available for the peasants be increased tenfold and advocated a characteris-tic solution to the problem of red tape: put one person in charge (instead of a collegium) and make that person responsible to the point of being shot in the event of failure.[8]

As late as May 1919 an appeal to the peasants of Kostroma declared that a full equivalent for peasant grain was being provided. After asking the peasants to fulfill their "moral duty to the socialist fatherland and the Red Army," the appeal told the peasants not to worry about who got more, the worker or the peasant: "the state demands from the peasant and for the worker only that amount that the worker can give [in return] to the peasant." This appeal shows the Bolsheviks' effort to allay the peasants' suspicion that a state authority based on the workers was cheating them. A local activist (evidently of peasant origin) described at the Eighth Party Congress how he closed all the shops in his home town, called the peasants in, and showed them the empty shelves to prove to them that the town was not deliberately withholding items from the countryside. Afterward grain deliveries picked up.[9]

The new policy certainly did not imply any letup on the hard line toward the kulak; but now *kulak* was defined even more exclusively in political terms, as someone who resisted the authorities and only for that reason would be mercilessly crushed. The shift can be seen in some dialogue from a story by Mikhail Sholokhov entitled "The Food-Supply

7. Kheisin, *Istoriia*, 226, 260–64; Kabanov, *Kooperatsiia*, 227–57. E. H. Carr exaggerates the importance of the cooperatives to the success of Bolshevik policy in *The Bolshevik Revolution* (New York, 1950–53), 2:227–28, 235ff. On this, see Claus, *Kriegswirtschaft*, 147–49; Chambre, Wronski, and Lasserre, *Les coopératives de consommation en URSS*, 28–32.

8. Lenin, *PSS*, 37:394–401 (speech of 25 December 1918).

9. *Prod. i snab.* (Kostroma), no. 8–10, 15 April and 15 May 1918, 16–17; Eighth Party Congress, 263–64. The possibility of a full equivalent was denied in *Pravda*, 22 June 1919, by a Food-Supply Commissariat official.

Commissar." The scene is a confrontation between the commissar and his kulak father. The father has been arrested for speaking out in the village meeting against giving grain to the Bolsheviks and for beating up two Red Army soldiers. Father and son meet in the courtroom, and the father says bitterly, "Go ahead and loot—you've got the power." The argument heats up as the son replies:

> "We don't loot the poor peasant but we rake away from those who live off other's sweat. You more than anybody squeezed the peasant laborer all your life!"
> "I myself worked day and night. I didn't knock around the wide world like you."
> "Those who work sympathize with the workers' and peasants' sovereignty, but you meet it with a pitchfork."[10]

At first the Bolsheviks tried to combine conciliation of the middle peasant with even further repression of the kulak. Although the Bolshevik leaders were aware that the peasant uprisings of the summer had been provoked by Bolshevik policy and although they were taking steps to change that policy, they were also deeply scared by the conjunction of these uprisings with the civil war that had just broken out. In an appeal of 6 August Lenin and Tsiurupa compared the peasant uprisings inside Russia to the onslaught of the international bourgeoisie outside Russia and concluded, "The answer to the treason and betrayal of 'our' bourgeoisie should be the intensification of merciless mass terror against the counterrevolutionary part of it." Kulaks and rich peasants (*bogatei*) with undelivered surpluses were declared enemies of the people.[11]

In a speech on 11 August before the Petrograd Soviet Zinoviev gave the following admiring account of a detachment in Viatka. The leader of the detachment called the peasants together and said that the Petrograd workers had sent them because the workers had no bread and the peasants did. The workers would take the bread from the kulaks, leave some in the area, and give the peasants town items for the rest. The Committees of the Poor, not the kulak shopkeepers, would distribute these items. "If anyone wants to give peacefully, fine; if not—a bullet between the eyes." The detachment leader then told everybody for the Committees of the Poor to move to the left, and everybody against to the right. What resulted from this sort of thing in Viatka we have seen already.[12]

---

10. The father is shot. The son is killed shortly thereafter in a peasant uprising, partly because his escape is slowed down by his efforts to help a freezing child. The story was written in 1925. *Sobranie sochinenii* (Moscow, 1965–), 1:57–62.
11. *Dekrety,* 3:178–80.
12. Zinoviev, *O khlebe.*

Frustration over the failure to enlist the poor peasants led to an exaggeration of kulak power. The official journal of the Food-Supply Commissariat proclaimed:

> On the one side, [the kulaks'] organizational ability, solidarity, and clear understanding of their own interests; on the other, extreme fragmentation, helplessness, and lack of awareness. The kulaks know precisely what they want, have a definite program of action, and clearly perceive who is friend and who is enemy. In contrast, the peasant masses will smash the landowner's estate today and tomorrow will go to the kulak to give him the authority in the masses' own soviet. "Trofim Semyonich best knows all the rules and can understand best." The kulaks act according to plan, carefully, and with organization, using all the circumstances that life presents. That is their method of struggle.[13]

This fear of the kulak as an alternative leadership for the peasantry led to violent anti-kulak rhetoric, which was used to cover up the loss of independence by the soviets and their transformation into the base of a centralized apparatus. As Zinoviev put it in the fall of 1918, "We are very well aware that we cannot carry through the proletarian revolution without crushing the village kulaks and without annihilating them psychically and, if necessary, physically. . . . The revolution in the village should take the kulak by the throat and strangle him according to all the rules of soviet art; it is precisely for this that we need a genuine, operative worker-peasant machine for strangling kulaks."[14]

This style of rhetoric was hardly compatible with the move toward partnership with the middle peasant. In December 1918 Lenin went out of his way to emphasize that the kulaks would not be completely expropriated in the same way the landowners had been but that any resistance by the kulaks to "necessary measures such as the grain monopoly" would be crushed.[15] The word *kulak* also tended to drop out of official decrees (although top officials still thought in these terms, as can be seen from various early drafts and marginal comments). Bolshevik rhetoric preserved the theory that resistance to the government was caused by inveterate class-based hostility toward the socialist revolution, but in practice the concern of the regime was simply to repress any open opposition that interfered with collecting the razverstka and prevent the formation of any alternative leadership for the peasants. The kulak remained an enemy, but he was no longer the key to resolving the food-supply crisis.

13. *Izv. NKP*, no. 20–21 (October 1918): 52–53.
14. Sixth Congress of Soviets, 89–92.
15. Lenin, *PSS*, 37:360–61 (speech of 11 December 1918).

The new strategy for dealing with the peasantry led to new methods for providing the food-supply apparatus with a secure base in the village. In the chaotic summer of 1918 the Committees of the Poor were found wanting: instead of splitting the village, they united it—in rage and fury against the Bolsheviks. The disillusionment that set in was so rapid that it can be seen happening within the pages of Orlov's 1918 book on food-supply policy. At first Orlov talked proudly of the new revolutionary force called forth by the decree on the Committees of the Poor and denied that the decree entailed any great political cost to the revolution. But by the end of the book enough reports from the localities had come in to show him the extent of the disaster. He now referred to the Committees of the Poor as

> pitifully small, self-seeking and benighted groups of poor peas-
> ants, making claims to *all* the grain of their area and conquer-
> ing the resistance of the entire peasant mass only by help of
> detachments from the cities and the north. . . . In the grain
> regions, where there is a special need for them, they will be
> weak, or the idea behind them will be distorted. In the hungry
> regions, where they will be strong and active, there will be no
> need for them in the fulfillment of the tasks that the legisla-
> tion had in view.[16]

According to Orlov, the Committees of the Poor often kept the grain for themselves, for purposes of speculation, so that "in the place of each large-scale kulak would appear ten petty swindlers." Things came to such a pass that the Committees of the Poor would prevent the owners of grain from delivering it to the state. This is an expressive image of the topsy-turvy world of the Russian time of troubles: kulaks stealing away in the dead of night so that they could give their grain to the state rather than to their hated fellow villagers.

In August 1918 the Bolsheviks sent out instructions ordering the Committees of the Poor to end the harassment of middle peasants. In a survey based on local reports and published in December, however, the most serious charges against the Committees of the Poor seemed to be timidity and sloth.[17] Looking through the pages of the local food-supply publications in a province such as Kostroma, we find many more complaints about lack of initiative than about an excess of militance. The provincial food-supply committee noted that the only time it heard from a Committee of the Poor was when it wanted money; even then so little supplementary

16. Orlov, *Rabota*, 68–75, 366–80.
17. *Izv. NKP*, no. 24–25 (December 1918): 26–30. See also V. N. Aver'ev, *Komitety bednoty* (Moscow, 1933), 2:70–204.

information was given that the provincial committee felt unable to provide financial support. Indeed, the food-supply authorities had only the vaguest idea of how many Committees of the Poor had even been organized, especially on the village level.[18] The authorities were frustrated because even the Committees of the Poor continued to be "kulak-dominated"—in other words, they had failed to break down the solidarity of the village. The situation in Vetchuzhskii county was described as follows:

> It would seem that the Committees of the Poor would play an extremely significant role. At first, however, they were completely disorganized. Even when the detachments applied pressure and the Committees of the Poor were elected, they were new organizations, often consisting of rich peasants, [and as such] they were completely useless for the goals put before them.
>
> In the villages—especially the small ones—practically all peasants are connected by family ties. In one village in Khmelevitskoe district the chairman, members, and secretary of the Committee of the Poor all signed themselves as "Galochkin"; it turned out that the whole village consisted solely of Galochkins, and all were related. Under these conditions there is no chance that Chairman Galochkin will tell us that his close relation the rich Galochkin really has a fifty-pood surplus—no, he will try to cut the figure in half.
>
> And then I would hear conversations like this: "If I show that Sidor Petrov has a hundred-pood surplus, then it will all be taken away, but maybe in the spring Sidor Petrov will help me out and loan me some bread since I can't get by on my half-pood norm." Literally everywhere the unenlightened poor peasant covers up for the rich peasant simply for fear of losing someone who will give loans.
>
> In such cases one must resort to repressive measures such as arresting the Committees of the Poor.[19]

In December 1918 the food-supply commissar in Kazan, D. P. Maliutin, issued a booklet of instructions criticizing the many committees that remained "stillborn." To remedy the situation, committees that showed no sign of life or disobeyed orders on grain delivery would get no money and no city goods. They were reminded that kulaks could not be members and

18. *Prod. i snab.* (Kostroma), no. 11, 1 December 1918; no. 12, 15 December 1918, 14, 27.

19. *Prod. i snab.* (Kostroma), no. 3–4, 1 and 15 February 1919, 35–37. For an example of similar extended families on the Bolshevik side, see V. A. Potapenko, *Zapiski prodotriadnika, 1918–1920 gg.* (Voronezh, 1973), 47.

that making deals with the sackmen or agitating against fixed prices were not activities appropriate to a Committee of the Poor. In cases of stubborn insubordination a "food-supply detachment on special assignment" would be sent out.[20] The exasperated Sverdlov asked in a speech on 14 October: "Only one question arises for us: the necessity of evaluating the performance of the Committees of the Poor as a food-supply organ. In this or that grain collection point the delivery of grain is halted, [and] it turns out that it is the Committee of the Poor that is preventing delivery. If they are not food-supply organs, then what exactly are they needed for?"[21]

Since the Bolshevik leaders naturally did not want to say that the Committees of the Poor had simply been a mistake, they stressed other tasks besides food supply. One of these tasks was leading the village to collective forms of agricultural production, a way of shunting the Committees of the Poor off into a less vital line of activity than food supply. In a speech to a congress of Committees of the Poor at the time of their demise in late 1918, Lenin defined their task as the creation of a new socialist agriculture, but he stressed that it would require a long period of detailed work encompassing many transitional steps and that it could only proceed by raising the consciousness of the rest of the peasantry. This call was as far as possible from the crusade against the kulak of the original food-supply dictatorship.[22]

Another task was more real: providing the Bolsheviks with a wedge in the village. They of course still referred to it as class war in the villages, but little effort was made to hide the facts. As Zinoviev stated, the Committees of the Poor were a small group of unelected people often created by some traveling agitator. Nothing wrong with that, he added: "You can't start a revolution with elections. First you have to deal with the scoundrels." What was important was to have a group of people who knew what they wanted and who pursued a single goal: to give a hitherto urban political authority a secure point of support in the village.[23]

In October 1918 the Bolsheviks announced that the Committees of the Poor would be absorbed by the local soviets. From the Bolsheviks' point of view, nothing in the life of the Committees of the Poor became them like the leaving of it, since the absorption of the committees into the soviet system helped the Bolsheviks change the soviets themselves into some-

20. D. P. Maliutin, *Knizhka v pomoshch krest'ianinu-truzheniku (o komitetakh bednoty)*, 2d. ed. (Kazan, 1918), 26–27.

21. Sverdlov, *Izbrannye proizvedeniia*, 222–26.

22. Lenin, *PSS*, 37:352–54 (speech of 11 December 1918).

23. Zinoviev, *Chto delat' v derevne* (Petrograd, 1919), 3–16; Sixth Congress of Soviets, 86–89.

thing resembling the lowest echelon of a centralized hierarchy. The new soviet could be represented as a meld of the two previous institutions, soviet and Committee of the Poor. Orlov put it this way: "Instead of the old soviet of the peasantry as a whole into which kulaks managed to penetrate 'owing to muzhik darkness,' and instead of the Committees of the Poor, which owing to the same darkness often became a nest of genuine lazy louts—[we see a] unified soviet of deputies elected by the toiling [but not kulak] peasantry."[24]

I agree with Orlov, but I would phrase it differently: from the old soviet came the idea of an institution that would represent the peasant population. From the old Committees of the Poor came both the idea of a task-oriented organ that was the lowest rung of a central hierarchy and the idea of class purity. Under the banner of class purity the central authority gave itself the right to purge local soviets of any voice of opposition—for what better sign of class essence could there be than one's attitude toward the decrees of the workers' and peasants' authority?

A basic aim of the razverstka system was to involve these new soviets in food-supply work. The attitude of the central authorities was the same as that of the tsarist government toward the zemstvos. As the tsarist legal scholar N. M. Korkunov explained: "Local self-government does not imply an opposition between local society and the state nor does it imply their isolation, but rather it is the means for organizing local society in the service of the state."[25] The food-supply official P. K. Kaganovich set forth the same logic: "In essence [the razverstka] was the first attempt at enlisting the district and village soviets in the fulfilling of state tasks. They had previously somewhat considered themselves to be representatives of local interests before the state central authority—it was necessary to compel them to become representatives of state interests before the local population."[26]

Under the razverstka system the local officials were handed a quota and told to fulfill it or else lose their jobs and possibly go to prison. This directive prevented the foot-dragging that was possible under the registration system, when local officials would inform the higher levels that their investigation showed that there was no surplus in their district; indeed,

---

24. *Prodovol'stvennaia politika v svete obshchego khoziaistvennogo stroitel'stva sovetskoi vlasti* (Moscow, 1920), 144–49 (hereafter cited as *Prod. politika*). There is some indication that the Committees of the Poor turned into the food-supply section of local soviets. Potapenko, *Zapiski*, 77.

25. Quoted in George Yaney, "The Imperial Russian Government and the Stolypin Land Reform," Ph.D. diss. (Princeton University, 1961), 274.

26. *Prod. biulletin* (Siberia), no. 2–3, 1 October 1920, 3–6.

they would plead a deficit and ask that extra grain be sent. Members of the local soviet were also supposed to fulfill their obligation before anybody else. This not only refuted any claim that the razverstka was unfulfillable but also gave the soviet members an extra incentive to put pressure on their fellow villagers.

If a local soviet executive committee refused to accept the razverstka quota, pressure could be applied to this small and exposed group of people in their capacity of "bearers of soviet sovereignty." Wider forms of enlistment made it more difficult to do so, and for this reason food-supply officials rejected proposals to convene a special district congress to decide on razverstka distribution. Indeed, it was best to avoid direct contact between the central authorities and the population. If the local soviet carried out the razverstka, all complaints about irregularities would be addressed to them and not to the central food-supply apparatus. A whole village united in protest against the razverstka quota would be more difficult to deal with than individual villagers protesting only against their own particular assignment. These somewhat Machiavellian considerations led the Bolsheviks to adopt traditional tsarist methods of dealing with the peasants through collective responsibility and through a peasant leadership that could be easily pressured.[27]

Somewhat to his surprise Kaganovich found that villages in Simbirsk in 1919 would fulfill their razverstka assignment in order to get their soviet executive committee out of jail. In the summer of 1918 Lenin had been demanding that the rich peasants in a district be taken hostage to ensure full grain deliveries. The Bolsheviks now discovered that more grain could be taken under the razverstka system, when it was the members of elected soviets who were taken hostage.[28]

FROM MONOPOLY TO RAZVERSTKA

One central pillar of the grain monopoly was registration of the grain surplus. The limited supply of grain made registration seem a practical necessity, and the commitment to equality and socialist principles made it seem a moral necessity. Regulation justified the drive of the food-supply dictatorship to split the village and centralize the apparatus: the Committees of the Poor would obtain the necessary information, and the centralized apparatus would then be able to shuffle grain resources on a national scale.

27. P. K. Kaganovich, *Kak dostaetsia khleb* (Moscow, 1920), 16–21; reprinted in *Prod. politika*, 181–85, 242–44.
28. Lenin, *PSS*, 50:144–45; M. Vladimirov, *Udarnye momenty prodovol'stvennoi raboty na Ukraine* (Kharkov, 1921), 9.

The food-supply workers felt that the new political situation had made registration not only necessary but also possible. A food-supply worker in Kostroma writing in the summer of 1918 listed the reasons for the earlier failure of registration in 1917: the best statistical workers were in the army; the continual reorganization of local organs hindered work; the population was hostile to the incessant demand for information (not only by food-supply committees but also by land committees, electoral committees, and the like); hostility was further fanned by the "dark forces"; finally, of course, the peasants were afraid of losing their reserves. But now these reasons had lost their force. The statisticians had returned, and local organs were acquiring experience. Most important, the population was no longer hostile to a government that belonged to the people; it would cooperate now that it saw the necessity of registration.[29]

Various appeals tried to convince the peasants that it was in their interest to continue the revolutionary movement toward putting the whole country on register: "THE CITY HAS ALREADY BEEN PUT ON REGISTER, but without a correct registration of the village, work on commodity exchange is impossible. Citizens, do not hinder registration—with your cooperation, help put in order the provisionment of the Socialist Army, the village, and the town with all that is necessary."[30]

The urgency of registration was intensified for those deficit provinces that were thrown back on their own resources in the summer of 1918. The Food-Supply Commissariat announced that it would not undertake to transport grain to these provinces since it was not satisfied with their efforts to mobilize grain already existing within each province. These provinces were among the first to discover the dilemma expressed by Shlikhter: "Either registration, or grain."[31]

Registration imposed extensive tasks on local officials. Local Committees of the Poor were lucky if they had one literate member, and yet they were asked to carry out a complete enumeration of the population and of each household's harvest, equipment, and items of mass consumption. Special attention was to be given to "known kulaks and those having surpluses from earlier years."[32] These demands were made at a time when official statistical bureaus had only the vaguest idea of the population of a given province.

29. *Prod. i snab.* (Kostroma), no. 3, 1 June 1918, 14–17.
30. Maliutin et al., *Knizhka*, 1st ed. (Kazan, 1918), 29.
31. A. G. Shlikhter, *Agrarnyi vopros i prodovol'stvennaia politika v pervye gody sovetskoi vlasti* (Moscow, 1975), 411–14. These words were written in 1920. On the origins of the razverstka in the deficit provinces, see *Prod. i snab.* (Kostroma), no. 6–7, 15 March and 1 April 1919, 11–13.
32. Maliutin, *Knizhka*, 1st ed. (Kazan, 1918), 12–13.

The problem was not just the lack of trained personnel: local officials did not want to cause trouble, and outsiders were easily fooled. The Kostroma food-supply committee held a county food-supply committee up to scorn because in one district the agent responsible for registration was a priest's son. Chosen because he was "powerful learned" (*silen v gramote*), this young seminarian stuck his head into the peasant's hut, asked what surplus the peasant had, and duly recorded the answer even when he himself knew it was completely absurd. Outsiders to the county were also helpless because of their ignorance of peasant life, agricultural terms, and local conditions. The following example was given of peasant doubletalk: a peasant showed his rye to the food-supply official and said, "Well, I harvested twelve barns worth; for my family I need sixty poods; for sowing, forty poods; to pay my spring debts, ten poods. For the reapers, sixteen of rye for their work, by contract. And for the provision of the carpenters who work here, we have to keep six poods." By the end the food-supply official, his head spinning, agreed that the peasant really had a deficit, not a surplus. The resulting registration was "so fantastic that even the provincial food-supply committees who carried it out and are responsible for its correctness did not dare to rely on it."[33]

It was no wonder that food-supply officials let themselves dream of a "food-supply passport" system: each person would carry a little book with a record of the "entire economic food-supply life" of the bearer.[34] But in reality various attempts were made to simplify registration, all of which failed, as Bolshevik food-supply commissar Kaganovich found in Simbirsk in 1919. At first a complete household-by-household (*podvornyi*) registration was tried but quickly abandoned. It was useless to rely on voluntary declarations: the only truthful ones were made by poor peasants who had something to gain by them. To verify each of these declarations would be an extremely arduous and perhaps impossible task, for the peasants were better at hiding than the Bolsheviks at finding. Besides, why go to all the trouble of getting a figure for a peasant's total supply when most of it would still have to be left with him under the consumption norm?

A new device was then tried out: village (*posel'nyi*) registration based on a test threshing. The idea was to establish the total amount for a village before the harvest was completed and the grain vanished into the peasants' hiding places. A sample field was selected and the amount of grain ex-

33. *Prod. i snab.* (Kostroma), no. 3–4, 1 and 15 February 1919, 35–37; no. 8–10, 15 April and 15 May 1919, 5 (Vetchuzhskii county, circular of 10 April 1919).

34. *Prod. i snab.* (Kostroma), no. 3, 1 June 1918, 14–17. See also *Prod. delo* (Tver), 15 August 1918, 29–30, where the Cheka is to be called in if anyone (especially district soviets) agitates against registration.

tracted from it served as the basis for an estimation of the village total. But the muzhiks simply led the food-supply officials by the nose when carrying out this test threshing. A poor field was chosen for the sample; the threshing was done inefficiently (by striking too hard); the sheaves were shaken on their way to the storehouse so as to lose grain; and of course there was a considerable amount of stealing. The result was that Simbirsk magically changed from a surplus province to a deficit province.

In some localities the officials tried a reregistration and threshed a sample field themselves. This approach was a disaster: less was obtained than during the original village registration. By that time registration had ceased to be a weapon of the authorities and had become a weapon of the peasants, who Kaganovich reported "beat us with our own figures."[35]

Thus the technical difficulties paled before the political one, the absence of peasant cooperation. The October revolution had not altered this situation in the slightest. Various explanations were suggested: kulak agitation, a rational attempt to lay in emergency reserves, the predominance of single-owner agriculture, or simply an expression of maddening peasant contrariness.[36] Whatever the reason and whomever to blame, it was clear that any attempt to proceed on the basis of the enlistment of the population in state tasks and its confidence in the new state authority was doomed to failure.

How then to proceed? Not by building up a statistical pyramid from the bottom but by making a global approximation of the available surplus and simply assigning it to a collectivity to fulfill. Registration gave the state the residual, after deducting a specific consumption norm; the razverstka gave it to the peasant, after deducting a specific state obligation. Harvest statistics came into play only during the bargaining by which this total was broken down and assigned to provinces and counties. In the words of the Food-Supply Commissariat, "the razverstka given to a district is already in and of itself a determination of the surplus."[37]

Although the razverstka was sometimes portrayed as a shortcut to an approximate registration, it was in reality an abandonment of the whole registration strategy. The same can be said about equivalent exchange, another pillar of a proper grain monopoly. The razverstka was presented as a temporary adjustment to an extreme shortage of exchange items. Its motto was "with exchange equivalents if possible, without exchange equivalents if necessary."

35. Kaganovich, *Kak dostaetsia khleb*, 16–18; reprinted in *Prod. politika*, 181–85. See also *Prod. biulletin* (Siberia), no. 2–3, 1 October 1920, 3–6.
36. *Prod. politika*, 189–92 (N. Osinskii).
37. M. I. Davydov, *Bor'ba za khleb* (Moscow, 1971), 136–37.

Since the razverstka was supposed to be based on exchange, there was no paradox in its coexistence with the tax in kind introduced in October 1918. In the minds of officials there was a clear distinction between grain collected under the razverstka and grain collected as a tax for which no compensation was promised. The tax was not supposed to be an exchange transaction but an equalizing measure based on progressive rates. The peasants had more trouble keeping the two distinct since the financial officials who administered the tax used the services of the food-supply apparatus for the physical collection of the grain. More important, the exchange equivalents promised under the razverstka were not forthcoming.[38]

Food-supply officials were quick to acknowledge that the razverstka resembled a tax. N. P. Briukhanov, a top official of the Food-Supply Commissariat, called at the beginning of 1919 for a "wide, obligatory, taxlike razverstka." In a circular sent out to provincial food-supply committees in March 1920, Tsiurupa argued that food-supply organs were asking for the minimum necessary to feed the army and the towns. Therefore "for the peasant there is a direct interest to sow more, for then more will remain to him. With a good harvest and a large sown acreage it could happen that in actuality more than the [consumption] norm will be left to the peasant."[39] The razverstka imposed on other foodstuffs was even more like a tax since in many cases the requested amounts were far below available surpluses.[40] As a food-supply official argued in 1923, the razverstka meant that the "alienation from the population of products for the use of the state took on in factual terms the form of a tax [based on] a complicated [system of] collective responsibility."[41]

Although a tax took grain without compensation, it included a promise from the authorities to stop harassing the peasant once the tax had been

38. The best discussion is I. A. Iurkov, *Ekonomicheskaia politika partii v derevne* (Moscow, 1980), 113–20. See also Kabanov, *Krest'ianskoe khoziaistvo*, 165–74. Malle, *Economic Organization*, 372–73, and Carr, *Bolshevik Revolution*, 2:249, incorrectly imply that the razverstka replaced the civil-war tax in kind.

39. *Prod. i snab.* (Kostroma), no. 3–4, 1 and 15 February 1919; Iu. A. Poliakov, *Perekhod k NEPu i sovetskoe krest'ianstvo* (Moscow, 1967), 251. See also Shlikhter's remarks in *Izv. NKP*, no. 1–2 (January 1919), 19.

40. Frumkin, *Tovaroobmen*, 16–17.

41. S. Bychkov, "Organizatsionnoe stroitel'stvo prodorganov do NEPa," *Prodovol'stvie i revoliutsiia*, 1923, no. 5–6:183–95. A. L. Okninskii, who lived in a Tambov village during the civil war and left before NEP, usually refers to a *prodnalog* (food-supply tax), not a *prodrazverstka*. Although Okninskii wrote his memoirs years later, this is evidence of how the peasants themselves viewed the matter. Okninskii, *Dva goda sredi krest'ian: vidennoe, slyshannoe, perezhitoe v tambovskoi gubernii* (Riga, 1936).

paid. The razverstka system moved in this direction as well. A decree dated 22 October 1919 promised that a village that fulfilled its quota would be freed from any supplementary demands and from the mill tax. (This promise shows that food-supply officials knew that it was impossible for the razverstka to get the entire surplus.) The village would also be given priority attention not only in the distribution of available industrial items but also in any other petition it might bring before the authorities. The village would be freed from searches: "Food-supply army members and food-supply detachment members should not even show themselves in such villages for whatever reason."[42]

The central Bolshevik metaphor for the razverstka was a loan given by the peasants to the state and to industrial workers. The state would invest the loan in victory and in industrial reconstruction along socialist principles and thus be able to repay it at a high rate of interest. (The Bolsheviks themselves did not stress the commercial origins of the metaphor, avoiding words like *invest* and *interest*.) The loan metaphor was an application of the exchange imagery of the grain monopoly to the reality of a tax. Under the monopoly the state was supposed to buy the grain, not simply take it. Although the Bolsheviks had nothing to give in exchange for the grain and therefore took it without compensation, they did promise future benefits. In reality they were no different from any wartime government that taxed the population while pointing out the benefits of victory.

A third pillar of the monopoly strategy was prohibition of independent purchases. In this area, as well, rhetorical devotion to the monopoly accompanied practical compromises. Industrial workers, the most influential category of urban consumer, were impatient with restrictions on individual and collective purchase. They disliked the requirements imposed by the food-supply officials—to register themselves in various central offices, to accept the authority of local officials, and to leave part of the grain in the localities. They wanted to be able to deliver the grain directly to the factory that sent them without going through the food-supply apparatus. The workers also wanted the list of nonmonopolized products available for direct independent purchase to be as wide as possible. They strongly resented the blockade detachments that interfered with the workers' transport of food despite central directives prohibiting such harassment.[43]

The food-supply officials were wary lest the workers become a centrifugal force of disorganization. Although accepting that the energy of the

42. *Dekrety,* 6:222–23.
43. Most of these aims can be inferred from Zinoviev's speech of 11 August 1918, in which he defended the provisions of the August decree on workers' detachments. Zinoviev, *O khlebe.*

consumers would add a necessary "corrective" to work in the surplus regions, the food-supply officials wanted to make sure that they were strictly monitored so that they did not destroy the fixed price by competitive bidding—the bane of food-supply officials since 1914. If that happened, the system of enlisting consumers would "change from a corrective of the grain monopoly (a primitive corrective, to be sure) . . . to a negation of the idea of the monopoly—the idea of the equitable distribution of food among all citizens."[44]

The contours of food-supply policy during the civil-war years wavered as the political leadership adjusted to the relative strengths of centrifugal and centralizing forces. One struggle was over the division of foodstuffs into various purchasing categories. The highest category was fully monopolized basic foods such as grain products, sugar, meats, and salt. These were subject to a razverstka, and nonstate purchasers were excluded. The next category might be called a passive monopoly: only state purchasers were allowed, but sale by the producer was not mandatory. For the time being, this category, which included dairy products, vegetables, poultry, and mushrooms, relied on voluntary sale, although full monopolization was still the goal. Foodstuffs that were not distributed to consumers by state organizations were at least theoretically available to nonstate purchasers.

Particular food items shuttled between these categories according to pressure from consumers and the organizational ambitions of the food-supply apparatus. Potatoes, for example, started off in the middle category of passive monopoly. Halfway through the 1918–1919 procurement year they were moved down to the category of items available for independent purchase. This designation proved unsatisfactory and at the beginning of the 1919–1920 procurement year they achieved the status of an obligatory razverstka.

Another struggle was over the freedom of action granted to individual and collective purchasers. Individual purchase was furthest from the monopoly, yet several times worker pressure compelled the government to permit individual workers to go to the countryside to obtain a limited amount of grain for themselves and their families. The food-supply officials felt that these "one-and-a-half-pooders" were little better than sackmen, and they tried to restrict such concessions as much as possible. The political leadership did not dispute that this practice was an unfortunate derogation from the principles of the monopoly. Lenin said that permission to make individual purchases was a "rotten concession," although a politically necessary one.[45]

44. Orlov, *Rabota*, 83–88. See also *Izv. NKP*, no. 1–2 (January 1919), 27; Vladimirov, *Udarnye momenty*, 5–6.
45. Lenin, *PSS*, 50:297 (April 1919). For the workers' joy at these concessions,

There was more controversy over the rights of factories, cooperatives, and other collective units to make independent purchases. At the same time as the razverstka became official policy in early 1919, major legislative enactments reaffirmed the right of these collective purchasers to obtain foodstuffs in the nonmonopolized category without harassment from blockade detachments. Local officials protested even this limited concession, declaring that it made state provision of these products impossible.[46] But a commission set up by the Central Executive Committee and headed by Kamenev argued that the food-supply question could not be solved before the war was over, that monopolization should therefore proceed only gradually, and that in the meantime worker organizations should be allowed to make purchases without harassment. The battle between the workers and the food-supply apparatus over this issue did not end here. The food-supply officials later managed to get six provinces declared off limits to collective purchasers, and other provinces simply went ahead and declared themselves off limits as well.

The general tendency of the razverstka system was to whittle away these concessions and to extend the range of monopolization. But the legal position did not reflect reality since the underground market was never effectively repressed—if anything, enforcement became more lax.[47] Thus the razverstka system meant that the three pillars of the monopoly strategy—registration, exchange equivalents, and prohibition of independent purchases—were all honored more in the breach than in the observance.

REAL FORCE

The food-supply dictatorship relied on hastily assembled requisition detachments to give the food-supply apparatus a source of real force (*real'naia sila*) and desperate urban consumers an outlet for their dissatisfaction. The disastrous results of this policy led to more specialized institutions. Under the razverstka system the worker detachments, the Food-Supply Army, and the blockade detachments all played distinct roles.

In the chaotic summer of 1918 haste and lack of discipline resulted in a vindication of the Menshevik and Left SR critique: the village became united in resistance to the city. One-fifth of the workers in the food-supply

---

see the contemporary novel *Golod* (1922) by Sergei Semenov, reprinted in *Izbrannoe* (Leningrad, 1970), 79.

46. *Prod. i snab.* (Kostroma), no. 3–4, 1 and 15 February 1919, 21. A discussion of this episode is in V. P. Dmitrenko, "Bor'ba sovetskogo gosudarstva protiv chastnoi torgovli," in *Bor'ba za pobedu i ukreplenie sovetskoi vlasti* (Moscow, 1966), 318–22.

47. Discussion of the underground market during the civil war will be found in chapter 8.

detachments were killed between May and December; in the months of July through September the conflict with the peasants led to more than ten thousand state and party casualties.[48]

The disillusionment of the center took place even as Orlov was writing his book on the Bolshevik food-supply system. Early in the book he asserted that reports coming in about the requisition detachments had refuted those who foresaw "fire and blood" as the inevitable outcome. He does mention that the detachments could have used more "exact and detailed instructions." By the end of the monograph he saw the detachments as a tragic necessity: "Going with a heavy heart to the 'grain war,' the central authority relied on the workers and hungry peasantry of the north and center." The resulting split between town and village, he said, made it possible for insignificant foreign forces to become a real threat.[49]

The Bolsheviks tried to impose some order on the chaotic crusade they had conjured up. A Bolshevik pamphlet with instructions on how to form a worker detachment allows us to deduce the faults of the previous requisition detachments. Who should join the detachments? it asks. The emphasis should be on quality not quantity. Unreliable elements have crept in: people who are just going to have a vacation or to get something for themselves—the kind of people who ask questions about overtime pay instead of being filled with the spirit of communism.

What are the tasks of the detachments? The first is economic: to help in the harvest, assist in carrying out the registration of grain, and so on. The second is political: to join with the poor peasants and help them fight the kulaks. "The greatest possible restraint and skill" is required so that the village will not look on the detachment as "looters from the city."

How should the detachments behave in the localities? Here a series of thou-shalt-nots paints a vivid picture of what had previously been going on. Use restraint in carrying out registration: do not take the last pood of grain from a poor peasant, and do not leave a rich peasant without enough to feed his family. *"You must not allow any elemental raids or undisciplined seizures of grain,* for that simply raises people against you and even causes unneeded clashes." Do not use armed force at the slightest opportunity— the peasants have suffered enough as it is. Keep the peasants themselves from elemental outbursts such as destroying houses or burning the grain supplies of other peasants. Explain to them that instead the grain should be

48. Total casualties on the Bolshevik side for 1918 equaled twenty thousand. Osipova, "Razvitie," 62; Mints, God 1918, 390.
49. Orlov, Rabota, 101–2, 179–82, 355–62. Orlov's remarks are the basis of Roy Medvedev's interpretation of the food-supply dictatorship in October Revolution.

put on register. And, of course, do not neglect to bring to them "spiritual bread"—that is, political propaganda.[50]

A less destructive outlet had to be found for worker participation in the food-supply apparatus. The new outlet was the worker detachments, whose institutional history began in August 1918 with a decree entitled "On Enlisting Worker Organizations in the Procurement of Grain." This decree told the workers that their salvation lay not in crusading against the kulak but rather in helping the food-supply apparatus procure grain at fixed prices. Great attention was given to matters of legality, monitoring, and supervision; force was contemplated not against the peasantry but against the detachment commanders, who were threatened with being turned over to the Cheka if they did not follow regulations.[51]

The new worker detachments fell under the direct control of a subsection of the central trade-union council, the Military Food-Supply Bureau (Voenprodbiuro). This title, an accident of administrative genealogy, is so misleading that I will henceforth refer to this organization simply as the trade-union bureau for food supply.[52] More than thirty thousand workers had volunteered for the detachments by the end of 1918, but as the trade-union bureau ruefully admitted, it had organizational control over no more than eight thousand.

The leader of one of these units, a Petrograd worker named Vasilii Potapenko, wrote later that his unit consisted mainly of nineteen- and twenty-year-olds who were the children of longtime Petrograd workers. One-fourth of his unit consisted of women. The unit was armed ad hoc: Potapenko himself used a Smith-Wesson that he obtained during the February revolution and kept during his time as a member of the Red Guard at the Westinghouse plant. Potapenko reveals a sense of humor about his ignorance of the countryside and tells a story about how he was misled by a local dialect and bought a pumpkin, thinking it was a watermelon. But he has less perspective about the way he was subjected to fierce rhetoric about class struggle during his two-week training period. He remembers looking through the train window on his way to the countryside and seeing shabby huts as well as occasional brick houses with iron roofs: "I wanted to bring down that sea of poverty onto those islands of wealth, to carry them away so that not a trace remained."[53]

50. K. Samuilova, *Prodovol'stvennyi vopros i sovetskaia vlast'* (Petrograd, 1918), 44–52.

51. *Dekrety*, 3:142–43; Orlov, *Delo*, 23–25.

52. Iu. K. Strizhkov, *Prodovol'stvennye otriady v gody grazhdanskoi voiny i inostrannoi interventsii, 1917–21* (Moscow, 1973), 114–16.

53. Potapenko, *Zapiski*, 13–17. On participation of the Red Guards in food-supply work after October, see Wade, *Red Guards*, 316–17.

A bureaucratic battle began between the trade-union bureau and the Food-Supply Commissariat over control of these worker detachments. The dispute took on ideological overtones; the trade unionists (in the mode of the later "workers' opposition") attacked the bureaucratic nature of the food-supply apparatus and wanted to replace it from below with worker delegates. After a sharp intervention by Lenin this recrudescence of the enlistment solution was defeated, and in February 1919 operational control of the detachments was given to the Food-Supply Commissariat. The trade-union bureau received a new collegium after a member of the old collegium, M. M. Kostelovskaia, made a strong plea for the worker detachments at the Eighth Party Congress. The hostility of trade-union officials toward the food-supply apparatus did not lessen over the years: in late 1920 Lenin was forced to remove Aleksei Sviderskii and Moishe Frumkin from the collegium of the Food-Supply Commissariat because of trade-union antipathy, and at the Tenth Party Congress the leader of the workers' opposition, Aleksandr Shliapnikov, accused Tsiurupa himself of criminal negligence.[54]

It was still not clear in 1919 whether the worker detachments were an appendage of the food-supply apparatus or agents of the organization that sent them. Pressure from the workers resulted in an experiment in the summer of 1919. Factories could send their own detachments to Simbirsk province, and these detachments were allowed to send all of the grain they obtained directly to the parent organization. The food-supply officials waited until the failure of this experiment became manifest and then managed to reassert control. Grain obtained by the detachments was no longer sent to the parent organization but put into the "common cauldron" (*obshchii kotel*) of food distributed centrally by the food-supply apparatus. Many of the detachments stayed on to help with the harvest under the direction of the food-supply committees. The inundation of outsiders that had threatened to destroy the food-supply apparatus in Simbirsk was now integrated into a more organized framework, and Simbirsk became a relative success story for the razverstka of 1919–1920.[55]

It was often far from clear that the worker detachments really helped food-supply work. Many food-supply officials were irritated at the naivete of the detachments, who assumed that all they had to do was make an eloquent appeal and then transport the grain. The workers were skilled neither in the use of arms nor in technical food-supply work so that in

---

54. Strizhkov, *Otriady*, 121, 154–58; Lenin, *PSS*, 52:31–32. For Kostelovskaia's views, see also *Izv. NKP*, no. 1–2 (January 1919), 23.
55. Strizhkov, *Otriady*, 181–88; Kaganovich, *Kak dostaetsia khleb*.

these areas they could only be used as backup resources. Because they lived in the villages, the worker detachments made a small, but vital, contribution to the effective use of force. As Kaganovich's report from Simbirsk asserted, "several armed men at village meetings and in everyday life force the kulaks and open counterrevolutionaries to keep quiet while they quickly get in with the poor and middle peasants and have a significant effect on them."[56]

For the most part the detachments turned into "travelling squads of agitators."[57] Food-supply officials stressed that agitation was worthless unless the workers demonstrated that the city was willing to offer concrete help to the village; hence often the real contribution of the worker detachments was help with the harvest or repairs. The leading Soviet authority on this subject, Iurii Strizhkov, estimates that one hundred thousand persons served in the worker detachments.[58]

The failure of the requisition detachments did not remove the need for real force. The direct descendant of the requisition detachments was the Food-Supply Army (Prodarmiia). As time went on, the Food-Supply Army was recruited increasingly from peasants in the deficit provinces who for one reason or another were unfit to serve in the Red Army. Indeed, the Food-Supply Army can almost be seen as the garrison force of the Red Army—or perhaps the Red Army should be seen as the expeditionary force of the Food-Supply Army. After reaching an enlistment of twenty-nine thousand in early November 1918, the Food-Supply Army was reduced within a month by more than half because of transfers to the Red Army—a graphic illustration of the priority of war demands over internal needs. The Food-Supply Commissariat fought to build up its forces again, and by the end of 1919 the Food-Supply Army had grown to around forty-five thousand persons. After the civil war ended in 1920, lack of competition from the Red Army and the greatly expanded territory under Bolshevik control led to enlistment swelling to seventy-seven thousand. A 1986 Soviet study estimates that a total of somewhere between 152,000 and

56. Kaganovich, *Kak dostaetsia khleb*, 26–29; reprinted in *Prod. politika*, 253–56.
57. These words are taken from an interview by the English journalist W. T. Goode with A. I. Sviderskii. Goode notes that "this interview was for me one of the clearest and most convincing. Sviderski is a master of his subject in all its details, and the clearness of his replies, together with the sequential character of his statement, made him impressive." *Bolshevism at Work* (New York, 1920), 69–76. The transition to a greater emphasis on agitation is noted in A. N. Chistikov, "Prodovol'stvennaia politika sovetskoi vlasti v gody grazhdanskoi voiny (na materialakh Petrograda). Avtoreferat," diss. abstract (Leningrad, 1984).
58. Strizhkov, *Otriady*, 299.

155,000 persons served in the Food-Supply Army during the time of troubles.[59]

Between the summer of 1918 and the summer of 1920 there were few significant uprisings in the countryside under permanent Bolshevik control.[60] Besides guarding grain depots and the like, the job of the Food-Supply Army was mainly to show itself at appropriate times and punish resistance on the part of individual villages in a suitably visible way.[61] The Food-Supply Army was never held in high esteem, even by Bolshevik officials. The members of one detachment complained that they were not issued tobacco on the grounds that they were fighting peasant women while others were fighting at the front. Only when Tsiurupa himself interfered did they get something to smoke.[62]

The Food-Supply Army, which collected the tax, was distinct from the blockade detachments, which enforced the monopoly by preventing illegal transport of grain. The blockade detachments were without a doubt the most hated institution of the civil-war period—more hated even than the Cheka. They predated the food-supply dictatorship, but the retreat to the razverstka system led to an effort to limit the damage they did. In his August theses Lenin insisted that the blockade detachments give receipts (with two or three copies) to any passenger whose goods were requisitioned: "For requisition without giving receipts—shooting." (This use of a violent threat to impose a bureaucratic formality is characteristic of both Lenin and the times.)

A decree issued on 4 August 1918 reveals that the blockade detachments often operated without clear authority; slowed down transportation (in cases of extreme necessity, the decree said, the detachments could delay the train for no more than an hour); were overbearing (the detachments "must preserve courtesy"); embezzled (strict records must be kept of confiscated goods); took excessive amounts (a definite norm for the amounts to be left to each passenger is given); used unnecessary force (the detachments "must avoid clashes not made necessary by the interests of the common cause"). Orlov reports that not much had been done about this decree by the end of the year. He was puzzled by the "strange slowness" of the government in coming to grips with this problem, but now he hoped the

59. A. M. Aleksentsev, "K voprosu o chislennosti Prodarmii," *Istoriia SSSR* no. 3–4 (1986): 155–67.

60. For discussion of peasant uprisings, see J. M. Meijer, "Town and Country in the Civil War," in Richard Pipes, ed., *Revolutionary Russia*, (Cambridge, Mass., 1968), 259–77, esp. 276–77, and Peter Scheibert, *Lenin an die Macht* (Weinheim, 1984), 385–408.

61. *Prod. politika*, 248–50; *Izv. NKP*, no. 1–2 (January 1919): 29–30.

62. Tsiurupa, *Kolokola pamiati*, 129.

time had come to end the scandal of these detachments, which he considered to be composed of the dregs of the population and more often in business for themselves than operating with authorization from an identifiable official. At best they protected the purely local interest of keeping food in the area.[63]

But with all their faults, the blockade detachments were necessary to enforce the monopoly.[64] The roots of the "war against the railroad passengers" reached back beyond the food-supply dictatorship to the Provisional Government period. An English eyewitness describes this central institution of civil-war Russia:

> At nine [the train] reached the straggling buildings of the Okhta Station [in Petrograd] . . . and there I saw a most extraordinary spectacle—the attempted prevention of sackmen from entering the city.
>
> As we stood pushing in the corridor waiting for the crowd in front of us to get out, I heard Uncle Egor [a peasant] and his daughter conversing rapidly in low tones.
>
> "I'll make a dash for it," whispered his daughter.
>
> "Good," he replied in the same tone. "We'll meet at Nadya's."
>
> The moment we stepped on to the platform Uncle Egor's daughter vanished under the railroad coach and that was the last I ever saw of her. At each end of the platform stood a string of armed guards, waiting for the onslaught of passengers, who flew in all directions as they surged from the train. How shall I describe the scene of unutterable pandemonium that ensued! The soldiers dashed at the fleeing crowds, brutally seized single individuals, generally women, who were least able to defend themselves, and tore the sacks off their back and out of their arms. Shrill cries, shrieks, and howls rent the air. Between the coaches and on the outskirts of the station you could see lucky ones who had escaped, gesticulating frantically to unlucky ones who were still dodging guards. "This way! This way!" they yelled wildly, "Sophia! Marusia! Akulina! Varvara! Quick! Haste!"
>
> In futile efforts to subdue the mob the soldiers discharged their rifles into the air, only increasing the panic and intensifying the tumult. Curses and execration were hurled at them

63. *Izv. NKP*, no. 24–25 (December 1918): 2–3; no. 1–2 (January 1919): 7–11. Throughout 1919 and 1920 central decrees continued to insist that only the Food-Supply Commissariat had the right to form blockade detachments.

64. *Prod. i snab.* (Kostroma), no. 1–2, 1 and 15 January 1919, 5–6.

by the seething mass of fugitives. One woman I saw, frothing at the mouth, with blood streaming down her cheek, her frenzied eyes protruding from the sockets, clutching ferociously with her nails at the face of a huge sailor who held her pinned down on the platform, while his comrades detached her sack.

How I got out of the fray I do not know, but I found myself carried along with the running stream of sackmen over the Okhta Bridge and toward the Suvorov Prospect. Only here, a mile from the station, did they settle into a hurried walk, gradually dispersing down side streets to dispose of their precious goods to eager clients.

Completely bewildered, I limped along, my frost-bitten feet giving me considerable pain. I wondered in my mind if people at home had any idea at what a cost the population of Petrograd secured the first necessities of life in the teeth of the "communist" rulers.[65]

A NEW POLITICAL FORMULA

There was only one element of continuity between the razverstka system and the food-supply dictatorship, but it was a central one: the drive to impose the discipline of the center on the food-supply apparatus as a whole. The assignment of razverstka quotas to local officials, the legalization of independent purchases by worker organizations, the conciliatory line toward the middle peasant—all required control over local officials who either lacked initiative or were too militant or felt more responsible to the local population than to the central state authority. In a speech to the Central Executive Committee on 17 January 1919 Lenin remarked that it was perhaps strange to speak of compelling local food-supply organs to carry out the will of the committee (whose will in this case was to allow independent purchase). But, he continued, "better to speak the truth: we must compel our local organs unswervingly and mercilessly." Lenin got applause only twice in this speech, for this remark and another one of similar import.[66]

The drive to unify and discipline the administrative apparatus faced great difficulties, given the centrifugal pressures of the time. It should be seen in the wider context of a political formula that defined sources of recruitment, authority relations, and political mission for the new political class.

65. Dukes, *Red Dusk,* 196–98.
66. Lenin, *PSS,* 37:421–24.

The enlistment strategy that had failed as a crusade against the class enemy could still be used to recruit cadres for the new political class. This was the advice of Miron Vladimirov, who was in charge of food-supply work in the Ukraine in 1920. Recognizing that the "iron logic of political development" meant that the position of peasant officials was more burdensome than advantageous, Vladimirov still felt that they were the most promising source of genuine support, on the basis of the following quid pro quo: "While helping the poor villagers and the loyal strata of the middle peasantry rise up on the social ladder, securing their political and social dominance in the village, providing them with a wide and genuine participation in overall soviet construction and turning them into conscious supporters of the Soviet Republic, it is necessary at the time to ask them to solve and carry out tasks that will lead to the strengthening of the soviet authority and ipso facto to the strengthening of their own position."[67]

The political formula for the authority relations of the new political class was *democratic centralism*. To understand the power of this formula, it is perhaps less useful to read Lenin's *What Is to Be Done*, about the problems of underground revolutionaries, than to consider the connection between solidarity and survival during the time of troubles. Maliutin boasted that "to others we are strict but to ourselves we are cruel"—the message of the Bolshevik political class to its unworthy agents was "Up against the wall."[68] The new political class accepted this discipline because, as another revolutionary had once put it, if they did not hang together they would assuredly hang separately. This dictum was especially true of the food-supply apparatus, which had continually to face a hostile and dissatisfied population of both consumers and producers. To break ranks was to invite the excesses from below that had destroyed the apparatus in the fall of 1917, so it is not surprising to hear of the gratitude with which "each food-supply worker feels upon himself the heavy but saving hand" of the food-supply dictatorship and its strict centralization.[69]

A political formula gives a political class a sense of mission. The political class led by the Bolsheviks derived its sense of mission from many sources, but one that should not be overlooked was its origin in a time of troubles and its perception of itself as a thin dam holding back the flood of anarchy. Orlov expressed this feeling poignantly: "The inhuman energy of a handful of dreamers—the progressive proletarians and party workers—is sustaining the chain of state and class that as yet holds us together. It seems

67. Vladimirov, *Udarnye momenty*, 8–10.
68. Maliutin, *Rech'* (Kazan, 1918).
69. *Prod. i snab.* (Kostroma), no. 8–10, 15 April and 15 May 1919, 12–14.

that if this handful vanished tomorrow, we would be scattered and torn apart from each other like the atoms of a substance subjected to strong heat."[70]

THE TWO SOLUTIONS

The adoption of the razverstka method led to the rehabilitation of Rittikh. For the Provisional Government, Rittikh was a prime symbol of the incompetent desperation of the tsarist regime. In historical overviews written by Bolshevik food-supply officials during the civil war, he became instead the representative of the sound and healthy part of the tsarist bureaucracy who, however, arrived too late and was too isolated to save the regime.[71] As this reevaluation suggests, the razverstka system was based on the gubernatorial solution—a strict definition of priority tasks to be accomplished by plenipotentiary agents of the center in complete subordination to the overall goal of efficient support for the war effort.

In the popular mind the razverstka was not one particular method of grain collection but a synonym for the state grain obligation itself. As a comparison, when we hear our neighbor say, "This damned income tax!" we assume he or she is referring not to the disadvantages of an income tax as opposed to a sales tax or a value-added tax but to the burdensome fact of being taxed at all. The food-supply razverstka became associated with— indeed became the prime symbol of—all the hardships of the complete economic breakdown of 1920, when the economy was rapidly spiraling toward utter destruction.

It is therefore something of a shock to realize that when the razverstka was introduced by the food-supply apparatus in 1918 and 1919, it was viewed as a concession to the peasantry and a move away from the village-splitting tactics of class struggle. The peasant population was also given greater control over distribution of the burden of the grain obligation. The razverstka assigned a definite amount to the village; the food-supply apparatus promised to leave the village alone once the amount was paid. Although the food-supply apparatus had guidelines on the proper principles of distribution, these had less and less relevance the further down one went in the hierarchy.[72] Another aim of the razverstka method was to put the provision of exchange items on a more secure basis. These advantages may not have been apparent to the peasants since the food-supply officials

70. Orlov, *Rabota*, 384–96.
71. A. I. Sviderskii, *Prodovol'stvennaia politika* (Moscow, 1920), 141–43; Orlov, *Delo*, 13–14.
72. *Prod. politika*, 189–92 (Osinskii).

could not keep their commitments. The officials admitted they could not, but they felt this failing was due more to troubled times than to the razverstka method itself.[73]

The disillusionment with registration reflected a new realism about the scarcity of administrative resources and the small likelihood of popular cooperation. In Tsiurupa's words, the Bolsheviks realized they had to cut their coat to their cloth.[74] The razverstka was still called an approximation of the surplus since the concept of registering the surplus made "excellent agitational material." Although the phrase *taking the surplus* is enshrined in later historiography as an expression of Bolshevik ruthlessness, it was used during the civil war to project a strong but reasonable image: the state was taking only the surplus and not anything that was really needed for consumption and farm needs.[75]

The attention of the Bolsheviks had shifted from enlisting the population in a revolutionary crusade to building up an apparatus that would earn respect and compliance by its competence and staying power. The Bolsheviks would use whatever force was necessary to crush resistance but try to avoid any show of force that was wasteful and irritating and caused more political damage than benefit. In late 1918 Zinoviev compared the middle peasant to the middle strata in the towns. At first the petty-bourgeois (*meshchanskii*) intelligentsia in the towns was hostile to the Bolsheviks and tempted to resort to sabotage, but soon it realized that "we weren't fooling around and that there was no other master [but us] nor could there be." In the village this realization would occur when the kulaks were crushed and the middle peasant saw that the poor peasant was now the "true master of the Russian land."[76] The Bolsheviks realized that the confident use of force attracted support, even though they expressed the thought in class terms. As a speaker at the Eighth Party Congress put it, the peasants accepted Bolshevik leadership in October because, among other reasons, "we were strong—and this is important for the petty-bourgeois strata."[77]

The civil war meant that the grain monopoly as a means of socialist transformation could not be a high priority: the Kamenev commission at the end of 1918 officially announced that the food-supply problem could

73. *Prod. i snab.* (Kostroma), no. 6–7 (March–April 1919): 11–13. For a defensive discussion of the move away from village splitting, see *Izv. NKP,* no. 13–16 (July–August 1919): 2–3.

74. Frumkin, *Tovaroobmen,* 7.

75. Shlikhter, *Agrarnyi vopros,* 411–14; *Izv. NKP,* no. 6 (November 1920): 13–14.

76. Sixth Congress of Soviets, 90; Zinoviev, *Chto delat' v derevne,* 3–16 (speech given in the fall of 1918).

77. Eighth Party Congress 227–40 (V. V. Kuraev).

only be solved by winning the war and that all efforts should be bent toward that goal. But a full state grain monopoly based on accurate registration and equivalent exchange remained the ideal: the razverstka was a compromise forced by the urgency of military survival and the breakdown of the war-torn economy. It was assumed that after the end of hostilities the monopoly would resume its place as the basis of socialist distribution. But in the meantime the razverstka, regarded as a makeshift substitute, came to be the basis on which the Bolsheviks were able to construct a serviceable food-supply apparatus.

8 Leaving Troubled Times

There was snow falling as I walked home. Two workmen,
arguing, were walking in front of me. "If only it were not for
the hunger," said one. "But will that ever change?" said the
other.

Arthur Ransome, Russia in 1919

Although each individual peasant family has not yet seen any
great advantage or relief for themselves from the revolution,
still, taken all in all, we have gone from victory to victory and
we have now approached the time when month by month each
family will begin to feel some small relief, will see and
evaluate what the revolution has given, and [will understand]
that life has really begun anew.

Grigorii Zinoviev, spring 1920

One common view of the later years of the time of troubles is as a period
when the Bolsheviks and the peasants grew dangerously apart after their
alliance in 1917. Only after a series of peasant revolts in late 1920 and 1921
did the Bolsheviks come to their senses by making the long-overdue
changes necessary to placate the peasants.

The course of food-supply policy reveals a different story: the Bolshe-
vik-peasant alliance of 1917 was compatible with mutual incomprehension,
and it was only in 1918 that the Bolsheviks and the peasants realized how
little they understood each other. In the years that followed, this lack of
knowledge began to be overcome, thus laying the groundwork for the
introduction of the food-supply tax. The policy changes of 1921 were not a
repudiation of the achievements of the civil war period but their continuation.

The Bolsheviks could not do much to lighten the burden of large and
uncompensated grain collections. Tsiurupa argued in late 1919 that "there
are only two possibilities: either we perish from hunger, or we weaken the
[peasant] economy to some extent but [manage to] get out of our temporary difficulties."[1] Just for this reason the Bolsheviks were eager to propiti-

1. Seventh Congress of Soviets, 163–66.

ate the peasants. The peasant revolts of 1920–1921 show the limits of what they felt they could do. The fact remains that each direction of change in food-supply policy during the years 1919–1921 was to some degree a response to peasant grievances.

FROM CLASS WAR TO STATE OBLIGATION

The Bolsheviks' class outlook did not sit well with the peasants, who strongly resented what they felt was the politically, ideologically, and materially privileged position of the workers. One "nonparty conference" held for peasants in Tambov wanted to change the wording of a telegram of greeting to Lenin, from "Long live worker-peasant sovereignty" to "Long live peasant-worker sovereignty."[2] "Help the workers" was thus bound to be a much weaker appeal than "Help the Army" (as Rittikh had discovered earlier). Cases were reported of peasants who wanted to take their grain back when they learned that it was not going to the Red Army but to nearby workers.[3]

There was also great dislike of Bolshevik attempts to set "muzhik against muzhik." Many peasants, not just those out of favor with the government, felt it unseemly. They also resented what they felt was persecution of the industrious and encouragement of the shiftless. When addressing a conference of "nonparty peasants" in the spring of 1920, Zinoviev could not understand why anyone in his audience would take offense at his violent attack on the kulaks. "If a kulak takes offense, that's understandable—his turn is coming. But among you there are no kulaks." Zinoviev complained that "the worker is not offended when we unmask the town kulak [the factory owner]. At peasant meetings as well, an attitude must be created toward the village kulak as an enemy, a spider, an oppressor."[4] In response peasants posed questions that the Bolsheviks found difficult to answer: "All right, you place [the burden of] the razverstka on the kulak. But you see, the kulak isn't a source that will never dry up. Over three years many *have* dried up. . . . What are you going to do when there are no more kulaks?"[5]

Food-supply officials found many reasons in their day-to-day experi-

2. Lev Trotsky, *The Trotsky Papers, 1917–1922*, ed. J. M. Meijer (The Hague, 1971), 2:518–24 (report of Antonov-Ovseenko).

3. A. Khvoles, "Voenno-prodovol'stvennoe delo za period revoliutsii," *Prod. i rev.*, no. 1 (1923): 56–57.

4. G. Zinoviev, *Krest'iane i sovetskaia vlast'* (Petrograd, 1920), 38–39, 42. See also Okninskii, *Dva goda*, 188–92.

5. *Pravda*, 27 November 1920 (account of a mass meeting in the Moscow region). Ellipsis in original.

ence to respond to the peasants' dissatisfaction with the class outlook. They discovered that the kulak was not the key to the food-supply problem; Potapenko explicitly states that in Voronezh in 1919 the difficulties arose not from the kulaks, who mostly fulfilled their obligations, but from the passive resistance of many of the middle peasants. Shlikhter observed in 1920 that in Tambov the "kulak element" did not think of refusing the orders of the food-supply committees "even when, it would seem, from the point of view of common sense, it might have to be recognized that these kulaks as citizens have to a certain extent a right to discuss these orders."[6] The comically careful language shows how difficult it was for a Bolshevik to say in public that a kulak might have genuine grievances. Still, as with any tax-collecting bureaucracy, there were strong pressures to see the kulak as a sort of milk cow to be protected.[7]

Officials also found that the poor peasants and semiproletarians were more a nuisance than a staunch ally. One official from Tambov observed that the poor peasants in his province would rather help the kulak hide his grain than tell the government where it was located. Other officials treated them as importunate consumers and a drain on the city's resources. The poor peasants who had benefited from the revolution were likely to be the ones most irritated by civil-war pressures that prevented them from consolidating their new position.[8]

It was indeed a revelation for many food-supply officials from the city to find themselves putting pressure on the middle peasant rather than serving as lieutenants in the class war. Potapenko describes such a case:

> I once noticed that one food-supply worker, Ignat Kiselev, was in a gloomy mood and asked him, "Why are you so glum, Ignat? Are you ill?" "No, I'm fine," he answered unwillingly and added after a short silence, "It's not good, you know." "What's not good?" "Our work's not good." "In what way?"
>
> Ignat started to explain. "We go today into one hut. We say hello—the old owner mumbles something in response. We get suspicious glances from the women. I turn to the old man and ask him how much grain he's delivered. He answers gruffly that he's given only ten poods, and he hasn't got any more. He's supposed to give fifteen poods. We look through the storehouse. Yes, there's grain and flour and so on, but just barely enough to last to the next harvest. We return to the hut

6. Shlikhter, *Agrarnyi vopros*, 398–402.
7. Vladimirov, *Udarnye momenty*, 39; Potapenko, *Zapiski*, 77.
8. *Biulletin NKP*, 2 July 1920; Vladimirov, *Udarnye momenty*, 39–40; Kaganovich, *Kak dostaetsia khleb*, 15–16, 19–21.

and appeal to the conscience of the owner: 'After all, you're not a kulak and you should help the soviet authority in its difficult moment.' We try to persuade him for about an hour, and he looks away and says nothing. As I go, I tell him that if he doesn't give those five poods in three days, we'll come and take it. Both women raise a cry and start to wail. We leave the hut accompanied by their weeping. Okay, I can give the orders, but my heart aches for pity. . . . No, I didn't think our work would turn out to be so difficult!"[9]

The middle peasant was the key not only to grain collection but also to political stability. Under these circumstances many officials began to feel that the fixation on the kulak could be dangerous. Representatives of the center such as Kaganovich argued that local officials, paralyzed by fear of kulak uprisings, at the same time increased the potential for uprisings by treating the middle peasant as a kulak. He was shocked when Simbirsk officials in 1919 told him that a recent visit by Mikhail Kalinin to popularize the new line on the middle peasant was bad for food-supply work. Kaganovich refused to see the kulak as an inveterate enemy; he argued that kulaks were "not so much as an economic force as a psychological phenomenon" and should be dealt with as such. The "kulak mood" in Simbirsk was therefore the result of a "mutual misunderstanding" caused in large part by the apparatus itself.[10] In 1920 Lenin went further and announced in the name of the entire Central Committee that "we got carried away with the fight against the kulaks and lost all sense of measure."[11]

Neither central nor local officials were prepared to abandon the class outlook completely. The well-off peasant did have more grain; he was visible and isolated, and attempts to take grain from the rest of the peasantry would not be credible until it was shown that the apparatus could deal with him. At the same time as Lenin made the comment just cited, he was asked the following question by a local activist: "Holy Cross county of Stavropol province, where I work, was supposed to pay 10 million poods of grain before 1 December 1920. The fulfillment was 3.2 million poods. In connection with this poor fulfillment, we intensified property confiscation from kulak elements. Therefore I would like to ask once more: how to proceed? Carry out confiscation, or do this only in extreme cases so as not to destroy the [peasant] economy?" Lenin's reply was evasive: "In strict correspondence with the decree of the soviet authority and your commu-

9. Potapenko, Zapiski, 83–84 (ellipsis in original).

10. Kaganovich, Kak dostaetsia khleb, 15–16, 19–21. For continued suspicion of so-called kulak soviets, see Pravda, 24 October 1920.

11. Lenin, PSS, 42:195.

nist conscience, continue to act freely in the future as you have acted up until now."[12]

The rhetoric of the class war prevented local officials like Potapenko from completely assimilating the lessons of experience. If the kulak failed to cooperate, it was sabotage, and if he cooperated, it was only from fear of repression. When the middle peasant failed to cooperate, Potapenko was more sympathetic and saw it as understandable wavering.[13] Despite all the changes in policy, the sabotage outlook remained embedded in the Leninist class vocabulary like a dormant virus, ready to spring to life when conditions were right.

If officials were reluctant to completely abandon the class outlook in their own thinking, they were less inhibited in the appeals they made to the peasants. The key Bolshevik message to the middle peasant was based on the gubernatorial solution: we are trying to limit what we demand of you, but we intend to get what we demand. A party circular in late 1919 listed the benefits to the middle peasant: "liquidation of private landowning estates, periodic raising of the fixed price for grain of the new harvest, provision of the village with industrial items, and struggles with the arbitrariness of [our own] local authorities." The circular stated that the peasant's reproach about the lack of industrial items was accurate but also unjust, since the shortages were not the fault of the Bolsheviks. It admitted that the razverstka was indeed a heavy obligation (*povinnost'*), but like any obligation in time of war, refusal to meet it would be treated like desertion. This Bolshevik circular used the same logic as Prokopovich two years earlier, when he argued that the doubling of fixed prices gave the Provisional Government the moral right to use force.[14]

Bolshevik posters did not ignore the desperate economic situation: "Peasant, you are dissatisfied: you have no iron, salt, cloth—no medicine if you are sick—no way of buying boots. You work well, your children help, and yet your life is poor and squalid." But, they warned, the peasant should not see the razverstka as a cause of these difficulties: "Success in the struggle against economic breakdown—the tragedy of the people—depends on the success of the republic's food-supply organs."[15]

12. Lenin, *PSS*, 42:192; see also Potapenko, *Zapiski*, 89–93.
13. Potapenko, *Zapiski*, 52–55, 125.
14. *Biulletin NKP*, 3 October 1919.
15. B. S. Butnik-Siverskii, *Sovetskii plakat epokhi grazhdanskoi voiny, 1918–1921* (Moscow, 1960), 452; Zubareva, *Khleb Prikam'ia*, 46–47. A Bolshevik journal in 1920, *Vestnik agitatsii i propagandy*, criticized posters that did not try to convince peasants that grain deliveries were in their own direct economic self-interest. Stephen White, *The Bolshevik Poster* (New Haven, 1988), 115–16.

The supporting argument relied less and less on class-war rhetoric, as shown by this 1920 list of suggested agitational themes:

1.   The razverstka has great significance for the existence and development of the Republic.

2.   "The provisionment of the Red Army is a question of victory, peace, and security for the Republic." Why is victory important for the peasant? Because "if [Wrangel] is not quickly liquidated, his forces could advance, and he could cut Soviet Russia off from the grain of the Kuban, the coal of the Donets region, and the oil of Baku, and this threatens great losses for our still damaged economy."

3.   The village relies on town industry, which cannot work without bread.

4.   The old regime actually took more out of the village "with the help of vodka, taxes, and various other methods."

5.   Grain exports previously paid for goods for the bourgeoisie, whereas the first thing the Bolsheviks will buy is agricultural machinery.

6.   If the peasant thinks about it, he will realize that the Bolsheviks are giving the village an equivalent for what they take.

7.   The larger part of the razverstka goes to the Red Army, in other words, to fellow peasants. The grain also goes to peasants working outside their villages and to regions suffering from harvest failure.

8.   Every peasant has a stake in this system of insurance in case of harvest failure.

9.   The razverstka is part of the soviet authority's general program, and the socialist character of food-supply policy means that all toilers have an interest in it.[16]

Bolshevik propagandists also tried to convince the peasants that the workers were not a privileged class and that wartime burdens were not imposed in a discriminatory way. A textbook for food-supply propagandists recommended the following arguments: the government had a "whole system of repressions in relation to self-seekers [*shkurniki*] and saboteurs" among the workers. The recent law against absenteeism was an example. Factory disciplinary courts could impose a series of sanctions: deprivation of bonuses, then deprivation of food rations, and finally arrest. The guilty party either worked off his penalty at the factory or was sent to a concentration camp for compulsory labor: "It is obvious that the soviet au-

16. *Krasnyi put'*, no. 2, 1 November 1920, 10–12, 42–43. For propaganda aimed at the workers, see L. Sosnovskii in *Pravda*, 22 March and 14 July 1920; *Pravda*, 10 June and 24 June 1920.

thority is not particularly gentle with lazy louts [*lodyri*] found among the workers."[17]

In much of their propaganda the Bolsheviks had moved away from class struggle to the idea of a state obligation imposed in the name of the common interest. In the words of a *Pravda* editorial of November 1920, "Hunger is the common enemy. It does not distinguish between parties and convictions. It tortures in similar fashion the worker, the intellectual, the communist, the Menshevik, and the nonparty people. . . . Let all citizens of Russia close ranks behind the soviet authority, and it will be able to defeat hunger."[18] Some Bolsheviks even began to believe that they were in truth what they claimed to be, not so much revolutionaries as national leaders working to prevent a common disaster.[19]

CREATING A SERVICEABLE APPARATUS

A tsarist bureaucrat who lived in Tambov during the civil war, A. L. Okninskii, was surprised to find that despite the powerless parody to which soviet self-government had been reduced, the peasants still favored it in principle:

> Our soviets are a good thing. All that's necessary is for the party people not to interfere in our business so that we our-selves can decide our affairs according to our own standards [*po sovesti*] and for the party people not to weigh us down—in a word, without them. . . .
> Yes, we're ready to pay taxes—but let them be reasonable [*po Bozheski*] and without excess so that a person can still live. Also we should know ahead of time how much a person is sup-posed to pay so you can pay what you owe, and that's it—not a kopeck more. [*Zaplatit' svoe i shabash—bol'she ni-ni.*] How it is now, you know well: today I pay everything that's de-manded of me for a year—and tomorrow look what happens: again it's give this and give that to some boss or other. Where do all these bosses come from, that we have to give everything to them? This sort of thing was unheard of in the past.[20]

It is not accurate to say the peasants only wished to be left alone; in fact,

---

17. *Prod. politika,* 131–32; see also P. K. Kaganovich, *Velikaia trudovaia razverstka: front, derevnia i gorod v sovetskoi respublike* (Omsk, 1920), 10.

18. *Pravda,* 12 September 1920.

19. Arthur Ransome, *Russia in 1919* (New York, 1919), 49; Ransome, *The Crisis in Russia* (London, 1921), 124–32 (interview with Rykov).

20. Okninskii, *Dva goda,* 289–90. "Soviets without Bolsheviks" was a key slogan of the Kronstadt rebels.

they were eager for economic contact with the towns. They did not deny the need to support the government with taxes and other services. What they objected to was the way they were treated: requisitions came in an unending stream with no regard for the convenience of the peasant and were accompanied by flagrant cheats and swindles. As Okninskii put it, "Anyone who lived then in Russia knew well that without any reason they would take anything they wanted—that's what they called 'requisition.' "[21]

The dislike of administrative lawlessness was compounded by contempt for incompetence. In a document circulated among peasants by opposition forces in late 1920, the local officials are called "mostly bungling, inefficient, incompetent persons, real good-for-nothings. . . . Nobody respects them, and no one could ever regard them as real authorities."[22] The peasants felt it proper that there be a strong state to ensure order and national independence but also were accustomed to some minimum of competence from the local representatives of the state. They wanted "real authorities." Particularly infuriating to the peasants were the scandalously inefficient yet coddled state farms (*sovkhozy*) and the way in which food taken from hungry peasants was wasted through incompetent storage and transport.[23]

The accuracy of the peasants' view of the food-supply apparatus was documented in a devastating report by the short-lived People's Commissariat of State Monitoring in the spring of 1919:

> A whole round of reports, and even more the results themselves of the food-supply apparatus, indicates that the apparatus is completely worthless. . . . The worker detachments and the Committees of the Poor find neither in the center nor in the localities a crystallizing and unifying center and so they lose focus and scatter their efforts, often distorting the economic policy of the Soviet Republic. . . .
>
> The food-supply institutions have neither experienced agents, nor a quick, clear accounting system, nor exact statistics. The question arises: what are they doing out there? . . .

21. Okninskii, *Dva goda*, 268.

22. The document from which this material is taken was published in the *New York Times*, 19 October 1920. According to the article, it was a resolution circulated and passed by various peasant village meetings. Although it was obviously drafted by a political activist, probably an SR, I believe that whoever wrote it listened closely to actual peasant complaints and tried to express them. Therefore despite the vagueness of the origin of the document, I believe it can serve as one indication of the peasants' view. It is reprinted in *Soviet Society Since the Revolution* (New York, 1979), 19.

23. Vladimirov, *Udarnye momenty*, 24–27; *Na bor'bu s golodom* (Moscow, 1921), 70–72.

If we turn our attention to the center and consider the endless sections, subsections, and directorates of the Food-Supply Commissariat, we will see the same picture: a flood of paper, top officials weighed down with trivial correspondence, bureaucrats who have no initiative, who are bored and oppressed with their work, and who have a strikingly unsympathetic attitude toward visitors.[24]

One ever-present temptation was to blame the failures of the apparatus on sabotage. The peasant rebellion in Tambov inspired this example of the philosophy that was later called wreckerism: "Special attention was given [by SR rebels in Tambov] to discrediting food-supply work in the village. Illegal actions in relation to the peasantry in the collection of the razverstka and deliberate spoilage before the eyes of the population of food-supply raw materials had the provocational aim of calling forth the indignation of the peasantry."[25]

But there were many voices in the new political class that challenged this type of explanation. The State Monitoring report explicitly ruled out evil intent as the reason for the absence of a basic bureaucratic system and poured scorn on the local officials mesmerized by the "kulak" (quotation marks in the report).[26] If sabotage was not the problem, "proletarianization" was not the answer. Lenin had long argued that the Food-Supply Commissariat without the workers was worth exactly nothing.[27] But in 1920 an article published in the journal of the Food-Supply Commissariat "for purposes of discussion" rejected this "red-over-expert" view and argued that the civil war had forced a retreat in economic policy from a class principle to a "national" principle, on the model of the cooperation with tsarist officers in the Red Army. The article went so far as to assert that the food-supply dictatorship, defined as a class policy of reliance on workers alone, was now only a fiction.[28]

---

24. A. P. Mashkovich, *Deiatel'nost' prodovol'stvennoi organizatsii* (Moscow, 1919), 29. This report is discussed in Lancelot Lawton, *An Economic History of Soviet Russia* (London, 1932), 1:139–40. On the short-lived Commissariat of State Monitoring (NKGosKon), see E. A. Rees, *State Control in Soviet Russia: The Rise and Fall of the Workers' and Peasants' Inspectorate, 1920–34* (New York, 1987), 12–20.

25. A. Kazakov, *Partiia s-r v tambovskom vosstanii 1920–1921* ([Moscow, 1922]), 5.

26. Mashkovich, *Deiatel'nost'*, 25–26, 34, 12–14.

27. Lenin, *PSS*, 50:140–41; *Izv. NKP*, no. 1–2 (January 1919): 15–18; Mashkovich, *Deiatel'nost'*, 20–24, 12–14; Kaganovich, *Kak dostaetsia khleb*, 8–9, 26–29.

28. *Izv. NKP*, no. 1–2 (January–February 1920): 13–20 (S. V. Rozovskii). Frumkin called for more reliance on the cooperatives in *Izv. NKP*, no. 1–2 (January 1919): 21–23.

Top food-supply officials were not so outspoken, but they also shifted their emphasis from proletarianization to professionalization. They saw 1918, the year of the food-supply dictatorship, as a year of amateurism and irregular attacks on the food-supply problem—what Briukhanov called *prodpartizanshchina*. The attention of the Bolshevik food-supply officials was now directed toward acquiring what Orlov called state art. Tsiurupa even implicitly acknowledged that the Bolsheviks were building on the heritage of pre-Bolshevik governments when he apologized in 1919 for abuses and failures: "I can say about myself that I am at fault as well. I have worked for five years on food-supply procurement, but that is not enough in such a difficult moment. It must be admitted that we do not know how to work—but the fact that we are aware of this is also important."[29] The State Monitoring report succinctly summed up the problem: "Centrifugal forces are great, and centripetal ones are inadequate. The resultant is tearing the apparatus to pieces."[30] The Bolsheviks were thus faced with a series of challenges as they tried to create an apparatus in the uncongenial environment of the time of troubles.

The first challenge was to provide material support for the local members of the apparatus. Some of the few available exchange items had to be traded for political services rather than food products. This necessity led to the policy of collective exchange, whereby a whole village rather than individual grain producers, received goods. As Moishe Frumkin explained, "We had an exceedingly small amount of commodities, and our provision or 'distribution' was more in the way of a bonus, not for delivery of grain, but for rendering political help in the extraction of grain." During the food-supply dictatorship the grain taken from rich fellow villagers was the principal form of payment. But the central authorities soon concluded that grain was too scarce to use in this way, and so payment had to be made in the form of industrial items. The benefit to the poor peasants consisted not only in the goods themselves but also in the influence that came from control of distribution.[31]

The peasants were told that because there were so few commodities, individual exchange would mean that only the rich would receive items, and the poor would be left with nothing.[32] But collective exchange was not

<hr>

29. Seventh Congress of Soviets, 163–66; Orlov, *Delo*, 26–28; *Ekonomiche-skaia zhizn'*, 30 June 1920; *Biulletin NKP*, 9 November 1920.

30. Mashkovich, *Deiatel'nost'*, 25–26, 34, 12–14.

31. Frumkin, *Tovaroobmen*, 7; *Prod. politika*, 195–96. The Provisional Government rejected individual exchange for similar reasons; see the speech by A. A. Titov in TsGVIA, 12593-36-69/31–32.

32. *Izv. NKP*, no. 6, 7 November 1920.

adopted out of egalitarian motives: although distribution *within* a grain-producing district may have discriminated against the actual producers, distribution *between* districts discriminated in favor of those with a grain surplus. Peasants from deficit districts, both producers and nonproducers, had to be satisfied with long explanations about the temporary difficulties faced by the country.[33]

The policy of collective exchange was unpopular within the apparatus itself since the peasants' dislike of the system created difficulties, and the required paperwork was intimidating. But the center continued to defend it by the logic of the time of troubles. In late 1919 Tsiurupa told a conference of provincial food-supply officials that "one should not even speak of individual commodity exchange—it is absolutely excluded. . . . At the present time, when we do not have enough commodities, when our reserves are not being replenished and we are living on what was bequeathed to us, [we must realize that] the forms of the future are not available for us. For the most part, we have to resort to surrogates and cut our coat according to our cloth. . . . While a fire is burning, we cannot permit the luxury of experiments."[34]

Writing in early 1921, Miron Vladimirov pointed to a growing paradox: the collective-exchange policy was losing its effectiveness at the same time that razverstka fulfillment was going up. Grain producers who delivered their grain would often tear up the receipts needed to document the village's fulfillment of the razverstka: if they received no goods, why should anybody else in the village? Even the poor peasants began to complain that only the local activists got the few goods available. Vladimirov's explanation for the improvement in grain collection was the growing strength and prestige of the new state authority.[35] In other words, with a working apparatus in place, the political services of the poor peasants were no longer so valuable.

The next challenge presented by the time of troubles to the builders of

33. Kaganovich, *Kak dostaetsia khleb,* 21–24; Orlov, *Rabota,* 179–203. Malle's discussion of collective commodity exchange overemphasizes the ideological factor and overlooks completely the political dimension (*Economic Organization,* 338–49). For references to commodity exchange as socialist, see Lenin, *PSS,* 36:517, Shlikhter in *Izv. NKP,* no. 1–2 (January 1919): 19.

34. Frumkin, *Tovaroobmen,* 7–8; Vladimirov, *Udarnye momenty,* 9; Kritsman, *Geroicheskii period,* 174; Orlov, *Sistema,* 61–67; Prokopovich, *Narodnoe khoziaistvo SSSR,* 153–54. For the food-supply officials' dissatisfaction with collective exchange, see *Tri goda,* introduction; M. I. Davydov, "Gosudarstvennyi tovaroobmen mezhdu gorodom i derevnei v 1918–1921 gg.," *Istoricheskie zapiski* 108 (1982): 45–47.

35. Vladimirov, *Udarnye momenty,* 17–20.

the new apparatus was lack of knowledge: the dream of registration had yielded to the reality of acting in the dark. The apparatus had a hard time getting information about its own actions, much less those of the peasants. When Potapenko's worker detachment met with a county food-supply committee early in 1919, the committee was surprised to learn there was a worker detachment in the area, and Potapenko was surprised to learn about the razverstka legislation of January 1919.[36]

Reliable information about the doings of the peasants was even scarcer. The statistics underlying razverstka assignments were completely inadequate; local officials were often no better informed, and even less realistic, than the center. Kaganovich relates how the Simbirsk food-supply committee in the summer of 1919 came up with the fantastic figure of 78 million poods for the upcoming harvest surplus; under pressure from Kaganovich it was reduced to 11 million. The haphazard distribution of the razverstka to lower levels was fraught with political perils, for the peasants felt keenly the unfairness of assessments that made some peasants pay thirty-five poods per desiatin and others only five.[37]

At the village level the main source of information was still informers. Mutual denunciation was motivated by class hatred but even more by the pressures of collective responsibility. A. M. Bol'shakov wrote later that mutual informing destroyed neighborly relations in his Tver village: "Everybody registered each other down to the last detail—if you had a dog, for example, you would hear about it, and people would say, 'You can feed a dog, you can pay more than I.'" As a result, not only good will but dogs disappeared from the village.[38]

Multiple sovereignty presented yet another challenge: the new political class had to not only defend its claim to sovereignty against other contenders but also sort out basic lines of authority within itself. The fledgling food-supply apparatus had to acquire sufficient political prestige to hold its own against other forces in the Bolshevik government. An important case was relations with the Red Army. In 1918 the newly created units of the Red Army played the same role as the units of the disintegrating tsarist army: it was a centrifugal force that relied on destructive self-provi-

36. Potapenko, *Zapiski*, 66–68. See also Kaganovich, *Kak dostaetsia khleb*, 13–14; *Tri goda*, 25ff.; D. S. Baburin, "Narkomprod v pervye gody sovetskoi vlasti," *Istoricheskie zapiski* 61 (1957): 358–59.

37. Kaganovich, *Kak dostaetsia khleb*, 16–18. See also Potapenko, *Zapiski*, 46–47, 71ff.; Mashkovich, *Deiatel'nost'*, 29, 15–17; *Tri goda*, 15–16; N. M. Vishnevskii, *Printsipy i metody organizatsionnogo raspredeleniia produktov prodovol'stviia i predmetov pervoi neobkhodimosti*, ed. V. Groman (Moscow, 1920), 157–58, 187–88.

38. A. M. Bol'shakov, *Derevnia 1917–1927* (Moscow, 1927), 90–91.

sionment. Only in September 1918 was "a bridle was thrown on the wild horse of military self-provisionment" by an interdepartmental commission that later came under the full control of the Food-Supply Commissariat.[39] But real progress in providing a workable substitute for military self-provisionment came from local organs called *oprodkomy*; these operated with scant regard for instructions from the center, which seemed glad to stay out of the way. The *oprodkomy* usually applied razverstka methods and often were the creators of new civilian food-supply committees in outlying areas. Looking back, food-supply officials felt that the *oprodkomy* had proved a great success in meeting the special demands of military provisionment while preventing dualism in food-supply policy.[40]

The battle among civilian institutions was no less rough and ready. Kaganovich described how agents of military and transport organizations searching for wood fuel would descend on Simbirsk and requisition carts needed for grain transport, using not only impressive-looking mandates but also salt and other material incentives that violated official prices for cartage. The local food-supply apparatus would not have been able to sustain these attacks without Kaganovich's extra authority as an agent of the center, and even he had to threaten force against other civilian and even military organizations.[41]

The shortage of trained and reliable personnel set severe limits on the professionalization of the apparatus. The center had to send out agents they knew little about; the local committees had to mobilize anyone who was at all literate.[42] The low quality of personnel galled not only the center but the peasants as well, who were forced to submit, in John Locke's words, to the "inconstant, uncertain, unknown, arbitrary will of another man."[43] The State Monitoring report confirmed the justice of the peasants' complaint that "too many products and commodities spill over into the pockets of the soviet bureaucracy, their families, lovers, acquaintances, and rela-

39. Bychkov, "Organizatsionnoe stroitel'stvo," 189.

40. The acronym *oprodkomy* is derived in part from *okrug*, "military district." My account is based on A. Khvoles, "Voenno-prodovol'stvennoe delo." N. P. Briukhanov, ed., "Kak pitalis' i snabzhalis' Krasnaia Armiia i flot prodovol'stviem," in *Grazhdanskaia voina* (Moscow, 1928–1930), 2:306–26, is substantially based on the Khvoles article, although no credit is given. Malle, *Economic Organization*, 440–44, incorrectly portrays the *oprodkomy* as army institutions. See also Kritsman, *Geroicheskii period*, 220.

41. Kaganovich, *Kak dostaetsia khleb*, 24–25, 30–34, 39–40; Mashkovich, *Deiatel'nost'*, 20–24, 51–53; Vladimirov, *Udarnye momenty*, 28.

42. Orlov, *Delo*, 19; Potapenko, *Zapiski*, 71; Kaganovich, *Kak dostaetsia khleb*, 39–40.

43. John Locke, *Second Treatise of Government*, ed. C. B. Macpherson (Indianapolis, 1980), chap. 4, 17.

tions."[44] In late 1920, Shlikhter observed that "the provincial food-supply committee has not found in itself the resources and capacity to carry out a sharp distinction between what can and what cannot be done in the Soviet Republic. As a result—and this is really unfortunate—there has grown up a feeling among the population, precisely in connection with the food-supply question, that for a food-supply official in the Soviet Republic, everything is possible. This is not the case, comrades; this is not true."[45]

Local officials might well have replied that they had been handed an impossible task by the center. They were told to get as much grain as possible out of the province but preserve "good-neighbor relations" with the peasantry; to crush mercilessly any resistance but stay within the bounds of strict legality; to subordinate unhesitatingly local interests to state interests but involve the local population in the work of the apparatus.

The difficulty of finding the small amounts held by the middle peasant goaded the food-supply officials into simply taking what they found, on the assumption that the peasant could subsist on what was hidden. Potapenko asserts that despite the many protests such confiscations caused, the peasants seemed to eat well enough during the winter. But he also admits that abuses took place; abuses or not, the political cost of this kind of pressure was high.[46]

Top officials tried to improve the work of the lower rungs of the apparatus by resorting to campaign methods. Kaganovich sent out forty top provincial officials on a mission to rouse local food-supply officials from their amateurish lack of initiative and dependence on local influence.[47] In the second half of 1919 this strategy took the form of food-supply conferences (*prodsoveshchaniia*). These consisted of the chairmen of the relevant food-supply committee, soviet executive committee, and party committee; the food-supply conference itself was chaired by a representative of a higher level (often a member of the provincial soviet executive committee). This new institution was useful not only for campaign purposes but also for popularizing food-supply policy in state and even party circles that had little understanding or sympathy for it.

One supporter of the new strategy, N. Osinskii, argued that the food-supply conferences could replace the "vanished base [*opora*]" earlier provided by the Committees of the Poor.[48] The shift from enlisting the masses

44. Mashkovich, *Deiatel'nost*, 44–47.

45. Shlikhter, *Agrarnyi vopros*, 398–402 (describing Tambov). See also Dukes, *Red Dusk*, 296.

46. Potapenko, *Zapiski*, 101–2, 125.

47. Kaganovich, *Kak dostaetsia khleb*, 24–25, 34.

48. *Prod. politika*, 189–92. See also *Pravda*, 24 November 1920; Zubareva, *Khleb Prikam'ia*, 46–50; Kaganovich, *Kak dostaetsia khleb*, 34; *Tri goda*, 25–30; Vladi-

for crusades to enlisting cadres for limited campaigns reveals the growing importance of the gubernatorial solution, with its emphasis on building a centralized and technically adequate apparatus, working out a modus vivendi with the population, and concentrating scarce administrative resources on priority tasks. The gubernatorial solution was also seen in the continued reliance on the energetic pressure of agents from the center. Kaganovich's response to unexpected bottlenecks in grain transport is a model: "I fired people, arrested them, even threatened shooting; I sent out plenipotentiary agents and traveled around myself."[49]

The Bolsheviks faced severe challenges in their effort to create a serviceable apparatus: finding material incentives for political services, obtaining adequate information, preventing open warfare between bureaucracies, limiting local arbitrariness and abuse. One reason food-supply officials were loyal to the razverstka system is that it was devised to compensate for the weaknesses of the fledgling apparatus. The same thinking helps explain their opposition to the introduction of a food-supply tax.

In the spring of 1921 two important changes were made in food-supply policy: the replacement of the razverstka by a food-supply tax and the decriminalization of private grain transactions. In 1920 no one defended decriminalization, whereas the food-supply tax found many defenders. One food-supply official from the Kuban area, L. G. Prigozhin, even argued that it was not necessary to replace the razverstka with a tax but only necessary to realize that the razverstka had already become a tax.[50] But a majority of food-supply officials rejected this proposal.

No food-supply official would have disagreed with A. E. Badaev when he argued in 1920 that under present conditions, "say what you will, we lack a socialist mode of procurement." Even Frumkin, a strong supporter of the razverstka method, granted that it was introduced by bourgeois governments and that it was not socialism but a temporary necessity.[51] But Frumkin argued that the apparatus was simply too weak to realize the political and economic advantages of a tax system. Whereas the razverstka

---

mirov, *Udarnye momenty*, 5; *Chetvertaia godovshchina Narkomproda* (Moscow, 1921), 15–23.

49. Kaganovich, *Kak dostaetsia khleb*, 30–34.

50. *Biulletin NKP*, 2 July 1920; Iurkov, *Ekonomicheskaia politika*, 121–22; *Pravda*, 3 October 1920. Many food-supply officials from the southern surplus regions favored the food-supply tax. The usual translation of *prodnalog*, "tax in kind," is in one respect unfortunate: the English-speaking reader has a tendency to read it as a "tax in *kind*," that is, as opposed to a money tax. But in 1921 the *prodnalog* was opposed to the *prodrazverstka*; hence the term should be read as "*tax* in kind," as opposed to "*razverstka* in kind."

51. *Biulletin NKP*, 30 June 1920; *Ekonomicheskaia zhizn'*, 30 June and 1 July 1920; *Prod. politika*, 173–79; *Tri goda*, 15.

relied on a quota assignment to the village as a whole on the basis of collective responsibility, a tax gave an assignment directly to the individual taxpayer. This necessity imposed a strain on what continued to be the weakest aspect of food-supply work, namely, accurate registration.[52] There were indeed many arbitrary assessments under the razverstka system— but these were due to the difficulties of registration that would also cripple a tax system. In addition, food-supply officials predicted that most peasants would claim to have less than the taxable minimum, and grain would have to be collected again by the old methods of confiscation, requisition, and arrests. Furthermore, they argued that given the continued absence of industrial items, a tax system in itself would not solve the problem of stimulating the production of surpluses above the minimum.[53]

The food-supply tax as it was introduced in 1921 tried to take account of these realities. In fact, one may go further and argue that the tax was a continuation of long-standing efforts to improve the apparatus and over-come uncertainty. It was carefully designed not to require exact data. Individual assignments were based on the crudest of indicators: amount of sown acreage and number of dependents ("eaters"). Other factors, such as quality of land, amount of equipment, hiring of labor, and other sources of income, were ignored.[54]

The penchant of local officials to add supplementary assignments was another target of the food-supply tax legislation. The razverstka had implied a promise to leave the peasant alone after it was fulfilled, but Lenin himself admitted that officials had tended to collect the razverstka not once but two or three times.[55] The essence of the new system was, as Shlikhter argued, to give firm "juridical recognition" to the promises of the old system. Even after the introduction of the tax system, it required the full authority of the center to keep local officials from breaking this promise.[56] It was no wonder that Mikhail Tukhachevskii reported to Lenin in July that one of the difficulties of the pacification campaign in Tambov was peasant cynicism about the new decrees. The peasants had heard soothing words before, and now their reaction was, "These are good decrees, all right, but in the localities they are somehow redecreed."[57]

52. Tenth Party Congress, 415–25 (Tsiurupa).
53. *Biulleten NKP,* 2 July 1920. Supporters of a food-supply tax advocated using foreign exchange to obtain exchangeable goods.
54. Vladimirov, *Udarnye momenty,* 13–15; V. P. Danilov, "Sovetskaia nalogovaia politika v dokolkhoznoi derevne," in *Oktiabr' i sovetskoe krest'ianstvo* (Moscow, 1977), 164–91.
55. Lenin, *PSS,* 43:312–13. See also *PSS,* 40:337–39 for an expression of confusion about the nature of the razverstka.
56. Shlikhter, *Agrarnyi vopros,* 440–41.
57. Vladimir Antonov-Ovseenko, quoting peasants, in Trotsky, *Trotsky Papers,*

To reassure the peasantry, a highly visible crackdown on local abuses and the exemplary punishment of food-supply officials had already begun in February 1921. Food-supply officials realized that on this occasion they were being used as whipping boys and were understandably bitter. Tsiurupa defended his people at the Tenth Party Congress: "Yes, among us are many crooks, and we have made many mistakes, but among us there are also heroes of food-supply work, and this we must remember."[58]

The food-supply tax legislation set up local committees to monitor the tax assignments. In an early draft of the legislation these committees were supposed to represent only the poorest peasants, but this was quickly changed to representation of all categories of taxpayer. In his commentary on the legislation Sviderskii especially wanted to avoid the impression that these taxpayer committees would be a "sort of Committee of the Poor."[59] These assurances reflected the logic of the gubernatorial solution. In the words of an official commentary, "The taxpayer is obliged to fulfill his tax obligation to the state: the state in turn has the right to set in motion all the force of state coercion in order to guarantee the fulfillment of the demands of the law—but along with this the state is also obliged to give a definite guarantee to the taxpayer against any breach of the law tending to his harm."[60]

A food-supply official pointed out in 1921 that the razverstka had created the technical preconditions for the tax.[61] This was true not only because the Bolsheviks had created a workable, if clumsy, apparatus, which after the reforms of 1921 was able to apply the necessary pressure without excessive political damage, gather enough statistical information to distribute the tax burden fairly equitably, and physically receive and transport the grain. It was also true because policy-makers had moved away from proletarianization toward professionalization of the apparatus and had striven for several years to overcome their own lack of knowledge and give the peasantry some small measure of predictability.

2:518–24, 480–85. The visible reluctance of local food-supply officials did not help; Kaganovich in Siberia was reprimanded for still referring to the food-supply tax as a kulak proposal, even after the Tenth Party Congress. Poliakov, *Perekhod,* 244.

58. Tenth Party Congress, 415–25. A later speaker sarcastically gave an example of one such hero in Siberia, who rode around saying, "I will stop at nothing to see that the razverstka is fulfilled 100 percent. If you don't do it, I'll put a bullet in my head, but before I do, I'll lay a thousand of you down." The razverstka was only fulfilled 40 percent—to what extent the "hero" carried out his threat is unknown. Tenth Party Congress, 428–31.

59. *Na bor'bu,* 48; E. B. Genkina, *Gosudarstvennaia deiatel'nost' V. I. Lenina* (Moscow, 1969) 87–88. On peasant skepticism about these committees, see Eighth Central Executive Committee, 103–4 (Osinskii).

60. *Na bor'bu,* 60 (article by A. A.).

61. *Chetvertaia godovshchina,* 9–14 (S. Aktov).

DECRIMINALIZING FREE TRADE:
OVERCOMING THE FEAR OF CHAOS

The Russian time of troubles meant an increase in state interference in daily life, not only because of the material burden of state obligations but even more because of demands to help the new bureaucracy and make its life easier by providing registration information, filling out forms, and obeying regulations. The peasant saw these requirements as a nuisance and as a reflection of a profoundly distasteful worldview.

In Leonid Leonov's novel *The Badgers* a peasant rebel entertains his comrades with a fable on this subject, set in an "olden time when there was more elbow room everywhere, and the air was purer and clearer." When Kalafat was nine years old, he told his father, the king, Your kingdom has no order. Do you know how many blades of grass there are in the field? How many trees in the wood? Fishes in the river? Stars in the sky? And he set about numbering each one: "He branded the fish, issued passports to the birds, and wrote down every blade of grass in a book. . . . The bear pined away, not knowing whether he was man nor beast, now that he'd been given a passport." But Kalafat went too far when he tried to label the stars, for when he climbed the tower he had ordered prisoners of war to build, it sank beneath his own weight, and he never got any nearer the stars. Yet although Kalafat was in despair, "the fields were sweet with the smell of flowers, and the birds sang over them. Nature had thrown off Kalafat's passport and was herself again."[62]

The food-supply officials were aware of this attitude. But they could not seem to help themselves: even when they set out to give something to the peasantry, they imposed further bureaucratization. The commodity-exchange system is a good example. In his pamphlet of 1918 Maliutin promised the peasants that the new state authority would "not allow the middleman-merchant to get big money in any way for any reason." To replace this wasteful middleman, the following system was instituted. The peasant delivers his grain for which he gets a receipt, and he turns his receipt in to the village Committee of the Poor. When that institution has gathered a sufficient number of receipts, an overall account is made and sent to the district Committee of the Poor. After the district committee gets enough of these, they draw up a list to send to the county food-supply committee. The county committee, armed with all these receipts, obtains the release of a certain amount of consumer goods. These are sent back to

62. Leonid Leonov, *The Badgers* (1923–1924), trans. Hilda Kazanina, (New York, 1947), 234–41. Kalafat's parable can also be found in *The Fatal Eggs*, 2d. ed., trans. Mirra Ginsburg (New York, 1987), 135–41. A similar point is made in Panteleimon Romanov's "Inventory" ("*Opis'* ") in *Fatal Eggs*, 6–11.

the district Committee of the Poor, which distributes them among the village committees in proportion to the amount of grain delivered and the number of residents. (How these two factors are combined is not explained.) The village committee hands out the goods not only to the peasants who delivered the grain but also to those without any grain surpluses. By that time the peasant must surely be blessing the day the Bolsheviks got rid of the middlemen—all those "parasites and spiders, merchants, dealers, and kulaks."[63]

There was only one way the state could substantially reduce this kind of interference: decriminalize free trade in grain and allow the private market to take on the major burden of collecting and distributing it. A tax system did not necessarily imply decriminalization. The essence of the tax system was to assure the peasant by giving him an individual assignment before the harvest. This policy implied individual control over any grain that remained, but it was still compatible with continued prohibition of free trade. When the food-supply tax decision was made at the Tenth Party Congress in the spring of 1921, Frumkin made exactly this point in supporting the tax but rejecting decriminalization.[64]

Yet for all their willingness to accommodate the peasants in other ways, food-supply officials refused even to consider decriminalization. Various explanations have been given for this refusal: devotion to socialist principle, complacent habituation to the use of force, or simple lack of imagination.[65] An examination of the debates over food-supply policy in 1920 does not support any of these but shows rather that the main motive was the fear of losing control and allowing the centrifugal forces of chaos to sweep over the fragile barriers the food-supply officials had erected at such cost.

The greatest source of scholarly confusion on this topic has been the failure to make a careful distinction between three issues: exchange versus coercion, monopoly versus free trade, and razverstka versus tax. In each case the reasoning of the food-supply officials was tied closely to the realities of the time of troubles.

It would hardly seem to be worth documenting the commitment of the Bolsheviks to the use of material incentives and the justice of equivalent exchange, except that the opposite impression is often left both by Western and Soviet historiography.[66] In the summer of 1918 Orlov wrote that along

63. Maliutin et al., *Knizhka,* 1st ed., 23–26.
64. Tenth Party Congress, 431–34.
65. See Malle, *Economic Organization,* esp. 488, and Vasilii Seliunin, "Istoki," *Novyi mir,* 1988, no. 5:162–89.
66. For examples, see Carr, *Bolshevik Revolution,* 2:169; Alec Nove, *An Economic History of the USSR* (London, 1969), 66; Poliakov, *Perekhod,* 223. Davydov comments on the neglect of material incentives by Soviet historians in "Tovaroobmen," 51–52.

with its demands for grain, the revolutionary state authority "strives to implement the principle, long put forward by the working masses and continually developed on the pages of the journal [of the Food-Supply Commissariat], of the equivalent exchange of economic goods between town and country, industry and agriculture."[67] The Bolsheviks were serious about the metaphorical description of the razverstka as a loan. In 1920 Evgenii Preobrazhenskii described "peasant weeks"—campaigns in which workers came to the village to help with the harvest and with repairs—as the "beginning of the payment for grain and for labor obligations. . . . We must show the village that soviet authority takes the peasant's surplus, while giving him almost nothing in return, only because of its poverty."[68]

The food-supply apparatus did not scorn the use of money, the sign and symbol of material value. If the razverstka was a loan, the IOUs were given in the form of money. By late 1920 inflation had reached such awe-inspiring heights that municipal authorities disposed of the formality of payment for certain services. This action did not signify a plunge into a moneyless economy, for the state still needed money to give to the peasants. The state also paid the workers in money so that they in turn could give it to the peasants via the black market.[69] In 1920 fears arose that the peasants would finally shed their money illusion, with unfortunate consequences for grain procurement. To prevent this, any agitation among the peasants to demand goods instead of money was deemed counterrevolutionary.[70]

According to food-supply officials, it was the economic breakdown of the time of troubles that made coercion necessary. In Tsiurupa's words, "We say to the peasant, 'Give us all you owe according to the razverstka. Then you will receive from us all that we are able to give you.' [But] we do not fool ourselves nor hide the fact that what we give is not an equivalent of what we receive. The means for the extraction of agricultural products is the force of state coercion."[71]

67. *Izv. NKP* (August 1918): 2; see also *Izv. NKP* (January 1919): 15–18 (Briukhanov and Shlikhter); Gol'man, cited in Strizhkov, *Otriady*, 106 and in Lars T. Lih, "Bolshevik *Razverstka* and War Communism," *Slavic Review* 44 (1986): 681; Potapenko, *Zapiski*, 47.

68. *Pravda*, 28 April 1920. Order of passages reversed.

69. Kritsman, *Geroicheskii period*, 138; A. Terne, *V tsartsve Lenina* (Berlin, 1922), 333–57.

70. Orlov, *Delo*, 28–30; Zubareva, *Khleb Prikam'ia*, 45–46; Lenin, *PSS*, 41:146–47 (June 1920); E. Preobrazhenskii, *Bumazhnye den'gi v epokhu proletarskoi revoliutsii* (Moscow, 1920), 48–58, 78–84; Kritsman, *Geroicheskii period*, 138.

71. Frumkin, *Tovaroobmen*, 7; *Prod. politika*, 195–96.

The frank reliance on coercion was in its way a tribute to the primacy of material incentive: once the means of material incentive were absent, there was no alternative but to rely on force—certainly the weak reed of revolutionary enthusiasm and loyalty would be almost useless. If anything, food-supply officials were somewhat naive about the ease of getting grain by economic methods once the emergency had passed. After noting that "everybody understands that there is no way to destroy Sukharevka [the Moscow bazaar that became a symbol of the illegal market] simply by decrees," Iurii Larin went on confidently to assert that "when the state has more products [under its control,] the need for Sukharevkas will disappear and all you will see at the Food Supply Commissariat will be happy faces."[72]

The changeover to a tax system in 1921 did not alter the realities that made coercion necessary. As Tsiurupa observed at the Tenth Party Congress, "Whether it is a tax, a razverstka, a monopoly, or perhaps some other procurement method, the procurement can still come only from the peasant's consumption norm, [and] nobody allows food to be ripped out of his mouth without resistance, either active or passive." In August 1921 Lenin echoed his demands of August 1918 by calling for the exemplary punishment of a few rich peasants in each district.[73]

If in fact less coercion was necessary in 1921 than earlier, it was not just because of the abandonment of the razverstka but also because of its achievements. The evidence points to a drop in the use of coercion taking place already by late 1920, especially in areas with long-standing food-supply institutions. Many food-supply officials commented on this drop in 1920, and their assertions are confirmed by the size of the Food-Supply Army, which began to decrease in December 1920. By January 1921 the Food-Supply Army was less than two-thirds of its size in September 1920.[74] This reduction seems difficult to square with the widespread peasant revolts of 1920–1921. But the presence of peasant rebels did not necessarily mean that day-to-day food-supply operations required the use of force. In the summer of 1920 Potapenko's worker detachment closed up shop in Voronezh despite troubles in the spring from agitators sent by the peasant rebel Antonov in neighboring Tambov. According to Potapenko, the peasants said to these agitators, "If the White generals Krasnov and Denikin couldn't handle the Reds, you surely won't succeed. And the

72. *Pravda*, 4 May 1920 and 17 October 1920.

73. Tenth Party Congress, 415–25 (Tsiurupa); Lenin, *PSS*, 53:92–93; *Na bor'bu*, 50–52 (Sviderskii); Baburin, "Narkomprod," 366.

74. Aleksentsev, "K voprosu," 163–64; *Biulletin NKP*, 9 September and 30 November 1920; Zubareva, *Khleb Prikam'ia*, 50; *Chetvertaia godovshchina*, 9–14.

razverstka—what can we say, it was also introduced because of the war. We have to stop making war right away."[75]

Other food-supply officials agreed that the key to peasant acceptance was the stability of Bolshevik authority.[76] The peasants realized that political reconstitution was the key to ending the time of troubles and that the Bolsheviks were the only viable candidate for a sovereign authority. Coercion could recede only when this basic uncertainty was removed.

The question of coercion versus exchange did not prejudge the question of the proper form of exchange—state grain monopoly or free trade. No one questioned that a state monopoly was better than free trade in the long run. The introduction of the food-supply tax did not mean any change in this proposition, which remained axiomatic throughout the 1920s. The real question was one of strategy: since the lack of exchange equivalents at the disposal of the state meant that a flourishing private market was unavoidable, should that market be prohibited and driven underground or should it be decriminalized?[77]

In 1920 everybody—including advocates of a food-supply tax—supported the prohibition strategy. The consensus was not confined to the Bolsheviks: the Menshevik David Dallin proposed a food-supply tax at the Eighth Congress of Soviets in December 1920 but vehemently denied that he wanted free trade.[78] On this subject the food-supply officials did not differ from accepted opinion.

The hostility of food-supply officials to the free market was based not only on a principled rejection of "speculation," which they shared with wide sections of Russian society, but also on their own experience with procurement efforts outside the framework of the monopoly. Sackmanism was stronger than ever in 1920. Starting from about the middle of 1919, the attempt to stamp out the illegal free market became progressively more pro forma, until by the middle of 1920 it had almost been abandoned in practical terms.[79] Despite this hostile tolerance, sackmanism was still a

75. Potapenko, *Zapiski*, 142, 159. Tambov is presented as a success story by Briukhanov in *Ekonomicheskaia zhizn'*, 28–29 September 1920; see also *Biulletin NKP*, 14 December 1920.

76. Vladimirov, *Udarnye momenty*, 17–20, 38–42; *Tri goda*, introduction by Sviderskii.

77. Various opinions were expressed about the proper rate of trade nationalization outside the grain monopoly and about the role of the commodity exchange program. See *Dekrety*, 4:41 (November 1918), 6:12 (5 August 1919); Kaganovich, *Kak dostaetsia khleb*, 21–24; Orlov, *Rabota*, 68–75, 351–55; Frumkin, *Tovaroobmen*, 5–6; *Prod. politika*, 256–60; Dmitrenko, "Bor'ba."

78. Eighth Congress of Soviets, 197–99. Trotsky advocated a food-supply tax in February 1920, but his proposal contains no hint of a legalized market. Lev Trotsky, *Novy kurs* (Moscow, 1924), 57–58. See also Lenin, *PSS*, 39:408 (July 1919).

79. Bychkov, "Organizatsionnoe stroitel'stvo"; *Ekonomicheskaia zhizn'*, 23 September 1920.

potent source of demoralization and corruption; all citizens, no matter what their attitude was toward the Bolsheviks, were forced to act according to the maxim "He who does not speculate, neither shall he eat."[80]

Food-supply officials had reason to doubt that the horde of small-time sackmen increased the amount of grain available. The sackman system did not itself bring new goods into circulation: it mainly relied on items embezzled from state stores so that, as Vladimirov expressed it, goods put on state register ended up on the register of the speculators. Inefficient in themselves, the sackmen were the cause of inefficiency in the state system: they broke the discipline of the state fixed price and undermined the commodity-exchange program by giving the peasant an alternate source of supply. Furthermore, the flourishing urban markets proved to the visiting peasant that the soviet authority was lying when it asserted that the city had nothing to give to the peasant.[81]

Food-supply officials were also exasperated with the "legal sackmanism" of workers who were allowed at various times to go into the countryside and make individual purchases of one or two poods of grain. Besides all the problems caused by regular sackmen, the *otpuskniki* (workers making purchases while on leave from their factories) caused political confusion by presenting the spectacle of workers making friends with kulaks and agitating against the monopoly. Sometimes opposition went beyond agitation: after observing a group of sailors on leave disarm a food-supply worker detachment, peasants in one Simbirsk village observed, "Now here is the real sovereign."[82]

Even official state procurement efforts helped solidify the loyalty of food-supply officials to the monopoly when they were conducted outside the monopoly framework. Kaganovich argued that the competition among agencies caused officials to lose the state point of view; he was appalled to see chains of middlemen form up within the government procurement agencies. The state purchase of honey in Simbirsk in 1919 illustrated his point. The Food-Supply Commissariat signed a contract with the Chief Confectionary Committee (Glavkonditer) for honey. Since the committee did not have its own procurement apparatus, it made a deal with Tsentrosoiuz, the central cooperative organization, which in turn made a deal with an organization called Petserkop. This body contracted with a local organization, the Alatyr county union of consumer societies. The county

80. Terne, *V tsarstve*, 333–57. The authorities often connived at the workers' involvement in sackmanism by giving them items produced at their factories as part of their pay—a sort of workers' equivalent of the private plot.

81. M. K. Vladimirov, *Meshochnichestvo i ego sotsial'no-politicheskoe otrazhenie* (Kharkov, 1920); Kaganovich, *Kak dostaetsia khleb*, 12; Simon Zagorsky, *La république des soviets* (Paris 1921), 147–48.

82. Kaganovich, *Kak dostaetsia khleb*, 12–15; *Biulletin NKP*, 9 October 1920.

union gave the job to district and village cooperatives, which hired private purchasing agents. These last were the only ones to make contact with the beekeepers. This intricate arrangement did not lead Kaganovich to reflect that perhaps the existence of middlemen had all along been due to objective economic circumstances rather than private greed; he concluded instead that the poor results of this system of honey purchases demonstrated that state procurement should be directed by a single will.[83]

Popular attitudes toward free trade were complicated. There is evidence that at least the workers in the capitals supported the prohibition of free trade. Yet at the same time that these workers insisted that Sukharevka be closed down, they expressed their hatred of the blockade detachments. The main complaint against these detachments was the corruption that caused the poor to starve while the speculators waxed rich. But the workers demanded impartial enforcement, not decriminalization: by 1920 many had been priced out of the black market, and they now saw it as a "source of depravity and embezzlement."[84] An editorial in *Pravda* summed up the popular attitude as follows: "Yes, the masses are for the razverstka—but only one that can really be paid and is carried out without scandalous abuse. Yes, the masses are for the monopoly—but a complete one that does not leave room for Sukharevkas."[85] When the Moscow Sukharevka was finally closed down in late 1920, there was no complaint from the workers.[86]

The loyalty of food-supply officials to the monopoly was thus based on a perception, grounded in their own experience, that "unity of will" was a necessary bulwark against centrifugal forces.[87] This perception determined their attitude on the separate question of the best method of collecting the state grain obligation: tax or razverstka. As Frumkin argued, taxes were "unacceptable methods in principle since they exclude the monopoly."[88] Their feelings on this point, however, were not based on any love of state regulation in and of itself. Contrary to stereotype, a hostility to bureau-

83. Kaganovich, *Kak dostaetsia khleb*, 35–38; *Izv. NKP*, 1920, no. 3–5:2. Relying on purchasing was criticized as drift (*samotek*); see *Ekonomicheskaia zhizn'*, 15 June 1920; *Prod. i snab.* (Kostroma), no. 8, 15 October 1918, 2–3; *Prod. politika*, 256–60, 173–79; *Prod. biulletin* (Siberia), no. 2–3, 1 October 1920, 5.
84. *Pravda*, 27 November 1920; Sergei Semenov, *Golod*, in *Izbrannoe* (Leningrad, 1970), 76. According to Okninskii, the main customers of the bazaars were railwaymen (rich from bribes) and professionals such as doctors. *Dva goda*, 278–86.
85. *Pravda*, 27 November 1920.
86. Badaev, *Desiat' let bor'by i stroitel'stva* (Leningrad, 1927), 87–90. Vladimirov, *Udarnye momenty*, 31–33, gives a different picture of worker outlook in the Ukraine. See also Lih, "Bolshevik *Razverstka*," 679–80; Dmitrenko, "Bor'ba," 327–30.
87. Kaganovich, *Kak dostaetsia khleb*, 35–38.
88. *Biulletin NKP*, 2 July 1920.

cratic overregulation was part of Bolshevik political culture during the civil-war years. A 1919 resolution on the subject of local handicrafts stated, "Given that a break in the whole structure of handicraft, [or] its restructuring [by] excessively inhibiting regulation, would hold up the flow of craft items for commodity exchange, [the food-supply conference] considers it necessary to liberate handicraft production [from such regulation]."[89] The food-supply officials' fear of the tax system stemmed rather from the feeling that the food-supply apparatus was already barely holding its own against the illegal market; it would not stand a chance if the market was further strengthened by surpluses remaining under producer control.

The main reason for this feeling of weakness was the state's own poverty. The state had never been able to rely on exchange equivalents; as Frumkin stated flatly in late 1921, "commodity exchange never existed and still does not."[90] Yet food-supply officials were unanimous that, in Sviderskii's words, "no matter how chaotically commodity exchange was set up, it was undoubtedly one of the most powerful factors in the state's grain procurement operation."[91] At the very least it showed that the state was making a good-faith effort to supply the village.

By early 1921, the growing crisis in the availability of exchange items meant that any kind of commodity exchange was becoming impossible. Tsiurupa gave the following statistics at the Tenth Party Congress: the amount of nails being received by the village (forty thousand poods) was less than the amount of castor oil received before the war (sixty thousand poods). When this remark got a laugh, Tsiurupa commented that although it was perhaps funny, it was tragic at the same time.[92] Indeed the situation began to take on the air of tragicomedy, as the Bolsheviks reached beyond basic items such as cloth and nails to whatever they could lay their hands on to give to the peasants. The list of items to be exchanged included the following:[93]

Agricultural equipment	19,000 poods
Nails	1,000 poods
Powder	540,000 boxes

89. *Izv. NKP*, no. 1–2 (January 1919): 27.

90. Frumkin, *Tovaroobmen*, 4; Iu. K. Strizhkov, "Priniatie dekreta o prodovol'stvennoi razverstke i ego osushchestvlenie v pervoi polovine 1919 g.," in *Oktiabr' i sovetskoe krest'ianstvo* (Moscow, 1977), 154–56; *Prod. politika*, 195–96; Orlov, *Rabota*, 362–66; Mashkovich, *Deiatel'nost'*, 35–36, 48–51; Kaganovich, *Kak dostaetsia khleb*, 12–15.

91. *Prod. politika*, 253–56, 166–73.

92. Tenth Party Congress, 415–25.

93. Terne, *V tsarstve*, 258.

Perfume	240,000 vials
Rope	5,000 poods
Glazed crockery	3,000,000 pieces
Church bells	3,000 pieces

Lenin was a little apologetic about the church bells and noted that some comrades hoped that the bells would soon be melted down and used for electrical wiring. But at least, he continued, the state was not relying on harmful items such as vodka. Lenin tried to make the best of it by asserting that "if we are able to run our affairs properly, we can build up heavy industry on the basis of pomade." For if nothing else was available, he concluded, even pomade could be traded with the peasant for grain.[94]

Lenin's speech provoked a revealing parody. It was now clear how to save Russia, people said. Declare a mandatory pomade obligation. Start a crash campaign by announcing a Communist Pomade Week. Set up head offices such as Glavpomade. (*Glavkizm*, or chief-committeeism, was the popular name for bureaucratic overcentralization.) Insert articles in *Pravda* about the "antipomade policies of the counterrevolution." Then use the three thousand church bells to announce the onset of a new prosperous life and wait for the perfumed, powdered, and rouged peasants to bring grain to the starving cities in glazed crockery.[95]

The food-supply officials might have responded that it was indeed the poverty of the state that forced it to resort to the methods satirized here. As Osinskii declared in December 1920:

> People say: establish a definite rate per desiatin. And what is hidden behind these words? [The expectation is that] a surplus will remain, and this free surplus will be used as pleases the producer, that is, he can trade freely with it. . . . We do not have any goods fund [and therefore] no state procurement— tax or razverstka, call it what you like—will produce anything if a free grain trade begins alongside it. In that case, all products will flow into that channel. . . . He who opens that little door to free trade will lead us to the collapse of our food-supply policy and to the destruction of the national economy.[96]

In the context of 1920, when decriminalization was not an option, the food-supply officials clearly had the stronger case. Giving the peasant an

94. Lenin, *PSS*, 43:326 (speech of 27 May 1921).
95. Terne, *V tsarstve*, 259. This is an early example of a new postrevolutionary folk art form, the political anecdote.
96. Eighth Congress of Soviets, 146–47. See also Potapenko, *Zapiski*, 133ff.

individual assignment before the harvest would bring few advantages and make enforcement of the monopoly impossible. Even in the context of 1921 and a decriminalized market the gloomy predictions of the food-supply officials were more justified than has been thought. Economic breakdown did negate many of the benefits of a tax. The state was just scraping by as it was, so the promise of lower grain-collection targets could not be met. Already under the razverstka the amounts given to the Ukraine and Siberia in 1920 were significantly below the estimated surpluses for those regions, and owing to the drought, the razverstka had been lifted from many of the central provinces.[97] The party commission that worked out details of the food-supply tax after the Tenth Party Congress first decided (with an estimated available surplus of 500 million poods) to set the tax at 300–350 million poods—that is, above the 1920–1921 razverstka figure of 285 million poods. At the insistence of the Central Committee the tax was lowered to 240 million poods. But the tax represented only the amount to be taken without compensation. For a true comparison with the razverstka we should add the amount the state hoped to obtain through commodity exchange, 160 million poods. This addition makes a total target figure of 400 million poods to be obtained by the state in 1921–1922.[98] Furthermore, individual tax assignments still remained dependent on the size of the harvest: a schedule with eleven categories was announced, and the tax rate per desiatin was calculated on the basis of the category that matched the local harvest.[99]

In the short term the tax system ran into other problems predicted by the food-supply officials: grain procurement *did* collapse, and the free market *was* uncontrollable. The hope of using permission to trade as an incentive for razverstka fulfillment proved groundless since the peasants interpreted the decision of the Tenth Party Congress as an immediate authorization of free trade everywhere. The state barely scraped by with grain procurement for the rest of the 1920–1921 agricultural year. Both this remnant of the razverstka and the collection of the new tax in 1921–1922 required the liberal application of coercion. The state's attempt to procure grain through voluntary commodity exchange was, as predicted, a

97. Strizhkov, *Otriady*, 218; Davydov, *Bor'ba za khleb*, 137–38, 144–63.

98. In some localities the tax alone was higher in 1921 than in 1920 because hay and straw were added to grain deliveries. Bol'shakov, *Derevnia*, 456–57. In the event, commodity exchange gave almost nothing, and the tax figure was reduced in December 1921 because of the drought. The lowered tax—133 million poods—was almost entirely obtained by March 1922. Genkina, *Gosudarstvennaia deiatel'nost'*, 111, 296; Lenin, *PSS*, 44:9.

99. *Na bor'bu*, 54–59. For objections to a tax independent of harvest size, see Eighth Congress of Soviets, 146–47 (Osinskii).

failure: the creaky apparatus of food-supply committees and cooperatives proved no match for the legalized sackmen, and barter at state-determined ratios could not compete with the demand for money-mediated exchange. If it had not been for the unexpected intervention of Herbert Hoover's American Relief Agency in the second half of the year, it is doubtful whether the new food-supply policy would have sustained the challenge of the famine in the Volga region.[100]

In the long term, contrary to their experience during the time of troubles, the food-supply officials found that the decriminalized market was a force not for disintegration but for reconstitution. The main benefit of decriminalization was an end to the unavoidable costs of repressing the market. Speculation was a victimless crime, and the consequences of its prohibition are strikingly similar to those of the prohibition of drugs, liquor, or prostitution. Two present-day criminologists have summarized the effects of the "overreach" of the law when it prohibits victimless crimes: "The criminal law operates as a 'crime tariff' which makes the supply . . . profitable for the criminal by driving up prices and at the same time discourages competition by those who might enter the market were it legal." They argue that these high prices in turn have a "criminogenic" effect because of the need for users to obtain cash, which helps create a much wider criminal subculture with a romantic aura of rebellion. Police resources become enormously overstrained and pressing priorities are neglected. The prohibitions are hard to enforce because of the lack of complainants; arbitrary enforcement and bribery flourish.[101]

The attempt to outlaw private grain transactions had exactly the same range of effects. Without decriminalization the Bolsheviks were faced with a no-win choice between the political costs of tolerating corruption and the costs of attempting to crack down on the illegal market. Massive corruption throughout Russian society, political disaffection resulting from the ineffective harassment by the universally hated blockade detachments, scandalously inefficient methods of individual grain provisionment—most of these heavy costs could be avoided at a stroke.

The food-supply officials regarded the grain market as a mighty competitor to state procurement—which it was, in the context of market

100. Bolshevik reactions to the famine are discussed in two articles by Charles M. Edmundson: "The Politics of Hunger: The Soviet Response to Famine, 1921," *Soviet Studies* 29 (October 1977), and "An Inquiry into the Termination of Soviet Famine Relief Programmes and the Renewal of Grain Export, 1922–1923," *Soviet Studies* 33 (July 1981).

101. Norval Morris and Gordon Hawkins, *The Honest Politician's Guide to Crime Control* (Chicago, 1969), 5–6.

prohibition. But a decriminalized market could also be a partner for the state. It strengthened the incentive for fulfillment of state tasks by making the reward of fulfillment more enticing, in the manner of a private plot on a collective farm: the peasant could trade openly and without harassment only after paying his tax. The market could also take over portions of the major task of food collection and distribution, leaving the state free to concentrate its attention on its own priorities.

Even before 1921 there had been a movement in distribution policy toward a reduction of the number of people for whom the state guaranteed a ration. Instead of distributing available food more or less equally to everybody at amounts no one could live on, it was decided to guarantee ("armor") a livable ration for workers in the most important industries. This policy of purposive provisionment (*tselevoe snabzhenie*) meant that the state was already relying on the existence of a market for all other consumers. Decriminalization made it official. Andrei Vyshinskii, working at the time in the distribution section of the Food-Supply Commissariat, used class rhetoric to describe the result:

> So you see that when the state removed the prohibition on fending for oneself from the disorganizing spontaneity that surrounded it, it received both the right and the possibility of concerning itself with those in whose name the struggle went on, for whom mortal sacrifices were made, and for whom the future is being constructed.
>
> So you see that the state has the right to say to the mass of bourgeois parasites entangling it and draining away its blood and vital fluids: "Begone! Fend for yourselves! Use your freedom for the sake of your stomach. I have nothing to do with you—my strength, cares and thoughts belong to another."[102]

Given the Bolshevik consensus in 1920 against free trade, the food-supply officials could only discover these advantages *after* the market had been decriminalized. And indeed, when we inquire into the decision to decriminalize the grain trade, we find that it was not really made by the Bolsheviks.

Since any advocacy of decriminalization was taboo, there was only one place where such proposals could emanate, and that was the very top: Lenin and the Politburo. Kalinin observed in the spring of 1921 that if he

---

102. A. Ia. Vyshinskii, *Voprosy raspredeleniia i revoliutsiia* (Moscow, 1922), 20. In 1918–1919, 12 million people were maintained by the state; this number grew to 35 million in 1920–1921 and fell to 5 million by 1921–1922. Prokopovich, *Economic Condition*, 133.

had suggested a legalized market four months earlier, Tsiurupa would have sent him to a lunatic asylum.[103] But Tsiurupa could not send Lenin to a lunatic asylum, and so he had to go along with the Politburo on 8 February 1921 when it made the decision both to impose a tax and to allow "local economic circulation" (Tsiurupa's own grudging euphemism for local markets).[104]

Lenin's decision was a response to a sudden burst of strength in the centrifugal forces of disintegration. The harvest failure of 1920 meant that by December the razverstka figure for European Russia was lowered from 224.5 million poods to 193 million (it had been set at 327 million the previous year). Even so, food-supply officials grimly realized that diminished peasant resources meant more resistance from both peasants and local officials. Increased pressure on well-off peasants meant more room for administrative abuse. Since the amount of exchange items was less than ever before, the use of force was again the only guarantee of the razverstka. At the same time officials realized that greater reliance on peasant recruits would make the Food-Supply Army a shaky instrument for putting the necessary pressure on the peasantry.[105]

At best the Bolsheviks could offer the workers only the same wretched conditions of 1920. More likely, even the grain acquired with so much difficulty would be of little benefit, given transport difficulties (both cartage and rail) about which food-supply officials could do little. Urban rations were prematurely increased in late 1920, and as a result reserves became exhausted, and the plight of city dwellers seemed desperate. By February 1921 the conditional support observed in the summer and fall of 1920 was melting away. Peasants in Siberia cutting railroad lines, sailors mutinying in Kronstadt, workers striking in Petrograd—the centrifugal forces could no longer be contained.[106]

Lenin's label for the forces of disintegration was "petty-bourgeois disorganizing spontaneity [*stikhiia*]." The petty-bourgeois nature of the peasant, it seemed, craved the security of a food-supply tax. But as the food-

103. Genkina, *Gosudarstvennaia deiatel'nost'*, 105.

104. Genkina, *Gosudarstvennaia deiatel'nost'*, 91.

105. *Biulletin NKP*, 7 December and 28 December 1920; *Ekonomicheskaia zhizn'*, 28–29 September 1920; *Pravda*, 9 September 1920. On the decline in worker participation and the growth in peasant recruits, see Aleksentsev, "K voprosu," 165; Chistikov, "Prodovol'stvennaia politika."

106. Lenin, *PSS*, 42:216–27, 306–9, 333, 348–50, 353–66; Genkina, *Gosudarstvennaia deiatel'nost'*, 79–80; Oliver Radkey, *The Unknown Civil War in Soviet Russia*, (Stanford, 1976), esp. 229; Bertrand Mark Patenaude, "Bolshevism in Retreat: The Transition to the New Economic Policy," Ph.D. diss., Stanford University, 1987. The Provisional Government on the eve of its downfall faced the same problem of grain that was unavailable because of transport problems.

supply officials themselves argued, "free disposal" of the surplus meant that prohibition of free trade would be utterly ineffective. Lenin saw the validity of this argument, and so when he decided "to satisfy the desire of the nonparty peasant" for the tax, he felt it only made sense to take the next step of decriminalizing local markets.[107]

Up to this point the decision to introduce the food-supply tax was similar to earlier temporary concessions to the weary masses, such as allowing individual workers to purchase two poods of grain. The food-supply officials had always argued that these concessions only strengthened the centrifugal forces of disintegration. But they had built better than they knew, and to their surprise they now found themselves able not only to withstand these forces but also to use them to make reconstitution more secure.

The food-supply officials were thus in a better position than many other Bolsheviks to appreciate these various benefits once they became evident. Many of them became staunch supporters of NEP and even members of the right opposition. The list includes Tsiurupa and Vladimirov (who both died in the mid-1920s) as well as Osinskii and possibly Sviderskii.[108] Special mention should be made of Frumkin, whose brave defense of NEP is enshrined in Stalin's speeches.[109] These men showed no nostalgia for the razverstka of the civil-war years.

It remains true that at the time of the changeover to the food-supply tax in the spring of 1921, the Bolsheviks still hoped to decriminalize markets only on a local basis. The Bolshevik publicist R. Arskii assigned the market a modest place in his description of the new policy: "The tax consists of this: having handed over a certain amount of grain for the needs of the soviet authority, the rest may be disposed according to whim [*po proizvolu*]. You can use it for minor consumption, or for sowing, or feed it to livestock, or exchange it for state products, or even sell it at the market or bazaar."[110] The Bolsheviks quickly found they could not hold the line and

---

107. Lenin, *PSS*, 43:29, 57–73.

108. Vladimirov is treated as a model "right communist" by N. Valentinov in *The New Economic Policy and the Party Crisis After the Death of Lenin* (Stanford, 1971), chap. 7. My speculation concerning Sviderskii is based on his sudden switch of jobs in early 1929 from a high post at the People's Commissariat of Agriculture to diplomatic representative in Latvia. An exception is Kaganovich, who joined the Trotskyist opposition.

109. Stalin, *Sochineniia*, 11:116–26, 270–77. According to Terne, Frumkin (who had responsibility for the razverstka campaign in the Cossack regions) was particularly notorious for fierce repression, and Frumkin himself says in his speech at the party congress that he was known as a "fairly tough food-supply official [*prodovol'stvennik*]." Terne, *V tsarstve*, 219–24; Tenth Party Congress, 431–34.

110. Arskii, *Nalog vmesto razverstki* (Novocherkassk, n.d.).

that they had to accept the existence of a national free market. The real decision that brought the time of troubles to an end was thus made not by them but by the Russian people, when they refused to accept the half loaf of local markets. In truth, the Bolsheviks discovered the New Economic Policy just as Columbus discovered the New World—by hoping it was something else.

9   Reflections on
a Time of Troubles

The miseries of the poor are such as cannot easily be borne;
such as have already incited them in many parts of the
kingdom to an open defiance of Government, and produced
one of the greatest of political evils—the necessity of ruling by
immediate force. . . . We have often deliberated how we
should prosper, we are now to inquire how we shall subsist.

Samuel Johnson, writing of the dearth in 1766

[In those days] even the arguments of reason could be accepted
more easily from someone with a rifle, if the someone was a
worker or a peasant as well.

A food-supply official in 1923

In 1924 the People's Commissariat of Food Supply was abolished and its
functions taken over by the Commissariats of Finance and Internal Trade.
The Food-Supply Commissariat was a direct descendant of the Special
Conference on Food Supply created in 1915. The Special Conference gave
rise to the Ministry of Food Supply in 1917, which in turn served as the
basis for the Food-Supply Commissariat. Given the time lag of institutional inertia, the time of troubles was marked by the existence of a special
central institution whose mission was to carry out what was normally the
routine job of food-supply distribution. The demise of the Food-Supply
Commissariat also ended the publication of its short-lived journal *Food
Supply and Revolution*. The trauma of the time of troubles seemed on its
way to becoming a memory.

But the scars left by the time of troubles could not be forgotten easily,
and the whole future development of the Soviet Union was deeply affected
by the drama of the years 1914–1921. In retrospect this drama first appears as a titanic struggle between the centrifugal forces that accelerated
social breakdown and the centralizing forces that strengthened reconstitution. But a closer look reveals the characteristic instability and lack of
clarity of a time of troubles: forces that are constructive one day are
destructive the next—rebellion against authority turns into support for
authority—policies devised to strengthen the center provoke anarchy at
the periphery.

This instability leads to the dilemma of Hobbes's choice. A time of troubles is a period that lies between two possibilities: breakdown and reconstitution. Each of these possibilities imposes its own special logic on behavior. The logic of breakdown resembles the anarchy of international relations, and the logic of reconstitution resembles a country with a generally recognized authority. The two logics are well described by Kenneth Waltz:

> In a self-help system [such as the one created by breakdown], each of the units spends a portion of its effort, not in forwarding its own good, but in providing the means of protecting itself against others. . . . In every age and place, the units of self-help systems—nations, corporations, or whatever—are told that the greater good, along with their own, requires them to act for the sake of the system and not for their own narrowly defined advantage. . . . The very problem, however, is that rational behavior, given structural constraints, does not lead to the wanted results. With each country constrained to take care of itself, no one can take care of the system. . . . The international imperative is "take care of yourself!"
>
> Insofar as a realm is formally organized [or reconstituted], its units are free to specialize, to pursue their own interests without concern for developing the means of maintaining their identity and preserving their security in the presence of others. They are free to specialize because they have no reason to fear the increased interdependence that goes with specialization. . . . The domestic imperative is "specialize!"[1]

The basic uncertainty of a time of troubles is which of these two logics will prevail. It leads to the importance, and the difficulty, of Hobbes's choice: support the central authority if it has a chance of being effective, but sabotage the central authority and look out for yourself if it appears to be ineffective. For many participants, this dilemma is not just a matter of self-interest but a painful moral choice as well.[2]

The dilemma of Hobbes's choice was imposed on all social groups and classes during the Russian time of troubles. Leadership groups, whether tsarist or Bolshevik, tended to locate the drive toward anarchic breakdown in the impulses of the people and interpret this drive as a product of "darkness" or "petty-bourgeois psychology." But the elite itself could not

1. Kenneth N. Waltz, *Theory of International Politics* (Reading, Mass., 1979), 104–9. Order of passages rearranged.
2. African intellectuals have been known to formulate the choice before them in just these terms (Craig Murphy, personal communication).

avoid the self-help logic of anarchy. Faced with an absence of overarching authority, all social units—army divisions, industries, classes, localities— were forced to resort to protective self-help actions that were equally rational and equally anarchical. Conversely, there were strong reservoirs of support for reconstitution among the people, who were tired of bloodshed, deprivation, and radical uncertainty.

The process of breakdown and reconstitution can be divided into three stages: (1) "things fall apart," the period before the collapse of the center; (2) "the center cannot hold," the period of breakdown when centrifugal forces dominate; (3) the "rough beast" appears, the period of reconstitution when centralizing forces begin to take the upper hand. These headings, borrowed from Yeats's "Second Coming," can be applied directly to Russia's time of troubles. In describing the first stage—from July 1914 to February 1917—I can do no better than Boris Kadomtzeff, an émigré economist writing in England in late 1918. Kadomtzeff felt that the basic cause of breakdown was the de facto blockade that wrenched Russia out of the world economy.

> [The] whole power [of the Blockade] does not develop immediately. The first symptoms have not the appearance of leading to a great national disaster; people regard them lightly, and blame the "bad government" or the "greedy speculators" for the lack of goods. But where the Blockade had laid its paralysing finger, notwithstanding the most energetic Government measures against speculation, one by one the necessaries of life vanish from the market; prices begin to rise; the family budget loses its meaning, proportions and stability; existence becomes insecure. . . . The Blockade crosses all frontiers, penetrating into the house of every citizen, greeting every citizen at his morning awakening, shares his meals with him and accompanies him darkly as he goes about his business or his pleasure; it speeds him to his bed and companions his dreams.
>
> The whole life of the people becomes infirm; customs and habits must be changed continually in an attempt to conform to the novel prices of goods. The masses begin to grumble; dissatisfaction, like a fire among dry grass, spreads quickly over the whole country; and as it were marking singular conflagrations, hunger-riots and violence consume and destroy the bonds of civil order. . . . Government steps in, we will suppose, and rations the nation's food, but to meet the demands of even the narrowest rations supplies of some sort must be forthcoming from somewhere; not to mention that the Governmental Machine itself is seamed with the common discontent, for the servants of a bureaucracy will suffer from high

prices not less than any labor-socialist. The social structure cracks from top to bottom—and the country quests eagerly for ministers to mend it. Energetic ministers succeed each other with the rapidity of a cinematograph picture, and by the very fact of rapid change introduce new disorder into disorder. . . .

The Blockade, having ruined that enormous and very complicated economic organism, the Russian empire, compelled the people to return to the primitive form of self-supplying communities. . . . Before the war all the Separatists—and the Bolsheviks—could have been put in a student's room. But when the economic soil of Russia grew sterile of healthful growth, the bright, poisonous weed of Separatism spread like a dull fire. . . .

Blockade crushes the old order very effectively, but it does not create a new one.[3]

Thus the ground is prepared for second stage, "the center cannot hold," which covers the period from early 1917 to the middle of 1918. After the tsarist political authority collapsed in February 1917, the centrifugal "Separatism" of Kadomtzeff's scenario becomes full-fledged multiple sovereignty (*mnogovlastie*). The more familiar concept of dual sovereignty concentrates on the conflict between the forces that wish to complete the revolution and those that wish to stop it.[4] Multiple sovereignty emphasizes less the social problem of class warfare than the political problem of the splintering of all authority and leadership. In 1917 a speaker warned the Main Land Committee that "each hour that you drag out [the land reform] means the creation of new republics."[5] It was these new republics, these competing centers of political authority, that presented the basic challenge during the time of troubles.

The Provisional Government did not long remain a serious contender for a reconstituted authority; indeed, as the year wore on, it hardly could be called even the arena where other political forces confronted each other.[6] Peshekhonov describes the situation in 1917 before and after the Bolshevik takeover in October:

On 27 February 1917 the old state authority was overthrown. The Provisional Government that replaced it was not a state

3. Boris Kadomtzeff, *The Russian Collapse* (New York, 1919), 20–21, 45. Order of passages rearranged.

4. For an application of the dual-power concept to workers control, see S. Smith, *Red Petrograd;* for an application of multiple sovereignty to political problems, see Ferro, *La révolution,* 2:14–15, 293ff. See also Koenker, *Moscow Workers,* 142, on the problem of "friction" between the new organizations.

5. *Ek. pol.,* pt. 2, doc. 172 (July 1917).

6. Ferro, *La révolution,* chap. 7, esp. 337.

authority in the genuine sense of the word: it was only the symbol of authority, the carrier of the idea of authority, or at best its embryo. . . . In this process of destruction the Bolsheviks played an outstanding role. They were also the main obstacle for the establishment of a new state order. With their takeover they so to speak finished off any effective Russian state authority, [for] there was in reality no legislative, no judicial, and no administrative authority. Anyone who wanted could legislate as best suited him. The Litovskii regiment, quartered in the Vasileostrovskii section of Petrograd, issued decrees for all of Russia—but of course, even in Vasileostrovskii, where these decrees were posted, their authority was to say the least doubtful.

The legislative authority of Smolny [home of the new Bolshevik government] was just a little bit stronger. It wasn't always in the position even to get its decrees posted in public places. Even in Petrograd we would stroll at first into the revolutionary tribunal [the punitive organ aimed at "enemies of the revolution"] as into a theater where a new and merry farce was playing. The tribunal itself was evidently far from sure of its strength and at first limited itself mainly to "public censure."[7]

The dimensions of this breakdown in authority posed the basic challenge to the "rough beast" stage of reconstitution. Centralizing forces had always been present, but now they had the extra challenge of building a new center from almost nothing in the face of tremendous centrifugal forces. A new authority had to be built up using the crude methods available. In 1917 the liberal and moderate socialist activists of the Provisional Government had been swept away by methods that in quieter times would be called those of lynch mobs. But after this period—christened by Lenin "looting the looters"—there came a period with a different dialectical negation: lynching the lynchers.

An episode in an obscure Tambov village is emblematic of a process that was going on all across Russia. A Red Army detachment was billeted in the village, and the officer in charge was worried that the peasant soldiers would dissolve into their "native element [*stikhiia*]." A visiting officer moved to restore discipline. First he made the soldiers wait at attention for some time in the bitter cold. Then he came out and addressed them as follows: OK, you swine, you probably think this is still 1917, when the army was being run by Kerensky, the persuader in chief. Well, times have changed. I'm giving the officer in charge strict orders to shoot anyone who

7. A. V. Peshekhonov, *Pochemu ia ne emigriroval* (Berlin, 1923).

gets out of line, and *he* will be arrested if he fails to follow this order. The visiting officer then asked for the names of the worst offenders, and when these seven individuals stepped forward, he struck them across the face with a whip. Thus was authority restored by traditional tsarist methods infused with the brutal vitality of the soviet revolution.[8]

Much of the actual damage to Russian society was sustained during this stage. Some conclude from this that it was Bolshevism that wrecked Russia, and not—as the time-of-troubles concept would suggest—wrecked Russia that produced Bolshevism.[9] But that is the same as saying that under owner A the house sustained only the relatively minor damage of having its foundations sawn through, whereas under owner B the house collapsed. The conditions for economic and political breakdown were in place before the Bolshevik takeover. The shortfall in the production of the industrial items needed to sustain economic contact between city and village had taken place by late 1916. The disintegration of political authority had occurred by late summer 1917.[10] This context explains why Bolshevism as a destructive, centrifugal force acquired such power, and at the same time it reveals the dimensions of the paradoxical achievement of Bolshevism as a centralizing force for reconstitution.

The food-supply crisis was a barometer of the relative strength of centrifugal and centralizing forces in each of the three stages: the growing separatism of the first stage, the energetic yet anarchic self-help of the second stage, and the crude but adequate reconstitution achieved in the third stage. The course of food-supply policy can also help us determine the sources of some of the forces that pushed toward either breakdown or reconstitution. Although for the sake of convenience I shall examine the economic and political crises separately, it should never be forgotten that the forces operating in the two realms were inextricably intertwined.

BREAKDOWN AND RECONSTITUTION: BREAD

There is no one word for the set of institutions whose breakdown in Russia threatened to leave much of the population without bread. In each of the developed countries of the time these institutions made possible the

8. Okninskii, *Dva goda*, 68–70.
9. Robert Conquest, *The Harvest of Sorrow: Soviet Collectivization and the Terror-Famine* (Oxford, 1986), 54–55.
10. Oliver Radkey convincingly shows in *The Sickle Under the Hammer: Promise and Default of the Russian Revolutionaries in the Early Months of Soviet Rule* (New York, 1963) that the Constituent Assembly could never have provided the basis for a vigorous sovereign authority, given the political and regional divisions within the shaky SR majority.

mobilization of grain on a national scale. Such mobilization required the physical mobility of a transport system to and from the great economic centers; it also required the mobility of ownership and control created by credit and merchandising systems. Although the intricate and evolving set of practices known as the market may have created much of this mobilization potential, once in existence it could be used directly by the state.

Flexibility was the key to the survival of these mobilizing institutions under the terrific strain of the world war. As R. G. Hawtrey wrote, "A community of people accustomed to factory discipline and to productive processes, and led by a body of industrial employers, together with an adequate administrative and technical staff, . . . is something alive and organic. Once it has grown up, it can turn itself to new tasks."[11] In the Western countries, elites in science, industry, and public administration had been coalescing for some decades before the world war, and during the war an amalgam of market and bureaucracy was able to carry out mobilization for total war. This administrative community could and did turn itself to new tasks during the world war. But domestic administrative flexibility was only effective if some contact with the world economy remained.[12]

In Russia the de facto, and then de jure, blockade was much more effective than in the West, whereas the domestic industrial-administrative community was much less flexible.[13] This situation made economic breakdown almost inevitable. Many of the forces that helped or hindered secure economic reconstitution revealed themselves in the production and distribution of grain (see Chart 1).

Nationwide institutions for grain mobilization could only succeed if grain producers had both the incentives and the resources to orient their activities toward a nationwide network. The time of troubles first affected those parts of the economy that were most dependent on the cohesion of the whole—those that relied most on imported raw materials, credit, and transportation.[14] Large landowner estates had always been more oriented toward the market than had the peasant producer, but by 1918, the lack of a secure political authority to protect them and of a secure market where they could buy and sell what they needed spelled their ruin. Landowner agriculture could hardly have survived the time of troubles even without Bolshevik hostility.

11. R. G. Hawtrey, *Economic Aspects of Sovereignty* (London, 1930), 86.
12. William H. McNeill, *The Pursuit of Power* (Chicago, 1982).
13. Boris E. Nolde, *Russia in the Economic War* (New Haven, 1928), chap. 2.
14. Gert Meyer, *Studien zur sozialökonomischen Entwicklung Sowjetrusslands 1921–1923: Die Beziehungen zwischen Stadt und Land zu Beginn der Neuen Ökonomischen Politik* (Cologne, 1974), 11–26.

Chart 1. Forces Affecting the Bread Crisis

Production
  Incentives: Subsistence, Industrial Items, Money
  Resources: Industrial Items, Manpower, Livestock, Seed, Land
  Control of the Productive Process
Distribution ("Speculation" vs. Political Authority)
  In Time (Hoarding and Squandering)
  In Space (Interregional Competition)
  Within Society (Entitlements Among Population Categories)

The primary incentive for the peasant producer who remained was continued survival for himself and his family. Insofar as the Bolsheviks stuck to their promise of taking only the surplus above the amount needed for personal consumption and continued production, this primary incentive was not damaged. Despite Lenin's admission in 1921 that sometimes more than the surplus had been taken, it was no part of the razverstka policy to do so. It would have been just as shortsighted as cruel if the Bolsheviks had indeed systematically taken more than the surplus since that would have left the peasant without the necessary minimum for the next year's production.[15] The continued production of *samogon* (home-distilled vodka) and the thriving black market show that in most places a surplus remained under producer control (see Table 2).[16]

The various governments tried to ensure that sufficient material incentives were given to agricultural producers, but their success became progressively worse as the time of troubles wore on. The underlying cause of this failure was the demands of the army and the effect of the blockade (Russia had always depended on imports for agricultural equipment). Exact value comparisons of what was given to the countryside in comparison to what was taken from it are impossible, given the arbitrary assumptions needed to compensate for extremely abnormal economic conditions. In 1920 Briukhanov used official fixed prices to assert that in 1918–1919 peasants had received considerably more than they had given (a tribute to the poor procurement of that year), that in 1919–1920 the amounts had been about equal, and that only afterward did the state really become a debtor of the peasantry. Frumkin wrote that only one-fifth of the razverstka was matched by exchange items.[17] This figure is very low, but

15. Strizhkov, "Priniatie dekreta," 131–63.
16. Bol'shakov, *Derevnia*, 97–101; V. V. Kabanov, *Krest'ianskoe khoziaistvo*, 123.
17. *Ekonomicheskaia zhizn'*, 28–29 September 1920. Frumkin, *Tovaroobmen*, 8.

Table 2. Share of Free Market in Food Consumption

Percentage share of free-market procurement in the consumption of urban worker families and other families in 1919.

Article	March–April		July		December	
	Worker	Other	Worker	Other	Worker	Other
Bread	48.5	52.5	44.0	46.8	32.8	33.2
Flour	—	—	75.8	78.8	62.4	59.8

Original source: *Statisticheskii ezhegodnik, 1918–1920*, 1:8, 16, 24–25. Source: L. Szamuely, *First Models of the Socialist Economic System: Principles and Theories* (Budapest, 1974), 18.

given the usual summary statement that starting in 1918 the Bolsheviks took grain without compensation, it is perhaps more enlightening to say that the glass was one-fifth full rather than that it was four-fifths empty.

Although the Bolshevik government could do little to increase the availability of industrial items, the distribution of these items within the village did lie within their control. But Bolshevik distribution policies were determined more by the imperatives of political reconstitution than those of economic reconstitution. In 1918 the aim of collective exchange was primarily to enlist a coercive apparatus for grain collection rather than to motivate expanded production. After the introduction of the razverstka, commodity exchange was used as a fine for an unpaid grain tax. A certain amount of goods was set aside to be given to the peasants at so much per person—an amount bearing no relation to grain delivered. The peasant had the right to these goods *if* he and his village fulfilled their grain obligation—otherwise not.

Given the absence of any material incentive to produce more than the consumption norm, the level of prices may seem irrelevant. But despite the runaway inflation and the economic chaos, money provided some sort of incentive until the very end of the period. Central officials continually raised the fixed prices for grain and other foodstuffs, and the demand of local officials for money was insatiable. The power of the money incentive weakened as the economy went into its final tailspin in 1920–1921. But money remained the central nexus between town and country, and the printing presses never stopped rolling.[18]

Industrial items were important not only as an incentive but also directly as resources in production. Peasant agriculture could weather the

18. Preobrazhenskii, *Bumazhnye den'gi*; Lenin, *PSS*, 41:146–47 (June 1920); Boris Pasternak, *Doctor Zhivago*, chap. 13.11.

storm longer than landowner estates, but even the peasants could not hold out indefinitely. Equipment finally gave out and could no longer be repaired. Already in 1917 peasants were afraid of breaking scythes.[19] The peasant producer needed, if not new plows, then at least scrap metal, horseshoes, nails, kerosene, and bags for milling operations.

The long years of war and civil war began to tell as well on the living productive resources of manpower and livestock. The world war caused a massive depletion of manpower, and the nation's agriculture was preserved only by the *baba*, the peasant woman. Livestock was severely damaged by military disruption, requisitions, and droughts. The areas with the greatest damage were those that were the theater of military action during the civil war, not those that were regularly obligated to hand over the razverstka burden.[20] When drought hit wide regions in 1920 and 1921, the problem of seed for the next year's harvest became severe, especially because it was compounded by the transportation crisis. By that time there was no longer a question of whether the peasant would produce a surplus but whether he could.

Scarcity of land did not create a bottleneck in production in the same way as equipment and livestock did. More important were the changes and uncertainties caused by massive redistribution of land, first from the landowner to the peasantry and then among the peasants. The Bolsheviks quickly allied themselves with long-standing Russian government efforts to provide minimal security by stabilizing land tenure and preventing communal redistribution. They were in no position to interfere in the productive process to impose ideologically desirable forms other than by showing some ineffective favoritism toward collective farms and egalitarian communes. In Simbirsk Kaganovich even told worker detachments to help communes and state farms only after they had satisfied all requests for help from individual citizens.[21] More important forms of interference were the requisitions and labor services demanded by both sides during the civil war as well as the sheer disruption caused by its shifting fronts. Grain production was harmed not only by economic breakdown but also by the costs of this struggle for political reconstitution.

Turning from production to distribution, we come to a central interpretive problem: was speculation a force for reconstitution or for breakdown? I define speculation broadly as any middleman activity aimed at private profit and not under the control of political authority. It is usually seen as a

---

19. Poole, *Village*, 93–99.
20. Malle, *Economic Organization*, 437.
21. Kaganovich, *Kak dostaetsia khleb*, 26–29; Robert G. Wesson, *Soviet Communes* (New Brunswick, N.J., 1963).

force for breakdown, and a good case can be made for this view. Speculation was not just a reaction to shortage but a cause of it since speculators withheld grain from the market to drive up the price. It also crippled the regulatory efforts of the state. Before the revolution speculation defeated local efforts at price regulation. If the price was set below market prices, goods simply would not be forthcoming, and price wars developed, such as the meat war between Moscow and Petrograd described by Chaianov (see chapter 1). After the revolution the sackmen not only continued to undermine fixed prices but also intensified the strain on transport capacity by carrying grain in minute amounts. This inefficiency was a basic argument for the grain monopoly. The cover of one Bolshevik pamphlet had two pictures, one showing the small amount of grain carried by a train filled with sackmen and the other showing the huge amount carried by a train with only one or two guards.[22] The high prices caused by speculation put bread beyond the reach of the poor and led to discontent that made political reconstitution more difficult.

Hostility to speculation was shared by the left and the right, by elites and the people, and therefore it often became a central political issue. An example from the right is a letter to the Special Conference on Food Supply from General N. V. Ruzskii on the subject of sugar. Ruzskii argued that the organization that united the sugar industry, although it was officially condoned, was "in fact a 'syndicate,' with the harmful properties that belong to such an organization. The biggest factories were founded by completely loyal people such as Bobrinskii, Tereshchenko, Kharitenko, and Brodskii, but lately in the 'union' there has been a regrouping, and at the head of it now stand two Jews: Gepner and Abram Dobrii."

Ruzskii felt that these "sugar kings" were holding back supplies to be able to dictate terms and that the civilian authorities were doing nothing. He argued that these authorities should form their own sugar reserves to beat down the price by competition and "paralyze the [harmful] work of the private banks." (He did not realize that a policy of forming reserves would drive the price up.)

The reaction of the Special Conference to this letter was exasperated: chiding Ruzskii for his many inaccuracies, it informed him that no drastic change in the participation of banks was possible.[23] The Special Conference did investigate bank policy in response to this as well as other complaints. It polled its commissioners and found them split about evenly on whether

22. D. Kuznetsov, *O prodovol'stvii* (Moscow, 1919).
23. 457-1-262/82–83 (16 December 1915). The general's suspicions were unallayed, and he later had Gepner and Dobry arrested. In January 1917 Protopopov arranged a pardon for them.

the loan policy of the State Bank helped speculators. The Special Conference itself concluded that bank policy was not a harmful factor in food-supply procurement.[24] The Bolsheviks' crusade against speculation should thus be seen less as an offshoot of socialist ideology than as a precapitalist attitude they shared with the rest of the Russian political community. Analogues to medieval English laws against "engrossers," "forestallers," and "regrators" are still on the books in the Soviet Union.[25]

The case in defense of speculation as a force for reconstitution is a much less common one, although it was sometimes made in commercial circles in the early years of the time of troubles. According to this view, the real cause of high prices was scarcity of food, and the speculative middleman was only the messenger blamed for the bad news. Indeed, the speculator played a positive role by distributing available grain supplies more evenly. If the speculator withheld supplies, it was only because he foresaw a time when grain would be even more scarce—and therefore when consumers would need his supplies even more. Thus, limited supplies would not be depleted before they were replenished by the new harvest or new deliveries. Following this logic, Adam Smith argued that under conditions of competitive decentralization "it is the interest of the people that their daily, weekly, and monthly consumption should be proportioned as exactly as possible to the supply of the season. The interest of the inland corn dealer is the same."[26]

A further argument in defense of speculation is the poor job done by political authority when it took over the task of distribution. Political authorities operated within a shorter time horizon than speculators because of the direct political, and often physical, pressure of the consumer. In the winter of 1917–1918 the shaky new revolutionary authority distributed any supplies it found as quickly as possible, thus hurting the situation in the not-so-long run. A similar hastiness in distribution exacerbated the crisis in the winter of 1920–1921.

Distribution in space posed similar problems for political authority. The

24. 457-1-260/16–20; 457-1-263/37–39; 457-[2]-20/9–16.
25. Exact definitions of these terms can be found in Forrest McDonald, *Novus Ordo Seclorum: The Intellectual Origins of the Constitution* (Lawrence, Kans., 1985), 14–15, which also documents the importance during the American Revolution of legislation against the "wicked arts of speculators." One tsarist official remarked that a speculator was anyone who had a "large supply of oats and did not want to sell it at the fixed price." 456-1-18/5–8. Compare a Soviet historian's description of 1916: "Speculation took on a genuinely fantastic character. Merchants transported grain in the first place to where it could be sold most advantageously." Laverychev, "Politika," 177.
26. Adam Smith, *The Wealth of Nations*, ed. Edwin Cannan (Chicago, 1976), 2:30–34. A recent empirical study of Bangladesh casts doubt on the quality of the middleman's information. Martin Ravallion, *Markets and Famines* (Oxford, 1987).

speculative middleman represented the public interest in an equal distribution of scarce goods among all sections of the country, whereas local authorities wanted only to protect the grain supply of their own region. Many forms of popular struggle throughout Europe developed out of the attempt of local populations to keep grain in their area. When the state took over the task of distribution from private middlemen, it ran into the same localist hostility, whether in the form of tsarist generals imposing embargoes, revolutionary soviets protesting razverstka assignments, or peasant guerrillas such as Nestor Makhno opposing central pressure on the Ukraine. Officials were still being arrested in 1921 for protecting "their" areas.[27]

It is true that uncontrolled price rises imposed unfair burdens on the poor. But even there political authority provided an inadequate substitute. The growth of the ration system was haphazard and depended mainly on the initiative of local authorities: the Bolsheviks did not try to rationalize the system until 1919. Unlike earlier governments, the Bolsheviks were not committed to an egalitarian rationing system. The so-called class-ration system introduced in various places in 1918 was meant as something comparable to a progressive tax, whereby people in the lower ration categories would free up resources and ease the burden on more favored categories. But a study by N. M. Vishnevskii showed that the class ration could not live up to these expectations, given the small number of people in the bottom categories and the inflation in the upper categories. Further changes in the system tended to hurt those involved in heavy physical labor and favor "responsible workers" (top officials), civil servants, and women and children (see Table 3).[28]

Inflation—the generation of entitlements without relation to the actual quantity of available food—occurred in the ration system as well as the market because it was easier to print money and ration cards than it was to provide the bread to which a person was then entitled (see Tables 4 and 5). In 1919 and 1920 an attempt was made to impose a devaluation on the rationing system by introducing "armored" or reserved rations to protect those in high-priority employments, in effect creating a new privileged class. By that time the Bolsheviks were moving away from the principle of "social protection" (*sobez*) toward a policy of using the rationing system to enforce labor discipline and increase labor productivity—in other words, as a substitute for the market.[29]

27. E. B. Genkina, *Gosudarstvennaia deiatel'nost'*, 272; Lenin, *PSS*, 52:197, 211–12.

28. Vishnevskii, *Printsipy i metody*, 37–55.

29. Vishnevskii, *Printsipy i metody*; N. Fidelli, "Ocherk istorii kartochnoi sistemy," *Prodovol'stvie i revoliutsiia*, 1923, no. 7–12:142–62. See also Paul Ashin,

Table 3. Changes in Distributive Principles
(Comparison of Petrograd weekly rations (a) before the class ration, (b) class ration, first edition, summer 1918, (c) class ration, second edition, November 1918.)

	Ration (in Calories)			
	(a) *Previously existing system*	*(b)* *Class ration, 1st edition*		*(c)* *Class ration, 2d edition*
Type of Person		*announced average*	*factual average*	
Physical labor	24,182	24,318	22,224	18,545
Nonphysical labor	12,091	12,159	13,590	13,908
Executive positions	12,091	12,159	13,590	18,545
Professions	12,091	6,080	10,374	4,636
Unearned income	12,091	3,040	5,018	4,636
Women: nursing, pregnant, large families	12,091	24,318	22,224	18,545
Women: housewives in average families	12,091	6,080	10,374	13,908
Infants (under 1 year)	12,091	5,111	8,721	10,548
Children 1–3 years	12,091	6,080	10,374	18,545
Children 3–12 years	12,091	12,159	13,590	18,545

Source: N. M. Vishnevskii, *Printsipy i metody* (Moscow, 1920), 40.

The case for speculation is strongest when pointing to the deficiencies of political distribution, just as the case against speculation is strongest when pointing to the deficiencies of market distribution. But instead of asking whether political regulation or speculation was more destructive, we should ask why state and market did not work together in the manner of the other warring countries.[30] Comparisons can profitably be made on this score to England during the Napoleonic Wars, as described by Mancur Olson:

"Wage Policy in the Transition to NEP," *Russian Review* 47, no. 3 (1988): 293–313; William J. Chase, *Workers, Society, and the Soviet State: Labor and Life in Moscow, 1918–1929* (Urbana, 1986), chap. 1. On market prices, see Demosthenov, "Food Prices," 269–79; Kondratiev, *Rynok khlebov*, 248ff., 292ff. For the importance of entitlements in the study of famines, see Amartya Sen, *Poverty and Famines: An Essay on Entitlement and Deprivation* (Oxford, 1981).

30. Gerd Hardach, *The First World War* (Berkeley and Los Angeles, 1977), chap. 5.

Table 4. Price of Rye Flour (rubles per pood)

Date	Moscow	Petrograd	Saratov	P/M	S/M
1914	1.1	1.23	0.8	1.12	0.73
1917, July	5.1	5.3	—	1.04	—
1918, spring	200	420	431	—[a]	2.2
1918, autumn	290	420	431	1.45	—[a]
1919, March–May	920	1,600	50	1.74	0.05
1919, September–November	2,400	4,000	600	1.67	0.25
1920, January	8,000	12,000	—	1.50	—
1920, April	13,500	16,600	2,200	1.23	0.16
1920, June	19,600	17,200	3,500	0.88	0.18
1920, September	26,500	24,000	12,000	0.91	0.45
1921, January	32,000	32,000	16,000	1.00	0.50
1921, March	120,000	100,000	45,000	0.83	0.38
1921, May	103,000	120,000	—	1.17	—
1921, July	161,000	140,000	270,000	0.87	1.68
1921, August	120,000	120,000	160,000	1.00	1.33

Source: S. G. Wheatcroft, "Famine and Factors Affecting Mortality in the USSR," CREES Discussion Paper, SIPS nos. 20 and 21, pp. 26–27. (Ratios corrected from source.)
Original Source: *Vestnik statistiki*, 1921, no. 1–4:210.

[a] Data in original not comparable.

Table 5. Inflation of Top Ration Categories
Distribution of the Population by Categories of the Petrograd Class Ration, 1918

	July	August	September	October
Category 1	43.0	46.25	52.56	54.21
Category 2	43.13	41.0	39.08	38.92
Category 3	12.71	12.0	8.16	6.75
Category 4	1.16	0.75	0.20	0.12
Total	100.0	100.0	100.0	100.0

Source: N. M. Vishnevskii, *Printsipy i metody* (Moscow, 1920), 35.

> The persecution of the middlemen, who performed useful
> functions and were in no way responsible for the high prices,
> no doubt made the price system far less effective than it could
> have been. The destruction by mobs of the facilities of millers,
> bakers and grain dealers could only be harmful. The same was
> true of the legal punishment promised to those who sold grain
> for a higher price than they paid for it. . . . Thus, it is not
> only that Britain did not have the competence to develop an
> effective system of control; the government and the people did
> not have the economic knowledge needed to make the price
> system function as well as it might have done.[31]

If speculation means responsiveness to information provided by the market, then it too was infected by the uncertainty and distortions of the time of troubles. In a careful study of accusations made by tsarist officials against the banks, S. S. Demosthenov concluded that the responsibility of the banks arose from their lack of policy so that they merely followed and amplified market swings and thus intensified market disruption.[32] It was this disruption that led to the exaggerated reaction against speculation, as exemplified by Ruzskii's anti-Semitic charges of sabotage. It was not simply the strain of mobilization that broke down the trade network; many public activists and bureaucrats were determined to use mobilization as an excellent opportunity to replace what they saw as parasitical intermediaries. Later, when mobilization pressures were more extreme, many of them wished that the trade network were still in place. Even so, speculators and sackmen played a major part in getting grain to where it was needed most.

This summary of the food-supply crisis shows that there were powerful forces helping and hindering economic reconstitution. The forces that were undercutting the productive base and destroying the unity of the national economy seemed dominant, but both the state and the population continued their struggle to put the economy back together. Although these efforts often seemed at tragic cross-purposes, they succeeded in protecting the possibility of economic reconstitution. But this possibility would remain unrealized without the prior reconstitution of political authority.

BREAKDOWN AND RECONSTITUTION: AUTHORITY

Because it would be difficult to examine the whole course of the crisis of authority, I shall use the politics of food supply to throw light on the

31. Mancur Olson, *The Economics of the Wartime Shortage: A History of British Food Supplies in the Napoleonic War and in World Wars I and II* (Durham, N.C., 1963), 134–35.

32. Demosthenov, "Food Prices," 376–85. Uncertainty also led to hoarding, a centrifugal self-protection strategy adopted by all social units.

Chart 2. Influences on the
Authority Crisis

Learning (Creation of a Political Class)
   Political Formula
   Building an Apparatus
   Working Unity
Loyalty (Overcoming Multiple Sovereignty)
   Overcoming Passive Resistance
   Overcoming Active Resistance

---

specific question of Bolshevik success. But instead of the traditional question, Why did the Bolsheviks win? I will ask, How did the Bolsheviks manage to reconstitute political authority? This inquiry will shift the focus from power competition to the wider problems that confronted any contender for sovereign authority.

A political authority can be said to exist when, in the words of Peshekhonov, the center "can rest assured that its orders will go out without any special distortion to any point in its territory and almost everywhere there will be organs that will observe these orders and carry them out."[33] The positive precondition for a political authority is the existence of a political class—people who can be relied on to carry out the orders of a decision-making center. A new political authority requires a new political class, based on new sources and styles of recruitment, authority relations and leadership, and a new definition of its political mission.[34] The negative precondition is the absence of a serious alternative center of authority. An effective political authority can be kind and gentle, or ruthless and repressive, but in either case it cannot tolerate a condition of multiple sovereignty—like Leviathan, it must overawe them all.

The positive precondition can be called *learning* since a new political class must undergo a rapid learning process as it adopts a political formula, builds an apparatus, and achieves a working unity. I will call the negative precondition *loyalty*—not necessarily a do-or-die loyalty but at least a recognition of a political authority as the only legitimate one. Gaining this loyalty involves overcoming passive resistance, or reluctance to obey orders, as well as active resistance, or attempts to set up alternative centers of authority (see Chart 2).

One of the forces leading to disintegration of political authority was the sheer lack of knowledge about an effective response to the unexpected

---

33. Peshekhonov, *Pochemu*, 51–60.
34. On the Bolsheviks as a new political class, see Marc Ferro, *Des soviets au communisme bureaucratique* (Paris, 1980).

challenge of a food shortage in agricultural Russia. The crisis first baffled experienced tsarist bureaucrats and then the more inexperienced activists who replaced them. But along with the floundering and the mistakes, I should also stress the remarkable learning process through which these activists shed their illusions and learned to govern. The gubernatorial and enlistment solutions—the two contrasting strategies available in Russian political culture for tackling practical problems—will allow us to trace this learning process. Under each government there was a journey from the enlistment solution to the gubernatorial solution. Under the tsar the strategy that had led to the Special Conference on Food Supply and the imposition of fixed prices for all grain transactions was replaced by Rittikh's razverstka. The Provisional Government's shift from a monopoly carried out by food-supply committees to the gubernatorial solution remained embryonic at the time of its downfall. The Bolsheviks moved from the food-supply dictatorship to the razverstka system.

This cycle repeated itself three times because each new government thought that the failure of the previous government was due to the reluctance of that government to implement the enlistment solution consistently and thoroughly. Hence both the Provisional Government and the Bolsheviks began by introducing an even more radical version of the enlistment solution. The population to be enlisted was found deeper and deeper in the midst of the people until it included the poorest peasants and workers and excluded the former elite of wealth and education. The population's confidence was to be earned by ever more radical measures. With the introduction of the Committees of the Poor, the Bolsheviks tried to base a nationally centralized apparatus on social elements that previously had barely participated in the life of the village, much less in national politics. The Provisional Government addressed the peasant as a citizen, saying in effect, We now have a republic, and the government belongs to the people, so give grain, citizen peasant. The Bolsheviks addressed him as a comrade: "Peasant! The worker helped you take land from the landowner; help the worker take bread from the kulak."[35]

The dark side of the enlistment solution was the sabotage outlook. When a government was confronted with hostility and resistance even though enlistment advocates felt it had earned the people's confidence, an explanation had to be found for the anomaly. Gubernatorial advocates were prone to blaming difficulties on saboteurs, but they were less tempted by the sabotage outlook because they were less sanguine about the chances for

---

35. The second statement is taken from the title page of a 1918 Zinoviev pamphlet, *Pis'mo k krest'ianam.*

enthusiastic popular cooperation. The danger of the sabotage outlook was the illusion that the "dark forces" were the main obstacle to solutions of pressing problems.

Under the tsar the villain class was restricted to the speculative grain dealer and, to some extent, the greedy landowner. Advocates of the enlistment solution under the Provisional Government expanded the list to include profiteering businessmen who resisted economic regulation and peasant shopkeepers who saw the grain monopoly as a threat to their way of life. The Bolsheviks broadened the scope of the villain class further to include a worldwide bourgeois conspiracy terrified by the advent of socialism and determined to choke it with the "bony hand of hunger." The kulak became a fiend incarnate whose greed and class-based hostility were the basic explanation for the failure of the village to cooperate.

Viewing the kulak as the principal source of food-supply difficulties led to a shift in the meaning of *kulak*. When the massive grain reserves supposedly in the hands of the kulak-middleman failed to materialize, *kulak* began to mean the efficient peasant producer, in sharp contrast to the prewar connotations of the term. But crushing the kulak did not solve the food-supply crisis—indeed, it created many new difficulties. Why work hard to produce if the result was not even gratitude but a declaration of being fair game for local officials or traveling commissars?

There were countervailing tendencies against this discrimination among food-supply officials. In 1918 Orlov pointed out the shift from the "poor peasant—assistants in the campaign for grain—[to] the actual producer of marketable grain supplies, that is, for the most part, the middle peasant and the kulak who has not yet broken away from the land."[36] During the years that followed, the food-supply apparatus showed a growing appreciation of productive capability and made a sharper distinction between the deserving poor and the undeserving loafer.[37] This development reached a high point in late 1920 with the canonization of the "industrious owner" and Lenin's admission that the Bolsheviks had gotten carried away with the struggle against the kulak.[38]

The French Revolution provides an instructive contrast because Jacobin economic regulation was based on a sabotage theory of economic difficulties, whereby grain producers and *accapareurs* (speculative middlemen)

36. Orlov, *Rabota*, 182–203. The phrase *ne porvavshii s zemleiu kulak* shows the prewar concept of the kulak as someone who was part of the peasant estate without being part of the peasant class.

37. *Prod. i snab.* (Kostroma), 1919, no. 5:31 (Kaganovich).

38. For further discussion of this point, see Lars T. Lih, "The Bolshevik Sowing Committees of 1920: Apotheosis of War Communism?" forthcoming.

were viewed as conscious enemies of the revolution. This definition of the situation led the Jacobins to abandon their own preference for laissez-faire and introduce in 1793 a program of extensive price regulation called the maximum. The economic centralization required by the maximum and the political centralization of the Terror went hand in hand, and the excesses of both contributed to the Jacobin downfall in 1794.[39] The Bolsheviks managed to modify their own sabotage theories in time to avoid a similar fate.

The learning process that modified the emphasis on sabotage in the Bolsheviks' original political formula also played a role in the evolution of the apparatus from simply awful (in 1918 and early 1919) to barely adequate (in 1921). Peshekhonov observed that

> the Bolsheviks had to take even longer to reestablish the state
> apparatus than to recreate the army—and not because this
> task was inherently so difficult, but because they had no idea
> of how to go about it. It was no help that they tried for so long
> to give the state apparatus a class character. In each and every
> part, they would time and again build and pull down, build
> again and again pull down. The observer was forced to say,
> "No matter how much you practice, you'll never be musi-
> cians." And indeed there were no experienced "musicians" in
> their number whatsoever. But bit by bit they learned, and
> among them some talent even became evident.[40]

The enlistment of the village poor in 1918 might be justified as a step toward the creation ex nihilo of a village-level tax-collecting apparatus, but the political cost was exorbitant, and there was no way to incorporate the Committees of the Poor into a national apparatus. The Bolsheviks moved away from the poor peasant to the middle peasant, and this shift was mirrored by a shift in emphasis from proletarianization to professionalization as a recipe for improving the apparatus.

There were political limitations on Bolshevik freedom of action. Orlov pointed out already in the summer of 1918 that the impossibility of adopting a policy of free grain trade stemmed in the first place from the inconceivability of Bolshevik rifles being used to protect grain dealers against hungry proletarians.[41] Indeed, it can be argued, if the tsarist government found such protection to be beyond its political means, what can one expect

39. Albert Mathiez, *La Vie chère et le mouvement social sous le terreur* (Paris, 1927). Shingarev alluded to the French experience in *Izv. po prod. delu*, 1(32): 61–62.

40. Peshekhonov, *Pochemu*, 51–60.

41. Orlov, *Rabota*, 355–62. According to Conquest, the various White governments also used nonmarket methods. *Harvest of Sorrow*, 50.

from a shaky new revolutionary authority? In 1920 food-supply officials felt that a free market in grain was intolerable primarily because of their perception of the weakness of the apparatus and its inability to stand up to the competition of the private trader. The Bolsheviks were able to relent on this point in 1921 not only because economic recovery had become a possibility but also because they now had a serviceable tax apparatus as well as what Osinskii in 1920 called a disciplined population.[42]

The creation of the apparatus was a political achievement as much as an administrative or economic one because it depended on the prior unity of the political class. In practice the criterion for effective unity was a crude one—avoiding the fundamental splits and schisms that afflicted every other Russian party and government. Lenin's *What Is to Be Done?* explains little about Bolshevik unity, which should be seen both as evident common sense and as an impressive political feat.[43] In the realm of food-supply policy the Bolshevik achievement can be gauged by observing the secure tenure of Tsiurupa as Commissar of Food Supply in contrast to that of his predecessors, none of whom (after Krivoshein) lasted more than a few months. This stability did not go deep into the apparatus, as figures for provincial food-supply commissars show.[44] The unified party acted as a rubber band to keep the jerry-built apparatus from collapsing.

In addition to learning how to govern, the political class had to ensure the loyalty of the nonelite classes. The food-supply crisis made this job more difficult in many ways, but hunger in itself is neither a centrifugal nor a centralizing force. Although the food-supply situation under the Bolsheviks was much worse than the food-supply difficulties that undermined the tsarist and Provisional governments, the Bolsheviks were often able to use hunger as a source of support. In pamphlets urging the Bolsheviks to take power, Lenin asserted that the ruthless use of power over food

42. *Biulletin NKP,* 30 November 1920.

43. Common sense: "An oligarchy at one with itself is not easily overthrown from within." *The Politics of Aristotle,* ed. Ernest Barker, (Oxford, 1962), 219. Impressive political feat: this statement by an Iranian applies to Russia: "One Iranian will never yield to another. Each believes in his own superiority, wants to be first and foremost, wants to impose his own exclusive I. I! I! *I* know better, *I* have more, *I* can do everything. . . . Any group of Iranians immediately organizes itself according to hierarchical principles. I'm first, you're second, you're third. The second and third ones don't go for that, but immediately start trying to nose ahead, intriguing and maneuvering to unseat number one." Quoted in Ryszard Kapuscinski, *Shah of Shahs* (New York, 1982), 38–39.

44. Out of 59 "food-supply units" between November 1919 and November 1920, 18 kept the same commissar, 24 saw one change, 11 saw two changes, 6 saw three or more. About half the changes were initiated by the Food-Supply Commissariat. *Tri goda,* 7–10.

supply could solve one of the major difficulties foreseen by skeptics—overcoming the passive resistance of "bourgeois specialists." The Bolsheviks never had sufficient reserves to carry out this policy systematically, and the black market always provided an escape route. It would nevertheless be hard to overestimate the importance of the ration entitlement attached to government employment in securing at least the minimal cooperation of otherwise hostile sections of society. Perhaps in a more subtle way the dependence on the state for food helped destroy even the spirit of opposition. Several participant observers remarked that the degradation implied in accepting a ration played a role in the demoralization of the Russian intelligentsia.[45]

Special rations were used to solidify support among the classes the Bolsheviks felt were their natural constituency. Chief among these was the Red Star ration, the top-priority ration given to Red Army personnel and their dependents. Paul Dukes recounts a meeting with a completely apolitical lad who joined the Red Army solely for the ration. Confirmation comes from Andrei Vyshinskii, who wrote that the Red Star ration had performed an "invaluable service to the cause of the revolution."[46]

Rationing policies also strengthened loyalty by appealing to the class hostility and the sabotage outlook of the population. The original idea of the so-called class ration was to give only half-rations to various categories of "bourgeois"; in practice no food at all was available for them. But the symbolic importance of the class ration remained: a ration card showing a bourgeois category was a badge of pariah status that effectively declared a person outside the law. The class ration was part of what the Menshevik S. O. Portugeis called relative enrichment (in contrast to Marx's concept of relative impoverishment): although the living standards of the working class went down, those of the former elite sunk even lower. Sviderskii once gave statistics showing that workers' families got a slightly less miserable diet than other families and commented: "Yes! In Soviet Russia hunger and need have not yet been conquered. But in Soviet Russia the workers no longer go hungry in order that the bourgeoisie make profits and flourish."[47] Thus if the sabotage outlook was a centrifugal force when it led to

45. Okninskii, *Dva goda*, 34–36; Pitirim Sorokin, *Hunger as a Factor in Human Affairs* (Gainesville, Fla., 1975), 147–48; S. O. Portugeis (S. Ivanovich), *Piat' let bol'shevizma: nachala i kontsy* (Berlin, 1922), 133.

46. Dukes, *Red Dusk*, 42, 118–21, 223; Vyshinskii, *Voprosy*, 9. For more on Red Army rations, see Mark Von Hagen, *Soldiers in the Proletarian Dictatorship: The Red Army and the Soviet Socialist State, 1917–1930* (Ithaca, 1990).

47. *Prod. politika*, 166–73; Portugeis, *Piat' let*, 44–49; Tyrkova-Williams, *Why Soviet Russia Is Starving*; Pasternak, *Doctor Zhivago*, chap. 7.10; Kritsman, *Geroicheskii period*, 78–80.

disastrous policy mistakes, it was a centralizing force when it led to popular support, and for this reason the Bolsheviks could not completely abandon the sabotage outlook even if they had been so inclined.

The food-supply crisis played an unappreciated role in the Bolshevik success in overcoming active resistance during the civil war since the wavering front between the White armies and the Red Army tended to follow the division between grain surplus and deficit regions. After listing the twenty-one deficit provinces and the twenty-four surplus provinces, Arskii pointed out that all of the deficit provinces were under permanent Bolshevik control, but only five surplus provinces. Portugeis argued that "this 'war' was no more than a punitive food-supply expedition on the part of the hungry and a food-supply boycott on the part of those with food."[48]

This split in the peasantry, already evident in 1917, did not give equal strength to all contenders. Whereas the peasants in the White armies were protecting their grain, the peasants in the Red Army were either net grain consumers themselves or were producers under intolerable pressure unless and until the outlying regions were conquered. When the White armies went on the offensive, they often made rapid gains, striking deep into Bolshevik territory, but then they would collapse and even more rapidly retreat. One reason for this pattern was that the White generals were moving from grain-rich regions to grain-poor regions. The peasants in the White armies could therefore only lose from a reunification of the country.[49]

Many of the Bolsheviks' agitational slogans promised an end to food-supply difficulties when the outlying regions were conquered. Posters proclaimed, "Only the Red Army will give us bread. Denikin occupies Kharkov and Ekaterinoslav. In Moscow and Petrograd there is no grain. The Red Army attacks, and the bread in Soviet Russia will increase."[50]

The final crisis of the time of troubles arose in 1920 when the Bolsheviks experienced great difficulty in making good on these promises. In the summer of 1920 the central authorities frantically informed officials in

48. R. Arskii, *Transport i prodovol'stvie* (Moscow, 1920); S. O. Portugeis (S. Ivanovich), *Krasnaia Armiia* (Paris, 1931), 132–33. Other observers who made passing comments to this effect include Struve (Introduction, xx), Kritsman (*Geroicheskii period*, 63–68, 108), and Sorokin (*Hunger as a Factor*, 215). Sorokin's work was about to be published in Russia in 1922 when he was exiled; it was published in America after his death as a memorial. See also Launcelot Owen, *The Russian Peasant Movement, 1906–1917* (1937; New York, 1963), 232; Yaney, *Urge to Mobilize*, 437.

49. Pasternak, *Doctor Zhivago*, chap. 13.11, shows the effect on Siberia of being joined to devastated central Russia.

50. Butnik-Siverskii, *Sovetskii plakat*, 329.

Siberia, the Ukraine, and the northern Caucasus that "citizens guilty of evading [obligatory] threshing and delivery of surpluses, as well as all responsible representatives of the central authority who permit this evasion, are to be punished with confiscation of property and imprisonment in a concentration camp as traitors to the cause of the worker-peasant revolution."[51] But once they had weathered this political crisis, the Bolsheviks could again rely on wide support, despite the devastating famine, because people realized that any existing authority was better than the chaos arising from further uprisings and civil war.

Once political authority was firmly established, loyalty was not shaken by the final tragedy of the 1921–1922 famine in the Volga region. It was the damage wrought by the time of troubles that changed the natural disaster of a severe drought into the social disaster of famine. The long delay in establishing a single political authority over the entire country led to pressures that increased the vulnerability of the Volga region. The drought region had supplied almost 60 percent of state procurements in 1918–1919 and more than a third of state procurements overall. The inability to get at the supplies of Siberia and the Ukraine meant that those provinces were hit again and again when the outlying regions did not live up to expectations. Bolshevik officials admitted that the severity of the famine was due in part to this extraordinary pressure.[52] The severity of the famine was compounded by the breakdown in transport that prevented the usual methods of the tsarist government in dealing with recurrent drought. But since the famine occurred when in most respects the time of troubles had passed and political authority had been successfully reconstituted, it did not lead to further breakdown even though it claimed more lives than all previous food-supply difficulties.

Overcoming the "horrifying lack of knowledge" characteristic of a time of troubles required a mutual learning process. The Bolsheviks were able to move past their own lack of knowledge about the job of governing and the nature of the Russian people, and society in turn learned where authority was located, as the ceaseless contention ended and the Bolsheviks showed they could endure. Amid the tragedy and conflict caused by breakdown and civil war, this constructive process should not be entirely forgotten.

ROLE OF THE RAZVERSTKA

The razverstka was designed as a response to both economic and political breakdown, but it is not easy to decide whether it really contributed to

51. *Dekrety*, 9:241; 10:238–40.
52. *Na bor'bu*, 28–31 (Sviderskii), 25–28 (Kalinin).

Table 6. Comparative Reliance on
Direct Taxes by Period

Year	Percentage in Direct Taxes	All Others (Including by Currency Inflation)
1912	28.3	71.7
1918–1919	56.5	43.5
1920–1921	96.3	3.7
1921–1922	83.6	16.4
1922–1923	67.0	33.0

Source: Al'bert Vainshtein, *Oblozhenie i platezhi* (Moscow, 1924), 118.

reconstitution or rather led to continued breakdown. Judgment is possible only after recognition of the dilemma posed by the time of troubles: economic breakdown increased the challenge faced by the government, whereas political breakdown diminished the resources needed to respond to it.

Economic breakdown—the lack of exchange items and the devaluation of paper money—meant that grain had to be collected in the form of a direct tax in kind (see Table 6). This necessity imposed a difficult task on the government—in fact, one far beyond that faced by the tsarist government before the war. Direct taxes were only a small part of the tsarist tax structure and were mostly collected to meet local needs (see Table 7).[53] The central government mainly relied on indirect sales taxes on consumer items, which allowed it to increase its revenues without preventing a rising peasant standard of living.[54] Although it is often maintained that the tsarist government used the tax mechanism for squeezing grain out of the peasant for export purposes, there was in fact no apparatus for doing so in the absence of economic incentives.

The razverstka, as well as being a direct tax, had to be collected in kind. Any tax in kind will have an inequitable distribution, falling most heavily on people who happen to have the required kind of goods. In the case of the

53. Al'bert L. Vainshtein, *Oblozhenie i platezhi krest'ianstva v dovoennoe i revoliutsionnoe vremia* (Moscow, 1924), 47.
54. Paul R. Gregory, *Russian National Income, 1885–1913* (Cambridge, 1982), Appendix D; J. Y. Simms, "The Crisis in Russian Agriculture at the End of the Nineteenth Century: A Different View," *Slavic Review* 36 (1977): 377–98.

Table 7. Comparative Reliance on Direct Taxes
Between Countries Before the War

Country	Percentage of Direct Tax	Indirect, Customs, Monopolies	Taxes on Circulation
Russia	13.7	76.8	9.5
Germany	28.3	56.8	14.9
Austria	28.2	58.1	13.7
France	19.5	47.1	33.4
Great Britain	31.5	45.0	23.5
Italy	29.8	52.6	17.6

Source: Al'bert Vainshtein, *Oblozhenie i platezhi* (Moscow, 1924), 128.

Table 8. Distribution of the Razverstka Within the Village

Arable Land per Household	Income per Household	Razverstka, Horse Confiscation, Taxes (in prewar rubles)	Burden as Percentage of Income
Deficit Provinces			
1–2 desiatins	404.8	17.43	4.3
2–4 des.	526.5	32.20	6.1
4–6 des.	714.2	83.86	11.7
6–8 des.	683.2	44.11	6.5
more than 8 des.	647.3	93.69	14.5
Surplus Provinces			
1–2 desiatins	312.1	76.47	24.5
2–4 des.	339.7	30.05	8.8
4–6 des.	418.8	55.62	13.3
6–8 des.	505.7	61.67	12.2
more than 8 des.	712.6	142.71	20.0

Source: Al'bert Vainshtein, *Oblozhenie i platezhi* (Moscow, 1924), 71.

razverstka there could be no consistent principle for allocation of the burden among peasant farms of varying size (see Table 8). By 1921 there were some fifteen categories of foodstuffs being taxed; even when the rates were low, the taxation seemed irritatingly endless.[55]

A tax in kind is the most inefficient variety of tax and requires the

55. Bol'shakov, *Derevnia*, 92.

Table 9. Breakdown of the Tax Burden by Type and
Province, 1920–1921
(Per Household in Prewar Prices; Budget Survey of Central Statistical
Administration)

Province	Razverstka and Horse Confiscation	Losses from Labor Obligations	Percentage of Net Individual Income
Deficit Region			
Moscow	10.11	4.70	3.6
Vladimir	34.12	20.29	21.3
Ivanovo-Vosnesensk	15.26	12.94	10.1
Novgorod	42.57	30.15	25.7
Severodvinsk	29.63	32.03	23.2
Average	26.36	20.02	16.8
Surplus Region			
Ufa	44.70	38.80	45.2
Orel	74.58	18.75	26.8
German Volga Commune	165.45	6.44	51.0
Tula	78.90	13.76	31.1
Kursk	41.60	10.75	12.4
Average	81.03	17.70	33.3

Source: Al'bert Vainshtein, *Oblozhenie i platezhi* (Moscow, 1924), 66–67.
Note: These figures should be regarded as minimum approximations.

bulkiest apparatus to collect. This was a central reason for the expansion of
the government apparatus in 1920. In January 1920 local employees of the
Food Supply Commissariat numbered 147,500 people; by January 1921
the figure was 245,154. The food-supply tax in 1921 did not reverse this
pattern, and a reduction in staff only occurred after the transition to a
money tax.[56]

The razverstka was only one part of the tax burden imposed by the
government. Table 9 shows the importance of imposed labor obligations
(*trudguzhpovinnosti*): cartage for public purposes, aid to families of Red
Army soldiers, the cutting and delivery of wood, road maintenance, removal of snow from railroads. The razverstka imposed by the center was

56. Bychkov, "Organizatsionnoe stroitel'stvo," 192; Baburin, "Narkomprod,"
gives a figure of 300,000 central and local employees of the Food-Supply Commissariat in October 1921. See also Bol'shakov, *Derevnia*, 174; Danilov, "Nalogovaia politika."

Table 10. Comparative Tax Burden, Prewar and Time of Troubles

	1912	1918–1919	1920–1921	1921–1922	1922–1923
Average per person (in prewar rubles)					
Direct taxes	1.80	3.9	10.3	6.11	4.07
All others	4.56	—	—	0.10	0.93
Total taxes	6.36	3.9	10.3	6.21	5.00
Insurance	0.27	—	—	0.04	0.20
Lease and land payments	3.74	—	—	—	1.08
Total nontax payments	4.01	—	—	0.04	1.28
Percentage of net income					
Direct taxes	3.06	9.7	25.1	17.4	10.6
All others	7.73	—	—	0.3	2.5
Total taxes	10.79	9.7	25.1	17.7	13.1
Insurance	0.48	—	—	0.1	0.5
Lease and land payments	6.37	—	—	—	0.2
Total nontax payments	6.85	—	—	0.1	0.7
Taxation by currency inflation (in prewar rubles)					
Average, whole population	—	4.9	1.2	2.6	3.6
Average, rural population	—	3.0	0.4	1.1	1.4
Total taxes (including inflation)					
Per person (in prewar rubles)	6.36	6.9	10.7	7.3	6.4
Percentage of net income	10.79	16.7	26.1	20.9	16.9

Source: Al'bert Vainshtein, *Oblozhenie i platezhi* (Moscow, 1924), 116.

Note: Net income equals gross income per household minus seed and forage.

probably equaled by local additions for military and other needs.[57] Calculations made by A. L. Vainshtein show that in comparison with prewar taxes, there was a substantial increase in the absolute burden and an even larger increase in the relative burden. The relative burden increased even if we add to the prewar total an amount equal to rent and other payments abolished by the revolution (see Table 10).

The imperative of imposing a heavy, direct tax in kind was thus an unprecedented challenge, and political breakdown did not make it any

57. Vainshtein, *Oblozhenie*, 63–66. Malle writes, "Vainshtein showed that the total sum extracted from peasants through the regime of *razverstka* was more than twice that of foodstuffs only." *Economic Organization*, 410. Vainshtein said no such nonsensical thing; this statement is unfortunately typical of the muddle that pervades Malle's discussion. On the burden of labor obligations, see Kabanov, *Krest'ianskoe khoziaistvo*, 190–202.

easier for the Bolsheviks. The necessarily inexperienced and insecure Bolsheviks had to build an apparatus out of almost nothing and impose a heavy tax on a population quickly losing the habit of unthinking obedience, after a period when the revolution had seemed to promise a much lighter tax burden.

It is usually assumed that the razverstka contributed to economic breakdown: since the Bolsheviks took the entire surplus, the peasants had no incentive to sow more than was necessary for their own consumption. But even if the Bolsheviks had not taken a single pood, the peasants would have had no reason to produce anything above personal needs, given the impossibility of using the grain to obtain needed items. Conversely, if the Bolsheviks had taken even more grain but at the same time provided an equivalent in industrial items, the peasants would have much more willingly parted with their surplus. Indeed, under the conditions of a goods famine it was only Bolshevik demands that provided any incentive to produce a surplus because the Bolsheviks began to threaten to cut into the already low consumption norm to force the peasant to sow. An appeal in late 1920 warned the peasants not to lower sowing to the level of their own consumption: "Since this is a matter of the common interest, the state will in any case take just as much as it needs for the satisfaction of everybody, but the difference will only be that the person who suffers will be the one who purposely thinks to sow only for himself, or the person who is lazy, in the hope of living off the labor of others."[58]

One might indeed argue that razverstka collections were insufficient since the absolute amount taken by the Bolshevik razverstka even at its height was less than the grain procurements of either the tsarist government or the Provisional Government (see Tables 11 and 12). Bolshevik grain collections fell woefully short of even the Bolsheviks' somewhat arbitrary targets. But both the actual collection of previous governments and the Bolshevik's own targets impose irrelevant standards. Indeed, no statistical calculation can tell us what a reasonable standard of performance would have been under the circumstances of the time of troubles.

The fall in agricultural production is not an irrelevant standard, but I. A. Iurkov has shown that it is better explained by shortages in the means of production than by a lack of incentive created by the razverstka. In the major agricultural regions the amount of sown acreage per plow or per unit of livestock hardly decreased (see Tables 13 and 14). The peasantry evidently did not lack incentive to use the available equipment to the fullest extent possible.[59]

58. *Prod. politika*, 192–95.
59. Iurkov, *Ekonomicheskaia politika*, chap. 1.

Table 11. Grain Procurement, 1914–1920 (in thousands of poods)

	Total Grain and Forage						
	1914	1915	1916	1917	1918	1919	1920
Jan		8,347	55,792	57,000	2,801	13,112	22,864
Feb		37,803	67,078	41,000	2,510	7,676	22,770
March		51,712	62,790	69,000	2,881	13,580	22,511
Apr		53,590	35,741	30,000	2,338	4,291	8,388
May		36,582	54,713	77,000	220	1,386	6,095
June		23,704	34,479	62,000	91	2,292	7,154
July		3,096	12,967	28,000	430	5,529	6,264
Aug	20,431	37,837	6,407	4,470	1,599	4,007	
Sept	30,008	38,199	19,444	15,128	7,677	6,510	
Oct	20,313	32,831	48,956	19,052	23,273	25,700	
Nov	11,475	39,205	39,000	39,125	14,875	21,189	
Dec	5,850	28,328	63,000	8,329	14,933	27,089	
Total	88,077	391,234	500,367	450,104	73,628	132,361	96,046

Source: N. D. Kondratiev, *Rynok khlebov,* 244–45 (material of the Food Supply Commissariat).

The difficulties under the razverstka were caused not so much by what was taken out of the countryside as by the failure to put anything back in. The reasons for this failure lie in the war and the de facto blockade: the great drop in the production and import of items needed by the peasant occurred in 1916 (see Table 15).[60] Both the Provisional Government and the Bolsheviks had to struggle with the heritage of this collapse, which led first to a lack of incentives to market grain and later to a lack of capacity to produce it.

The usual assertion that the razverstka policy was responsible for the fall in agricultural production thus overlooks the terrible dilemmas of the time of troubles. Without a revival of industry, agriculture was doomed as well—and without burdensome and uncompensated grain collections, industry could not revive. As much as peasant agriculture suffered in these years, it suffered less than the town economy, as shown by population movement—people migrated in large numbers from the towns back to the countryside[61]—and food consumption (see Table 16). Under these circum-

60. Demosthenov, "Food Prices," 426–27; *Ek. pol.,* pt. 2, doc. 75, 78, 82.
61. V. Z. Drobizhev, "Demograficheskoe razvitie strany sovetov (1917 g.–seredina 1920-kh godov)," *Voprosy istorii,* 1986, no. 7:15–25.

Table 12. Razverstka Fulfillment

Year	Razverstka Target	Actual Collection	Percentage of Target	Percentage of 1916–1917 Collection
1916–1917	426,264	323,090	75.8	100.0
1917–1918	no target	47,539	—	14.7
1918–1919	260,100	108,147	41.6	33.5
1919–1920	326,000	212,507	65.2	65.8
1920–1921	446,000	285,000	63.9	88.2

Source: M. I. Davydov, *Bor'ba za khleb* (Moscow, 1971), 167.

Table 13. Amount of Sown Land per Plow (in desiatins)

Region	Arable Land per Plow		Sown Land per Plow	
	1917	1920	1917	1920
Central Agricultural Region	20.0	28.9	13.6	10.9
Middle Volga	23.2	28.3	15.1	13.6
Lower Volga	21.9	19.5	12.6	10.3
Central Industrial Region	8.9	6.9	5.4	2.9
Belorussia	5.1	6.3	3.5	2.7
Lake Region	6.6	8.3	4.7	3.5
Ural	72.0	61.1	44.7	27.6
North	9.4	10.9	6.9	5.4
Ukraine	13.2	7.0	9.7	7.0
Southeast	18.3	22.1	11.4	10.2
Steppes	22.4	17.3	12.7	11.4
Siberia	18.7	23.0	9.0	9.8

Source: I. A. Iurkov, *Ekonomicheskaia politika partii* (Moscow, 1980), 21. Original source: *Na novykh putiakh*, vol. 5, part 1 (Moscow, 1923), 88, 620.

stances the enforced loan of the razverstka was a force for economic reconstitution.

The razverstka should be judged not only by the size of the burden it imposed but also by its success as a method of collection. The necessity of direct taxation meant an unprecedented intrusion of the central govern-

Table 14. Amount of Sown Land per Unit of Livestock

Regions	Working Livestock per Household			Sown Land per Unit of Working Livestock (in desiatins)		
	1916	1920	1922	1916	1920	1922
Central Agricultural Region	1.2	0.3	0.6	4.0	3.9	4.9
Middle Volga	1.1	0.7	0.6	4.0	3.9	4.5
Lower Volga	2.6	1.6	0.6	2.5	2.8	4.7
Central Industrial Region	0.8	0.7	0.7	2.7	1.9	2.7
Belorussia	1.3	1.0	1.1	3.1	2.0	2.5
Lake Region	1.0	0.8	0.8	2.8	1.8	2.1
Ural	1.2	1.0	0.8	3.6	3.2	3.3
North	0.8	0.8	0.8	2.2	1.6	1.7
Ukraine	1.4	7.0	1.0	3.8	7.0	3.3
Southeast	2.8	1.8	1.0	3.0	3.0	3.6
Steppes	4.0	2.9	0.9	1.3	1.6	2.5
Siberia	2.8	2.4	1.9	1.7	1.9	1.2

Source: I. A. Iurkov, *Ekonomicheskaia politika partii* (Moscow, 1980), 24.
Original Source: *Na novykh putiakh*, vol. 5, part 1 (Moscow, 1923), 70, 621.

Table 15. Production and Import of Agricultural Machinery (in thousands of gold rubles)

Year	Production	Percent of 1913	Import	Percent of 1913
1913	60,508	100.0	48,678	100.0
1914	54,017	89.3	40,909	84.0
1915	30,254	50.0	120	0.2
1916	12,101	20.0	481	1.0
1917	9,076	15.0	1,286	2.6
1918	6,382	10.5	2,770	5.7
1919	4,212	7.0	152	0.3
1920	2,840	4.7	2,000	4.1
1921	3,125	5.2	14,000	28.8

Source: I. A. Iurkov, *Ekonomicheskaia politika partii* (Moscow, 1980), 11.
Original Source: *Plan sel'skokhoziaistvennogo mashinostroeniia RSFSR v 1922–1931 gg.*, no. 2 (Moscow, 1922), 5.

Table 16. Town-Country Differences in Consumption
(Summary of food consumption in K calories per day per adult.)

	Moscow		Leningrad		Saratov	
	Town	Rural	Town	Rural	Town	Rural
1918–1919						
Mar. 1919	2066	—	1598	—	2773	—
July 1919	2554	—	2415	—	2766	—
1919–1920						
Dec. 1919	2791	—	2976	—	3156	—
Jan.–Feb. 1920	—	2845	—	3299	—	4474
May 1920	3430	—	2690	—	2275	—
1920–1921						
Oct. 1920	2744	—	3041	—	2425	—
Nov. 1920	—	3320	—	3333	—	3626
Feb. 1921	—	2924	—	3041	—	3196
Apr. 1921	2411	—	2420	—	2723	—
1921–1922						
Sept. 1921	2760	—	2606	—	2025	—
Oct. 1921	—	3576	—	3757	—	2615
Feb. 1922	2749	3716	2668	3724	1901	1762
June 1922	—	—	—	—	—	1945
1922–1923						
Oct. 1922	3219	3943	2949	3896	2827	4242
Feb. 1923	3337	3783	3287	3645	2739	3892
1923–1924						
Feb. 1924	3326	4081	3069	3932	3041	4295
June 1924	—	4258	—	4045	—	4323
1924–1925						
Oct. 1924	3547	—	3512	—	3281	—
Feb. 1925	3444	—	3636	—	3005	—

Source: S. G. Wheatcroft, "Famine and Factors Affecting Mortality in the USSR," CREES Discussion Paper, SIPS nos. 20 and 21, 1981, 35.

ment into daily life; payments in kind were inefficient and inequitably distributed; labor obligations were a reminder of serf status and an invitation to local arbitrariness; the central provinces had to be taxed beyond their strength; the lack of industrial items meant a degradation of daily life and productive activity; the benefits stemming from the black market were illegal and demoralizing. Under these trying conditions the razverstka method sought to economize on administrative resources, maximize the impact of the extremely limited goods fund, and reduce the politically costly side effects of coercion.

Like previous governments, the Bolsheviks found that they had to cut their coat to their cloth, as Tsiurupa put it; they had to put aside dreams not only of socialism but even of state capitalism in its original meaning of effective centralization of the economy. The razverstka, which started out as a compromise improvisation, proved to be the basis of a relatively serviceable tax-collecting apparatus. Like any set of middlemen, the food-supply apparatus was cursed by those from whom it took and those to whom it gave, and the resulting bad press still dominates our view of it. Nevertheless, it should on balance be accounted a force for reconstitution that successfully, if crudely, carried out the task of a middleman apparatus, to move goods from low-priority uses to high-priority uses—or, in the words of one Bolshevik official, to take from the hungry to give to the hungrier.[62]

REVOLUTION IN A TIME OF TROUBLES

We can imagine two extreme views of an upheaval such as the one that took place between 1914 and 1921. In one view, long-term causes completely determine short-term events, which have no independent significance. In the other view, only the short-term crisis and its internal dynamics have long-term effects. The first view can be called the pure revolutionary view, and the second the pure time-of-troubles view.

The pure revolutionary view, whether liberal or Marxist, has its roots in the Enlightenment philosophy of human progress as steady and incremental. It did not dispute this philosophy but added a conservative element that resists progress. This addition leads to a steady growth of tension, of "inner contradictions." The elements of the new society are slowly developing in the womb of the old society, to use the ubiquitous birth imagery of the revolutionary view. A revolutionary break is needed to clear away conservative resistance and allow unimpeded growth, but this birth of a new society, like a human birth, is causally important in itself only if something goes wrong. In Marx's theory the revolution can be carried off well or badly, but there is little suggestion that the event of revolution itself is of fundamental creative significance.[63]

The pure view cannot be sustained, as the Bolsheviks found, and perhaps the greatest Bolshevik contribution to Marxist theory is the analysis of the effects of the revolutionary process itself. Under the label *revolution-*

62. Arskii, *Transport;* Malle, *Economic Organization,* 425–50.
63. An example of Marx's gradualistic rhetoric can be found in *Das Kapital* (*Capital*), vol. 1, chap. 24, pt. 7. Georgii Shakhnazarov uses the birth imagery of Marxism to refute a revolutionary voluntarism associated with Stalin. "Vostok-Zapad," *Kommunist,* 1989, no. 3:70.

ary situation Lenin described the necessary preconditions of an actual revolution, such as a crisis in the ruling elite, which might occur before the new society is fully formed. He also argued that revolution itself was a sharply accelerated learning process through which the workers and peasants gained much greater class awareness. For the most part Lenin assumed that what the revolutionary crisis taught people was valid. The realization that the revolutionary crisis could in and of itself have long-term effects lay behind Bukharin's concept of the production costs of revolution. These observations provide the basis for a modified revolutionary view.

The opposite extreme, the pure time-of-troubles view, is implicit in Thomas Hobbes's emphasis on the establishment of an overarching political order as the basic creative social act. Although Hobbes's work is often considered ahistorical, a theory of history can be derived from it in which the fundamental rhythm of historical change is determined by the breakdown and reconstitution of order. Theorists who approach this Hobbesian view are Frederick Teggart and Pitirim Sorokin; both see the incremental changes that occur in normal times as typically less significant for explaining major social change than calamities such as epidemics or invasion.[64]

This pure view also needs some modification to be useful. Events in Russia cannot be understood apart from the world historical change variously called industrialism, modernization, or the spread of capitalism. This change can perhaps be assimilated to the time-of-troubles view by treating modernization as a vast global time of troubles that forces societies to transform themselves.[65] Another modification comes from the realization that neither breakdown nor reconstitution can be understood apart from the weaknesses and resources created by a society's past internal development; as Gaetano Mosca remarked, the new building is usually created out of materials left by the wreckage of the old.[66] The heritage of the past includes the revolutionary visions that inspire efforts at political and social reconstitution—although it is usually a complicated question to determine whether loyalty to a specific image of reconstitution is a centrifugal or centralizing force.

These modifications bring the two views closer together, but there remains a fundamental difference of perspective. Marx and Hobbes would each see the events of 1914–1921 as a drama, but a drama with a different

64. Frederick J. Teggart, *Theory of History* (New Haven, 1925); Pitirim Sorokin, *Man and Society in Calamity* (New York, 1942). See also Harry Eckstein, "A Culturalist Theory of Political Change," *American Political Science Review* 82 (1988): 789–804.

65. Theodore Von Laue, *The Global City: Freedom, Power and Necessity in the Age of World Revolutions* (New York, 1969); Von Laue, *The World Revolution of Westernization: The Twentieth Century in Global Perspective* (Oxford, 1987).

66. Mosca, *Ruling Class*, 378.

pathos. The one would see it as the dialectically painful transition to a higher stage, the other as the collapse of a workable society and a traumatic object lesson in the necessity of order. Or, in terms of biblical archetypes, one sees a Moses defeating the forces of established society, leading an oppressed people out of bondage, giving them new institutions during a search for the promised land, and setting the scene for final establishment of a more advanced political order; the other sees a Noah hastily constructing a small ark against imminent disaster, trying to save as much as possible of the doomed old society, living a stripped-down and impoverished life as the floods rise, and starting over in a devastated land when the waters have receded.

In more practical scholarly terms the two views boil down to different interests and a different set of questions: one view focuses on the causes and effects of the revolution, and the other view focuses on breakdown and reconstitution. A perspective is thus partly a matter of choice and experience. Memoirs and novels have persuaded me that the time-of-troubles view is closer to the outlook of those who lived through the actual events.[67] I would also argue that the time-of-troubles view leads to more accurate interpretations. To illustrate, I will contrast the findings of my inquiry with an interpretation that is derived from the revolutionary view, one that focuses on the concept of war communism. In this study I have avoided the term *war communism* for Bolshevik policy during the years 1918–1921. It was invented after the fact to justify the New Economic Policy, and there is a great danger of anachronism in importing it back into descriptions of goals and methods prior to 1921.[68] There are many different conceptions of war communism, but almost all, I would argue, are answers to the following questions: what went wrong with the revolution? why did it degenerate into a repressive authoritarianism? how could Stalinism grow out of the revolutionary experience? As one of the characters says in a 1988 play by Mikhail Shatrov: "October was a pure spring—it was the civil war that muddied it."[69]

67. Two works of literature by participants that evoke the time of troubles are Viktor Shklovskii, *A Sentimental Journey: Memoirs, 1917–1922,* ed. Richard Sheldon (Ithaca, 1974), and Osip Mandel'shtam, *Tristia* (Petersburg, 1922). Published diaries include *A Russian Civil War Diary: Alexis Babine in Saratov, 1917–1922,* ed. Donald J. Raleigh (Durham, N.C., 1988), and *Time of Troubles: The Diary of Iurii Vladimirovich Got'e,* ed. Terence Emmons (Princeton, 1988). For an outsider's view, see H. G. Wells: "Our dominant impression of things Russian is an impression of vast irreparable breakdown . . . The fact of the Revolution is, to our minds, altogether dwarfed by the fact of this downfall." *Russia in the Shadows* (New York, 1921), 17.

68. For more discussion, see Lih, "Bolshevik *Razverstka,*" 673–89.

69. Mikhail Shatrov, "Dal'she, dal'she, dal'she!" *Znamia,* 1988, no. 1:3–53. For similar sentiments, see S. Smith, *Red Petrograd,* 264–65; Kingston-Mann, *Lenin*

One of the most plausible and well-supported answers to these questions points to a process of "statization."[70] According to this line of thought, the civil war led the Bolsheviks to a new emphasis on the power of the state in word and deed. Not only political methods but also the very conception of socialism became more centralized and authoritarian. Although NEP represented a return by Lenin and others to the more moderate Bolshevik outlook of old, the new statist outlook eventually triumphed during the Stalin era.

The statization interpretation rests on many hard facts, yet these same facts look different when viewed in the full context of the time of troubles. The Bolsheviks certainly had great faith in the state, but this faith can hardly be ascribed to the civil war. It was the time of troubles that led to a new emphasis on state regulation of society, which predated the Bolsheviks and encompassed almost the entire political spectrum. In December 1916 the liberal Peter Struve already saw Russian society as a besieged fortress:

> This war is being decided not by the clash of armed vital forces
> as such but by a competition of entire national organisms in
> conditions of mutual siege or blockade. . . . We must have a
> harmonious, fully thought-out organization of all the aspects
> of life in conformity with the objectives of a war of indetermi-
> nate duration. . . . The problem of the war [is not only mili-
> tary but also one] of the all-around organization of the
> nation—economic, political, and perhaps above all, spiritual.[71]

Struve argued that the technical solution of this problem required a registration (*uchet*) of national forces and that the political solution required confidence (*doverie*) and a purging (*ochishchenie*) of reactionary elements.

This statist conception was manifested in the grain monopoly, an idea

---

and *Peasant Revolution*, 193–94; Ronald G. Suny, "Revising the Old Story: The 1917 Revolution in Light of New Sources," in Daniel H. Kaiser, ed., *The Workers Revolution in Russia, 1917* (Cambridge, 1987), 19; Rabinowitch, *Bolsheviks*, 310. Sheila Fitzpatrick, *The Russian Revolution, 1917–1932* (Oxford, 1982), 63–65, and Ferro, *La révolution*, 2:422ff, trace the roots of some of the unpleasant features of the civil war to 1917.

70. Moshe Lewin, *Lenin's Last Struggle* (New York, 1968); Lewin, *Political Undercurrents in Soviet Economic Debates* (Princeton, 1974), chap. 4; Lewin, *The Making of the Soviet System: Essays in the Social History of Interwar Russia* (New York, 1985), 260–62, 204–6. In his earlier work Lewin sees Trotsky as the most likely ally of Lenin's final position. See also Robert C. Tucker, *Political Culture and Leadership in Soviet Russia* (New York, 1987), esp. 86–88; Cohen, *Bukharin*. Many Soviet reformers have favored this interpretation; for discussion, see Lars T. Lih, "NEP: An Alternative for Soviet Socialism," in Stephen F. Cohen and Michael Kraus, eds., *The Soviet Union under Gorbachev* (New York, 1990).

71. Struve, *Collected Works*, vol. 11, no. 510; Richard Pipes, *Struve: Liberal on the Right, 1905–1944* (Cambridge, Mass., 1980), 224.

that the Bolsheviks took over bodily from the Kadets and the Mensheviks. Already by May 1917 representatives of the deficit regions argued that the "basic principle by which we should be guided is the statization (*ogosu-darstvlenie*) of food supply," according to which "there exist only obligations *to* the state and the right to demand *from* the state."[72] The grain monopoly itself was no feverish assault on socialism but one part of state capitalism as understood prior to 1921. The ideal of the grain monopoly—state control of all grain transactions—was never abandoned by the Bolsheviks, and steady progress was made toward it throughout the NEP period.

It is not helpful to say that the Bolsheviks underwent a process of statization, as they were strongly pro-state from the beginning. Their enthusiasm for the state derived both from their Marxist principles and the Russian political environment. Lenin's vision of the withering away of the state was based on the premise that the democratic enlistment of the masses into the state apparatus would overcome the coercive and alien nature of the state. But as the concept of the enlistment solution suggests, there was no contradiction in the minds of enlistment advocates between this far-reaching democratization and highly centralized economic regulation—indeed, the two were seen as mutually reinforcing. The enlistment solution was not confined to socialists; Neil Weissman has described the "cherished liberal goal of uniting the entire populace equally in a hierarchical chain of democratized zemstvos stretching from the provincial capital to the village" so that authority and sovereignty flowed not from the top down but rather from the bottom up.[73]

Although the Bolsheviks took over the program of state economic regulation from the other parties, they responded to the popular mood in 1917 and 1918 by claiming that food-supply difficulties were the result of deliberate sabotage motivated by class hostility. This definition of the situation was translated into policy in the spring of 1918 with the food-supply dictatorship. To label this period moderate in contrast to the civil-war years does not square with easily available rhetorical evidence—for example, the use of the word *kulak* in Lenin's writings. Starting in January 1918, the violence of these references increases steadily to a murderous climax in August 1918. Lenin's antikulak intensity then subsides rapidly, until he can admit in December 1920 that the Bolsheviks had gotten carried away with the struggle against the kulak.[74] If Stalin's onslaught in the late

72. *Izv. po prod. delu* 1 (32), O.O., 76–79, 101–3.
73. Neil Weissman, *Reform in Tsarist Russia* (New Brunswick, N.J., 1981), 108, 111.
74. Lenin, *PSS*, 35:323–27, 37:41–42, 42:195.

1920s was a return to anything, it was to the sabotage outlook and the class-struggle radicalism of 1917 and early 1918.

The privations of the civil war did mean that the Bolsheviks had to impose great burdens on the peasantry, but for just this reason they were anxious not to irritate the peasants more than necessary. There was no inhibition about using coercion, but its aims shifted away from revolutionary goals such as the transformation of production relations toward national goals such as national independence and economic recovery. The methods used in applying coercion shifted away from class-struggle methods to more traditional methods such as collective responsibility. A decree in November 1918 showed the evolution of Bolshevik attitudes under the pressure of civil war. It announced the government's desire to give to the "laboring peasantry the possibility of fulfilling its duty to the socialist fatherland"; it defined a rich peasant (*bogatei*) as anyone who had surplus grain after 1 February 1919—that is, not in class terms but in terms of fulfillment of civic duty.[75] The concept of the gubernatorial solution helps bring out the possibility, too often neglected by historians, of this juxtaposition of a brutal imposition of burdens with an offer of partnership in achieving common goals.

The statization hypothesis also leads to an inappropriately negative valuation of the state-building process. Contemptuous terms for bureaucrats such as *chinovnik* and *apparatchik* have closed off thought on this matter for observers from both the right and the left. Perhaps the only thing worse than too much bureaucracy is too little bureaucracy.[76] The creation of an effective state apparatus was a necessary precondition for what H. G. Wells called the recivilizing of Russia, and we should be less surprised by the crudity of Bolshevik methods than by their achievement in building a relatively serviceable state apparatus out of nothing.[77]

In contrast to the statization hypothesis I have argued that the civil-war period should not be dismissed as war communism but should be viewed more favorably as a time when a group of extremist revolutionaries shed their inexperience and took on responsibility for complex national problems. I am far from denying, however, that the time of troubles had many long-term destructive consequences. Indeed, it is not too fanciful to say that the time of troubles cast its shadow into the past as well as into the future since many developments in prewar Russia were caused by preparations for the testing time to come. Many observers have blamed the war for

75. *Dekrety*, 4:83–84 (November 1918).
76. My father made this observation after spending several months as a volunteer doctor in Kenya.
77. Wells, *Russia in the Shadows* (New York, 1921), 106.

cutting off the evolution of Russia toward a modern society. But paradoxically this evolution—manifested in industry, urbanization, education, and
middle-class professionalism—would have been weak indeed without the
threat of war and the Tsar's reluctant decision to create modern sources of
national strength.[78]

The shadow cast into the future by the time of troubles was caused by
the weakening of society. The physical weakening is perhaps best shown by
typhus rates: rates for 1919 were 74 times higher than for 1918 and 515
times higher than for the period 1901–1910.[79] According to Stephen
Wheatcroft, hunger "probably contributed indirectly to most of the up-
surge in mortality that occurred after the 1918 harvest and before the 1922
harvest." He supports this statement by showing the congruence between
the movement of mortality rates and the scarcity of bread as indicated by
price movement in Moscow, Petrograd, and Saratov.[80]

The moral and psychological weakening was caused by what Alexander
Berkman called the abolition of the established, not just in politics, but in
every sphere of daily life. Berkman, an anarchist who came to Russia
toward the end of the time of troubles, was exhilarated by the breakdown
of an overarching order:

> The abolition of the established—politically and economically,
> socially and ethically—the attempt to replace it with some-
> thing different, is the reflex of man's changed needs, of the
> awakened consciousness of the people. To them revolution is
> not a mere change of externals: it implies the complete dis-
> location of life, the shattering of dominant traditions, the an-
> nulment of accepted standards. The habitual, measured step of
> existence is interrupted, accustomed criterions become in-
> operative, former precedents are void. Existence is forced into
> uncharted channels; every action demands self-reliance; every
> detail calls for new, independent decision. The typical, the fa-
> miliar, have disappeared; dissolved is the coherence and inter-
> relation of the parts that formerly constituted one whole. New
> values are to be created.
>
> This *inner* life of revolution, which is its sole meaning, has
> almost entirely been neglected by writers on the Russian Rev-
> olution.[81]

78. Dietrich Geyer, *Russian Imperialism: The Interaction of Domestic and Foreign Policy, 1860–1914* (New Haven, 1987).

79. Drobizhev, "Demograficheskoe razvitie," 19.

80. S. G. Wheatcroft, "Famine and Factors Affecting Mortality in the USSR:
The Demographic Crises of 1914–1922 and 1930–1933," Centre for Russian and
East European Studies (University of Birmingham) Discussion Paper, SIPS nos. 20
and 21, 1981, pp. 29, 17, 12.

81. Alexander Berkman, *The Bolshevik Myth: Diary, 1920–1922* (New York,
1925), vii.

Perhaps a more common reaction of people who lived through that time was expressed by Pitirim Sorokin, who wrote that "one's whole life becomes a painful series of surprises and fantastic changes, permeated by constant uncertainty."[82]

This prolonged uncertainty had its effect on the new political class, which made a fetish of unity of will as a bulwark against the centrifugal forces that seemed so powerful during the time of troubles. When Stalin really wanted to scare the elite, he warned opposition would lead to renewed civil war.[83] It was neither Leninist doctrine nor the antifaction resolution of 1921 that led to the bedrock insistence on party unity, but rather the shared memory of the time when the party seemed an ark of reconstitution threatened by a flood of anarchy and breakdown.

The effect of the time of troubles was not just on the new political class. Its wider effects are revealed in Boris Pasternak's novel *Doctor Zhivago* (being published for the first time in the Soviet Union as these words are written in 1988).[84] Pasternak insists that the troubles began with the war. After war was declared "everything started going toward destruction: the movement of trains, food-supply for the towns, the bases of family life, and the foundations of moral consciousness." Zhivago contrasts the comfortable novelties of prewar life—the sense of progress and modernity, including the hope of revolution—with a different kind of novelty that imposed itself brutally after the beginning of the war. Because the "artificial interruption" of normal life sent Pasternak's characters journeying across Russia, the longing to return home and resume their lives became their most intense dream, impossible as it was.

A central aspect of the period started by the war was the lack of knowledge (*neizvestnost'*) that Miliukov found so horrifying: "People in the cities were as helpless as children in the face of an approaching lack of knowledge that cast out of its path all established habits, leaving a wasteland around itself." This uprooting of settled life brings Zhivago at first an exhilarating sense of unbounded freedom but later a feeling of emptiness. The kind of people who thrived in this environment and became leaders were comfortable in the element of plebeian upheaval but were narrow and rigid—more interested in proving their theories right than in helping people live. Pasternak does not consider the possibility that perhaps this

82. Sorokin, *Man and Society*, 109, 116, 119, 78–79.

83. Stalin, *Sochineniia*, 11:314. As late as 1964 the first reaction of Mikhail Suslov to the plot to remove Nikita Khrushchev as party leader was that it would risk civil war. Alexander Rahr, "Shelest Remembers," *Report on the USSR*, 1989, no. 4:14–16.

84. Pasternak, *Doctor Zhivago*. I have sometimes used the translation by Max Hayward and Manya Harari (London, 1958). Most quotations are taken from chap. 4.14; chap. 5.15; chap. 6.5; chap. 13.14.

narrowness was necessary to preserve some sort of continuing order amid breakdown and upheaval.

The collapse of social order meant that the fields were neglected but not dead: "They were astir with an incessant crawling that suggested something foul and repellent"—a plague of mice. The resulting privation meant that the period "confirmed the ancient proverb, 'Man is a wolf to man.' Traveler turned off the road at the sight of traveler, stranger meeting stranger killed for fear of being killed. . . . The laws of human civilization were suspended." Beyond this material and moral disintegration the time of troubles led to a more subtle deformation. The key symptom for Pasternak was a misuse of language: the inflated heroics first of monarchist and then of revolutionary rhetoric. Without a secure reality people stopped being themselves and were playing an unknown part. Because they were no longer sure of who they were or who other people were, hypocrisy and suspicion were rampant. The feeling of being two-faced, ripe for exposure, sometimes even led to frenzies of self-accusation.

Doctor Zhivago describes how radical uncertainty creates an attitude of automatic suspicion. This attitude can still be found in the Soviet Union. In 1987 a Soviet journalist, E. Maksimova, wrote about the campaign to give soldiers who were missing in action in World War II full recognition for honorable service, which is important to family and comrades. She notes that the main obstacle is the suspicious attitude exemplified by an official who said, "Maybe your father deserted to the Germans, and you think his name should be on a monument?" Maksimova comments on this attitude: "A distorted notion of human nature emerged from the 1930s, from the depths of the 'cult' period, and began to spread and become implanted in people's minds—a notion holding that anyone could be guilty of any sin, according to the principle, 'If one person is capable of doing it, that means everyone is.' Ideals and morality were empty twaddle. Today someone is an upstanding individual, tomorrow he is a scoundrel."[85] The people described by Maksimova, who were officers in World War II and are pensioners today, were small children during the time of troubles. The insecurity of that period affected them not only directly but also through the anxiety of the adults around them. Perhaps the view of human nature she describes was not just a result of the Stalin era but a cause of it as well.[86]

85. *Izvestiia*, 21 August 1987, cited in *Current Digest of the Soviet Press*, 1987, no. 35:1ff.

86. Bruno Bettelheim, *A Good Enough Parent: A Book on Child Rearing* (New York, 1987), 38–45. See also P. Loewenberg, "The Psychohistorical Origins of the Nazi Youth Cohort," *American Historical Review* 76 (1971): 1457–1502; Theodore Von Laue, "Stalin in Focus," *Slavic Review* 42 (1983): 373–89.

These long-term effects of the time of troubles should make us respect all the more the achievements of those whose activities helped reconstitute society. If this study has any heroes, they are unlikely ones—the bureaucrats and middlemen of the entire period. Whatever their private motives, they helped to overcome the disintegration and demoralization that showed themselves so powerfully in the food-supply crisis. We who live in normal times can have little conception of what is required to restore the structure of everyday life and return efficacy and meaning to social activity. We should be more ready than we often are to extend our compassion and admiration.

Bibliography

1. ARCHIVAL SOURCES

Archival material is cited in the following fashion: *fond-opis'-delo/list*. For example, 1284-47-1288/9 is *fond* 1284, *opis'* 47, *delo* 1288, and *list* 9.

Tsentral'nyi gosudarstvennyi istoricheskii arkhiv (TsGIA) (Central State Historical Archive). Fond 398, Departament zemledeliia Ministerstva zemledeliia.
————. Fond 455, Otdel zagotovok prodovol'stviia i furahza dlia de-istvuiushchei armii Ministerstva zemledeliia.
————. Fond 456, Kantseliariia glavnoupolnomochennogo po zakupke khleba dlia armii Ministerstva zemledeliia.
————. Fond 457, Osoboe soveshchanie dlia obsuzhdeniia i ob"edineniia meropriiatii po prodovol'stvennomu delu Ministerstva zemledeliia.
————. Fond 1276, Sovet ministrov.
Tsentral'nyi gosudarstvennyi voenno-istoricheskii arkhiv (TsGVIA) (Central State Military Historical Archive).

2. CONGRESSES AND CONFERENCES

Third Congress of Soviets, January 1918. Stenographic Report, 1918.
Fifth Congress of Soviets, July 1918. Stenographic Report, 1918.
Sixth Congress of Soviets, November 1918. Stenographic Report, 1919.
Seventh Congress of Soviets, December 1919. Stenographic Report, 1920.
Eighth Congress of Soviets, December 1920. Stenographic Report, 1921.
Central Executive Committee, 4th *sozyv*, March–June 1918. Stenographic Report, 1920.
Central Executive Committee, 8th *sozyv*, March–May 1921. Stenographic Report, 1922.

Eighth Party Congress, March 1919. Protocols, 1959.
Ninth Party Congress, March–April 1920. Protocols, 1960.
Tenth Party Congress, March 1921. Stenographic Report, 1963.

3. FOOD-SUPPLY PERIODICALS

Biulletin Narodnogo Komissariata po Prodovol'stvennomu Delu.
Izvestiia Narodnogo Komissariata po Prodovol'stvennomu Delu, Moscow.
Izvestiia po prodovol'stvennomu delu, Petrograd, 1917 (Ministry of Food
    Supply).
Krasnyi put', Omsk, 1920 (Omsk Communist party).
Prodovol'stvennoe delo, Kharkov, 1918.
Prodovol'stvennoe delo, Kostroma, 1917.
Prodovol'stvennoe delo, Moscow, 1917 (Municipal Food-Supply Commit-
    tee).
Prodovol'stvennoe delo, Tver, 1917–1918.
Prodovol'stvennyi biulletin, Siberia, 1920–1921.
Prodovol'stvie, Nizhegorod, 1917.
Prodovol'stvie, Poltava, 1917.
Prodovol'stvie, Tobolsk, 1917.
Prodovol'stvie i snabzhenie, Kostroma, 1918–1919.

4. BOOKS AND ARTICLES

Agurskii, M. *Ideologiia natsional-bolshevizma.* Paris, 1980.
Aleksentsev, A. M. "K voprosu o chislennosti Prodarmii." *Istoriia SSSR,*
    1986, nos. 3–4:155–67.
Andreev, V. M. "Prodrazverstka i krest'ianstvo." *Istoricheskie zapiski* 97
    (1976): 5–49.
Antsiferov, Alexis N., Alexander D. Bilimovich, Michael O. Batshev, and
    Dimitry N. Ivantsov. *Russian Agriculture During the War.* New Haven,
    1930.
Aristotle. *The Politics of Aristotle.* Edited by Ernest Barker. Oxford, 1962.
Arskii, R. *Nalog vmesto razverstki.* Novocherkassk, n.d.
———. *Transport i prodovol'stvie.* Moscow, 1920.
Ashin, Paul. "Wage Policy in the Transition to NEP." *Russian Review* 47,
    no. 3 (1988): 293–313.
Atkinson, Dorothy. *The End of the Russian Land Commune.* Stanford,
    1983.
Aver'ev, V. N. *Komitety bednoty: sbornik materialov.* 2 vols. Moscow,
    1933.
Avrich, Paul. *Kronstadt 1921.* Princeton, 1970.
Babine, Alexis. *A Russian Civil War Diary: Alexis Babine in Saratov, 1917–
    1922.* Edited by Donald J. Raleigh. Durham, N.C., 1988.

Baburin, D. S. "Narkomprod v pervye gody sovetskoi vlasti." *Istoricheskie zapiski* 61 (1957): 333–68.

Badaev, A. E. *Desiat' let bor'by i stroitel'stva.* Leningrad, 1927.

Berkman, Alexander. *The Bolshevik Myth: Diary, 1920–1922.* New York, 1925.

Bettelheim, Bruno. *A Good Enough Parent: A Book on Child Rearing.* New York, 1987.

Bol'shakov, A. M. *Derevnia 1917–1927.* Moscow, 1927.

Briukhanov, N. P., ed. "Kak pitalis' i snabzhalis' Krasnaia Armiia i flot prodovol'stviem." In *Grazhdanskaia voina,* 3 vols., 2:306–26. Moscow, 1928–30.

Brovkin, Vladimir. *The Mensheviks After October: Socialist Opposition and the Rise of the Bolshevik Dictatorship.* Ithaca, 1987.

Browder, Robert Paul, and Alexander F. Kerensky, eds. *The Russian Provisional Government 1917: Documents.* 3 vols. Stanford, 1961.

Bukharin, N. I. *Ekonomika perekhodnogo perioda.* Moscow, 1920.

———. *Selected Writings on the State and the Transition to Socialism.* Edited and translated by Richard Day. Armonk, N.Y., 1982.

Bukharin, N. I. and E. Preobrazhenskii. *Azbuka kommunizma.* Petrograd, 1920.

Bukshpan, Ia. M. *Voenno-khoziaistvennaia politika: formy i organy regulirovaniia narodnogo khoziaistva za vremia mirovoi voiny 1914–1918 gg.* Moscow, 1929.

Bunyan, James. *Intervention, Civil War, and Communism in Russia.* Baltimore, 1936.

Bunyan, James, and H. H. Fisher. *The Bolshevik Revolution, 1917–1918: Documents and Materials.* Stanford, 1934.

Burdzhalov, E. N. *Vtoraia russkaia revoliutsiia.* 2 vols. Moscow, 1967–1971.

Butnik-Siverskii, B. S. *Sovetskii plakat epokhi grazhdanskoi voiny, 1918–1921.* Moscow, 1960.

Bychkov, S. "Organizatsionnoe stroitel'stvo prodorganov do NEPa." *Prodovol'stvie i revoliutsiia,* 1923, no. 5–6:183–95.

Carr, E. H. *The Bolshevik Revolution.* 3 vols. New York, 1950–1953.

Chaadaeva, O. *Pomeshchiki i ikh organizatsii v 1917 godu.* Moscow, 1928.

Chaianov, A. V. *Prodovol'stvennyi vopros.* Moscow, 1917.

Chamberlin, W. H. *The Russian Revolution.* 2 vols. New York, 1935.

Chambre, Henri, Henri Wronski, and Georges Lasserre. *Les coopératives de consommation en URSS.* [Paris], 1969.

Chase, William J. *Workers, Society, and the Soviet State: Labor and Life in Moscow, 1918–1929.* Urbana, 1987.

Cherniavsky, Michael, ed. *Prologue to Revolution.* Englewood Cliffs, N.J., 1967.

Chetvertaia godovshchina Narkomproda. Moscow, 1921.

Chetyre goda prodovol'stvennoi raboty. Moscow, 1922.

Chistikov, A. N. "Prodovol'stvennaia politika sovetskoi vlasti v gody grazhdanskoi voiny (na materialakh Petrograda). Avtoreferat." Diss. abstract, Leningrad, 1984.

Claus, Rudolph. *Die Kriegswirtschaft Russlands bis zur bolschewisten Revolution*. Bonn, 1922.

Cohen, Stephen F. *Bukharin and the Bolshevik Revolution: A Political Biography, 1888–1938*. New York, 1971.

―――. *Rethinking the Soviet Experience*. Oxford, 1985.

Conquest, Robert. *The Harvest of Sorrow: Soviet Collectivization and the Terror-Famine*. Oxford, 1986.

Crisenoy, Chantal de. *Lénine face aux moujiks*. Paris, 1978.

Daniels, Robert V. *The Conscience of the Revolution: Communist Opposition in Soviet Russia*. Cambridge, Mass., 1960.

―――. *Red October: The Bolshevik Revolution of 1917*. New York, 1967.

Danilov, V. P. "Sovetskaia nalogovaia politika v dokolkhoznoi derevne." In *Oktiabr' i sovetskoe krest'ianstvo*. Moscow, 1977.

Davydov, M. I. *Aleksandr Dmitrievich Tsiurupa*. Moscow, 1961.

―――. *Bor'ba za khleb*. Moscow, 1971.

―――. "Gosudarstvennyi tovaroobmen mezhdu gorodom i derevnei v 1918–1921 gg." *Istoricheskie zapiski* 108 (1982): 33–59.

Dekrety sovetskoi vlasti. Moscow, 1957–.

Demosthenov, S. S. "Food Prices and the Market in Foodstuffs." In *Food Supply in Russia During the World War*, edited by P. B. Struve. New Haven, 1930.

Deviatyi s"ezd predstavitelei gorodov Petrogradskoi oblasti. Petrograd, 1916.

Diakin, V. S. *Russkaia burzhuaziia i tsarizm v gody pervoi mirovoi voiny, 1914–1917*. Leningrad, 1967.

Dmitrenko, V. P. "Bor'ba sovetskogo gosudarstva protiv chastnoi torgovli." In *Bor'ba za pobedu i ukreplenie sovetskoi vlasti, 1917–1927*, 286–338. Moscow, 1966.

Dobb, Maurice. *Russian Economic Development Since the War*. New York, 1928.

Drobizhev, V. Z. "Demograficheskoe razvitie strany sovetov (1917 g.– seredina 1920-kh godov)." *Voprosy istorii*, 1986, no. 7:15–25.

Dukes, Paul. *Red Dusk and the Morrow: Adventures and Investigations in Red Russia*. New York, 1922.

Eckstein, Harry. "A Culturalist Theory of Political Change." *American Political Science Review* 82 (1988): 789–804.

Eckstein, Harry, and Ted Robert Gurr. *Patterns of Authority: A Structural Basis for Political Inquiry*. New York, 1975.

Edmondson, Charles M. "An Inquiry into the Termination of Soviet Famine Relief Programmes and the Renewal of Grain Export, 1921–1923." *Soviet Studies* 33 (July 1981): 370–85.

―――. "The Politics of Hunger: The Soviet Response to Famine, 1921." *Soviet Studies* 29 (October 1977): 506–18.

Ekonomicheskoe polozhenie Rossii nakanune velikoi oktiabr'skoi sotsialisticheskoi revoliutsii. 3 vols. Leningrad, 1957–1967.

Evans, Alfred B. "Rereading Lenin's *State and Revolution.*" *Slavic Review* 46 (1987): 1–19.

Farber, M. D. *Tverdye tseny na khleb.* Publication of the Vserossiiskii Soiuz Gorodov. N.p., 1916.

The Fatal Eggs and Other Soviet Satire, 1918–1963. 2d ed. Translated by Mirra Ginsburg. New York, 1987.

Ferro, Marc. *Des soviets au communisme bureaucratique.* Paris, 1980.

———. *La révolution de 1917.* 2 vols. Paris, 1967–1976.

Fidelli, N. "Ocherk istorii kartochnoi sistemy." *Prodovol'stvie i revoliutsiia,* 1923, no. 7–12:142–62.

Field, G. Lowell and John Higley. *Elitism.* London, 1980.

Fitzpatrick, Sheila. *The Russian Revolution, 1917–1932.* Oxford, 1982.

Frenkin, M. *Russkaia armiia i revoliutsiia.* Munich, 1978.

Frumkin, M. *Tovaroobmen, kooperatsiia i torgovlia.* Moscow, 1921.

Genkina, E. B. *Gosudarstvennaia deiatel'nost' V. I. Lenina, 1921–1923.* Moscow, 1969.

Gerasimenko, G. A. *Nizovye krest'ianskie organizatsii v 1917–pervoi polovine 1918 godov: na materialakh Nizhnego Povolzh'ia.* Saratov, 1974.

Geyer, Dietrich. *Russian Imperialism: The Interaction of Domestic and Foreign Policy, 1860–1914,* New Haven, 1987.

Gill, Graeme J. *Peasants and Government in the Russian Revolution.* London, 1979.

Gimpel'son, E. G. *"Voennyi kommunizm": politika, praktika, ideologiia.* Moscow, 1973.

Gins, G. K. *Organizatsiia prodovol'stvennogo dela na mestakh.* Petrograd, 1916.

Golovine, Nicholas. *The Russian Army in the World War.* New Haven, 1931.

Goode, W. T. *Bolshevism at Work.* New York, 1920.

Gosudarstvennaia duma, IV sozyv, sessiia V. Petrograd, 1917.

Got'e, Iurii V. *Time of Troubles: The Diary of Iurii Vladimirovich Got'e.* Edited by Terence Emmons. Princeton, 1988.

Graf, Daniel W. "Military Rule Behind the Russian Front, 1914–1917: The Political Ramifications." *Jahrbücher für Geschichte Osteuropas* 22 (1974).

Graham, Stephen. *Russia and the World: A Study of the War and a Statement of the World-Problems That Now Confront Russia and Great Britain.* New York, 1915.

———. *Russia in 1916.* New York, 1917.

Gregory, Paul T. *Russian National Income, 1885–1913.* Cambridge, 1982.

Hagen, Manfred. *Die Entfaltung politischer Öffentlichkeit in Russland 1906–1914.* Wiesbaden, 1982.

Hamm, Michael. "Liberalism and the Jewish Question: The Progressive Bloc." *Russian Review* 31 (1972): 163–72.

Hardarch, Gerd. *The First World War.* Berkeley and Los Angeles, 1977.

Hasegawa, Tsuyoshi. *The February Revolution: Petrograd 1917.* Seattle, 1981.

Hawtrey, R. G. *Economic Aspects of Sovereignty.* London, 1930.

Hindus, Maurice G. *The Russian Peasant and the Revolution.* New York, 1920.

Hirschman, Albert O. *Exit, Voice and Loyalty: Response to Decline in Firms, Organizations and States.* Cambridge, Mass., 1970.

Hoare, Samuel. *The Fourth Seal.* London, 1930.

Iaroslavskii, E. *Otchego net tovarov v derevne, khleba v gorodakh.* Moscow, 1917.

Igritskii, I. V. *1917 god v derevne.* Moscow, 1967.

Iurkov, I. A. *Ekonomicheskaia politika partii v derevne, 1917–1920.* Moscow, 1980.

Iurovskii, L. N. *Denezhnaia politika sovetskoi vlasti, 1917–1927.* Moscow, 1928.

Iziumov, A. S., ed. *Khleb i revoliutsiia.* Moscow, 1972.

Jasny, Naum. *Soviet Economists of the Twenties: Names to Be Remembered.* Cambridge, 1972.

———. *To Live Long Enough: The Memoirs of Naum Jasny, Scientific Analyst.* Edited by Betty A. Laird and Roy D. Laird. Lawrence, Kans., 1976.

Kabanov, V. V. "Aleksandr Vasil'evich Chaianov." *Voprosy istorii,* 1988, no. 6:146–67.

———. *Krest'ianskoe khoziaistvo v usloviakh "voennogo kommunizma."* Moscow, 1988.

———. *Oktiabr'skaia revoliutsiia i kooperatsiia (1917 g.–mart 1919 g.).* Moscow, 1973.

———. "Oktiabr'skaia revoliutsiia i krest'ianskaia obshchina." *Istoricheskie zapiski* 111 (1984): 100–150.

Kadomtzeff, Boris. *The Russian Collapse.* New York, 1919.

Kaganovich, P. K. *Kak dostaetsia khleb.* Moscow, 1920.

———. *Velikaia trudovaia razverstka: front, derevnia i gorod v sovetskoi respublike.* Omsk, 1921.

Kaiser, Daniel H., ed. *The Workers' Revolution in Russia, 1917.* Cambridge, 1987.

Kalendar'-spravochnik prodovol'stvennika. Moscow, 1921.

Kapuscinski, Ryszard. *Shah of Shahs.* New York, 1982.

Karrik, V. V. *O khlebnoi monopolii.* Petrograd, 1917.

Katkov, George. *Russia 1917: The February Revolution.* New York, 1967.

Kazakov, A. *Partiia s–r v tambovskom vosstanii 1920–1921.* [Moscow, 1922.]

Keenan, Edward L. "Muscovite Political Folkways." *Russian Review* 45 (1986): 115–81.

Keep, John. *The Russian Revolution: A Study in Mass Mobilization.* New York, 1976.

Keep, John, ed. *The Debate on Soviet Power.* Oxford, 1979.

Khalatov, A. B. "Sistema zagatovok i raspredeleniia v period voennogo kommunizma." In *Vnutrennaia torgovlia soiuza SSR za X let,* 22–38. Moscow, 1928.

Kheisin, M. L. *Istoriia kooperatsii v Rossii.* Leningrad, 1926.

Khvoles, A. "Voenno-prodovol'stvennoe delo za period revoliutsii." *Prodovol'stvie i revoliutsiia,* 1923, no. 1:50–64; no. 3–4:172–86.

Kingston-Mann, Esther. *Lenin and the Problem of Marxist Peasant Revolution.* Oxford, 1983.

Kitanina, T. M. *Voina, khleb i revoliutsiia: prodovol'stvennyi vopros v Rossii, 1914–Oktiabr' 1917 g.* Leningrad, 1985.

Klier, John D. "Zhid: Biography of a Russian Epithet." *Slavonic and East European Review* 60 (January 1982): 1–15.

Koenker, Diane. *Moscow Workers and the 1917 Revolution.* Princeton, 1981.

Kondratiev, N. D. *Rynok khlebov i ego regulirovanie vo vremia voiny i revoliutsiia.* Moscow, 1922.

Krasil'shchikov, V. *Intendant revoliutsii.* Moscow, 1967.

Kritsman, L. *Geroicheskii period velikoi russkoi revoliutsii.* Moscow, [1924].

Krivoshein, K. A. *A. V. Krivoshein (1857–1921). Ego znachenie v istorii Rossii nachala XX veka.* Paris, 1973.

Kupaigorodskaia, A. P. *Oruzhiem slova: listovki petrogradskikh bol'shevikov 1918–1920 gg.* Leningrad, 1981.

Kuznetsov, D. *O prodovol'stvii.* Moscow, 1919.

L. L. *Prodovol'stvennyi vopros.* N.p., 1916.

Laverychev, V. Ia. "Gosudarstvenno-monopolisticheskie tendentsii pri organizatsii prodovol'stvennogo dela v Rossii." *Istoricheskie zapiski* 101 (1978): 100–159.

———. "Krupnaia burzhuaziia i prodovol'stvennyi vopros v 1917 g." *Istoricheskie zapiski* 99 (1977): 312–21.

———. "Prodovol'stvennaia politika tsarizma i burzhuazii v gody pervoi mirovoi voiny (1914–1917 gg.)." *Vestnik Moskovskogo Universiteta,* 1956, no. 1:141–80.

Lawton, Lancelot. *An Economic History of Soviet Russia.* 2 vols. London, 1932.

Leiberov, I. P. *Na shturm samoderzhaviia.* Moscow, 1979.

———. "Nachalo fevral'skoi revoliutsii (sobytiia 23 fevralia 1917 v Petrograde)." In *Iz istorii velikoi oktiabr'skoi sotsialistecheskoi revoliutsii i sotsialistecheskogo stroitel'stva v SSSR.* Leningrad, 1967.

Lenin, V. I. *Polnoe sobranie sochinenii.* 5th ed. Moscow, 1959–1965.

Leonov, Leonid. *The Badgers.* Translated by Hilda Kazanina. New York, 1947.

Levi, Edward H. *An Introduction to Legal Reasoning.* Chicago, 1949.

Lewin, Moshe. *Lenin's Last Struggle.* New York, 1968.

————. *The Making of the Soviet System: Essays in the Social History of Interwar Russia*. New York, 1985.

————. *Political Undercurrents in Soviet Economic Debates*. Princeton, 1974.

Lih, Lars T. "Bolshevik *Razverstka* and War Communism." *Slavic Review* 44 (1986): 673–89.

Linhart, Robert. *Lénine, les paysans, Taylor*. Paris, 1976.

Locke, John. *Second Treatise of Government*. Edited by C. B. Macpherson. Indianapolis, 1980.

Loewenberg, Peter. "The Psychohistorical Origins of the Nazi Youth Cohort." *American Historical Review* 76 (1971): 1457–1502.

Lotman, Iu. M., and B. A. Uspenskii. "Binary Models in the Dynamics of Russian Culture." In Alexander D. Nakhimovsky and Alice Stone Nakhimovsky, eds., *The Semiotics of Russian Cultural History*. Ithaca, 1985.

Lozinskii, Z. *Ekonomicheskaia politika vremennogo pravitel'stva*. Leningrad, 1929.

Malia, Martin. *Comprendre la révolution russe*. Paris, 1980.

Maliutin, D. P. *Knizhka v pomoshch krest'ianinu-truzheniku (o komitetakh bednoty)*. 1st and 2d eds. Kazan, 1918.

————. *Rech'*. Kazan, 1918.

Malle, Silvana. *Economic Organization of War Communism 1918–1921*. Cambridge, 1985.

Mandel'shtam, Osip. *Tristia*. Petersburg, 1922.

Mansbridge, Jane J. *Beyond Adversary Democracy*. New York, 1980.

Mashkovich, A. P. *Deiatel'nost' prodovol'stvennoi organizatsii*. Publication of the Narodnyi Komissariat Gosudarstvennogo Kontrolia. Moscow, 1919.

Materialy po voprosu ustanovleniia tverdykh tsen na prodovol'stvie. Petrograd, 1916.

Mathiez, Albert. *La vie chère et le mouvement social sous le terreur*. Paris, 1927.

Maynard, John. *Russia in Flux*. New York, 1948.

Mazon, André. *Lexique de la guerre et de la révolution en Russie*. Paris, 1920.

McDonald, Forrest. *Novus Ordo Seclorum: The Intellectual Origins of the Constitution*. Lawrence, Kans., 1985.

McNeill, William H. *The Pursuit of Power*. Chicago, 1982.

Medvedev, Roy. *The October Revolution*. Translated by George Saunders. New York, 1979.

Meijer, J. M. "Town and Country in the Civil War." In Richard Pipes, ed., *Revolutionary Russia*, 259–77. Cambridge, Mass., 1968.

Merl, Stephan. *Die Anfänge der Kollektivierung in der Sowjetunion: Der Übergang zur staatlichen Reglementierung der Produktions- und Marktbeziehungen im Dorf (1928–1930)*. Wiesbaden, 1985.

Meyer, Gert. *Studien zur sozialökonomischen Entwicklung Sowjetrusslands 1921–1923: Die Beziehungen zwischen Stadt und Land zu Beginn der Neuen Ökonomischen Politik.* Cologne, 1974.

Mints, I. I. *God 1918.* Moscow, 1982.

Morris, Norval and Gordon Hawkins. *The Honest Politician's Guide to Crime Control.* Chicago, 1969.

Mosca, Gaetano. *The Ruling Class.* New York, 1939. Originally published as *Elementi di scienza politica.*

Mstislavskii, Sergei. *Five Days Which Transformed Russia.* 1922. Bloomington, Ill., 1988.

Nabokov, V. N. "Vremennoe pravitel'stvo." *Arkhiv russkoi revoliutsii* 1 (1922): 9–96.

Naumov, A. N. *Iz utselevshikh vospominanii.* 2 vols. New York, 1954–1955.

Na bor'bu s golodom. Moscow, 1921.

Nevskii, S. N., ed. *Prodovol'stvennaia rabota v kostromskoi gubernii.* Kostroma, 1923.

Nolde, Boris E. *Russia in the Economic War.* New Haven, 1928.

Nove, Alec. *An Economic History of the USSR.* London, 1969.

Obzor deiatel'nosti osobogo soveshchaniia dlia obsuzheniia meropriatii po prodovol'stvennomy delu. Petrograd, 1916.

Okninskii, A. L. *Dva goda sredi krest'ian: vidennoe, slyshannoe, perezhitoe v tambovskoi gubernii.* Riga, 1936.

Olson, Mancur. *The Economics of the Wartime Shortage: A History of British Food Supplies in the Napoleonic War and in World Wars I and II.* Durham, N.C., 1963.

———. *The Logic of Collective Action: Public Goods and the Theory of Groups.* Cambridge, Mass., 1965.

Orlov, N. *Prodovol'stvennaia rabota sovetskoi vlasti: k godovshchine oktiabr'skoi revoliutsii.* Moscow, 1918.

———. *Prodovol'stvennoe delo v Rossii.* Moscow, 1919.

———. *Sistema prodovol'stvennoi zagotovki: k otsenke rabot zagotovnykh ekspeditsii A. G. Shlikhtera.* Tambov, 1920.

Osipova, T. V. *Klassovaia bor'ba v derevne v period podgotovki i provedeniia oktiabr'skoi revoliutsii.* Moscow, 1974.

———. "Razvitie sotsialisticheskoi revoliutsii v derevne v pervyi god diktatury proletariata." In *Oktiabr' i sovetskoe krest'ianstvo,* Moscow, 1977.

Owen, Launcelot A. *The Russian Peasant Movement, 1906–1917.* 1937. Reprint. New York, 1963.

Padenie tsarskogo rezhima. 7 vols. Moscow, 1924–1927.

Page, Stanley W. "Lenin's April Theses and the Latvian Peasant-Soldiery." In *Reconsiderations on the Russian Revolution,* edited by R. C. Elwood. Columbus, Ohio, 1976.

Pares, Sir Bernard. *The Fall of the Russian Monarchy: A Study of the Evidence.* 1939. Reprint. New York, 1961.

Pasternak, Boris. *Doctor Zhivago.* Translated by Max Hayward and Manya Harari. London, 1958.

Patenaude, Bertrand Mark. "Bolshevism in Retreat: The Transition to the New Economic Policy, 1920–1922." Ph.D. diss., Stanford University, 1987.

Paustovsky, Konstantin. *The Story of a Life.* Translated by Joseph Barnes. New York, 1964.

Pavlovsky, G. P. *Agricultural Russia on the Eve of the Revolution.* 1930. New York, 1968.

Perrie, Maureen. *The Agrarian Policy of the Russian Socialist-Revolutionary Party.* Cambridge, 1976.

Pershin, P. N. *Agrarnaia revoliutsiia v Rossii.* 2 vols. Moscow, 1966.

Peshekhonov, A. V. "Pered krasnym terrorom." *Na chuzhoi storone* 2 (1923): 200–220.

———. "Pervye nedeli." *Na chuzhoi storone* 1 (1923): 255–319.

———. *Pochemu ia ne emigriroval.* Berlin, 1923.

Pethybridge, Roger. *The Spread of the Russian Revolution.* London, 1972.

Pigou, A. C. *The Political Economy of War.* London, 1921.

Pipes, Richard. *Struve: Liberal on the Right, 1905–1944.* Cambridge, Mass., 1980.

Poliakov, Iu. A. *Perekhod k NEPu i sovetskoe krest'ianstvo.* Moscow, 1967.

Poole, Ernest. *"The Dark People": Russia's Crisis.* New York, 1918.

———. *The Village: Russian Impressions.* New York, 1918.

Portugeis, S. O. [Stepan Ivanovich]. *Krasnaia Armiia.* Paris, 1931.

———. *Piat' let bol'shevizma: nachala i kontsy.* Berlin, 1922.

Potapenko, V. A. *Zapiski prodotriadnika, 1918–1920 gg.* Voronezh, 1973.

Preobrazhenskii, Evgenii. *Bumazhnye den'gi v epokhe proletarskoi revoliutsii.* Moscow, 1920.

Prodovol'stvennaia politika v svete obshchego khoziaistvennogo stroitel'stva sovetskoi vlasti. Moscow, 1920.

Prokopovich, S. N. *The Economic Condition of Soviet Russia.* London, 1924.

———. *Narodnoe khoziaistvo SSSR.* 2 vols. New York, 1952.

———. *Narodnoe khoziaistvo v dni revoliutsii: tri rechi.* Moscow, 1918.

Protsess kontrrevoliutsionnoi organizatsii men'shevikov. Moscow, 1931.

Rabinowitch, Alexander. *The Bolsheviks Come to Power: The Revolution of 1917 in Petrograd.* New York, 1976.

———. *Prelude to Revolution: The Petrograd Bolsheviks and the July 1917 Uprising.* Bloomington, Ind., 1968.

Radkey, Oliver Henry. *The Agrarian Foes of Bolshevism: Promise and Default of the Russian Socialist Revolutionaries February to October 1917.* New York, 1958.

———. *The Sickle Under the Hammer: The Russian Socialist Revolutionaries in the Early Months of Soviet Rule.* New York, 1963.

———. *The Unknown Civil War in Soviet Russia.* Stanford, 1976.

Rahr, Alexander. "Shelest Remembers." *Report on the USSR*, 1989, no. 4:14–16.

Raleigh, Donald J. *Revolution on the Volga: 1917 in Saratov*. Ithaca, 1986.

Ransome, Arthur. *The Crisis in Russia*. London, 1921.

———. *Russia in 1919*. New York, 1919.

Ravallion, Martin. *Markets and Famines*. Oxford, 1987.

Redlich, Roman. *Stalinshchina kak dukhovnyi fenomen*. Frankfurt, 1971.

Reed, John. *Ten Days That Shook the World*. 1919. New York, 1960.

Rees, E. A. *State Control in Soviet Russia: The Rise and Fall of the Workers' and Peasants' Inspectorate, 1920–34*. New York, 1987.

Rickman, John. "Russian Camera Obscura: Ten Sketches of Russian Peasant Life (1916–1918)." In Geoffrey Gorer and John Rickman, *The People of Great Russia: A Psychological Study*. New York, 1962.

Rigby, T. H. *Lenin's Government*. Cambridge, 1979.

———. "The Soviet Regional Leadership: The Brezhnev Generation." *Slavic Review* 37 (1978): 1–24.

Robbins, Richard G. *Famine in Russia, 1891–1892: The Imperial Government Responds to a Crisis*. New York, 1975.

———. *The Tsar's Viceroys: Russian Provincial Governors in the Last Years of the Empire*. Ithaca, 1987.

Robien, Louis de. *The Diary of a Diplomat in Russia, 1917–1918*. London, 1969.

Rogger, Hans. *Russia in the Age of Modernization and Revolution 1881–1917*. London and New York, 1983.

Rosenberg, William G. *Liberals in the Russian Revolution: The Constitutional Democratic Party, 1917–1921*. Princeton, 1974.

———. "The Zemstvo in 1917 and Its Fate Under Bolshevik Rule." In *The Zemstvo in Russia*, edited by T. Emmons and W. S. Vucinich, 383–421. Cambridge, 1982.

Rosenberg, William G., and Marilyn B. Young. *Transforming Russia and China: Revolutionary Struggle in the Twentieth Century*. Oxford, 1982.

Samuilova, K. *Prodovol'stvennyi vopros i sovetskaia vlast'*. Petrograd, 1918.

Scheibert, Peter. *Lenin an der Macht: Das russische Volk in der Revolution*. Weinheim, 1984.

Selishchev, A. M. *Iazyk revoliutsionnoi epokhi*. Moscow, 1928.

Seliunin, Vasilii. "Istoki." *Novyi Mir*, 1988, no. 5:162–89.

Semenov, Sergei. *Golod*. 1922. In *Izbrannoe*. Leningrad, 1970.

Sen, Amartya. *Poverty and Famines: An Essay on Entitlement and Deprivation*. Oxford, 1981.

Serebrianskii, Z. "Sabotazh i sozdanie novogo gosudarstvennogo apparata." *Proletarskaia revoliutsiia*, no. 10 (57), 1926.

Shakhnazarov, Georgii. "Vostok-Zapad." *Kommunist*, 1989, no. 3:67–78.

Shakhovskoi, V. N. *"Sic Transit Gloria Mundi."* Paris, 1952.

Shanin, Teodor. *The Awkward Class: Political Sociology of the Peasantry in a Developing Society*. Oxford, 1972.

———. *Russia as a "Developing Society."* London, 1985.

Shidlovskii, S. I. *Vospominaniia.* Vol. 2. Berlin, 1923.

Shingarev, A. I. *Finansovoe polozhenie Rossii.* Petrograd, 1917.

―――. *The Shingarev Diary.* Strathcona, 1978.

Shirokorad, L. D. "Diskussii o goskapitalizme v perekhodnoi ekonomike." In *Iz istorii politicheskoi ekonomii sotsializma v SSSR 20–30e gody.* Leningrad, 1981.

Shklovskii, Viktor. *A Sentimental Journey: Memoirs, 1917–1922.* Edited and translated by Richard Sheldon. Ithaca, 1974.

Shliapnikov, A. *Semnadtsatyi god.* 2d. ed. 3 vols. Moscow, 1924–1927.

Shlikhter, A. G. *Agrarnyi vopros i prodovol'stvennaia politika v pervye gody sovetskoi vlasti.* Moscow, 1975.

―――. *Iz vospominanii o Lenine.* 2d. ed. Kiev, 1934.

Sholokhov, Mikhail. *Sobranie sochinenii.* 9 vols. Moscow, 1965–.

Shul'gin, V. V. *Dni.* Belgrade, 1925.

Sidorov, A. L. *Economicheskoe polozhenie Rossii v gody pervoi mirovoi voiny.* Moscow, 1973.

Siegelbaum, Lewis H. *The Politics of Industrial Mobilization in Russia, 1914–1917.* New York, 1983.

Sigov, I. *Arakcheevskii sotsializm.* N.p., 1917.

Simms, J. Y. "The Crisis in Russian Agriculture at the End of the Nineteenth Century: A Different View." *Slavic Review* 36 (1977): 377–98.

Smith, Adam. *The Wealth of Nations.* Edited by Edwin Cannan. Chicago, 1976.

Smith, R. E. F. and David Christian. *Bread and Salt: A Social and Economic History of Food and Drink in Russia.* Cambridge, 1984.

Smith, S. A. *Red Petrograd: Revolution in the Factories, 1917–1918.* Cambridge, 1983.

Solomon, Susan Gross. *The Soviet Agrarian Debate: A Controversy in Social Science, 1923–1929.* Boulder, Colo., 1977.

Sorokin, Pitirim. *Hunger as a Factor in Human Affairs.* Gainesville, Fla., 1975.

―――. *Man and Society in Calamity.* New York, 1942.

Soviet Society Since the Revolution. New York, 1979.

Sovremennoe polozhenie taksirovki predmetov prodovol'stviia v Rossia i mery k ee uporiadocheniiu. Petrograd, 1915.

Stalin, I. V. *Sochineniia.* 13 vols. Moscow, 1946–1953.

Startsev, V. I. *Vnutrenniaia politika vremennogo pravitel'stva.* Leningrad, 1980.

Stein, Arthur A. *The Nation at War.* Baltimore, 1978.

Stone, Norman. *The Eastern Front, 1914–1917.* London, 1975.

Strizhkov, Iu. K. "Iz istorii vvedeniia prodovol'stvennoi razverstki." *Istoricheskie zapiski* 61 (1961): 25–41.

―――. "Priniatie dekreta o prodovol'stvennoi razverstke i ego osushchestvlenie v pervoi polovine 1919 g." In *Oktiabr' i sovetskoe krest'ianstvo, 1917–1927 gg.*, 131–63. Moscow, 1977.

————. *Prodovol'stvennyi otriady v gody grazhdanskoi voiny i inostrannoi interventsii.* Moscow, 1973.

————. "V. I. Lenin—organizator i rukovoditel' bor'by za sozdanie sovetskogo prodovol'stvennogo apparata." In *Bor'ba za pobedu i ukreplenie sovetskoi vlasti, 1917–1918 gg.,* 236–85. Moscow, 1966.

Struve, P. B. *Collected Works.* Edited by Richard Pipes. 15 vols. Ann Arbor, 1970.

————. Introduction to *Food Supply in Russia During the World War,* edited by P. B. Struve. New Haven, 1930.

Sukhanov, N. *Zapiski o revoliutsii.* 7 vols. Berlin, 1922–1923.

Suny, Ronald G. *The Baku Commune, 1917–1918.* Princeton, 1972.

————. "Revising the Old Story: The 1917 Revolution in Light of New Sources." In Daniel H. Kaiser, ed., *The Workers Revolution in Russia, 1917,* 1–19. Cambridge, 1987.

Suslov, A. I. "Sovremennaia anglo-amerikanskaia burzhuaznaia istoriografiia o prodovol'stvennoi politike v pervye gody sovetskoi vlasti." *Istoriia SSSR,* 1978, no. 3:188–95.

Sverdlov, Ia. *Izbrannye proizvedeniia.* Moscow, 1976.

Sviderskii, A. I. "Prodnalog." In *Tret'e vserossiiskoe prodovol'stvennoe soveshchanie.* Moscow, 1921.

————. *Prodovol'stvennaia politika.* Moscow, 1920.

Szamuely, Laszlo. *First Models of the Socialist Economic System: Principles and Theories.* Budapest, 1974.

Taniuchi, Y. "A Note on the Urals-Siberian Method." *Soviet Studies* 33 (1981): 518–47.

Teggart, Frederick J. *Theory of History.* New Haven, 1925.

Terne, A. *V tsarstve Lenina.* Berlin, 1922.

Tri goda borby c golodom: kratkii otchet o deiatel'nosti NKP za 1919–1920 gg. Moscow, 1920.

Trotsky, Lev. *Kak vooruzhalas' revoliutsiia.* 3 vols. Moscow, 1923–1925.

————. *Novyi kurs.* Moscow, 1924.

————. *The Trotsky Papers, 1917–1922.* Edited by J. M. Meijer. The Hague, 1971.

Trudy komissii po izucheniiu sovremennoi dorogovizny. Moscow, 1915.

Trudy pervogo vserossiiskogo s"ezda sovetov narodnogo khoziaistva. Moscow, 1918.

Trutovskii, V. *Kulak, bednota i trudovoe krest'ianstvo.* Moscow, 1918.

Tsiurupa, Vsevolod. *Kolokola pamiati.* Moscow, 1986.

Tucker, Robert C. *Political Culture and Leadership in Soviet Russia.* New York, 1987.

————. *Politics as Leadership.* Columbia, Mo., 1981.

————. *The Soviet Political Mind.* rev. ed. New York, 1971.

————. *Stalin as Revolutionary, 1879–1929: A Study in History and Personality.* New York, 1973.

Tyrkova-Williams, Ariadna. *Why Soviet Russia Is Starving*. London, March 1919.

Vainshtein, Al'bert. *Oblozhenie i platezhi krest'ianstva v dovoennoe i revoliutsionnoe vremia*. Moscow, 1924.

Valentinov, N. *The New Economic Policy and the Party Crisis After the Death of Lenin*. Stanford, 1971.

Velikie dni rossiiskoi revoliutsii. Petrograd, 1917.

Vishnevskii, N. M. *Printsipy i metody organizatsionnogo raspredeleniia produktov prodovol'stviia i predmetov pervoi neobkhodimosti*. Edited by V. Groman. Moscow, 1920.

Vladimirov, M. K. *Meshochnichestvo i ego sotsial'no-politicheskoe otrazhenie*. Kharkov, 1920.

———. *Udarnye momenty prodovol'stvennoi raboty na Ukraine*. Kharkov, 1921.

Volobuev, P. V. *Ekonomicheskaia politika vremennogo pravitel'stva*. Moscow, 1961.

Von Hagen, Mark. *Soldiers in the Proletarian Dictatorship: The Red Army and the Soviet Socialist State, 1917–1930*. Ithaca, 1990.

Von Laue, Theodore. *The Global City: Freedom, Power and Necessity in the Age of World Revolutions*. New York, 1969.

———. "Stalin in Focus." *Slavic Review* 42 (1983): 373–89.

———. *The World Revolution of Westernization: The Twentieth Century in Global Perspective*. Oxford, 1987.

Vospominaniia o Vladimire Iliche Lenine. Vol. 3. Moscow, 1969.

Vserossiiskii Soiuz Gorodov. *Organizatsiia narodnogo khoziaistva*. Moscow, 1916.

Vserossiiskoe soveshchanie sovetov rabochikh i soldatskikh deputatov. Stenograficheskii otchet. Edited by M. N. Tsapenko. Moscow, 1927.

Vyshinskii, A. Ia. *Voprosy raspredeleniia i revoliutsiia*. Moscow, 1922.

Wade, Rex A. *Red Guards and Workers Militias in the Russian Revolution*. Stanford, 1984.

———. *The Russian Search for Peace, February–October 1917*. Stanford, 1969.

Waltz, Kenneth N. *Theory of International Politics*. Reading, Mass., 1979.

Weissman, Benjamin N. *Herbert Hoover and Famine Relief to Soviet Russia, 1921–1923*. Stanford, 1974.

Weissman, Neil B. *Reform in Tsarist Russia: The State Bureaucracy and Local Government*. New Brunswick, N.J., 1981.

Wells, H. G. *Russia in the Shadows*. New York, 1921.

Wesson, Robert G. *Soviet Communes*. New Brunswick, N.J., 1963.

Wheatcroft, S. G. "Famine and Factors Affecting Mortality in the USSR: The Demographic Crises of 1914–1922 and 1930–1933." Centre for East European Studies (University of Birmingham) Discussion Paper, SIPS nos. 20 and 21, 1981.

White, Stephen. *The Bolshevik Poster*. New Haven, 1988.

Wildman, Allan. *The End of the Russian Imperial Army: The Old Army and the Soldier's Revolt (March–April 1917)*. Princeton, 1980.

Yaney, George. "The Imperial Russian Government and the Stolypin Land Reform." Ph.D. diss., Princeton University, 1961.

———. *The Urge to Mobilize: Agrarian Reform in Russia, 1861–1930*. Urbana, 1982.

Zagorsky, S. *La république des soviets*. Paris, 1921.

Zaitsev, K. I. and N. V. Dolinsky. "Organization and Policy." In *Food Supply in Russia During the World War*, edited by P. B. Struve. New Haven, 1930.

Zinoviev, G. *Chto delat' v derevne*. Petrograd, 1919.

———. *Khleb, mir i partiia*. Petrograd, 1918.

———. *Krest'iane i sovetskaia vlast'*. Petrograd, 1920.

———. *O khlebe nasushchnom*. Petrograd, 1918.

———. *Pis'mo k krest'ianam: Zachem rabochie posylaiut prodovol'stvennye otriady v derevniu?* Petrograd, 1918.

Zubareva, L. A. *Khleb Prikam'ia*. Izhevsk, 1967.

Index

Abramovich, Rafael, 162
Administrative lawlessness, 206, 211–12, 214, 228, 263; disapproval of by center, 203, 215; under tsarist government, 50
Aleksandrovskaia (village in Viatka), 49–50
Alexandra, Empress, 33
All-Russian Food-Supply Council of Ten, 120
American Relief Agency, 226
American Revolution, 242n25
American trusts, 149
Anisimov, V. I. (Provisional Government food-supply official), 90, 112, 119
Antonov (peasant leader), 219
Aristotle, 4, 251n43
Army, 11, 25–26, 48, 50–51; and civilian interests, 10, 18, 25, 34, 45n; and peasantry, 51, 71–72, 80. See also Ministry of War; Red Army
Arskii, R. (Bolshevik publicist), 129, 229, 253

Badaev, A. E. (Bolshevik food-supply official), 213
Baku, 106, 168n2, 204
Banks, 36–37, 241–42, 246

Batrak, 143, 145. See also Rural proletariat
Beliaev, M. A. (tsarist minister of war), 54–55
Berkman, Alexander, 270–71
Black Hundreds, 37–38, 154
Blockade, of Russia, 9, 233–34, 237–38, 260
Blockade detachments, 131, 222, 226; precursors of, 79; and razverstka system, 185, 187, 192–94
Bobrinksii, Aleksei (tsarist minister of agriculture), 30, 105
Bogatko, General (Provisional Government military food-supply official), 116
Bol'shakov, A. M., 210
Bolshevism: attacks on, 119–21, 159–66; and breakdown and reconstitution, 97, 234–36, 246–54; and enlistment solution, 39, 98, 103, 151, 248; and property perspective, 93–96; and revolution view, 264–65
Brest-Litovsk, treaty of, 134, 150, 152, 164
Briukhanov, N. P. (Bolshevik food-supply official), 184, 208, 220n75, 238

291

Compositor:	Keystone Typesetting, Inc.
Text:	10/12 Aldus
Display:	Aldus
Printer:	Edwards Brothers, Inc.
Binder:	Edwards Brothers, Inc.